QUEEN BESS

QUEEN BESS

An Unauthorized Biography of Bess Myerson

JENNIFER PRESTON

CB
CONTEMPORARY
BOOKS
CHICAGO

BIOG
MYERSON

Library of Congress Cataloging-in-Publication Data

Preston, Jennifer.
    Queen Bess : the unauthorized biography of Bess Myerson /
Jennifer Preston.
        p.   cm.
    ISBN 0-8092-4530-2
    1. Myerson, Bess.   2. Beauty contestants—United States—
Biography   I. Title.
HQ1220.U5P74   1990
791.6′2—dc20

89-48268
CIP

Published by Contemporary Books, Inc.
180 North Michigan Avenue, Chicago, Illinois 60601
Manufactured in the United States of America
International Standard Book Number: 0-8092-4530-2

For my parents and for Chris

Contents

Acknowledgments

My very special thanks to my agent, Philippa Brophy of Sterling Lord Literistic, who guided me through a difficult process with wit and wisdom. From the beginning, she believed in this book and did not give up until it was published. Along the way, she read parts of the manuscript and offered critical insights. I will always be grateful for her constant support and encouragement. Every author should have such a caring, nurturing literary agent and friend.

Thanks also to my colleagues who offered their generous assistance. I am indebted to Jeanie Kasindorf of *New York* magazine for teaching me a lot about reporting and writing during the Bess Myerson trial and for helping me with the final chapters of this book. I am particularly grateful to Marcia Kramer, who broke the story of the Bess Myerson scandal in the *New York Daily News*, and Paul Moses, who covered the trial for *New York Newsday*, for steering me to documents and sources. Many thanks also to Wayne Barrett, Anne Bollinger, Edward Borges, Ben Bradlee, Jr., Jimmy Breslin, Maurice Carroll, Joe Conasan, John Cotter, Richard Cramer, Michael Daly, Hal Davis, Rita Delfiner, Doug Edelson, Al Ellenberg, Owen Fitzgerald, Kevin Flynn, Kristen Kelch, Murray Kempton, Steven Kroft, Diane McNulty, Jack Morrison, Patricia Morrisroe, Jack Newfield, Joyce Purnick, Marvin Smilon, F. Gilman Spencer, Sharman Stein, and Marilyn Thompson.

For allowing me to browse through their clip and photo files, a special expression of appreciation goes to Christine Baird and Mary Ann Skinner of *Newsday*, Faigi Rosenthal of the *New York Daily News*, Merrill Sherr of the *New York Post*, and Linda Uhrmann of the *Atlantic City Press*. I am also indebted to the many librarians who assisted me with my research at the New York Public Library at Lincoln Center, New York Municipal Reference Center, New York Municipal Archives, YIVO, and Hunter College's archives, where William Omelchenko gave me tremendous help.

More than two hundred people were interviewed for this book. While it is not possible to list all of them here or to name all of the people who offered their insights and advice over the past two years, I would like to note a special thanks to George Arzt, Virginia Freeland Berry, Pat Byrne, Lori Calabro, Nancy Capasso, Pam Chanin, Roma Conable, Maureen Connelly, Linda Daly, Michael Feldberg, Myrna Felder, Raoul Lionel Felder, Chester Feldman, Joseph Fitzpatrick, Walt Framer, Sam Fredman, Kevin Ford, Arnold Forster, Hortense Gabel, Dr. Milton Gabel, Sukhreet Gabel, Neal Gantcher, Steve Gersten, Jay Goldberg, Rema Goldberg, Phyllis Goldman, Barry Gray, Betty Ann Grove, Jeremy Gutman, Fred Hafetz, Steve Hyman, Candy Jones, Leland T. Jones, former Mayor Edward I. Koch, David Lawrence, Simon Lazarus, Paul Levinson, Tony Lombardi, Henry Morgan, Steve Mosley, Susan Mulcahy, Hope O'Connor, Murray Panitz, Steve Posner, Lisa Rayder, Vera Robinson, Philip Schrag, Ceci Scott, Henry Stern, Ruth Singer, Louise Sugarman, Gary Walker, Elaine Werbell, Dan Wolf, and Judith Yeager.

At _New York Newsday_, I would like to thank my editors, Tom Curran, Don Forst, and Jim Toedtman. A special debt of gratitude is owed to Bill Murphy, _New York Newsday_'s City Hall bureau chief, whose support during the final stage of this project I will always remember.

I am grateful for the research assistance that I received from Josh Kurtz and Dean Pelligra, as well as the comments on the manuscript that I received from Sue Weston, Bob Williams, Jan Winburn, and, particularly, Carolyn White. Thanks also to Michael Antonello, Pam Richardson, and Kathy Willhoite at Contemporary Books for their professionalism and hard work and to Chris Benton, who edited the manuscript.

Finally, I reserve my deepest thanks for my husband, Christopher Conway, who spent countless hours editing and discussing this project and whose love, support, and encouragement saw me through every day of work on it.

Preface

I first met Bess Myerson in October 1987. I was working as a
newspaper reporter for *New York Newsday*; she was promoting a
book about her early life and her reign as Miss America, 1945. We
arranged to meet in the office of her publisher in midtown Manhattan
at about three o'clock one afternoon. She had another appointment
earlier in the day: her arraignment on criminal charges that she had
bribed a state judge to lower her lover's substantial alimony payments.

Watching her walk up the steps of the U.S. District Courthouse in
Foley Square that morning, I found it easy to understand why over the
years she had become known as Queen Bess. Despite the tremendous
embarrassment that the indictment had caused her, she moved through
a crowd of curious onlookers on the courthouse steps with regal
bearing and her head held high.

It was her first public appearance since she had resigned in disgrace
six months earlier from her post as New York City's commissioner of
cultural affairs. She had stepped down after a specially commissioned
mayoral investigation concluded that she had abused her power as a
public official to help her boyfriend. Once a symbol of achievement,
dignity, and ethnic pride, Bess had been reduced to another politician
swept up in the city's municipal corruption scandal.

I was following Bess Myerson's troubles for *New York Newsday*. As I
interviewed her longtime friends and read dozens of yellowing newspaper clips detailing her victory as the first and only Jewish Miss America,
her career as a game show hostess and panelist during television's
Golden Age, and her ascent in New York politics as the city's crusading
consumer advocate, I became intrigued by her rise and fall.

Although she began her public life as Miss America, she aspired to be
more than just a beauty queen, and she succeeded like no other before
or since. With her crowning, she became a powerful symbol to Jews still
suffering from bigotry and discrimination at the end of World War II.
And long before American women rebelled against their traditional
roles of wife and mother, Bess had made a determined decision to try to

balance the demands of a family and career. Instilled with a fierce ambition, she went on to become one of the most powerful women in New York.

I had been trying since her indictment to arrange an interview, but nearly six months passed without a response to my letters or phone messages. Finally, in the fall of 1987, Bess relented, hoping an interview might help sales of her new book about her year as Miss America. Despite the federal indictment, she was embarking on a nationwide tour to promote *Miss America, 1945*, about her early life in the Bronx and the anti-Semitism that she encountered during her reign. But she warned that she would not discuss her present troubles or her boyfriend, Carl Andy Capasso, the multimillionaire sewer contractor then in federal prison for tax evasion. I reluctantly agreed.

Bess Myerson was waiting when I arrived at her publisher's office that afternoon. She rose to meet me as I entered, and my most immediate impression was of her size. Standing nearly six feet tall, Bess's mere presence in a room commands attention. Her thinness accentuates her height. And though she was then sixty-three and had endured nearly six months of scrutiny from the press and prosecutors, her face bore no sign of the strain. Her smile—a big, wide, dazzling show of perfect white teeth—completed the picture.

She was exceedingly gracious and solicitous, and her deep, resonant voice conveyed a sense of intimacy. As she spoke about the years leading up to her triumph in Atlantic City, she chose her words carefully, furrowing her brow in concentration as she turned thoughts over in her mind. She made her points clearly and forcefully, sweeping her hands slowly through the air for emphasis.

She spoke animatedly about growing up in the Bronx with her strong-willed Russian Jewish immigrant mother, who was determined that her three daughters be outstanding achievers. Hers was a tale of an awkward young girl whose dream of owning a Steinway piano led her to Atlantic City for a beauty contest, only to be handed the heartbreak and pain of bigotry along with her scepter and crown. As Bess described the difficulties she faced as the first Jewish Miss America, I became increasingly curious about how she had gone from Atlantic City to the federal courthouse. What had happened during those forty years?

My curiosity was not satisfied by the interview, and her life after 1945 was left unchronicled in her book. I began researching the rest of her life in the hope that she might agree to talk with me about her life after Atlantic City. But she was not interested in revisiting the past four decades.

"Much of what happened to me has been exciting, glorious, and some of what has happened to me was painful," she told me. She did not want to relive those painful times: the highly publicized custody battle with her first husband over their only child, the bitter divorce from her second husband, her arrests on shoplifting charges, her struggle against ovarian cancer, her devastating loss in the United States Senate race, and her obsessive jealousy over a man who had jilted her for a younger woman. And finally, she did not want to talk about the events that had led up to her fall from grace.

Over successive months, however, Bess was gracious enough to discuss and clarify some aspects of her life. For those discussions I am grateful because they helped me understand some of the choices and decisions that she has made during her life and tell the story of what happened to the nation's first "beauty with brains" after she left Atlantic City in 1945.

1
A Fall from Grace

At 7:00 A.M. Bess Myerson pulled open the blinds in her living room on a sunny, crisp autumn morning. It was Thursday, October 15, 1987, and from her apartment window on Manhattan's posh Upper East Side she could see the treetops of Central Park, where the leaves were beginning to turn, brightening the city with their red, orange, and yellow hues.

In just four hours she was due downtown at the U.S. District Courthouse in Foley Square. Four photographers had been waiting outside her apartment building since before dawn to chronicle her departure. Photographers seemed to follow her everywhere now—to the drugstore, to the supermarket, even to the Hamptons waterfront estate of her boyfriend, Carl Andy Capasso, where a photographer from the *New York Post* had caught her in his telephoto lens just that week, carrying a pair of andirons from the house to the car. She was shocked when she saw the paper's front page the next day. There she was, looking old and haggard in a rumpled gray sweatsuit, without any makeup, her unwashed hair pushed behind her ears, holding the andirons. And there was a story accusing her of stealing them. So there was little doubt that today the photographers would be out in force to document her trip to Foley Square.

She was to answer charges that she conspired with Andy to bribe a state supreme court judge to lower his $1,500-a-week alimony payments to the woman he had left behind for her. It was an untidy business that had been played for all it was worth, and more, on the front pages of New York's merciless tabloids. It seemed that the public could not read enough about the case and Bess's affair with Andy, who stood almost a head shorter than she and who was now in federal prison on an unrelated tax evasion charge.

Yet their very incongruity was fascinating enough. Andy was twenty-one years her junior, a heavyset, street-smart contractor who lacked a college education and Manhattan sophistication but who had made millions of dollars installing sewers under the streets of New York. Bess

1

was tall and statuesque, a woman whose beauty, even at age sixty-three, turned heads. She had parlayed her 1945 Miss America crown into a successful television and political career that had brought her wealth and admiration, even in a city of cynicism that seemed to take a special delight now in watching her fall.

This would be Bess's first public appearance since she had resigned six months earlier as New York City's commissioner of cultural affairs, and she selected clothes and accessories that would make her look every inch the former beauty queen that she was. From her closet, filled with size twelve and fourteen designer suits and dresses hung according to color, she chose a black knit Chanel-style suit with brass buttons, a crimson silk blouse, and low-heeled black patent leather shoes. From her toolbox-size jewelry case she picked out a strand of black beads and pearl earrings set in gold filigree.

Bess had spent enough years in television to know that she should apply a heavy foundation for the cameras and extra color over her high cheekbones. She brushed aquamarine eye shadow around her almond-shaped hazel eyes and dark red color onto her full, expressive lips. She put her chestnut-brown hair in electric rollers, and after she took them out she fluffed layers of curls on top of her head.

When she was dressed, the reflection in the full-length mirror contrasted sharply with the Bess Myerson in a sweatsuit who had stared from the front page of the *New York Post* only days before. She looked stunning in her black suit, weighing only a little more than the 136 pounds she weighed when she had competed for the title of Miss America forty-two years earlier.

Her younger sister, Helen, a retired high school music teacher, was due to arrive around nine o'clock and take her to the Conservative Synagogue of Fifth Avenue in Greenwich Village. Today was a Jewish holiday, Sh'mini Atzereth, and Bess wanted to attend Yitzkor, a memorial service for the dead. Perhaps prayer would help her face what promised to be the most difficult day of her life.

A few minutes after nine the doorman rang upstairs to announce that Helen had arrived and was waiting in the lobby. Bess took the elevator down and walked outside with her sister into what was now a crowd of photographers. Smiling for the cameras, she followed Helen into a waiting dark blue Cadillac, which pulled away, turning left on Fifth Avenue and heading downtown through heavy traffic in midtown Manhattan and into the Village. A reporter and photographer from the *New York Post* followed right behind all the way.

They reached the synagogue in twenty-five minutes and took a seat in the back, where Bess picked up a black Hebrew prayer book. In her prayers she asked her mother and father, Bella and Louis, for strength.

At the end of the service Bess hurried out of the synagogue before the rest of the worshipers, the prayer book still in her hands. Knowing the next few hours would be a media circus, she thought it would be best to go to the courthouse without Helen, so she kissed her sister good-bye. Her lawyer, Fred Hafetz, a former federal prosecutor–turned–defense attorney who had represented Andy Capasso on other matters, was waiting outside in the back of a chauffeur-driven black Lincoln Town Car.

It was a short ride downtown to the massive granite courthouse in Foley Square, a few blocks north of City Hall, where Bess had reigned for years as the city's unofficial first lady to her one-time friend, Mayor Edward I. Koch. Approaching the courthouse, she could see a mob of almost two hundred reporters, photographers, camera crews, and curious onlookers, all jostling for position as they awaited her arrival.

As the Lincoln pulled up, the crowd pushed and shoved its way down the courthouse steps, a human tide with microphones, flashing cameras, and tape recorders that seemed to engulf Bess as she stepped from the car. They shouted their questions:

"Any comment, Bess?"

"How do you feel, Bess?"

"Turn this way for the cameras, Bess."

She smiled into the cameras but ignored their questions as she inched her way into the swarm and up the courthouse steps. She would make a brief public statement after the arraignment. The crowd parted as she urged Hafetz to "go straight, go straight." It took a full two minutes to climb the thirteen steps to the revolving door entrance.

Once inside she sighed in relief and let her body sag. Three federal marshals blocked the entrance while she put her black purse and Hebrew prayer book on a conveyor belt that took them through an airport-style x-ray machine. Then she turned left down a long hallway, following her attorney to Courtroom 110.

Nearly a hundred reporters and spectators were waiting inside the vast courtroom with black marble walls and oak panels. When Bess entered the room all heads turned and watched her take a seat in the middle of the fourth row on the right. As she thumbed through her prayer book, state supreme court justice Hortense Gabel was arriving at the courthouse. She was the judge whom Bess and Andy had been accused of attempting to bribe, and she was here now because federal prosecutors had charged her with conspiracy in the alleged scheme.

A tiny woman with short brown hair, Judge Gabel, at age seventy-four, looked frail and almost lost inside the oversized silver-and-black brocade suit that she had borrowed from her daughter. Nearly blind, she peered out at the crowd through thick glasses, looking confused and frightened as she walked slowly on the arm of her eighty-one-year-old husband, Milton, a tall, slender, gray-haired dentist, now retired.

As the Gabels walked up the courthouse steps through the crush of reporters and the curious, their only child, Sukhreet, grabbed her mother's arm and whispered encouragement in her ear. "Just pretend you're Madonna, Mother," she told her as she smiled and waved for the cameras.

A big woman who was so round she looked as if she had been blown up like a balloon, Sukhreet had become a central figure in this drama after she agreed to cooperate fully with prosecutors and willingly point a finger at her own mother. It was Sukhreet to whom Bess was accused of having given a city job in exchange for her mother's lowering Capasso's alimony payments. And now it was Sukhreet's revelations that were threatening to bring down both her mother and Bess. For without Sukhreet's testimony it was unlikely the federal government would have been able to bring any charges at all.

Bess glanced over at Sukhreet, sitting between her parents. She thought Sukhreet looked like a clown in her bright green suit and black and green sweater. Bess was surprised, too, at how much weight Sukhreet had gained. She hadn't seen her for more than a year—since the night she learned a federal investigation was under way and went to Sukhreet's Upper East Side apartment to talk to her about the case.

A few minutes after eleven U.S. Magistrate Leonard A. Bernikow called the court to order. The first item on his calendar was criminal case no. 796, *United States of America* v. *Bess Myerson, Carl A. Capasso, and Hortense W. Gabel.*

Two federal marshals led Andy from behind a heavy wooden door and into the well of the court. He looked trim in his impeccably tailored dark blue suit, having lost almost forty pounds since the past June when he entered Allenwood federal prison in northcentral Pennsylvania to begin serving a three-year sentence for tax evasion. He looked older than his forty-three years, with dark circles under his large, heavy-lidded brown eyes. His chin faded into his white starched shirt, and his thin, jet-black, wavy hair barely covered a bald spot on the back of his head. As he took his place before the magistrate he appeared subdued and solemn. His arms hung loosely at his sides.

Bess never took her eyes off him as she waited in the back of the hushed courtroom for the clerk to call out her name. Finally she heard the clerk's voice shout, "Bess Myerson." She rose slowly from her seat, leaving the prayer book on the bench, and climbed over a few spectators into the center aisle. All eyes were on her as she walked slowly toward the well of the court, moving directly to Andy's side. He extended his arm. Taking his hand, she leaned toward him and kissed him on the cheek. He whispered something in her ear. She turned her head without a reply.

Moments later the clerk called out, "Hortense W. Gabel." The judge walked haltingly to the front of the court, nervously twisting a handkerchief in her hands. She stood next to her attorney, Michael Feldberg, and put her hand on his arm.

The court clerk asked the defense attorneys whether they wanted the charges of conspiracy, mail fraud, and use of interstate facilities to commit bribery read aloud in open court. They each said no.

"How do you plead, Ms. Myerson?" the clerk asked.

Bess, no longer smiling, tapped her teeth with the frame of her tortoiseshell glasses—a gesture familiar to millions of television viewers from her years on quiz and panel shows during the late 1950s and 1960s.

"Not guilty," she replied.

"How do you plead, Mr. Capasso?" the clerk asked Andy.

"Not guilty."

"How do you plead, Justice Gabel?"

"Not guilty," she said in an unwavering voice.

Bail was set at $250,000 for Bess, and she was ordered to surrender her passport. Andy was to return to prison. Judge Gabel was released on her own recognizance. The entire proceeding lasted eight minutes.

Afterward Bess leaned over and again kissed Andy on the cheek. She would see both him and the judge in just a few minutes in the booking room, where they would be fingerprinted and photographed.

Escorted by her attorney, Bess took the elevator to the third floor, where she was led into the U.S. marshal's booking room. A black steel door closed behind her. A cage door opened into a small room. Bess took a seat on a bench next to Judge Gabel and across the table from Andy. They exchanged a few formal pleasantries and then fell silent.

Bess was the first of the three defendants to be led into an adjoining room to be processed. Black ink was daubed on her fingers and thumbs. Each was pressed to three cards to produce three complete sets.

After washing the ink from her fingers, she took a seat in front of a camera. A deputy marshal handed her a black oblong frame with white plastic numbers underneath. She held the frame up to her chest while a photographer took color photos, front and profile.

Judge Gabel followed her into the room. Bess kissed Andy good-bye and joined Hafetz, who was waiting in the hallway. On her way to the elevators she rehearsed her short speech, the only public statement she would make about the federal charges until the end.

By the time she emerged from the courthouse more than five hundred people had filled Foley Square. Four bulky federal marshals pushed and shoved their way through a horde of photographers, carving a path for Bess to the battery of microphones set up at the bottom of the steps. When she finally reached the microphones, the marshals locked their arms around her. She looked directly into the cameras, as she had so many times before. Nervously fingering her prepared speech, she began in a slightly shaky voice:

"This morning I pleaded not guilty to the indictment. I am innocent of all charges brought against me and have not committed any illegal acts. These have been difficult and troubling times for me and my family. For a long time I have been the target of ugly accusations and false rumors. I now look forward to having my day in court and am totally confident that I will be vindicated there.

"I believe my work as a consumer advocate and as a spokesperson for the arts has made significant contributions to the people of the city of New York. I considered it a privilege to have had the opportunity to serve them and the many humanitarian causes to which I've lent support over the last forty years.

"This is the only statement that I will make about the case."

Refusing to answer reporters' questions, she lowered her head and stepped away from the microphones, moving slowly through the crowd to the waiting Lincoln Town Car.

"Bess! Good luck, Bess!" someone shouted.

She lifted her head and searched the crowd for her admirer. Then, still holding the black prayer book, she disappeared with her lawyer into the waiting car.

2
A Shtetl in the Bronx

Bella Myerson once dropped some change in the center of the kitchen table as her teenage daughter Bess was sitting down for dinner in their crowded three-room apartment in the Bronx. The money was Bella's meager earnings from a part-time job scrubbing the floor of a neighborhood restaurant. "See that?" she demanded of her middle daughter. "That's what I earned from all my work. If you don't go to college, if you don't turn out to be something, that's what is going to happen to you."

Bess took her mother's words seriously. Prodded and pushed by Bella to achieve from her earliest years, Bess would grow up to exceed virtually any mother's expectations for a daughter. "I think I spent a lot of time trying to get my mother's approval," Bess once said. Yet for all of her accomplishments—her Miss America title, the lucrative years as a television celebrity, the praise she won as New York City's tough and precedent-setting consumer affairs commissioner, and more—she was never able to win a single word of approval from her mother, Bella, the most domineering and influential person in her life.

Once, while Bess was campaigning for New York's U.S. Senate seat in 1980, she stopped by a Bronx hospital to visit her ailing, elderly mother, then in her eighties. All the polls showed Bess ahead of her opponents for the Democratic nomination. It was shaping up as another triumph for Bess, possibly her biggest yet. It was not enough, however, for Bella Myerson.

When Bess was turning to leave after the two had visited, Bella demanded to know where she was going. To Manhattan to campaign, Bess replied.

"Sure, for everybody else you have time. For me, you don't have any time. What do you care?" Bella retorted.

"I'll see you tomorrow," Bess assured her.

"You'll come tomorrow, I'll be dead."

"I'm not going to let you die," Bess countered. "I'm not going to let you die until you've told me I've done something right."

With that Bella rose up from her pillow and looked squarely at her daughter. "I'll never tell you you did anything right," she shot back, her head then falling back on the pillow.

I'm fifty-five years old, Bess thought at the time, and she's still telling me I don't do anything right.

A short, frenetic woman, Bella Podelaky Myerson arrived in New York from her native Russia in 1902 at the age of ten. Friends who grew up with her remembered her as a beautiful, outgoing teenager with flowing brown hair who was always quick to take to the dance floor or to tell a joke.

But Bess would never know that woman.

On December 19, 1922, almost two years before Bess's birth, Bella's first and only son died of bronchial pneumonia at the age of two after lying sick from whooping cough for weeks at Manhattan's Willard Parker Hospital for Communicable Diseases. One of 268 children to die of complications from whooping cough that year, little Joseph Myerson was buried the next day at the Baron Hirsch Cemetery on Staten Island.

Family friends remember that the death of Bella's little boy transformed her in a way that would cast a shadow over her family for the rest of their lives. It was as if Joseph's last pained breath had extinguished Bella's own sense of life, leaving her, at age thirty, a stern, bitter, and seemingly affectionless woman who was impossible to please.

Her depression lingered for months as Bella all but ignored her husband, Louis, and her only surviving child, five-year-old Sylvia. Her doctor, hoping to boost her spirits, finally advised Bella to try to have another baby. Within a year of her son's death Bella was pregnant again and wishing for another boy. On July 16, 1924, Bess Myerson was born instead. Named for her paternal grandmother, Bessie, she was such a beautiful child that her mother would tie a red ribbon in her hair to ward off the evil eye—an old Jewish superstition that warned of bad luck for anyone too rich, too successful, or too beautiful. Bess would ultimately come to believe that her blessings were also a curse and that her humiliation at the hands of federal prosecutors years later might have been a fulfillment of her mother's superstitious fears.

Bess grew up in a small but sunny one-bedroom apartment in Kingsbridge Heights in the northwest corner of the Bronx. The apartment was in a castlelike complex of eleven four-story red-brick buildings that had been built in 1926 as a cooperative by a group of Jewish intellectuals. Their hope was to protect secular Yiddish culture from assimilation into the American melting pot by living together in a community where their language, traditions, and art could be preserved and passed along to the next generation. They named the complex the Sholem Aleichem Cooperative Houses after the famous Yiddish writer whose story about

Tevye the dairyman was later made into the hit Broadway musical *Fiddler on the Roof.*

Perched on a hilltop on Sedgwick Avenue between 238th Street and Giles Place, the two hundred apartments encircled a courtyard and were a sharp contrast to the single-family homes that made up the rest of the neighborhood. The neighborhood and complex had everything Louis and Bella could want for their family. Across a quiet, tree-lined street was Fort Independence Park, a shaded playground with wooden benches for parents and swings for children. A newly built public school, P.S. 95, was nearby, and within the complex itself the children could study Yiddish in the afternoon at shul, the Yiddish folk school. Here the Myerson girls would grow up among their own, near uncles and aunts in a tightly knit working-class Jewish community that must have reminded Bella and Louis of the shtetls, the small Jewish towns they had left behind in their native Russia.

Louis Myerson was eighteen when he arrived in New York from Russia in 1907, five years after his future wife. Both Louis and Bella were part of a massive Jewish exodus fleeing from discrimination and violence in Eastern Europe and czarist Russia between the 1880s and the outbreak of the First World War. The violence of their homeland had touched Louis directly as a young boy when Russian soldiers were carrying out savage pogroms in the shtetls, terrorizing Jewish families and conscripting the young men of the villages into the Russian army. When soldiers descended on the shtetl where Louis and his family lived, his father hid him and his cousin under the floorboards of their kitchen. When his father removed the boards after the soldiers had left, he found Louis unconscious from lack of air and his nephew dead.

Like both Louis and Bella, many of the Eastern European Jews who emigrated to New York in the early years of the twentieth century first made their home in the crowded tenements of Manhattan's predominately Jewish Lower East Side. Discriminated against in Russia, they ran into religious intolerance in their newly adopted home as well. When they sought to move out of the inner city to the outer boroughs, they found some neighborhoods simply closed to them. This prejudice was summed up neatly by the owner of one Queens apartment complex, who posted a rental sign that advised "No Catholics, Jews, or dogs."

The wide-open spaces of the city's highlands in the Bronx were different. Jewish developers had bought large tracts of land there during the 1920s and had built dozens of new apartment buildings along the northward extension of the city's rapid transit lines. Attracted by this new development, thousands of Jews migrated north from the Lower East Side to the Bronx. So many made their way there during the 1920s that by the end of the decade Jews comprised more than 45 percent of the borough's 1.3 million people.

Louis and Bella were living in an apartment on Prospect Avenue in the South Bronx in 1926 when they first heard about the plans to build the Sholem Aleichem Cooperative Houses from Bella's sister, Fanny. Fanny's brother-in-law was building the complex, and she and her husband, Samuel Brodsky, were planning to buy an apartment there. Fanny convinced Bella and Louis to buy one, too. The following year the Myersons paid $1,000 for an apartment with five rooms, which they figured ought to provide plenty of space for their young family: Sylvia, who was then ten; Bess, three; and Helen, only a year old. Eventually Bella's other sister and her two brothers moved into the complex, as did Louis's two sisters and two brothers.

Bella decided soon after moving in, however, that she didn't like their new apartment, which faced the courtyard and, as a result, was dark and poorly ventilated. Worried that Helen's asthma might be exacerbated by the stuffy atmosphere, Bella asked Louis to find another flat in the complex. The problem was that the only apartment available had just one bedroom. But it was on the third floor, overlooking the Jerome Park Reservoir, and sunlight streamed through the windows. So Louis and Bella gave up their five rooms for three.

The three girls shared the only bedroom until they left home to be married. Bella and Louis slept in the living room on a bed that Bella covered each morning so it looked like a couch. The apartment's big eat-in kitchen became the center of the family's life.

Bella and Louis were among the original 135 members of the cooperative experiment, which included Yiddish poets and writers, sculptors and painters, meatcutters and garment workers. Their common thread was a love of their culture and Yiddishkeit, the Yiddish language. Peretz Kaminsky, a writer whose father was one of the founders of the cooperative, remembered, "We had to cry in Yiddish. That is what we did to preserve the language. What was central and important was the preservation of the culture. We had a very strong Jewish identity."

Culture was the glue of the Sholem Aleichem Cooperative Houses. Ruth Singer, a childhood friend of Bess's who grew up with her there, recalled, "Religion was nothing. Culture was the important thing. . . . I don't remember anybody being bar mitzvahed. I don't remember ever seeing a rabbi there. Bess's family was the same."

In keeping with the hope of preserving their traditions, the residents enjoyed a rich cultural and artistic life. The complex had been designed with artists' studios and an auditorium for lectures, concerts, and Yiddish theatrical performances. Abraham Maniewich, an artist who was widely known then for his painting *The Ghetto*, lived and worked there. So did writers Isaac Raboy, the author of seven novels, and Jacob Levine, whose textbooks were used in Jewish schools. Sculptor Aaron Goodelman, who also lived and worked at the apartment complex, sometimes invited Bess and the other children of the complex into his studio to see his work. And though not all who lived in the complex devoted their days to art or writing like Goodelman, many studied or wrote Yiddish poems and stories at night after returning home from their jobs in the factories or garment district.

While culture was the cohesive factor at the Sholem Aleichem Cooperative Houses, politics was the subject of considerable disagreement and heated debate. The rifts were not between Democrats and Republicans, however, but between Communists and Socialists. The disputes were such, recalled Judy Sanderoff, whose family lived upstairs from the Myersons, that "people of the same family wouldn't talk with each other." Her husband, Sam, who was also raised at the complex, said the politics could be "bitter. Neighbors would gather for a card game every weekend. One of the rules was that no one could talk politics."

Some former residents remember the Myersons as Communists, but Bess has said that her father stayed above the political divisions that beset the complex. Bess attended Yiddish shuls and day camps run by the Communists at some times and the Socialists at others. She recalls marching with her father in the Communist-sponsored May Day parades in New York's Union Square, but she also remembers her father joining the Socialist-run International Workers Order for its burial program.

Despite the political bickering, Bess would later say of the Sholem Aleichem Cooperative Houses, "You had a very safe and secure feeling here in this insulated communal place. Although the journey was only about forty minutes by train from Manhattan, it was as long a journey as coming from Muscatine, Iowa."

In the Myersons' small apartment Bella was the dominant personality, a matriarch who ruled her home with an iron hand and barked out commands to her three daughters with the force of a Marine drill sergeant:

"Eat!"

"Practice!"

"Homework!"

If the girls dared talk while eating supper, Bella would roar, "Finish!" She thought dinner conversation was a waste of time.

A stern and demanding taskmaster, Bella liked to argue, rarely paid her harried daughters a compliment, and almost never hugged or kissed them. When Bess and her sisters returned home from school, excited by the high marks they routinely got on their tests and report cards, Bella would demand, "Ninety-eight? What's ninety-eight? What happened to the other two points?"

The years at Sholem Aleichem were lonely ones for Bess, dominated by the impossible task of pleasing her irascible mother. "I was not allowed to have friends," Bess once said. "That made me feel different. I was envious of girls who could meet friends after school. I envied friends who could go to the movies together." In her mother's opinion having friends was an unproductive use of time that would be better spent studying or practicing the musical instruments her mother insisted her daughters master.

Bess found grade school difficult, too, because she was tall beyond her years, a thin, awkward, self-conscious child. "You know," she once told an interviewer, "when I was growing up, I realized that people just hugged little girls. And the big girls were asked to be the monitor and to fetch that and that. I was always wanting to be that little girl who would be taken care of and embraced. So I had to learn somewhere in life to put my arms around myself. To give myself comfort. To learn how to be supportive of myself, to approve of myself, to give myself love."

Her classmates taunted her about her height, which had soared to 5'10" by her twelfth birthday. "Hey, Stretch, how's the air up there?" they would yell to Bess. Her height figured in one of her worst memories as a child: being cast in the school play in the role of Olive Oyl, the tall, homely cartoon character. Bess begged her teacher to cast someone else, but her teacher told her she was perfect for the role. She was forced to pull her hair tightly behind her head, put on an ugly black dress, and complete the costume by wearing her father's shoes. She was mortified, but her mother waved off her complaints, telling Bess: "I would have been taller, but we couldn't afford it."

The constant drumbeat of the Myerson household was "Go to school. Get *A*s. And learn how to support yourself."

"Do something!" Bella would command her daughters on those rare occasions when she caught them unoccupied around the apartment.

"She taught me discipline. My mother was the constant who ruled my life," Bess later told a reporter. "I ingested my mother's attitude even when I wasn't with her. And her attitude was always 'You better do good.' "

There was an irony to Bella's nagging and her obsession that her three daughters succeed, however. Though she had lived in the U.S. since the age of ten, she was unable to read English and spoke it poorly. Some of her teeth were missing, and she paid little attention to the rest of her appearance. Despite all the time she spent cleaning and cooking—her daughters later concluded that this was her way of showing them affection—the Myerson apartment always seemed to be cluttered. And her cooking was terrible.

Bella and Louis, meanwhile, argued constantly. "My mother and father lived in conflict all of their married life," Bess once explained. "They were always fighting, always arguing, but there was a pact, you know. You could say rocks in his head fit the holes in hers. My mother argued incessantly. And my father surrendered."

Bess's father was in many ways her mother's antithesis. Soft-spoken and patient, he was the one Bess turned to for the affection she never seemed to get from her mother. He was also the one who instilled in her tremendous pride about her Jewish heritage. "Never forget who you are," he would tell little Bessie.

On the weekends Bess liked to tag along on her father's housepainting jobs. "His work was so good and they loved him, so he would say, 'Wait till you meet my daughter,'" remembered Bess. "He would drag me around to his clients who had pianos. I would give little concerts while he was moving buckets of paint."

Louis was painstaking in his work—a "craftsman," as one of his clients, Pearl Pochoda, later described him. Her husband, Sam, remembered that if Louis "would make a mistake and smudge one of the doorknobs, he would go out and buy one out of his own pocket. He did not rush his work. I don't think he got paid enough for the amount of time he put in."

Clients would write to him commending his work, though Bella would complain invariably that he was getting letters while other painters were earning more. During the 1930s, however, Louis was fortunate to find any work at all.

One of the stark realities of Bess's growing-up years and something she would remember with clarity years later was the Great Depression. By the time she was nine, in 1933, the Depression was at its very depth, with sixteen million people out of work—fully one-third of the nation's workforce. In New York its grim effects were everywhere: a shantytown of makeshift shelters arose in Central Park to billet the homeless, the unemployed sold apples from street corners, and long lines of the poor and dispossessed waited for meals outside the city's many soup kitchens.

The working-class families living in the Sholem Aleichem Cooperative Houses in the Bronx were not immune to the economy's ravages. When the Depression loomed in 1929, just two years after Louis and Bella had put down $1,000 for their apartment, the cooperative went bankrupt as more and more of its residents fell on hard times. The buildings were bought out by a private investor, and the Myersons and their neighbors suddenly found themselves tenants in the buildings they had once owned.

Some neighbors were cast out on the street soon afterward as the economy worsened and families became hard-pressed to pay their rent. Bess and her friends would sometimes return home on the bus from school to find a family evicted by the landlord, their furniture piled up around them on the street.

Despite the early evictions, the residents of Sholem Aleichem did not go sheepishly into tenancy. When forty families were issued eviction notices in 1932, a rent strike was organized by the cooperative—the first rent strike of the Depression in New York City. The residents

threatened to move out en masse (they advertised in the *New York Times*:
212 families looking for apartment building, reasonable rent) and
began constant picketing of the building. Norman Thomas, the Social-
ist candidate for president, took up their cause and addressed the
cooperative's residents. After several unsuccessful appeals of the eviction
proceedings in what organizers disparagingly called the city's "capital-
istic" municipal court, a truce with the landlord was reached in which
rents were reduced by 5 percent and a portion of the total rent was
placed in a special fund to subsidize the apartments of the cooperative's
unemployed. A victory dinner was held by the residents in celebration—
a "proletarian dinner," one of the strike organizers told the *Bronx
Home News* at the time. "We will charge regular prices, but it will be
herring and potatoes."

For all the hardship of the times, the Myersons survived—"independently poor," as Bess later described it. Bella and Louis were hard
workers. Her father brought home a steady income from his housepainting jobs, and Bella sometimes cleaned at the neighborhood restaurant.
During the summers she also took a boardinghouse in the Catskill
Mountains and rented out rooms. Her three little girls helped her make
the beds and clean up after the guests.

The Myersons were careful, too, not to spend their money foolishly.
Louis took home scraps of leftover wallpaper from his job to decorate
his daughters' bedroom. He also picked up other odds and ends to build
them doll carriages and other toys. Bella knew how to pinch pennies as
well. She sold her old housedresses for $1 each to the black cleaning
women who worked in neighboring apartments. Those who couldn't
pay the full dollar were put on an installment plan. When the cleaning
women were finishing up for the day, former neighbors remember, Bella
would be waiting outside in the hallway to collect that week's 25¢
payment.

Some of Bess's peers got allowances from their parents, but there
were no allowances in the Myerson household. Bess's father would tell
her, "Baby, I would give it to you, but I'll tell you what, I put my money
in the bank, you see. And then all those people come along like the
Rockefellers and Morgans, and they put all their money on top of mine.
I have to wait until they spend all their money to get to mine."

Despite the hardships, Bella's goal was to save enough money to buy a
piano and pay for music lessons for her daughters. To Bella music
represented a chance at upward mobility. In the Russia of her childhood
Jews were barred from attending universities, but they could leave their
shtetls to study at the great music conservatories in Moscow. The always
practical-minded Bella saw music as a way for her daughters to become
educated and to support themselves, if need be, as music teachers.

Bess was eight when a battered secondhand baby grand piano was hoisted up three stories and wheeled into her parents' crowded living room, and soon Bess's life revolved around music, like it or not. Every afternoon Bess would have to leave the neighboring children behind in the park and trudge home to the piano bench. Her mother would be waiting at the door, and whenever Bess objected to the daily practice sessions, Bella lectured Bess in Yiddish in her high-pitched voice: "You don't appreciate it now, but you'll thank me later. Now, practice!"

So Bess would take her seat at the piano and play the scales while Bella listened from the kitchen. Bella knew nothing about music herself, but every twenty minutes or so she would startle Bess by shrieking, "Wrong!"

At Bella's constant urging Bess advanced quickly on the piano, and when Bess was eleven her mother decided she had outgrown her teacher at the Sholem Aleichem Cooperative Houses and it was time for someone new. That's when Dorthea Anderson LaFollette entered Bess's life.

In Dorthea LaFollette Bess discovered a role model and a surrogate mother. She seemed to be everything that Bess's mother was not: refined, educated, and empathetic. "She was like Ingrid Bergman," Bess remembers. "She was very tall, and she had a wonderful, milky complexion and bright eyes."

Mrs. LaFollette's elegant apartment overlooking Central Park was a world away from the cramped apartment in the Bronx that Bess called home. Marble steps led into the apartment's front hall, and a spiral staircase led up to a salon with parquet floors and a big fireplace. Chandeliers hung from the ceiling.

Bess found her new teacher warm and a willing listener. When Bess complained about being teased about her height, Mrs. LaFollette told her, "It's not the altitude, Bess; it's the attitude."

She also was able to ease Bess's embarrassment at having only one presentable dress to wear for her piano recitals—a red dress with a full skirt and gathered bodice. Her father had declined her pleas for a new dress, telling Bess that she would look beautiful even in a burlap sack. But Mrs. LaFollette was able to coax Bess into the dress with aplomb.

"I don't know what you're planning to wear," she told Bess before each recital, "but would you, as a favor to me, wear that red dirndl you wore once before? . . . It's a lovely dress, and you look so lovely in it."

Tension hung in the air in the Myerson apartment in the days before a recital. Sylvia and Bess would fight for the piano bench, while Helen concentrated on the violin. The girls struggled to memorize their pieces because Mrs. LaFollette did not allow her students to bring their musical scores onstage. Bella granted them an occasional break by ordering them out the door for a brisk walk around the block. "Walk fast and don't forget to breathe. It's good for you," she would yell as they scurried down the stairs.

On the day of the recital Louis would have the old car ready for the trip from the Bronx to Mrs. LaFollette's apartment on Central Park West. Bella always invited a few friends or neighbors along, and Bess would squeeze into the backseat and visualize her lap as a piano keyboard.

Bess proved to be one of Mrs. LaFollette's best students, and by the age of twelve she was performing with a small symphony orchestra. Bess loved music and dreamed of becoming a concert pianist or possibly even a conductor. "My mother wanted for me what she never had," Bess said years later. "I remember her once saying to me: 'You hate me now. You'll love me later.'"

3
Beauty from the Bronx

The long hours Bess spent on the piano bench in her parents' living room paid off when she auditioned for and won acceptance into New York's High School of Music and Art in 1937. Only 120 children from throughout the city had been chosen to attend the new school, which had been created the year before by New York's music-loving mayor, Fiorello La Guardia, to offer artistically gifted children the opportunity to sharpen and develop their talents.

For Bess, who turned thirteen that year, the school opened a new and vastly different world from the one she had come to know. At the High School of Music and Art Bess found herself side by side with the best and brightest young talent the city had to offer. The students' enthusiasm was clear from the long commute many endured to attend. Some students from the far reaches of the city would travel for up to two hours by bus, subway—even ferry—to reach the school at 135th Street and Convent Avenue in Manhattan. Even so, the school posted one of the finest attendance records of any in the city.

Bess herself spent almost an hour riding the bus and the Broadway Local subway train down from the Bronx to the school, an imposing Gothic building that sat on the top of a hill and became known, appropriately enough, as "the Castle on the Hill." As her second instrument, Bess had been assigned the double bass because her teachers, seeing how tall she was, thought she would be able to handle the instrument. But after Bess explained the difficulty of her commute from the northwest Bronx, they allowed her to take up the flute instead.

Classmates of Bess remember her as shy, serious-minded, and a bit aloof during their freshman year. It took Bess time to develop close friendships, and even when she did she rarely revealed much about herself. "She was mysterious," said classmate Shirley Schwartz, who later had Bess as the maid of honor at her wedding. "She was very secretive about her life outside of high school."

Bess did not bring many friends home to her family's one-bedroom apartment in the Bronx. Her afternoons were filled mostly with practice, rehearsals, and part-time jobs.

By her junior year in high school Bess had grown from a tall, awkward, skinny girl into a beautiful, willowy young woman with amber-colored eyes, a wide smile, and thick, curly, dark brown hair that fell past her shoulders. She wore no makeup, only a touch of Vaseline on her lips. "In her middle high school years she began to blossom," said her neighborhood friend, Ruth Singer. By her senior year Bess's looks had impressed her classmates enough to vote her dual honors as "Prettiest Girl" and "Girl with the Most Charming Smile."

Bess paid little attention to comments about her looks. Beauty was something that her mother, Bella, had taught her not to value. "The one important thing about the way she treated me, and the way she treated my sisters, was that physical appearance had no meaning at all," Bess once said. "It wasn't anything one could rely on, depend on, or work towards."

What Bella Myerson did value was hard work, and during her high school years Bess did what she could, despite her hours of practicing and the long commute to school, to make money for her family. She did some baby-sitting and gave private piano lessons—an experience that provided a bit of a shock when she discovered that some parents allowed their children simply to give up on the piano rather than insisting, as her own mother had, that their children practice and master it.

With some of the money she earned Bess bought clothes for herself, but she was careful about bringing them home. "If I ever bought anything like something to wear, I always took the price tag and slashed it with a red pencil and wrote down a number that was exactly half of what it was on sale for. My mother thought it was terrible if we spent money and bought retail. She always thought we should buy everything on sale, because that's the way you save money," Bess recalled.

"I think the girls who grew up in the wealthier part of the city didn't have the work ethic that we did," Bess continued. "Also, you had to bring money home. If I got twenty-five cents for a lesson or eventually fifty cents for a lesson, I put that money on the kitchen table for my mom. We made that contribution to the house, as well as buy all our own things."

There were not many boys tall enough for Bess, who was 5'11", or for her close friend, Ruth, who was 5'8", so they joined a group of Ruth's friends who had formed a club for tall girls. Membership was limited strictly to girls who were 5'8" or taller. They went roller skating together at the old Columbus Circle rink, sometimes dressed alike in red sweaters and white skirts. Ruth remembers the time a sailor tried to pick Bess up at the roller rink. Bess thought he was too short for her. "She said her name was Bess O'Leary," Ruth said with a laugh.

As Bess progressed through high school, Ruth watched as she appeared to gain confidence in herself and become more outgoing.

"When I brought her into the group, she became a hit with them, I think mostly because she was level-headed, pleasant, and warm. They picked her to be president right away," Ruth recalled.

Bella didn't approve of the increasing interest Bess took in boys. "My mother sabotaged any attempt I made at dating because my mother thought that study and practicing were more important," Bess said years later. "And as a matter of fact, I remember times when I would meet a young man, perhaps I was playing in a symphony orchestra at Columbia University, and I'd say, 'Please call.'

"I'd give him the number, and I'd come home at night, and I would say, 'Mum, did anybody call?'

"And she'd say, 'Yeah.'

" 'Who?'

" 'I don't know. Name somebody.'

"I'd say, 'Milton?'

" 'Sounds like Milton. Another name.'

" 'Robert?'

" 'Oh, yeah. More like Robert. Not Milton. You know, I don't know because the phone rings all the time. It's so confusing for me, I can never remember names.'

"So that was the end. I mean, each time somebody would call I'd have to go through this charade with her."

There was one name Bella didn't forget: Frenchie. Bella was adamant that Bess stay away from this handsome young labor organizer she met during her senior year in high school. The problem for Bess's parents was that he was not Jewish.

One night Bess told her parents she was going to an orchestra rehearsal. Instead she went out on a date with Frenchie. When she returned home, her parents were waiting up for her. Her mother accused her of lying. Bess insisted that she was telling the truth.

"Hit her," her mother yelled.

Her father rolled up his newspaper and struck her in the face.

He later apologized, telling Bess that Bella made him do it and that he could not cross her.

Years later, in Susan Dworkin's book *Miss America, 1945: Bess Myerson's Own Story* (New York: Newmarket Press, 1987), Bess would say the incident made her realize for the first time that her father would always be on her mother's side. "Deep in my heart, I was in awe of my mother for the power she had over Dad," Bess told Dworkin. "She drove him crazy, but he loved her, committed himself to her, and could not leave her. I believe that when I married I looked for men who had the same controlling powers. . . ."

Bess's success at the High School of Music and Art led her to enroll as a music major at Hunter College, the city's public college for women. Even as a college student, though, her social life was limited—but not by her mother at this point. It was 1941, and all the boys were at war. "We lived four years without dating," Bess said.

Bess had thought about attending a music conservatory but realized she did not have the talent to become a concert pianist. And despite high test scores on state regent exams, she did not have the money to consider going away to college. Living at home and going to Hunter was her only alternative. It was free. Founded in 1870 to help meet the city's demand for teachers, Hunter graduated, as Bess once said, the city's smartest, poorest girls.

Bess spent her first two years with other freshmen and sophomores at the college's sixteen-acre campus in the Bronx, attending classes in ivy-covered Gothic buildings with large, cozy lounges. In 1943 the U.S. Navy took over the Bronx campus and turned it into a training station for the WAVES. All of Hunter's seven thousand students were forced to double up in classrooms at the Manhattan campus, a sixteen-story building on the Upper East Side.

With the creation of the WAVES, the noncombatant Women's Army Corps, and the Women Marines, Americans for the first time saw women in military uniform.

It was an extraordinary time for women. Between 1941 and 1945 more than six million women went to work for the first time. In newspapers, in magazines, and on the radio the national feminine model was a woman at work. "Rosie the Riveter" became a symbol of the times.

Most of the jobs were clerical positions or factory jobs. There were some opportunities for women in medicine and law, but few women moved into professional careers during the war. The top-level positions in government and business were left for men.

At Hunter College Bess juggled her classes and part-time jobs, working at Orbach's and Franklin Simon. She worked hard on her music and dreamed of becoming a conductor, but in major orchestras there were few opportunities for women to become performers, never mind conductors. The major orchestras would not even offer a woman an audition.

In any event, any dream of a life as a professional musician was secondary to what Bess and many of the other young women at Hunter wanted most of all: a husband and a family.

As a senior at Hunter Bess was nominated by her classmates as Hunter's "Personality Girl." She was chosen by her fellow students on the basis of charm, regardless of beauty or class standing. Her dazzling smile, however, must have helped her rack up a few votes.

"She was absolutely beautiful," Marjorie Wallis said. "I can remember the first time she came to my house on 86th Street. She was wearing a white turban. I can remember my mother opening the door. She gasped."

Bess did not take her success in the contest or the reports of her beauty too seriously. "You see, I did not live in a family where they said, 'Oh, isn't Bessie beautiful?' Nobody really said that. They said, 'So you are taking dancing lessons. So dance. Let me see you dance.' They didn't say you were beautiful.

"First of all, you were not allowed to say that. If you walked up to a baby carriage and said, 'Oh, the baby is so beautiful,' the woman would spit three times and say, 'Pooh, pooh, pooh' to protect the baby from the 'evil eye.' "

During her senior year a neighbor at the Sholem Aleichem Cooperative Houses suggested Bess earn some extra money modeling for a group of retired men who had formed an amateur photographers' club in Manhattan. Bess made an appointment and got the job.

Out of concern that her mother might disapprove, she did not tell Bella that John C. Pape, a retired steel executive from New Jersey, was paying her $5 an hour as a sitting fee. Her mother thought modeling was a disgrace.

Bess did, though, tell her older sister, Sylvia, who was now married and the mother of two baby girls. She could tell Sylvia almost anything. They had always been close, even though Sylvia was seven years older than she. She could count on Sylvia in ways in which she could not count on their mother. Sylvia knew and understood the way the world worked beyond the Sholem Aleichem Cooperative Houses. She was good-humored and warm and offered encouragement and hope when Bess felt depressed and pulled down by their mother's negative attitude and harsh criticism.

Sylvia encouraged her to pose for Pape: why not try to earn some extra money on her looks? Sylvia thought Bess had been an extraordinary beauty since Bess was sixteen. With her high cheekbones and almond-shaped eyes, Bess looked like their father. Sylvia looked more like Bella, with her large brown eyes, wide shoulders, and wide hips. Sylvia also suggested that Bess have John Pape take some photographs that could be used in a modeling portfolio even though a modeling career wasn't exactly the kind of profession that a smart Jewish girl like Bess might aspire to. They both thought, however, that she might be able to earn a lot of money and that it might even be fun.

As Bess was preparing to graduate from Hunter College in early 1945, Sylvia sent a couple of John Pape's photographs to Harry Conover and John Robert Powers, the two most powerful agents for models in New York, glamorous men who negotiated contracts with major

Hollywood studios, big advertising agencies, and the fledgling television industry. Sylvia was certain they would snap up her sister right away.

But John Robert Powers rejected her. So did Harry Conover. She wasn't the All-American type they were looking for to advertise products.

Bess was crushed. The rejection confirmed what she had thought about her looks. She put modeling out of her mind. Following graduation, she returned to the Birchwood Camp for Girls nestled in the Green Mountains in Brandon, Vermont, where she had worked as a music counselor for the past four summers. She had no idea what she would do in September other than give piano lessons. She didn't have any money to pursue graduate studies, and there had been no marriage proposals. "I felt that I wanted to be like everybody else, and I wanted to do what everybody else was doing, which was to get married and have children. And teach piano again."

4
Miss New York City

While Bess was away at camp that summer of 1945, Sylvia gave permission to John Pape to send a photograph of Bess to WJZ, a New York radio station sponsoring the Miss New York City contest. The winner would go to Atlantic City that September and compete for the Miss America title. The pageant was offering a $5,000 scholarship for the first time that year. Sylvia thought Bess could use the scholarship to continue her education or perhaps buy the black baby grand Steinway she had always longed for.

As it turned out, Bess was one of sixty contestants chosen from 1,200 photographs to participate in the contest. Sylvia called Bess with the good news and told her that she had to return to New York in a few days for the semifinal competition. At first Bess did not want to go. She took her position as music counselor very seriously, and she did not want to ask the camp's owners for the time off, remembers Louise Sugarman, who slept in the bunk next to Bess's. "She was very reluctant. We all had to push her to go."

Sugarman also recalled that Bess was hesitant about entering a beauty contest because she was shy and modest. "In spite of all of her beauty, she wasn't a show-off kind of person. She was very reserved."

Determined that Bess should enter the contest, Sylvia called the camp's owners and arranged for Bess to take a few days off. Helen, the youngest Myerson girl, was also working as a music counselor at the camp, so she took over the *HMS Pinafore* production that Bess was in charge of. Sylvia had made it almost impossible for Bess not to return to New York. With even the camp's owners now encouraging her to enter, Bess reluctantly agreed to go. She borrowed a white bathing suit from one of the camp counselors and took the train to New York.

On the stage of the Ritz Theater on a hot summer night in late July, Bess paraded past the judges in the two-piece bathing suit. She must have felt more comfortable when they began the talent part of the competition. After having performed so many times in school concerts and recitals, she looked confident playing a three-minute arrangement of Grieg's Piano Concerto in A Minor and Gershwin's "Summertime" on the flute in front of an audience. At the end of the night she was one of fifteen young women asked to return on August 15, for the Miss New York City finals.

On the afternoon of the finals she was rehearsing at the Ritz with the other finalists when she attracted the attention of Lenora Slaughter, executive director of the Miss America pageant, who was sitting in the front row. "She had a white scarf tied around her hair," Lenora remembered. "She was tall. She was a beautiful girl. I thought to myself that she looked like just the type of girl that we wanted in the pageant."

Bess was bright and talented, classy and educated, the kind of girl Lenora wanted to help change the image of the beauty contest. Lenora was looking for a Miss America more interested in furthering her education than pursuing a modeling or acting career in Hollywood. A smart, strong, outspoken woman whose southern charm helped make her a master saleswoman, she had single-handedly raised $5,000 for the college scholarship to be awarded to the winner that year. She had hoped the scholarship program would transform the seaside beauty contest into a national event. That had been her goal since she arrived in Atlantic City a few years earlier from St. Petersburg, Florida, where she had worked for the chamber of commerce.

"What I was fighting for was giving little girls a chance to go to college," said Lenora, who ruled the pageant through 1967. "My job was to help American girls get an education. I had a dream, and I saw the dream come true." The scholarship program now distributes $5 million each year to winners in local, state, and national contests.

After the rehearsal that day Lenora invited Bess to sit with her in the empty theater for a talk. According to Bess, Lenora told her that she had a good chance of becoming Miss New York City and asked what Bess intended to do with the scholarship money should she win the Miss America title. Bess was stunned by the suggestion that she might win. She assured Lenora that the scholarship money would be used to attend graduate school.

Lenora was visibly pleased. She then offered Bess some advice: why not change your name from Bessie Myerson to Betty Merrick?

Bess smiled and said no.

Lenora persisted. How about Betty Meredith?

Bess was adamant. She wasn't quite sure why, but she felt very strongly that changing her name would be terribly wrong. Her father's words floated back to her: "Never forget who you are." That meant "Never forget you are a Jew."

"Suddenly, when she said to me, 'Well, have you ever thought of changing your name?' what happened suddenly was 'Hey, Bessie, this may be far more important than you realize. She wants you to go through the process of denying a part of yourself. She must feel in some way that you may move toward winning.' The other side of it was 'If you are going to move toward winning, just think how 250 people who live up in the Bronx are going to feel when you win.' I mean my father was a housepainter. Someone else's father was a truck driver. Somebody else worked in a little shop. These were not people who had a lot of exciting, luxurious things happen to them. It was exciting and luxurious when they were able to luxuriate in my victory, and since we shared the bad times, I thought, why not share the good times?

"I lived in a place where everyone was Jewish. I lived in a city where people were what they were. I went to a school, the High School of Music and Art, where people were chosen for their talent, and I went to Hunter College, where people were chosen for their intense efforts to work hard and move along with their own lives and their careers. Being Jewish didn't matter."

Lenora does not recall asking Bess to change her name but acknowledges she might have out of concern that Bess would encounter anti-Semitism: "I thought it would be a good idea because I knew how Atlantic City felt about Jews. I figured that if I could get her name changed it would help because she didn't look Jewish or anything like that. There wasn't a damn thing wrong with that girl.

"There weren't many Jewish hotels. These Quakers who organized the pageant did not like Jews, but that didn't bother me one way or another, because I was a Southern Baptist. I didn't know a Jew from a gentile from a Quaker. And they were all changing names. You see, movie stars were always changing their names."

Later that night Bessie Myerson was crowned Miss New York City. She returned home to the Sholem Aleichem Cooperative Houses with a new watch and with a deeper understanding of her father's caveat.

5
Atlantic City, 1945

W hen Bess awoke the next morning, she soon found that a photograph of her in the two-piece white bathing suit appeared in almost all of the city's newspapers. Her victory took her parents by surprise.

Neither knew she had entered the Miss New York City contest, and when they saw their Bessie in a bathing suit, they were not pleased. It was only after Bess explained she might win a scholarship for graduate studies that they agreed she should pursue the Miss America title in Atlantic City. "When I explained that I might also bring back a black baby grand Steinway piano, and my mother knew, therefore, that I would be practicing the piano for forty years, she was fine," Bess said years later.

Her celebrity brought her invitations to New York City nightspots like the Monte Carlo and El Morocco. She drank champagne and flirted with men who promised to set up deals with Howard Hughes. She appeared on television and played the piano on radio. And she visited Mayor La Guardia at City Hall, where he made her promise to stick to her music.

It was a heady time for Bess, then twenty-one years old and still living with her parents in the Bronx. Yet within a week she began feeling anxious and depressed. Bewildered by her success, she belittled her appearance and her talent: "I thought I didn't have a good physical appearance. I felt like a skinny boy." Then the form letter Lenora Slaughter sent to all of the Miss America contestants in August 1945 arrived at the Myersons' home in the Bronx. It must have added to her anxiety:

> We are eagerly anticipating your arrival in this resort on Monday, Sept. 3, and we promise you the happiest experience in your life. We know you are going to enjoy every event we have planned for you, and we also know it is going to be a grand experience for you to meet the charming girls from every section of this great nation of ours, as well as Cuba and British Columbia. . . .
>
> Be sure to bring a minimum of three and a maximum of four evening

gowns. You will wear evening gowns at all formal appearances where you are judged. Street clothes should be simple and youthful. At no time are you judged in your street clothes. You appear in the Boardwalk Parade in an evening gown. Therefore, concentrate on your evening clothes, which do not have to be expensive but should be most flattering.

Evening gowns? A minimum of three and a maximum of four? Where was she going to get evening gowns? All she had was the one long white dress that she had worn in the Miss New York City contest. Unlike other local contests, the Miss New York City contest had not made any arrangements for a wardrobe with a department store or a sponsor.

After being informed of her problem, John Pape, the amateur photographer, offered to pay a seamstress to make her two daytime outfits: one a royal blue, the other chartreuse. And Samuel Kass, a Seventh Avenue clothing manufacturer, called to offer evening dresses from his showroom. Despite such good fortune and kindness, Bess still felt blue. Sylvia, sensing her younger sister's high anxiety, tried to comfort Bess with her good humor and by telling her to think of the pageant as a free vacation at the seashore. "We've never been away from home," Bess recalled Sylvia told her. "We've never been in a hotel. We're going to have a wonderful week. We'll enjoy ourselves and not to worry."

On Labor Day, September 3, Bess and Sylvia boarded an early morning train for Atlantic City, then a fashionable seaside resort for New Yorkers and Philadelphians. It was the home of the first Ferris wheel and saltwater taffy. The game Monopoly, which makes use of the city's street names, was invented there during the 1930s.

Bess saw hotels, shops, and amusements lining the six-mile boardwalk when she arrived that steaming hot day in 1945. The famous Steel Pier jutted out into the ocean. Rolling chairs offered tourists a pleasant ride down the boardwalk. It would be thirty years before legalized gambling would transform the resort into a gambler's mecca.

With World War II now finally over, the military was bringing the boys back home. For almost four thousand men that September their first stop was Atlantic City's Thomas N. England General Hospital. There had been a strong military presence in Atlantic City since the U.S. Army took over the town in 1941, turning the city's hotels and convention centers into barracks and stations to train thousands of soldiers. Almost all of those soldiers still in town would crowd into the old Warner Theater to watch the Miss America pageant that week.

When Bess and the other thirty-nine contestants arrived in Atlantic City, they first went to the Miss America pageant's headquarters at the Seaside Hotel for registration and their hotel assignment. They were instructed not to smoke, drink, or speak with men (including their fathers) during pageant week, or they would face disqualification.

On the registration forms that were distributed to the press Bess claimed to be 5'10", an inch shorter than her actual height. Her other measurements, mentioned in almost every news story: weight, 136 pounds; 35½-inch bust; 25-inch waist; 35-inch hips; 20-inch thighs; 14½-inch calves; even ankle, neck, upper arm, and wrist measurements were given. She wore a size thirty-six bathing suit, a size fourteen dress, and size nine shoes.

Bess and Sylvia watched the other contestants as they registered at the Seaside Hotel. "We got there, and here are these lovely girls, beautiful girls, shapely girls with their mothers," Bess told a reporter years later. "And I looked at those girls, and I said to Sylvia, 'I'm never going to make the final ten.' I was taller than anybody. I was skinny. I felt awkward, but I had felt that way most of my life, and I hadn't evolved to the point where I accepted my own attractiveness."

It also seemed to Bess that all the other girls were dressed in stylish clothes. Other than her Samuel Kass evening gowns, she had brought only the royal blue and chartreuse outfits made by John Pape's seamstress. As they checked into their room at the Brighton Hotel, Bess told Sylvia she didn't think she had brought enough clothes.

Sylvia told her not to worry. When they got upstairs and into their hotel room, she spread the outfits on the bed and showed Bess all of the possible combinations. "First you have the all-blue outfit," she said to Bess, dancing around the room as she held up the blue skirt and blue blouse, trying to get Bess to smile.

"Then you have the all-lime outfit. Then you can wear the blue top with the lime skirt and the lime top with the blue skirt."

"She made eight outfits," said Bess.

No one who watched Bess move around Atlantic City that week would have guessed that she felt so insecure. In fact, one of the other contestants said she believed from the beginning that Bess would take the crown.

"From the minute we got there, we were in awe of this big, tall, beautiful gal," remembered Miss Florida, Virginia Freeland Berry. "We knew that she was going to be Miss America from the time we arrived because she didn't look like the rest of us. She was so tall. She was really tanned. Her hair was black. She had beautiful hair. And she was just so confident. If she was nervous, she didn't show it."

Berry and some of the other contestants suspected that Bess was Lenora Slaughter's favorite and that pageant officials were guiding her to victory. Lenora adamantly denied ever choosing one girl over another during a contest.

"She was one of the girls that I admired tremendously," Lenora said. "But I trained myself never to have any feeling about one girl. If I had, it would have been the kiss of death."

Lenora remembered, though, that Bess did emerge as a potential winner early in the contest. "She was what they used to call 'a definite threat.' She wasn't a little southern beauty, you know. She stood out. She had a mouth of the most beautiful teeth you've ever seen. She had that dark tan and that gorgeous head of curly brown hair. She was just a beautiful girl. And then, of course, she was very talented, and we didn't have too many talented girls. It took years to get the talented girls they have on the stage today."

Bess got a chance to display her talent at the Warner Theater on Wednesday, September 5, which was the first day of official judging. The forty contestants were organized into three groups for preliminary competitions in talent, bathing suit, and evening gown. Thirteen finalists would be chosen from the preliminaries to compete for the Miss America title Saturday night.

At 8:00 P.M. Wednesday Bess and the other contestants arrived backstage at the Warner Theater on the Boardwalk for the pageant's opening night. Bess had practiced the piano and flute earlier that day at a rehearsal for those competing in the talent division that night.

More than thirty-five hundred people were jammed into the Warner Theater, including hundreds of servicemen who set the tone for the audience with their cheers and whistles. As the curtain rose, the U.S. Coast Guard Band, in dress whites, struck up "The Star-Spangled Banner" and a spotlight shone on a huge American flag draped against a black silk drop.

Gerald R. Trimble, owner of the Claridge Hotel, introduced the judges, and Venus Ramey, Miss America 1944, was presented to the crowd.

The talent competition opened with Miss Iowa performing a tap dance, followed by Miss Connecticut, who sang "I'm in the Mood for Love," and Miss Illinois, who belted out "The Sheik of Araby."

When Bess walked onstage, she looked confident and regal in her white dress. She first played George Gershwin's "Summertime" on the flute with the orchestra and then took a seat at the piano and performed once again her three-minute arrangement of Grieg's Piano Concerto in A Minor. She nearly brought down the house.

The ten judges, sitting in the first few rows, had difficulty deciding between Bess and Frances Dorn, Miss Birmingham, who won wild applause for a fast-paced tap routine. The judges finally announced a tie for first place. As a winner of a preliminary competition, Bess now had a chance of becoming a finalist Saturday night.

The next night Bess wore her new white Samuel Kass gown with long sleeves in the evening gown competition. While the judges revealed their scores in the talent and bathing suit competitions, they traditionally kept the winner of the evening gown competition secret to add to the suspense on Saturday night.

There was now only the bathing suit preliminary contest Friday night before the finals on Saturday. Winning the bathing suit contest would ensure her a place among the finalists. Surrounded by so many other beautiful young women, Bess felt unsure about herself, although she recalls being "filled with a flaming competitive spirit." She knew she had to keep going and try to win "no matter how insecure I felt," she later told a reporter. "I kept saying to myself, 'Move through the event. Stand tall.' I wasn't confident. But my mother had taught me the process of doing my best."

The importance of the bathing suit preliminary competition Friday night made it only more difficult for Bess when she learned on Thursday that the size twelve white bathing suit that looked great with her dark tan was too small. Lenora thought it rode too high in the back. She sent over a size fourteen for Bess to wear instead. Only it was not white. It was lime green and hung on her tall, thin frame like a potato sack. Bess was devastated.

"I looked like a frog," Bess remembered. "I had this suntan, a little darker than lime green. The fourteen was impossible. It was just silk jersey, had no built-in supports, anything like that, and I looked like a telephone pole draped in lime green."

Once again Sylvia saved the day. She thought of the perfect way to stretch out the size twelve white suit. She put it on over her own bulky frame. "She slept in it all night," Bess said. "She was at least two or three sizes larger than me."

On Friday morning Bess put on the white suit and joined the other contestants at the Thomas N. England General Hospital to entertain the wounded veterans. The suit was still too tight, but it looked great with her tan. She got the most whistles and the loudest cheers. It was not a surprise when they voted Bess the likely winner of the Miss America title.

Bess returned to the hotel early that afternoon and complained to Sylvia that the white suit was still too small to wear in the preliminary competition that night. Sylvia removed the buttons on the straps, loosening them enough for Bess to pull down the bottom of the suit even more. Then Sylvia sewed the straps shut. Bess was now sewn into her white suit. She had to wear an evening gown for the opening of the show, so she slipped her gown over the suit and headed to the theater.

As she joined the other contestants onstage at the Warner Theater, no one suspected Bess was wearing her bathing suit under her evening gown. When her name was called later that night for the bathing suit competition, she tried not to cough, sneeze, or laugh as she strode past the judges. "I heard this shriek in the audience. It was Sylvia," she said.

Bess won first place, making her the only winner of two preliminary competitions, talent and bathing suit. It was now clear she would be among the thirteen finalists. Some of the newspaper reporters were already picking Bess as the favorite to win.

But Bess saw signs that did not indicate a sure victory. She felt some people were uncomfortable selecting a Jew. She became certain when one of the pageant's photographers warned her, "They're going to take it away from you."

"I said, 'They can't take it away from me,'" Bess recalled. "'You can take it away from me because I am too tall or because my eyes are not light blue. But you cannot take it away from me because I'm Jewish.' And there was something in me; something that happened to me. It was like I was backed up against the wall and somebody was saying to me, 'You are going to go just that far and no further, unless you play the game our way.' I thought, 'If I keep in that stationary position, nothing is going to happen to me.'"

It was only a few hours until the finals. Bess tried to put out of her mind the photographer's grim warning and her troubling thoughts that some people associated with the pageant did not want her to win. She would learn years later that her suspicions were correct. Someone was plotting to rob Bess of the title, to make sure Miss New York City—a Jew—did not become Miss America that night.

The mysterious phone call came Saturday night to one of the judges, Harry Conover, as he was getting ready to leave his hotel room and join the other judges at the Warner Theater for the Miss America pageant finals.

"The caller did not identify himself," said Candy Jones, a former Miss Atlantic City and top New York model who later married Conover. "He said, 'We do not want a Jewish Miss America. And if you do vote for her, you will never be invited back again.'"

Jones, who had been invited to return to the pageant by Lenora Slaughter, said Conover slammed down the phone in disgust.

Conover wasn't the only judge who got a mysterious phone call that night. "It was well known that this nasty situation existed," said Jones, now a talk show host for New York's WMCA-AM radio, referring to the level of anti-Semitism at that time in Atlantic City.

Jones could not imagine another contestant taking the crown away from Bess Myerson that night. "Her talent was spectacular. She had the best smile. She had a good figure. She looked very refined but very wholesome. There had been so many cutie-poos, Bess should not have had any problem."

Conover had been marking high scores for Bess in the preliminary competitions all week, even though he had rejected her as a potential model a year before because she didn't look All-American enough for his agency.

What prevented anyone from stealing the crown from Bess that night was the elaborate scoring system used during the pageant's preliminary competitions. Even if judges had yielded to pressure, it would have been virtually impossible to ignore the fact that Bess was the only double winner in the preliminaries.

Bess did not know about the phone calls until years later, but she said that at the time she felt "there were people there who were not rooting for me, who were going to deprive me of something because I was of the Jewish faith. I think there was a lot of anti-Semitism then. Nobody said anything directly to me, but I was a difficult product for them, as it turned out."

That night at the Warner Theater, without any knowledge of the mysterious phone calls, Bess joined the other contestants backstage with the same hopes and dreams: to walk down the runway at midnight with a scepter, robe, and crown.

The Warner Theater was packed. Bess's younger sister, Helen, came down from the Bronx and sat in the audience with Sylvia. Their parents remained at home and did not even listen to the pageant broadcast live on radio.

Nearly ninety reporters, magazine writers, and photographers filled the press section. Camera crews from five newsreels and the American Broadcasting Company had their lights, cameras, and equipment set up along the front of the stage. For the first time in its history the pageant was to be carried on five hundred television stations around the country.

The curtain rose at 8:00 P.M. with the U.S. Coast Guard Band playing "The Star-Spangled Banner" and a spotlight once again illuminating the American flag. Then a gold-and-silver curtain parted, giving the audience its first glimpse of the forty contestants in their evening gowns.

Bob Russell, the master of ceremonies, then stepped to the microphone and to a hushed house announced the names of the thirteen finalists. As expected, Bess was among them.

As she stood onstage next to another finalist, Arlene Anderson, Miss Minnesota, Bess could not imagine herself as the winner. "She seemed to me to have complete beauty requirements," Bess said years later about Anderson, who was pretty and petite. "Looking down at her, I felt tall and thin and miserable. I wanted to go home."

Shortly before midnight, as the judges were ready to tally their scores, the thirteen finalists stood on a platform in their bathing suits behind Russell, who was trying to keep the audience's interest with a few jokes and songs. Finally a judge handed him a card.

The orchestra gave a drum roll.

"And the fourth runner-up is Arlene Anderson, Miss Minnesota," Russell announced.

Bess was numb. She had been sure that Arlene's looks would win.

"The third runner-up is Virginia Freeland, Miss Florida."

But she was such a pretty blond! And the judges had loved her performance in the talent competition.

"The second runner-up, Frances Dorn, Miss Birmingham."

Bess took a deep breath. Frances Dorn had been her toughest competition in the talent division.

"The first runner-up is Phyllis Mathis of San Diego."

"And Bess Myerson is Miss America."

The audience cheered and applauded wildly. Flashbulbs flickered throughout the theater as photographers captured the first shots of Miss America 1945, smiling her dazzling smile as she stepped down from a platform to the front of the stage to take Bob Russell's hand. She looked serene and composed as Miss America 1944, Venus Ramey, put an ermine robe around her shoulders and the glittering crown on her shiny, dark, wavy hair.

Still smiling, Bess strolled down the runway carrying a scepter in one hand and a bouquet of American Beauty red roses in the other. She paused at the end of the runway and waved her scepter to the cheering crowd before turning back toward the stage. Past winners had often wept, overcome by emotion, but Bess never shed a tear.

6
Pride and Prejudice

Lenora Slaughter was beaming as she took her new queen by the arm and led her through the crowd of well-wishers to the Coronation Ball at the Claridge Hotel. Lenora had what she wanted, a beauty with brains, a Miss America who could change the image of the Miss America pageant and would attract more money for the scholarship fund.

Bess danced until the early morning hours, returning to her hotel room at 6:00 A.M. Later that morning she was awakened by a telephone call from Earl Wilson, the columnist from the *New York Post*, who had a few questions for New York City's first Miss America.

"Haven't you got pretty long gams?" Wilson asked.

"Yes. They call me Long John," Bess quipped.

"What's your favorite cocktail?"

"Milk."

"Do you ever neck?"

"Neck? A little sometimes. Just from the neck up."

"Ever say damn or hell?"

"No. I say gee whiz."

"Are you a sweater girl?"

"Oh sure, I wore them all through college, but I don't wear them tight. I wear them long and sloppy."

"Do you care for Sinatra?"

"I can take him or leave him."

"Are you beautiful?"

"I thought a lot of the kids here were more beautiful. I'm just kind of attractive, a little different-looking. I'm not underestimating myself. I'm just being frank."

"Do you wear a girdle?"

"No."

"A brassiere?"

"Yes."

"Pads?"

"Me? No, sir."

"Tell me, did anything funny happen at the contest?"

"Yes," Bess replied. "I won it."

Wilson ended his column by describing Bess as "one of the smartest dolls I have ever talked to."

At her first press conference early that afternoon on the lawn of the Brighton Hotel, Bess met with more than seventy reporters and photographers, representing newspapers and magazines from around the country. She responded to dozens of inane questions ranging from her views on the end of the war to what color nail polish she preferred (dark red). She startled reporters when she said that she intended to decline the Hollywood screen test that went along with her scepter and crown. She proclaimed the only reason she had entered the pageant was to obtain the scholarship so that she could pursue a master's degree in music.

A Miss America who did not want to become a glamorous movie star? A beauty queen who wanted to go to Juilliard? The newspapers dubbed Bess "a very serious type" and America's "first beauty with brains."

Hollywood and Broadway press agents thought her decision to turn down the screen test was nothing more than a marvelous publicity stunt. But Bess knew her limitations and realized she had no dramatic abilities. She also believed that her parents would be furious if she had agreed to the screen test. "Hollywood to them meant bad girls, bad times, and I guess I never had the courage then to just go out and do it on my own. My father felt anything one did with his hands was respectable. My mother thought anything that one did with the hands and the mind was respectable," Bess said years later.

Bella was so concerned that the beauty pageant might have sullied her daughter's reputation that she set the record straight right away in the *New York Post*: "She's pretty and she's a nice girl and so she won. She's not one of those runaround girls, which is why we're proud of her."

Louis, who had been described in the newspapers as a "well-to-do interior decorator," said he thought the results were "very nice" but added that he may not have chosen Bess if he had been the judge: "I wouldn't say she's bad-looking, but maybe, if I was the judge, I would have chosen one of the other girls."

The Myersons' friends, family, and neighbors at the Sholem Aleichem Cooperative Houses were elated that someone from the complex had become Miss America, but underlying the congratulations was resentment among some neighbors, who wondered what Bessie Myerson had over their "Rosie."

"Some people were saying that," said Judy Sanderoff, who lived upstairs from the Myersons. "But we were so proud of her. She was one of our own."

"It became sort of a victory for the Jews," said Mildred Schwartzman, another neighbor. "It was more important that she was Jewish than that she was from the house."

The people of the Sholem Aleichem Cooperative Houses greeted her return with a bouquet of red roses. There was music and dancing in the cafeteria. "When I came back as Miss America, I felt like a lady," Bess said. "I had the world waiting outside. I went up to my apartment, and I wanted to share that with them because we had shared so much pain.

"Do you know what that would have meant to me if I had been Betty Merrick and I had disowned them? This was the only place I was nourished throughout my entire life. I have been nourished by my own Jewishness. That never leaves me."

Her friend Ruth Singer said the 1945 Miss America pageant was probably the first and last pageant the people of the Sholem Aleichem Cooperative Houses ever followed. "A girl walking down a runway with bare legs was not an attraction, but she was one of ours."

Before departing on a four-week vaudeville tour, Bess spent a few days in New York, beginning her new life as a glamorous celebrity. She stayed at the Ambassador Hotel and dined at the Pierre. She once again visited Mayor La Guardia. She went to a beauty parlor for the first time in her life, and she bought her first pair of high-heeled shoes, black satin pumps. She answered more questions from reporters and posed for more photographs.

"Men?" she said in response to a question posed during a press conference at the Ambassador Hotel shortly after she returned to New York. "Well, naturally, they must be tall since I'm so tall. About six-two, generally intelligent, kind of attractive, in a muscular way. And I'd like him to like music."

"Any boyfriends?"

"Sure, I have lots of boyfriends."

"Someone special?"

"We—ll," she said, smiling a secretive smile.

The truth was she had no one special at all.

Stacks of letters with proposals were, however, arriving at her family's home in the Bronx, and mothers were trying to interest her in their sons. A woman who had read about her in the *Bronx Home News* thought she would make an ideal daughter-in-law and urged her to meet her son, a dentist, who was also interested in music.

Bess was not intrigued. "Well, if the man can't ask me himself, then I don't want him," she told reporters.

The vaudeville tour, billed as the American Beauty Review, began at the Adams Theater in Newark, New Jersey, a week after the pageant. Bess's pronouncements that she was too serious about her music for a Hollywood screen test did not stop her from appearing on a live bill with "featured acrobatics, ventriloquial antics, the Marimba Co-Eds, and a vocalist singing a medley of romantic melodies." Lenora had signed up Miss America and the top five finalists with the William Morris Agency, which booked them into theaters in New York, Newark, Hartford, and Detroit. The tour paid $1,000 a week. Bess was glad to be finally earning some money. She expected the title to bring her not only fame but fortune as well.

Bess had never seen a vaudeville show before she arrived in Newark, and she did not like what she found. The theater was old. The dressing rooms were dirty and the audience unruly. "I came out in a high-necked gown and played 'The Ritual Fire Dance' and 'Malagueña' on the piano and flute. I could hear the boys in front complaining and muttering, 'Where's the bathing suit?' So in the finale I came out in a white bathing suit, and the boys would cheer. Toward the end of the tour I realized that they didn't want to hear my music, so I just came out in a bathing suit. Finally I was losing weight and not filling out the bathing suit, so I quit."

While the other finalists were accompanied by their parents on the vaudeville tour, Bess traveled alone. She was lonely and depressed. And she found it demoralizing that she had to play the piano and flute in between animal acts and second-rate comedians. In Detroit her friend Marjorie Wallis, who was living in Ohio, visited with her and was surprised to find her so blue. Bess told her that she wanted to go home. This is not how she had envisioned her Miss America reign. When the William Morris Agency offered to extend the American Beauty Review's tour, Bess refused to go on. She told Lenora she wanted out. Lenora agreed.

"In my heart I knew it wasn't the right thing," Lenora said about the vaudeville tour forty-three years later. "It was a colossal failure. In those days they had these acts running between the shows. She would come out and play the piano. And some of them made her come out in that damn bathing suit. And that I hated."

Virginia Freeland Berry, Miss Florida, remembers a different story. "We were told that Bess thought she could do better on her own and she wanted out. We kind of resented that."

Bess was ready to make money. On a postcard she sent to Lenora from Detroit on October 2, Bess wrote, "anxious to hear word from you about any recent developments on anything that's come up." She had bought her father a yellow station wagon with part of her earnings from the vaudeville tour, and now she expected pageant officials to line up endorsements and to schedule additional appearances. She assumed there would be dozens of corporations seeking her out to promote their products in the time of plenty right after the war. She dreamed that she would move her parents out of their apartment and into a building with an elevator. "During the Miss America pageant," Bess said years later, "we contestants listened to endless tales of sponsors who discussed glamorous plans for the new Miss America, a fashion show, for example, on Catalina Island, because Catalina Swimsuits was a sponsor."

But few offers to promote products came her way that fall of 1945, and she was stunned when she discovered that she could not depend on Lenora to seek out advertising and promotional campaigns. Unlike today, the Miss America pageant did not provide winners with a chaperon or with much help in managing their reign. Lenora was already busy putting together next year's pageant, and she did not have the time or the staff to help Bess find work. Lenora was expecting the William Morris Agency to arrange whatever bookings and endorsements that might come up.

Within a month after she was crowned, however, Bess found herself caught in a messy dispute between the William Morris Agency and her brother-in-law over the management of her career. Harry Kalscheim of the William Morris Agency assumed he would be her agent since he had a contract with the pageant. Sylvia's husband, William Grace, insisted that he was her manager and announced she would not appear on any radio program that paid less than $500.

When Kalscheim came up with radio appearances that did not meet the $500 rate, Grace rejected them. Lenora intervened. She sent Bess a letter suggesting that she ask her brother-in-law to step aside and allow the professionals at the William Morris Agency to manage her career. "I warned her to get herself an outsider, someone who was trained to be a manager," Lenora said.

Bess decided to stay with her brother-in-law, but eventually she turned to the director of the Vermont camp where she had been a music counselor. He signed her up with another agent. Still, the lucrative endorsements that Bess had expected did not materialize.

"I had my hands full trying to help her make some money," Lenora said. "Had she been a little sophomore, she would have gone back to college. But Bess was a college graduate, an ambitious kid. She had worked awfully hard, and she wanted to make money. She wanted to show her family that it would pay, and besides, Bess liked money. Who doesn't?"

That fall Bess visited wounded veterans in hospitals, attended bond rallies, and toured the White House, where she met Mrs. Truman. She was invited to appear at the Rose Bowl and Cotton Bowl parades. She modeled for a magazine layout for one of the pageant sponsors and posed in a shampoo advertisement for another. She also appeared at the National Canners' Association convention as a hostess. But she did not always collect a fee since the pageant sponsors had already contributed to her $5,000 scholarship.

Years later Bess would complain bitterly that she had earned less money than other Miss America queens because she was Jewish. She would blame anti-Semitism for the difficulties she faced in getting endorsements. "I wasn't invited to attend as many events as I should have been," she said. "In some instances I thought they really wanted a blond, not a brunette. I had to really cover. I had to really protect myself from the truth then."

Lenora insists that Bess had as many opportunities as past winners: "I don't know why she says they didn't use her. I think Bess is mistaken there."

Until Lenora Slaughter began providing some management and chaperons for the Miss America winners in the late 1940s, Bess and almost all of the other titleholders faced difficulty earning money during their reigns. Without the pageant's help, Bess made mistakes, inadvertently angering two of the pageant's five sponsors, first by appearing in a drugstore advertisement touting a competitor's shampoo and then by posing for a magazine layout in a bathing suit that was not a Catalina.

While Bess did encounter anti-Semitism at the pageant and during her reign, it is hard to tell what impact anti-Semitism had on her ability to cash in on sponsors and endorsements. She earned from sponsors and endorsements as much money as, if not more than, the two women who had been crowned Miss America in 1943 and 1944. In the first month of Bess's reign she earned at least $4,000 from her vaudeville tour, in addition to her $5,000 scholarship. During her reign in 1943, former Miss America Jean Bartel made 469 appearances and earned a total of $3,000. Venus Ramey, Miss America 1944, collected $8,500, but not from endorsing products. She chose to go directly into vaudeville, performing the tango and the rumba. She was able to cash in on her celebrity for only a few months, however, prompting her to write a little poem that ended with "But it's nice to be a Miss America, it makes life très gay/Now if I could only find a way to eat three times a day."

By late December Bess must have been thinking along the same lines when she was collecting mainly expenses for her travel. She did realize, however, that travel was a great teacher.

Growing up in the Sholem Aleichem Cooperative Houses, Bess had never encountered anti-Semitism. She had never been told she could not enter someplace because she was a Jew. Then, in Florida, she saw the signs outside of hotels that read "No Jews."

"Sometimes they said it subtly, and sometimes they said it quite obviously," she recalled. " 'No Jews. No Dogs.' I don't know what they called the blacks then. It was overt."

Not as overt was the conversation she overheard at a country club she had been invited to by one of the sponsors. She cannot remember where the country club was located, perhaps outside of Wilmington, Delaware, or Baltimore, Maryland.

"It was a lovely place," said Bess, remembering the beautiful landscaped gardens, the impressive architecture. "My memory on certain things is very clear. I can almost smell the fireplace. This lovely black woman came in, and she used these bellows to stoke up the fires. I got dressed.

"I was all dressed and standing tall and walking down the stairs, and I overheard this conversation."

"Well, you didn't tell us she was Jewish," said a member of the restricted club.

Bess froze on the stairs. Then she heard that voice explain, "This is a restricted country club. We do not have Jews, and we do not have Negroes."

"I think I was arrested in motion," Bess said. "I turned around and went up that stairway. I took off the gown. I just let it drop off my body. I took off the crown. I put it on top of the gown. I went over to where my own clothes were, and I got dressed silently.

"It was as though I had to get through these next few minutes, and I couldn't think about what it was that I had heard. I wanted to just get into my clothes, and I wanted to go home. Being Jewish was always a very important part of my life, and suddenly it didn't suit them."

Hurt and stunned, she went directly to the train station that night and waited for a train bound for New York to take her back home to the Bronx, where she felt safe and secure. She can still remember standing on the platform sobbing uncontrollably. "I couldn't stop crying because I wanted to go home. I wanted to feel safe and protected."

7

"You Can't Be Beautiful and Hate"

On the train back to New York Bess began to think that maybe her need to return to her protective, insulated community in the Bronx was wrong. She felt that as a public person, in a position of power, she could be a positive influence. Maybe, she thought, she should be doing something with her reign other than getting keys to cities, riding in parades, and sitting in department store windows. "And I realized that this title was mine, forever, that I didn't really lose it at the end of the year. I just didn't want to be remembered as a beautiful but dumb broad." She wondered what she could do to help end racism and anti-Semitism.

At the end of 1945 the horror of the Holocaust was just beginning to make its way into the consciousness of the American people. Six million Jews had died in Nazi death camps. "We can't live through a Holocaust and know we were not part of that," Bess said to herself. "We can't dismiss it as something that didn't happen to us."

Disappointed that she was unable to earn a lot of money and deeply hurt by her experience at the exclusive country club, she welcomed an opportunity to meet with members of the Anti-Defamation League (ADL) of B'nai B'rith, who proposed another way for her to spend her time. Harold Flender, a young writer who was dating her sister Helen, introduced her to his cousin-in-law Arnold Forster, who was counsel to the ADL. He thought Bess could be an effective speaker for the ADL's ambitious new campaign against racism and anti-Semitism.

"I had no idea who she was," said Arnold Forster years later, remembering the day Flender brought Bess to his office. "I did not know why he brought her in, and I made a big blooper. He said to me, 'She is ready to work for us.' And I said, 'Who is she? Should we be interested?' He said, 'Arnold, she is Miss America.'

"From there on in, she worked for us. She was a good name to use. She had personality. She was pretty and had achieved a kind of renown. We set her up to speak before high school audiences across the country. She did an excellent job."

41

The ADL, founded in 1913 to battle anti-Semitism, created an organization called Youth Builders Inc. to provide high schools and civic groups across the country with people to speak out against bigotry, anti-Semitism, and racism. Discrimination against Jews was rampant in post–World War II America, Forster recalled, "discrimination that no longer exists in any meaningful way in the United States today, which is to say it was difficult for Jewish applicants to get into colleges or graduate schools. It was impossible for them to get into jobs in big business, the utilities, and the banks. Insurance companies were virtually closed to them, except for sales jobs. It was rampant discrimination, to say it in one sentence, in housing, employment, education, and in the social areas, where it still exists."

With thousands of soldiers returning from war, competing for jobs, racial tensions were high, Forster said. The Ku Klux Klan, which now counts hundreds of people among its members, counted thousands then.

Bess embraced her new assignment with enthusiasm. She finally had a role that would allow her to display some substance with her style. "If I'm supposed to be representative of the American girl, I want to make constructive use of that fact," she explained to a reporter at the time.

In February 1946 Bess began her speaking tour in Chicago and Milwaukee, visiting schools and community groups. The title of her speech was "You Can't Be Beautiful and Hate."

"I talked to them about tolerance," Bess remembered. "I told them to be kind to people different from themselves, to strangers who might speak with foreign accents, reminded them that it would be impossible to hate and be beautiful." She also told groups about her experience in Atlantic City.

"I said, 'There were girls from big towns and little towns. Nobody asked if your parents spoke with an accent. Nobody called you, "Hey, Jewish girl. Hey, Catholic girl." Not there, and we competed and won on our merit.'"

In those first few months of 1946 Bess felt she was finally bringing her family honor. Not only was she now being taken seriously on the lecture circuit; she was also practicing the piano again for her Carnegie Hall debut.

On May 31, 1946, she appeared at Carnegie Hall with the New York Philharmonic. The concert opened with *Fantasia on Themes* by George Gershwin. Wearing an evening gown and flat shoes, Bess played "Full Moon and Empty Arms," based on a theme from Rachmaninoff's Second Piano Concerto. For an encore she played Chopin's *Fantaisie-Impromptu*. There was loud applause, and a young girl approached her and handed her a bouquet of long-stemmed red roses.

Bess harbored no illusions about her invitation to play at Carnegie Hall. "Of course I never would have had the chance to play at Carnegie if I hadn't been Miss America," she told the Associated Press in an interview four years later. "But the reviews were very nice, and they didn't say anything about bathing suits."

While the reviews were favorable in the next day's newspapers, Bess apparently did not perform well enough to satisfy her mother, who was in the audience that night.

"My teacher, Mrs. LaFollette, and my mother were backstage at the end of the concert," Bess recalled, "and Mrs. LaFollette went up to her and said, 'Mrs. Myerson, Bessie was wonderful.' And my mother looked up at her and said, 'I don't know why. She never practices.'"

Bess remembered thinking then how she had practiced the piano all of her life to please her mother: "And I thought, 'I'll never win.'"

With the Carnegie Hall performance Lenora Slaughter finally released the scholarship money that was being held for Bess until she was properly enrolled in school. But Bess did not enroll at Juilliard, the Curtis Institute, or anywhere else to obtain the master's degree she had talked about during and right after the pageant. Instead she bought a black baby grand Steinway and drew on the rest of the money to pay for piano lessons and later for courses in music, elocution, and television at Columbia University.

As her reign approached its end, Bess began to realize that the crown was losing its luster. "It seems incredible that all the doors won't stay open indefinitely, but toward the end of the year you begin to realize that the title is losing its magic touch," she said at the time. "Soon there's talk of the Miss America to come—next year's hot property."

When Bess returned to Atlantic City in September 1946 to crown her successor, Lenora had made sure that the new "hot property" would not encounter the same conflicts and difficulties Bess had experienced with sponsors and managers during her reign.

The new Miss America would be required to sign a contract giving pageant officials the exclusive right to serve as her agent. The sponsors spelled out exactly what they expected of the winner. A budget was set up to provide Lenora with an assistant and to provide the new Miss America with a chaperon.

Bess was hoping to earn some real money now that she was no longer required to make personal appearances for contest sponsors and the mayors of small towns. She made an appointment with modeling mogul Harry Conover about becoming one of his clients. Candy Jones remembered that Conover would not give her a job.

"She was not taken on, mainly because the look then was a more birdlike face," Jones said. "She had a perfect face for television, nice big strong features, but of course television wasn't around then. She was also a little bit taller than the average model. The average height then was five feet, eight inches."

What Bess was really yearning for was a man. She was a Cinderella at midnight about to slip back into the anonymous crowd without her prince. On her final walk down the runway that September of 1946 Bess could think only of marriage and of a handsome young soldier she had met a few months before.

8
A Practical Prince

Allan Wayne was twenty-seven years old, a tall, good-looking man with an athletic build, dark wavy hair, deep-set brown eyes, and a disarming smile. He was well mannered and knew how to turn on the charm. He must have cut an impressive figure in 1946, walking around Atlantic City in his captain's uniform in those months after the war.

He had spent three years as an artillery captain in the Pacific and had been back for only a few weeks when he first saw Bess Myerson sitting at a table in the Mayfair Lounge of the Claridge Hotel in Atlantic City. She was in an evening gown, having dinner with Lenora Slaughter and H. H. Wheeler, a supermarket owner and sponsor of the pageant's college scholarship who had hired Bess to attend a convention that week and sign autographs at his exhibit space.

Allan had heard about the Jewish girl from New York winning the Miss America title while he was overseas. As he studied her from across the room, he debated with his friend, another young officer, about whether they should introduce themselves. Finally they decided a polite approach might be the most successful. They sent over a note with a waiter to her chaperons, asking permission to meet her.

"They were both nice-looking young officers," Lenora recalls. "They just saw this beautiful girl, and the word was around—everyone knew who she was. They wrote me a little note and asked if they might come over and meet Miss America. And of course I didn't feel that I had the right to give them permission to, but I approved of it, so I gave the note to Mr. Wheeler, and he said, 'Of course.' Mr. Wheeler asked them to join our table, which was perfectly proper and right in every way.

"The two young officers danced with Bess. Every bit of it was just as nice as could be. A girl couldn't meet a boy any nicer than Allan. He was very handsome and very nice."

As Bess and Allan glided over the dance floor, he told her that he was in Atlantic City for a few days with his father, who was attending a convention for toy distributors and manufacturers. He asked to see her

45

again when they both returned home to New York City.

Bess said later she knew that evening that she wanted to marry Allan Wayne. Unlike other young men she had met during her reign, he didn't seem intimidated by her title. She felt comfortable with him.

Allan was enthralled with Bess. After they parted that evening, he had a white orchid and a note delivered to her hotel room, asking to meet her the next evening. "Then we started to go out with each other, and neither of us went out with anyone else," Bess said. Their romance blossomed into a steady courtship. It was sometimes difficult for them to see each other, though, because Bess was spending so much time traveling on behalf of the Anti-Defamation League and Allan, who was now working with his father in the toy business, was spending a lot of time on the road.

That summer of 1946 Bess took Allan home with her to meet her family in the Bronx. The Myersons approved of Allan, who was Jewish and whose family name originally had been Weinshenker. He was the first man Bess had brought home whom her mother liked.

Allan seemed to have just about everything Bess was looking for in a potential husband. He had been an officer in the war. He was now working in his father's business. He was from a seemingly prosperous Jewish family from West End Avenue on Manhattan's Upper West Side, which Bess would call years later the "golden ghetto."

His mother, Cathryn, was a beautiful redhead who wore sophisticated clothes and smoked one cigarette after another. Some of her cousins in Baltimore recalled that she had won a beauty contest in Maryland before she moved to New York. His father, Gus, was a friendly and generous man who made a lot of money in the toy business and liked to spend it. To Bess, who had grown up in a one-bedroom apartment in the Bronx, the Waynes represented upward mobility.

At the end of her reign Bess did not want to return to her family's cramped apartment in the Bronx, not after a year of roses and orchids, fur coats and first-class hotels. But leaving home to take an apartment on her own or with another young woman would have been unthinkable. "No woman left to get her own apartment and live on her own," Bess said years later. "If you left, it was to get married. And if you weren't getting married, you stayed there. And some of the girls who never got married never left home, ever."

She considered marriage her only option. Eight years after she was crowned she would tell a reporter that it was important for a beauty contest winner to find solid ground after a whirlwind tour: "The best thing that can happen to a beauty contest winner is to be engaged. Then, when the fanfare dies down, she can get married. It is a good excuse for not having a glamorous career."

At the time Bess could not have imagined parlaying her experience in public speaking into a career. "We were never taught as women or as girls that we could make it on our own," she said in an interview many years later. "You had to get married, and the man you married would take care of you. You'd never have to worry again, which never happens. That is a fairy tale. And that was an enormous problem because I think what I had built within myself was a history of dependency and being dependent on a man.

"I was the last of a flock," she said. "Imagine twenty-two, and I thought if I didn't marry this man, nobody would ever ask me."

It was Bess who actually proposed to Allan Wayne. When asked months later by a newspaper reporter how he had proposed to Bess, Allan didn't answer at first. Then he and Bess giggled.

"You mean, *who* proposed," said Allan, described in the newspaper *P.M.* as looking "like the man who smokes a pipe in those full-color ads."

"Sure," Bess said. "He was roped in."

"The first time you asked me. . . ," Allan began.

". . . was when I told you to stop seeing that blond I didn't like," Bess said, finishing his sentence.

". . . And I asked you whether your intentions were honorable," he said. "She said, 'Strictly.' "

"Provided he would reciprocate," Bess added quickly.

"I said I'd try," replied Allan. "One thing led to another, and then I said, 'I do.' "

"But even before I proposed to him he brought me this very beautiful doll, dressed in a bridal costume," Bess said. "I never would have proposed . . ."

". . . unless she knew that I'd say yes," Allan said.

"I just thought I'd help him out."

A month after the end of her reign as Miss America Bess and Allan eloped. They were married in a civil ceremony on October 19, 1946, in White Plains, north of New York City in Westchester County. The couple spent a few days in the Catskill Mountains at Grossinger's, a popular resort among Jewish families, and then drove around New England. Because of the housing shortage in New York after the war, they didn't have an apartment. Allan jokingly said that he would pitch a tent for them in Central Park. When they returned from their honeymoon, they moved into his parents' apartment on West End Avenue. Cathryn and Gus gave up their bedroom for the newlyweds.

Despite the elopement, Gus and Cathryn Wayne wanted to give Bess and Allan a formal wedding in a swanky midtown Manhattan hotel. On December 29 the stunning young couple was married in a Jewish religious ceremony followed by an elegant reception for 150 guests at the Waldorf-Astoria Hotel. "They were both so good-looking together that they looked like they stepped out of a movie," recalled Bess's cousin, Bebe Barkan.

"It was fabulous. High-class," recalled Allan's cousin, Gilda Kramer, whose husband, Sam, remembered that Allan's father gave Bess her first mink coat. "They were very, very good in-laws. She couldn't have had a better life."

Though Gus and Cathryn were kind and generous, it must have been difficult for the young couple to live with his parents during their first year of marriage, particularly since Allan was often away on business trips.

A longtime friend of the Wayne family remembers Bess disappearing into her bedroom whenever guests arrived: "She would always leave the living room. She was very cold. She was standoffish."

Bess kept herself busy in the first year of her marriage, using the pageant's scholarship money to pay for her lessons and courses at Columbia University. She had given up her dream of becoming a professional musician or conductor, but she still studied the piano and gave piano lessons. She also continued to deliver speeches against racism and anti-Semitism on behalf of the Anti-Defamation League of B'nai B'rith.

Seven months after she was married Bess was pregnant. She gave birth to her only child, Barbara Carol, on New Year's Eve in 1947. Barbara would later change her name to Barra. She would become one of the few anchors in Bess Myerson's personal life.

The Wayne apartment was not large enough for both Allan's parents and the young family. Finally Bess and Allan found their own apartment in a less fashionable neighborhood on the northern tip of Manhattan. "We used to go up to Dyckman with bags and bags of groceries," remembers a family friend. "Gus would go into her bedroom and put a few fifty-dollar bills in her purse. He would make sure they were taken care of."

Money was tight in those early post–World War II years. To earn extra money Allan opened a small store on Broadway during the Christmas season and sold stuffed animals. He also tried to boost his income by selling old records. With these extra earnings they were able to move to a better neighborhood, taking a small apartment at 155 East 93rd Street in Upper Yorkville.

As a young mother, Bess accepted a few modeling assignments and jobs working as a commentator for fashion shows. But she spent most of her time at home, giving piano lessons. Her marriage to Allan Wayne seemed strong, yet Bess felt somewhat discontented. Like most young women in 1945, she had wanted to get married, but now that she was someone's wife she felt that something was missing from her life. The words of one of her piano students struck her one day: "Isn't it strange, Miss Myerson, you were Miss America and all that, and this is all you're doing?"

Suddenly, teaching piano seemed like scrubbing the floor to Bess. "And I thought, that's right. This shouldn't be all I'm doing. So I heard my mother's voice again, even though she wasn't there, saying, 'So? What are you going to do next? What are you going to be good at?'"

9

The Lady in Mink

Bess had been interested in pursuing a career in television ever since she had spent some of her Miss America scholarship money on courses in the new medium at Columbia University. In the late 1940s she made a few appearances on local programs, playing the piano on "The Jacques Fray Music Room" and appearing as a guest on variety and audience-participation shows.

Television programming was sputtering into life now that World War II was over. TV's "Golden Age" had arrived, bringing with it lots of opportunities for performers. The networks were constantly looking for talent in New York, where most shows were broadcast live from old theaters on the West Side of Manhattan. The television industry did not shift production to California until the late 1950s, when film and tape were introduced and network executives discovered they could save money by producing shows in Hollywood studios rather than trucking equipment from theater to theater in Manhattan.

With her daughter approaching her third birthday, Bess began working regularly in September 1950 as the emcee of a musical quiz show on WPIX-TV, Channel 11, in New York. For posing the brain twisters and handing out the prizes, Bess earned $25 a week. "It was a tremendous training ground for me," she said ten years later. "I never had anything to do with the theatrical world. I never had the stage as my goal. But in those days I helped in the production and the writing of the show, which taught me a lot."

The quiz show led to other opportunities, and soon Bess was also working as the hostess of a weekly interview show for housewives. Bess sometimes invited old friends on the show as guests. Lenora Slaughter remembers making an appearance to chat about the Miss America pageant. Candy Jones was invited to talk about her life as New York's top model, and Virginia Freeland Berry, Miss Florida, who had become a successful model, recalls appearing on the show to share beauty tips.

Opting to work outside the home in those post–World War II years was a bold decision for Bess. While working women had been lauded for their efforts during the war, at its end they were expected to return to the home and resume their roles as housewives and mothers. The antifeminist rhetoric of the time assailed women who worked, accusing them of destroying their families.

Allan was supportive of Bess's blossoming television career—with the proviso that her role as wife and mother remain her top priority. "She takes only those jobs she thinks she can do without interfering with the family," Allan said at the time. In the beginning he helped manage her career, acting almost as an agent, handling the books and scheduling her television appearances and speaking engagements.

Still delivering her "You Can't Be Beautiful and Hate" speech for the Anti-Defamation League of B'nai B'rith in the metropolitan New York area, Bess kept a busy schedule. In 1951 she was also committed to raising money at dinners for bonds for the state of Israel. A masterful speaker, she would raise more than $1 million for Israel over the next thirty years.

It was at a fund-raising dinner on behalf of Israel that her poise and charisma at the podium impressed Walt Framer, a television producer. He thought she would be ideal to host his new giveaway show, "The Big Payoff."

Giveaway and quiz shows were popular with the new television audience in the 1950s. The shows were also inexpensive to produce. Manufacturers would swap millions of dollars in appliances, cars, clothes, airplane tickets, and cameras for the opportunity to reach a nationwide audience.

"The Big Payoff," first broadcast on December 31, 1951, became one of the most successful giveaway shows on television. "We felt that there ought to be something in television or radio that would glorify the American woman," Framer said years later. "The concept of 'The Big Payoff' at that time was that any man from the age of six to ninety-six could get up and tell the world about the woman behind the curtain and why she deserved the 'big payoff.' They could be wives, sweethearts, girlfriends, aunts, mothers, secretaries."

But before a man could tell the television audience about his wonderful wife, he would have to answer three questions correctly. At that point he could collect $600 in merchandise and become eligible for the fourth question and the opportunity to win the big payoff: a mink coat modeled by Bess and a trip to anywhere in the world. By the end of the program's first two years Framer had given away more than $2 million in prizes.

In Bess, Framer found an articulate, glamorous hostess, a woman who could both model and sell the stylish fashions he would give away as prizes. "She was the best thing around at the time," he said. "I thought she had a lot of possibilities. She was a wholesome Miss

America and the epitome of the American woman. She was beautiful. She still is. And she had a wonderful smile. She had personality."

Framer had to overcome only one problem to put Bess on the air: her height. Since he didn't want her towering over the host, Framer said, he launched a nationwide search for a host who was at least six feet tall. In Minnesota he found Randy Merriman, a tall, thin man in his early thirties with light brown hair and a booming voice.

Bert Parks and Robert Paige followed Merriman and worked with Bess, who remained on "The Big Payoff" during the entire eight years it aired on CBS television, weekdays at 3:00 P.M., right after "The Ernie Kovacs Show." At one time the show aired on two networks. In the summer of 1953 NBC broadcast the show as a replacement for "The Colgate Comedy Hour."

Soon after Bess took the job, she became known as "The Lady in Mink." At the show's climactic moment she stood with her back to the audience in a luxurious mink coat, then wheeled around to face the camera and lovingly caress the fur. She was the Vanna White of the 1950s. It was her job to introduce the contestants to Randy Merriman, and describe the prizes and the clothes that she and other models wore. In her mink coat and evening dresses from New York's leading designers, she was the epitome of high fashion and glamour.

On the set Jeff Hayden, who directed the show on NBC, remembers Bess as "gracious and charming, a very dear, sweet person. She was wonderful. She was a top, top professional. I adored her. She gave as much as anyone I had ever worked with. She was a very warm human being, and that came across on the air."

Betty Ann Grove, a singer and model on the show, recalled that Bess was a "mother hen" on the set. "She wanted everybody to be wonderful," Grove recalls. "We had only two-and-a-half hours of rehearsal, and as people were twirling around she wanted to know exactly what was going on. She was very smart and very professional."

On most afternoons, as soon as the show ended at 3:30, Bess was on her way home to her apartment on East 93rd Street. She would try to get home soon after Barra returned from school. She was very close to her young daughter, teaching her how to play the piano and taking her on horseback rides in Central Park. "I've always made it my business to see that my career doesn't interfere with my private life," Bess told the *Daily News* at the time.

During the first years of their marriage Allan and Bess often invited her sisters and Allan's brother to their apartment. Allan was very close to his family, and they saw his parents frequently. They would also often visit Bella and Louis in the Bronx. They rarely went to nightclubs or big parties. Allan liked to spend most nights and weekends at home.

Approaching the sixth year of her marriage, Bess's career was soaring as "The Big Payoff" led to more television appearances. They had talked for a couple of years about having another child, but Bess insisted they wait. She was only twenty-eight years old, and she was just beginning to earn a huge salary. Allan confided in a friend that he was unhappy with his marriage now that Bess was working at least five days a week, sometimes six, making appearances on television panel shows such as "The Name's the Same" and working as a commentator at fashion shows in New York and Philadelphia.

And every September she would return to Atlantic City for the Miss America pageant. At a time when most women would not have dreamed of working outside the home, Bess faced the difficult problem of balancing her family and her career and being married to a man who seemed to run into failure each time she achieved success.

Allan was no longer working with his father in the toy business. Too much travel was involved, and he did not like to be away from home. His father found him a well-paying job in sales for a lingerie company that was owned by the brother-in-law of an old family friend. Still, he was not earning as much as Bess.

"She was making a bigger income," said a longtime family friend. "There was a lot of aggravation between the two of them. I think all the problems started when she went into the television business. She would tell people, 'I let my husband handle my affairs' to make him feel big. Instead, to his family and old friends, it made Allan sound pathetic."

As Bess earned new fame as a television celebrity, Allan complained that her career was taking too much time away from him. He wanted her home more often, fulfilling the traditional responsibilities of a wife and mother. One night, over a couple of drinks in a bar on Broadway, he told his childhood friend Stephen Posner that he was no longer happy in his marriage. He warned Posner, who was to be married in just a few weeks, not to do it.

"It was a diatribe on marriage and unhappiness," Posner said. "He was vociferous about his dislike of the whole married state, except for his daughter."

Considering Allan's upbringing, Posner was surprised by his friend's discontent with his own marriage. Allan and his only brother, the late Colonel Leonard Wayne, had been very close to their parents. "It was a very, very tight family. They were very, very close to each other," Posner recalls.

"Allan was crazy about his dad," said another longtime family friend. "I think he tried to follow in his footsteps, but it was just too much. It was difficult for Allan to fill his father's shoes."

When his father, Gus, died on October 15, 1953, Allan was devastated. A private parlor car carried the family and a few close friends from New York to Baltimore, where he was to be buried. Allan rode in the railroad car with the coffin. "He did become very upset," remembers his aunt, Pearl Maged.

According to Bess, in the years following his father's death Allan underwent a radical change. She believes his overwhelming grief brought to the surface buried memories of the war and that he perhaps suffered postwar stress syndrome. He started drinking and didn't stop. He began staying out all night. When he was at home, he would awake in the middle of the night from terrifying nightmares. The drinking also made him impotent. He blamed Bess and her career for the difficulties they were facing in their marriage.

Her colleagues on the set of "The Big Payoff" could see the pain in her beautiful face. "She was very concerned," recalled Louise McKinney, the show's fashion coordinator. "She loved him very much. They were beautiful together. I loved Allan. He was a fine person. But you're dealing with a situation that was very difficult. Alcoholism was not out in the open then. It was hidden away in the closet."

Bess kept waiting for the drinking to stop. It didn't. In early 1956, three years after his father's death, she went to the Bronx and told her parents that she was going to leave Allan. She was hoping her mother and father would understand and provide her with support.

"I wanted some kind of emotional support," Bess remembered. "I wanted to go home again, and I said to my father, having this little nine-year-old girl with me, my daughter, 'I have to get a divorce.'

"My father looked at me. He shook his head and said, 'No divorce. You go back and make it better.' I was shocked by what he said. Then my mother said, 'How could you get a divorce? You just put up new drapes in the living room.'

"All of my energy and my hope and my will to move forward just left me. She had that power."

Bess returned home to her Manhattan apartment and tried to make it better, but it would not work. That summer of 1956 they argued bitterly. Then Bess said that Allan began to beat her after a night of heavy drinking. Betty Ann Grove remembers having to fill in as hostess of "The Big Payoff" a couple of times when the arguments and the beatings made it impossible for Bess to come to work. "I used to have to replace her at the last moment," Grove recalled.

On one hot August night, while Barra was away at camp, Bess said that during one of their arguments Allan beat her savagely with his fists, chased her into the street, and dragged her across the sidewalk. She told him that she wanted a divorce. But he refused to agree to a quiet separation, so Bess plotted an escape.

10
The Custody Battle

Four days later, at ten o'clock on Sunday evening, August 26, 1956, Allan was lying on the couch, half asleep, when he heard the apartment door buzzer. Bess went to the door and admitted two uniformed New York City police officers and two men she later identified as her "agents." Allan rose from the couch and demanded to know what was going on. Bess announced she was leaving him and led the men into the bedroom, where she had stored suitcases that she had packed earlier that day. Following Bess and the men into the bedroom, Allan ordered the men to leave, but they ignored him as they moved next into Barra's room and collected her things. When Allan protested her leaving and taking their nine-year-old daughter, Bess became hysterical.

The two hired men carried the suitcases out to a waiting car, and the police officers escorted Bess and Barra out of the apartment onto East 93rd Street. Allan followed them out into the street, shouting at Bess that she had no right to take their daughter away. But he was powerless to stop her that night. The police officers threatened to jail him if he impeded their departure.

Once inside the car, Bess must have felt relieved. She and Barra were whisked away to a hotel in midtown Manhattan. They remained there in hiding for several days. Bess told no one, except her lawyer and her parents, where she was staying.

Allan knew that he and Bess had been having problems, but he later said that he did not understand why she left that night. He called his lawyer, Richard Rudell, and three days later, on August 29, Allan filed court papers charging that Bess had deserted him and had "unlawfully spirited away" their daughter. He stated that he had been searching the city for his daughter since they left and that Bess "has no home and is physically, mentally, and spiritually unable to provide and care for the child."

Bess's lawyers responded with an affidavit in which she accused Allan of threatening to "do away with himself" and their little girl. She also

55

contended he was not a "fit or suitable person to have custody" and could not maintain a suitable home for Barra.

On Tuesday, September 4, for the first time since Bess's dramatic escape, the estranged couple met in a courtroom downtown. Photographers and reporters from the city's daily newspapers were waiting to record the bitter custody battle between the thirty-one-year-old former Miss America and the thirty-seven-year-old handsome war veteran whose romantic elopement had been chronicled in the city's tabloids only ten years before.

Bess arrived at the courthouse that morning in a crisp cotton striped shirtdress, dark sunglasses, and white gloves. Barra, her hair pulled back in a ponytail, was at her side. When the child walked into the courtroom and saw her father, she ran to his side and flung her arms around him. There were tears in Allan's eyes as he held his daughter close.

Since both Allan and Bess insisted on being with the child, they all shared a hard wooden bench in the front row. Barra, smiling as she sat between her parents, kissed one and then the other. Allan and Bess did not even look at each other.

When the proceedings began, state supreme court justice Matthew Levy called both attorneys to the bench. After hearing both sides, Levy postponed the hearing until 10:00 A.M. Saturday. "I hope I will not have to hear this case then and that further efforts at an amicable arrangement will be successful," Levy said. "I also hope the parents will become reconciled."

Barra gave her father a final hug and kiss in the corridor and then left with Bess to return to their midtown hotel hideaway.

Any hopes Allan may have had for a reconciliation were dashed on his way out of the courthouse, where he was served with a summons for a formal separation action.

On Saturday morning, September 8, 1956, Allan was the first to arrive at the courthouse with his mother, Cathryn, and his lawyer, Rudell. He was standing outside the courtroom, waiting for the proceedings to begin, when he saw Bess walking down the hallway with her parents, Louis and Bella, and little Barra. The child again rushed into her kneeling father's arms and showered him with kisses. Bess turned icily away as Barra grabbed her father's hand and then took her mother's. She looked up at her parents as if to try to make them smile, but Bess and Allan remained silent as they walked into the courtroom.

As soon as the court proceedings began, a nurse escorted Barra out of the courtroom. Allan, looking solemn and glum, took the witness stand. Denying under oath that he had ever assaulted Bess, he also insisted that he had never drunk to excess, nor had he dragged her across the sidewalk.

Under his lawyer's questioning he said he did not know why Bess had walked out on him, but under cross-examination he acknowledged that they had argued frequently in the last six months. Their difficulties, he believed, arose from Bess's "working like a horse for the past four years." He said her workload resulted in "extreme moments of anxiety and pressure for her."

He also said he had "never stopped trying" to effect a reconciliation: "My life has been centered around my home, my wife, and my daughter, whom I still love very much."

Bess appeared to be listening intently to Allan's testimony as she sat next to her lawyer at a large oak table. She did not take the stand herself.

After more than two hours of testimony and private conferences at the bench, Allan conceded that Bess was able to care for Barra. The judge then decided to allow Bess to retain custody and grant Allan visitation rights and scheduled a hearing on those rights for the following week. "Since I think both parents love the child, they ought not to fight to the last drop of the child's blood because of disagreement arising among themselves," Judge Levy said. "I think Barbara [Barra] deserves more than that."

The following week they worked out what Levy called a "mutually and agreeably resolved" custody arrangement in his chambers that allowed Allan to visit with his daughter on alternate weekends and for seven to ten days around the Christmas holiday.

But six months later Bess stopped her efforts to seek a legal separation. Allan had convinced her they should give their marriage another try for Barra's sake. They moved into a new apartment on the tenth floor of a luxury building on fashionable East 88th Street, near Madison Avenue. In the foyer of their apartment Allan had the words "Bess, I Love You" imprinted in gold letters on the large white tiles.

"Allan worshiped the ground she walked on," said Anne Rudell, widow of Allan's attorney. "He really loved her. . . . He was crazy about her. But he didn't fulfill her needs. I can't fault her for that."

Their reconciliation lasted less than a year. "He was in the background," said his cousin, Sam Kramer. "It was difficult for him. His ego could not take the fact that she wanted out. I would go up to New York many, many times to talk with him about it. He wanted her to raise a family. He wanted her to be a housewife and have more children."

Bess was uninterested, however, in being just Mrs. Allan Wayne. "She was beautiful and brilliant," Anne Rudell says. "She was not going to let her achievement as Miss America go down the drain and be a little nobody. She said, 'I am somebody.' And she proved it."

Allan was not going to let Bess go easily, though. Barra still remembers hiding in the closet during one of his rampages. Years later she told writer Patricia Morrisroe: "My father had a real Dr. Jekyll and Mr. Hyde personality. He was obsessed by my mother and didn't want to lose her. My mother physically protected me. Her main focus was that I survive."

When Allan Wayne's drinking worsened that fall, Bess once again planned to leave him—this time for good.

On Friday, November 1, 1957, after Allan had left for work, Bess changed the locks on their apartment and had a messenger deliver an envelope to his office. Inside was a court summons requiring him to appear in court the next week to hammer out a formal separation agreement. The court papers also demanded that he account for $100,000 in money she claimed belonged solely to her. With the court papers she enclosed a letter asking, for the sake of their daughter, that he get a hotel room and not return to the apartment that night.

Allan was furious. He returned to the tenth-floor apartment that night and broke the new locks with an electric drill. Inside the apartment he found Bess and an armed guard. Allan pleaded with Bess to reconsider. When she insisted it was over, he still refused to leave the apartment, contending that it was just as much his home as hers.

Bess then called her lawyer, and Allan called Rudell. Both attorneys agreed to go to the apartment that night. They sat around the living room until after 1:00 A.M., trying to work out an amicable separation agreement. When they got up to leave, they tried to persuade Allan to leave with them, but he refused.

Exhausted, Bess went into her daughter's room to sleep. Allan took their bed. The armed guard remained inside the apartment. At about 4:00 A.M., Bess later told the police, she awakened to find Allan standing over her. "He ripped my pajamas off and put his hands around my throat, hurting me," she told the police. She also claimed that he shoved her against a desk. Her screams alerted the guard, who was in the kitchen getting a glass of water. He ran into the room and separated them. Bess then called the police.

When the officers arrived, Allan went quietly with them to the nearby station house on East 104th Street, where he was jailed for about an hour, until his lawyer put up $500 bail. "We flatly deny the charges," Richard Rudell told reporters as he left the station house with Allan at his side. "There was no violence and no assault."

The assault accusations and the separation action were a "sneak Pearl Harbor attack," Rudell told reporters. "Everything was fine Friday. He kissed her good-bye in the morning, and they were supposed to go out in the evening. But during the day she changed the locks on the door."

Rudell claimed that Bess had accused Allan of assault as a ruse to get him out of the apartment. "The whole thing boils down to the same issue we had a year ago in court," he said, referring to the custody of Barra and the struggle over their property.

Turning to the reporters, Allan asked, "If I love her the way I do, could I assault her?"

"Do you love Bess?" a reporter asked.

"I always have, and I always will," Allan replied.

Bess looked nervous and upset later that day when she appeared at the station house and swore out a complaint against her husband. There was no visible evidence of the assault. When questioned by reporters, she dismissed Allan's comments about his love for her. "That's his statement," she said. "Only I know what I have been through. My daughter is my only concern. Her welfare and state of mind are paramount. Now let justice take its course."

On Monday Allan was scheduled to appear in Manhattan Criminal Court to face the assault charge. Bess showed up in a beige suit to testify against her husband, wearing her wedding band on a chain dangling from her neck. As they stood waiting outside the courtroom with their lawyers, they did not speak.

In her sworn testimony Bess again stated that Allan had ripped off her pajamas, put his hands around her neck, and shoved her against a desk. She said that in the past he had threatened "to get" her and their daughter. She also testified that he had pushed her around on "numerous other occasions, one necessitating hospitalization."

"This is a case with a history of violence," argued her attorney, Benjamin Robinson, "and we ask that the defendant refrain from threatening and intimidating the deponent."

Allan's lawyer, Rudell, denied the charges. "There has been no breach of peace by my client." Referring to the separation action, he said, "The complainant's charge is motivated by other causes." He asked the judge to transfer the case from the criminal courts to the family court, where he argued the case belonged. The judge agreed and asked Allan, "as a favor to the court," to take a hotel room and stay away from the East 88th Street apartment until the case was resolved.

After the court session Bess told reporters that she no longer loved her husband. "I don't really know when I stopped. I've had enough of his cruelty over the years, and I cannot stand it anymore. I tried to be a good wife and hide all of this, but I feel relieved I have gone this far." After she left the courthouse, she headed for her television show.

Allan refused to say anything negative about Bess to reporters. "She's still a wonderful girl," he said.

This time Bess went ahead with a divorce and another lawsuit, charging Allan with misappropriating $100,000 of assets she contended belonged to her. There was no hope for a reconciliation now. Divorce proceedings were under way.

In December 1957 she sought a court order barring him from

transferring stock that had been put in his name only. She contended that she had earned considerably more money than her husband had for several years and that the stocks were bought with her earnings. "I fear that he will attempt to sell these properties to avoid having to turn them over to me," she told the *New York Daily News*.

Allan responded with a lawsuit seeking custody of Barra. A month later, on January 17, 1958, Bess dropped her lawsuit for the $100,000. They reached an out-of-court settlement on property and child custody issues and finally were divorced. Bess won custody, but Allan retained visitation rights. "It took a long time finishing because he was suing for custody of my daughter, and you can't do that," Bess said years later. "He just wanted the money." She said she gave him money so she could end the bitter battle over Barra, get the divorce, and go on with her life.

Allan moved out of their apartment on East 88th Street and into an elegant, expensive residential hotel in midtown Manhattan. He was devastated by the divorce. His drinking increased. Over the next few months he became increasingly despondent. "He couldn't take what had happened to him. 'What, you can't hold on to Miss America?'" said a longtime friend of Allan Wayne's who had grown up with him on West End Avenue. "He was insane about her, and that's why he couldn't take it when she left. She was going forward. He wasn't. She is no good, no good. She was a cruel person to him. He gave her her start. . . . He was a very nice fellow, and he made the mistake of wanting this girl, and along the road she no longer needed him. I guess he was a stepping-stone."

Another woman, who dated Allan for two years after the breakup of his marriage, said she could never believe the charges that he had assaulted Bess. "He had too much respect for women," she said. "He was very bright. At the time I met him he had a very responsible position at M. Schrank, and he was just a loving person. He was just a very, very loving person. But I know there was another side to him. He drank a lot. That was a problem. I presumed it had started after they had separated and divorced."

At one point in their relationship she tried to persuade Allan to join Alcoholics Anonymous, but he wouldn't go. "He would just say he was busy," she said. "And by that time I had stopped seeing him. I felt then he was just beyond help."

By the summer of 1962, four years after his divorce from Bess, Allan's drinking was out of control and he was overwhelmed with despair. That spring his alcoholism had cost him his job at M. Schrank, a lingerie and underwear company. He ran out of money and lost his apartment. He had nowhere to go, but he felt too much shame to return to his mother's apartment on West End Avenue. His brother, Leonard, who lived with their mother, begged him to stop drinking and return home. But Allan did not want his mother to know what he had made of his life.

A woman he had worked with at M. Schrank offered Allan the use of her apartment on the East Side. She traveled frequently for the company and spent days at a time on the road.

Just after eleven o'clock on the morning of August 12, 1962, she returned home from a business trip. She had last talked to Allan on the telephone four days before.

When she opened the door, the stench must have been unbearable. Allan was lying fully dressed on a couch in the bedroom. His body was badly decomposed. The medical examiner's office concluded he had been dead for several days.

"Allan was a very sweet, mixed-up man," said the woman who had dated him in the years after his marriage with Bess ended. "He was very sick. In a way he took his own life, but I don't think he meant to."

The city's medical examiner conducted an autopsy and found no sign of fresh, traumatic injury. There was no evidence that he had committed suicide. Bess would later say that he died of a cerebral hemorrhage, but the report says the cause of death was "unresolved, indeterminable." The doctors told the Wayne family they suspected Allan had become sick while drinking and possibly choked to death on his own vomit. The coffin was closed at his funeral.

The funeral drew more than a hundred people to Manhattan's Upper West Side. Bess was not among the mourners at the West End Funeral Chapel, formerly located on West 91st Street. Neither was her daughter, Barra. Allan's mother, Cathryn, and brother, Leonard, were deeply hurt that Bess did not make arrangements for Barra to be there, according to other friends and relatives who attended. "They felt that Bess had deliberately kept her away," said a longtime friend of the late Cathryn Wayne. "But she never said a bad word about Bess. It was very, very sad. Allan died of a broken heart."

11

"I've Got a Secret"

After her highly publicized divorce Bess received a few kind letters from television viewers offering support and encouragement. Most of the letters that arrived on the set of "The Big Payoff," however, harshly criticized her for leaving her husband. Some people were cruel.

Bess was deeply hurt and overwhelmed by the emotional expense of having to undergo such a public divorce. "An Emma Schultz can go through it with dignity, but a celebrity cannot. The public can be cruel," she said bitterly four years later.

Besieged by financial insecurity now that she was a single mother at age thirty-four, Bess took on as many television and modeling appearances as she could fit into her schedule. She was growing bored with "The Big Payoff" after seven years of modeling the mink coat five days a week. She couldn't think, though, about giving up the steady paycheck. "It's hard to just pick up and go," she explained to a television columnist a year after her divorce from Allan. "I have to think of my obligations—my child, Barra, for example."

Instead of taking a vacation the first summer following the breakup of her marriage, she appeared in the summer stock version of Robert Anderson's *Tea and Sympathy* at the Gateway Playhouse in Somers Point, New Jersey. She portrayed a schoolmaster's wife who defends a sensitive student. While the reviews were favorable, she dismissed questions about becoming a serious actress. She said she was not ready to accept a dramatic role. Perhaps she was unwilling to risk failure at that point, when failure could have jeopardized her financial security and her ability to support her child.

By the late 1950s her picture-tube-perfect face could be seen all over the television dial. She made guest appearances on "The Name's the Same," filled in occasionally on NBC's "Today" show, and appeared regularly on the popular weekly prime-time show "I've Got a Secret" with host Garry Moore. In 1958 she replaced Jayne Meadows on the panel, where she would remain with Henry Morgan, Bill Cullen, and Betsy Palmer for the next nine years.

62

"I've Got a Secret" was a spinoff of Mark Goodson and Bill Todman's "What's My Line?" and was probably the most successful panel show in the history of television, making the top ten prime-time shows during most of the time Bess was there.

The show's format was simple. It was part quiz, part entertainment. Four panelists would try to guess a contestant's secret after it had been flashed on the screen for the television audience. Three contestants and a celebrity guest got a chance to stump the panel during each show. Then the contestants would demonstrate their secret on live television.

Thousands of people from all over the country wrote to the show's producers, hoping to interest them in their secrets. Some of the secrets were pretty strange. There was the young boy who could tap-dance on his hands and the dog who could churn butter. "It became almost like a superior vaudeville show," recalled Henry Morgan.

The panel guessed only about one-third of all of the secrets over the years. "They got some on intuition, very few on logical questioning," recalled Chester Feldman, who produced the show for years. "For the most part it didn't matter whether they guessed it or not. Unlike 'What's My Line?' where they could question for five or six minutes, the panelists on 'Secret' had a total of two minutes for questioning because we had to leave time for the demonstrations. The game playing was less important than the payoff."

Feldman remembers Bess joining the panel after Jayne Meadows moved to California: "She was just someone who was around who was intelligent and beautiful. Being a panelist is made to look easy, but believe me, a hell of a lot of auditions were held before we found someone who could think on her feet and ask questions logically.

"You never knew what your next question was going to be. So they had to really think on their feet. Panelists were really selling themselves. It was one of the hardest things to do, to be interesting as yourself. They have no role or script to hide behind, so they were just out there with their bare face."

"Nobody played a role," added Henry Morgan, who was a panelist on the show from 1952 until it went off the air in 1967. "They played what they thought was themselves. So they came out as themselves."

Bess knew she couldn't be the funniest panelist, so she played it straight, serving as the serious panel member who asked careful, thoughtful questions. At times, though, it appeared as if she were trying so hard to ask a serious question that she didn't realize it was all for fun and entertainment.

Morgan remembers with a laugh that she often repeated what had just been said. "She'd stall around—'Let's see, I understand that you have lived for twelve years in Podunket. It's already been established.' She would do it every goddamn time."

"Bess was like the schoolmarm on the show," Feldman said. "The others would go for the laughs. Betsy was a little kooky. Bill was very witty and bright, and Henry was the bad boy. They would take pride in their ability to come up with questions, but they didn't take it that seriously. Bess played it very straight, and that's what distinguished her from the others. It was good for balance."

Backstage Bess struck the people who worked on the set as moody. Sometimes she would be warm and friendly, but most often they found her aloof. When Henry Morgan first met Bess, she had just been divorced from Allan Wayne. "She was a pretty unhappy girl when I met her," said Morgan. "Things weren't all that great.... She was working to live, to eat."

Bess was lucky to have won a regular spot on "I've Got a Secret" in 1958. A year later CBS canceled "The Big Payoff," her bread and butter.

CBS swept all of the big-money giveaway and quiz shows off the air in the fall of 1959, in the wake of a congressional investigation that revealed some television quiz shows had been rigged to create more drama. In testimony before a congressional committee, contestants admitted they had been coached in advance, told when to lose, and, in some cases, supplied with the answers. While there had been complaints of skulduggery on "The Big Payoff" since 1952, the congressional committee did not turn up any evidence of wrongdoing.

Bess might have been secretly thankful that her eight years on "The Big Payoff" were over. "By the end it all boiled down to finding a new dress to wear every day," she said at the time.

Worried about not having enough money to support herself and Barra, she set out to capitalize on her celebrity and create as many opportunities as she could. Only three years before, she had told her agent, George Spota, to turn down offers to do commercials. Now she considered almost any lucrative offer, including television commercials. At that time a glamorous "pitchgirl" could earn between $75,000 and $100,000 a year. Bess became the "commercial hostess" for "The Jackie Gleason Show" and later sold Ajax in commercial after commercial.

In the late 1950s and early 1960s Bess worked hard, even producing a record album with MGM called *Fashions in Music*, which featured her piano versions of thirteen popular songs, including "Makin' Whoopee" and "Ain't She Sweet?" She appeared every September as an anchor at Convention Hall in Atlantic City, guiding millions of television viewers through the Miss America pageant. And she joined the parade circuit, providing the commentary with Arthur Godfrey for Macy's Thanksgiving Day Parade in New York City and with Ronald Reagan and later Michael Douglas at the Tournament of Roses Parade in Pasadena.

"She was kind of hot," said television director Lloyd Gross, who worked with Bess on the set of "I've Got a Secret" and behind the scenes at the Macy's Thanksgiving Day Parade. "She was somebody you could count on to do a solid performance in that type of thing. Not that she was a great actress, but as a hostess she was a fairly substantial person to put on a panel. You didn't have to worry about what was going to come out of her mouth. If something went wrong, you knew she wouldn't fall apart. People found her very professional."

That is because Bess did her homework. When the floats paraded past her glass booth, she knew everything there was to know about each and every one of them. "People in New York might say, 'What difference does it make?' But it makes a lot of difference to the people in California," she told a reporter years later. "They worked hard on those floats. I knew them so well, even if the TelePrompTer broke down I would remember. You can't rely on TelePrompTers."

Bess was earning almost $100,000 a year as a regular member of the popular panel show, but she still felt poor. And while her work and her projects and a trip to Israel were keeping her busy, she felt very lonely. She told a friend that she wanted very much to marry again. Only this time her prince had to be successful and wealthy.

12
A Pygmalion on Sutton Place

Arnold Grant sat on the dais at the annual dinner of the Anti-Defamation League of B'nai B'rith in New York in the fall of 1961, plotting how he would capture the attention of the stunning mistress of ceremonies. He had never seen Bess Myerson before that night, and he was struck by her beauty and her presence. A passionate speaker and dominating figure onstage, Bess held the attention of virtually everyone in the hotel ballroom as she made a brief speech and then introduced the ADL's honored guests and prominent members.

When she announced his name and spoke effusively about his efforts to raise money for Israel as chairman of the Joint Defense Appeal of the American Jewish Committee and Anti-Defamation League of B'nai B'rith, he knew exactly what to do. Grant rose from his chair, smiled, and told the audience that he would forgive such extravagant praise "only if the lovely mistress of ceremonies will have dinner with me after the dinner."

Many women might have been taken aback by such bravado, but Bess was intrigued by this man, who she knew was one of the richest and most powerful men in Hollywood and New York and who had been one of the most sought-after bachelors on both coasts since his divorce two years before. Flattered by such a gallant gesture, Bess turned and graciously accepted his invitation.

As Bess's longtime friend Lilly Bruck later recalled, "Arnold Grant represented security. He had everything she wanted."

A tall, trim man in his fifties, Grant was a well-connected lawyer who counted Eleanor Roosevelt, President John F. Kennedy, and Senator Hubert Humphrey among his friends. Polished and self-assured—some would say arrogant—Grant divided his time between the entertainment capitals of the East and West Coasts. He wore expensive suits, vacationed on the French Riviera and at the oceanfront resorts of Mexico, and did not hesitate to indulge his expensive tastes in art. As a multimillionaire who earned an estimated $300,000 a year—this in the sixties—

Grant had no trouble affording the jet-setting lifestyle he led.

Grant's success as a lawyer was rooted in his development of the concept of deferred compensation, a tax strategy that allowed highly paid entertainers and executives to reduce their tax liability and plan for their futures by agreeing to be paid their big salaries over a period of years instead of in a single year. This strategy had some of the most famous Hollywood stars flocking to his offices in Beverly Hills and Manhattan. His client list included Gary Cooper, Bing Crosby, Lana Turner, Mary Pickford, Darryl Zanuck, Earl Wilson, Ed Sullivan, and Orson Welles. Grant's tough bargaining style had also convinced Johnny Carson to hire him in his negotiations with NBC.

His reputation as a tax attorney and corporate strategist had also gained Grant entrance to the boardrooms of some of America's major corporations. He sat on the boards of directors of the Hertz Corporation and Continental Airlines and at various times had served as a director of some of Hollywood's biggest studios: 20th Century–Fox Film Corporation, Columbia Pictures, and RKO-Radio Pictures, where he was chairman of the board for a time.

Outside of business, he was active in Democratic party politics and strongly committed to Jewish causes. He had been born Arnold Goldstein, the son of a successful criminal lawyer from the Bronx who sent him to expensive private schools in New York. His mother, Hannah, had been among the founding members of the American Jewish Committee, which later would give Arnold its prestigious Human Relations Award "for sustained and active leadership on behalf of improved human relations."

Arnold was generous with his money. He donated millions of dollars to Israel to build a library and also underwrote the construction of the law school auditorium at Syracuse University, his alma mater. The school named the auditorium after him.

Within six months of the awards dinner where they had met, Arnold slipped a $60,000 diamond ring on Bess's finger and proposed marriage. Bess accepted. They celebrated their engagement at an elegant party at the posh New York restaurant 21. "I'm the luckiest man in the world," Grant proclaimed in an eloquent toast. His declaration of love for Bess compelled the other men at the party to rise and toast their wives as well.

On May 2, 1962, they were married in a civil ceremony. He was fifty-three; she was thirty-seven. The small private ceremony did not include Barra, then fourteen, or Arnold's two daughters, Sally and Nancy, who were both in their twenties. They were sent instead to a matinee theater performance. But that evening they all gathered together in a suite in the Plaza Hotel and sipped champagne in celebration.

A few days later Bess and Arnold departed on a Pan Am jet to London to begin a trip around the world that included a visit to Japan and two weeks touring the Greek islands on a luxury yacht. When they returned, they lived in a suite in the Plaza Hotel for almost seven months while decorators put the finishing touches on Arnold's triplex apartment at 25 Sutton Place, in one of the most prestigious neighborhoods on Manhattan's East Side.

The twelve-room maisonette included seven bathrooms and was enormous even by the standards of New York's well-to-do. Arnold personally oversaw the extensive and costly renovations. The walls on the first floor were knocked down to create a vast living room and a formal dining room large enough for the dinner parties he loved to give. He installed special lighting to illuminate his works of art, and the rooms were filled with French and English antiques. The air-conditioning alone cost $5,000 a year to run.

Henry Morgan, one of the panelists with Bess on "I've Got a Secret," was an occasional dinner guest of the Grants' and remembers the apartment being "very impressive. It was the kind of elegance that didn't oppress you. You were aware that it was elegant, but it didn't bite you. On his mantelpiece were four or five children playing blind man's bluff carved out of jade. . . . He had two Dalis. In fact, Salvador Dali was at dinner one night I was there. So was Johnny Carson.

"They always had very interesting dinner parties. They had quite a circle of friends. After dinner Bess would play the piano and two opera singers would sing. Name people who were dinner guests singing for their supper, I guess."

Arnold showered Bess with gifts, including a diamond necklace, diamond clasp earrings, and a gold and diamond bracelet watch from Tiffany. Now that she was married to a wealthy man, Bess was able to give up scrubbing sinks for Ajax on television. She continued working one night a week on the set of "I've Got a Secret," though, and still made appearances on daytime television shows and hosted television coverage of Macy's Thanksgiving Day Parade, the Miss America pageant, and the Tournament of Roses Parade. Arnold took over her finances and worked his tax wonders by arranging for CBS to defer her $100,000 annual salary over an extended period to save on their taxes. Bess didn't need to spend her money anyway, because Arnold paid for virtually everything.

For all he did for his wife, however, Arnold demanded a lot in return. He insisted that she move with grace and ease within his circle of wealthy and accomplished friends. Bess would later tell friends that he became her Pygmalion. He taught her how to entertain and how to run a household staff. A live-in French couple took care of all of the cleaning, cooking, and grocery shopping. On most mornings Bess would be served breakfast in bed by her French maid.

Bess had always been able to turn on an almost overpowering charm, and she turned it on for Arnold's big clients. With only a dozen or so strands of gray in her lush dark brown hair, she certainly looked the part of the "beautiful wife." Yet despite her seeming confidence and outgoing style, the glamorous Queen Bess felt very much like Bessie from the Bronx at Sutton Place. She was not at all comfortable in her new role as the wife of a "very important man."

Although Arnold's friends insisted that he loved his wife deeply, Bess soon came to feel trapped by what she regarded as Arnold's domineering personality. Bess would later tell friends that Arnold castigated her whenever she questioned his judgment, browbeating her until she broke down in tears. She complained that Arnold turned social occasions into personal lecture forums on whatever topic was at hand, embarrassing her and alienating her friends and relatives. She came to see his dominance as a compulsion that extended to even the most trivial matters of household management.

Whenever anything was amiss at one of their dinner parties, Bess later said, Arnold would fly into a rage and then refuse to speak to her for days. Sometimes he did not wait until the guests had left. Henry Morgan recalled one evening when Arnold lambasted Bess in the middle of dinner for not having two sets of salt and pepper shakers on the table.

Once again Bess found herself with a husband who could be described as Dr. Jekyll and Mr. Hyde. She later told the *New York Daily News*: "He was great fun around the track but awful in the stable. There were just tremendous flips and flops. We'd go and have a marvelous time at the opera, and suddenly at the end of the evening I'd say something and there would be four hours of argument."

Three years into the marriage Bess began seeing a psychiatrist. She was depressed and anxious and tired of listening to Arnold's endless complaining. She later said, "The bars on the windows of our home on Sutton Place began to look like a prison to me; I was so trapped by all the responsibilities of wealth that I had no chance to be me. There was no time to grow."

Even so, Bess was reluctant to walk away from Sutton Place and the financial security that Arnold provided her. Moreover, she had already had one failed marriage and didn't want a second. But those feelings seemed to change all at once at a dinner party one night in the fall of 1965 when Arnold again criticized the way she had set out the silverware. Suddenly, as she later remembered it, everything became clear.

"One night we had some political people over," Bess said. "It was a terribly stimulating dinner party. After it was over, I said, 'Arnold, I learned so much tonight, it was wonderful.' And he said, 'Yes, but Bess, sit down. I want to discuss something with you. These shrimp forks are too small.' I knew then I had to leave."

The psychiatrist Bess had been seeing advised the couple to separate, and they agreed to do so in October 1965. Bess remained at Sutton Place, while Arnold took a suite at the Pierre hotel on Fifth Avenue, across from Central Park. Within seven months, however, they were back together, and they embarked on a summer of travel. They visited the Aspen Institute in Colorado, where they heard eighteen businessmen-philosophers discuss Greek democracy and its relevance today. They also visited Santa Barbara's Center for the Study of Democratic Institutions. The intellectual stimulation failed to rekindle their marriage, though, and Bess told Arnold that she wanted a divorce.

On December 21, 1966, Bess and Arnold signed a separation agreement. There was no dispute over community property. Having been married for only four-and-a-half years, Bess would have had a difficult time winning alimony and property from him in court. She settled for $95,000 from Arnold so she could buy an apartment for herself and her daughter. Arnold, who had adopted Barra after Allan Wayne died in 1962, agreed to share responsibility for the eighteen-year-old, who was a student at Bryn Mawr College on Philadelphia's Main Line.

Bess took a Dali, her Picasso lithograph, their massage table, some pieces of furniture, and their wedding gifts. Two weeks after Arnold gave her the $95,000 check, she went to Mexico to finalize the divorce. It came through on January 5, 1967. When she returned to New York, she bought an apartment at 14 East 75th Street and moved into the Volney, a small residential hotel on Madison Avenue, to wait for her new apartment to be vacated.

At forty-two Bess was again a single woman, and with Barra away at college she was alone. At last she was free from her husband's domineering presence. Yet even though she was earning $100,000 a year, Bess, the daughter of poor parents and a child of the Depression, worried about her financial security. As it turned out, she would have reason to worry.

In March 1967, only three months after her divorce and departure from Sutton Place, CBS canceled both "I've Got a Secret," which she had appeared on for nine seasons, and "Candid Camera," where she had just begun as a hostess opposite Allen Funt. "I've Got a Secret" had just run its course, recalled Chester Feldman, the show's producer: "Television was changing. CBS wanted to drop all its game shows and concentrate mostly on sitcoms."

Within weeks of the cancellations Bess was living with Arnold again at Sutton Place. How this came about would later become a subject of bitter dispute between them. Bess claimed that Arnold had invited her to live there temporarily while she was waiting to move into her new apartment. Arnold claimed, however, that Bess had asked to move into the guest room at Sutton Place for a few weeks to recuperate from an illness.

Once back at Sutton Place, Bess later said, she found her ex-husband a seemingly changed man. He appeared to be more relaxed, gentle, and romantic. It wasn't long before they were sleeping together again in the master bedroom and attending parties and social events as a couple; Arnold sometimes even introduced Bess as his wife. Her new apartment on the Upper East Side was sold, and Bess remained at Sutton Place. This newfound romance in their once disastrous relationship continued for thirteen months and led to their remarriage.

Arnold later contended to a close friend that it was Bess who first broached the subject of marrying again. Claiming that he never understood what had gone wrong in their first marriage, Arnold quickly consented. But this time he was cautious. He asked Bess to sign a prenuptial agreement in which she promised to give up her rights to alimony and the Sutton Place apartment in the event of another divorce.

Bess signed the agreement, and they were married for the second time on May 28, 1968, in the fashionable oceanfront town of Deal, New Jersey, by Arnold's close friend, David Wilentz, New Jersey's former attorney general.

Once remarried, Bess told Arnold that she wanted another child— even though she was forty-four and had a daughter in college and despite the fact that Arnold was sixty with two daughters in their twenties. According to one close friend of Arnold's, "No way in the world did he want to have more kids."

Yet Bess insisted that summer on becoming pregnant, and she underwent surgery that August to make it possible for her to conceive. Bess was ecstatic when told that the surgery had succeeded.

Her husband had a different reaction. To Bess he seemed indifferent, almost disappointed that the surgery had been effective. Arnold withdrew from her, and they began arguing once again. He saw a sinister motive in Bess's desire for another child. He believed that it was a clever ploy by Bess to circumvent the prenuptial agreement so that she could obtain part of his fortune upon another divorce.

If things weren't bad enough at Sutton Place, the fall of 1968 was a difficult time for Bess professionally as well. Although she made frequent appearances on daytime television and radio shows and occasionally co-hosted "The Mike Douglas Show," she had not been a regular on a television show since CBS canceled "I've Got a Secret" and "Candid Camera."

Then, in September, Al Marks, the chairman of the Miss America pageant, told her she would not be asked back for next year's pageant. For years Bess had guided television viewers through the pageant's annual festivities, and she had become a familiar, expected presence to the viewers at home. But Marks thought the pageant needed updating and a younger former Miss America as a hostess.

Marks remembered that Bess did not take the news well. "Wasn't I good enough?" Marks recalled she asked when told she would not be invited back.

Despite that setback, Bess kept busy with appearances on daytime television shows and with raising money for Israel. She also worked that fall in the presidential campaign of Hubert Humphrey, a friend of her husband's, serving as a co-chair of Women for Humphrey. She attended rallies on his behalf in New York and in Anchorage, Alaska.

By the end of 1968 she found herself slipping again into depression, just as she had during her first marriage to Arnold. According to her friends, she realized that marrying him again had been a terrible mistake. The tension at Sutton Place was palpable, so she must have been grateful to escape to the West Coast for her annual New Year's appearance as the television commentator for the Tournament of Roses Parade.

When she returned to New York early in 1969, a message was waiting for her from a top aide to New York mayor John Lindsay, the liberal Republican who had promised reform when he took over City Hall in 1966. The aide was calling to find out whether she might be interested in meeting with the mayor to discuss a job in his administration.

13
An Urban Folk Hero

I t was mid-January 1969, and Mayor John Lindsay's senior aides were gathered at City Hall for their regular weekly staff meeting. On the agenda was the Department of Consumer Affairs. For months Lindsay and his aides had been struggling to come up with a big name to head the newly created city agency. Facing an uphill battle for reelection in November, Lindsay wanted a star, someone who could attract the media's attention and portray his administration as a protector of the little guy.

Deputy Mayor Robert Sweet reported that the mayor's first choice, Betty Furness, had turned him down. She had just completed a two-year stint as President Lyndon Johnson's special assistant for consumer affairs, and she wanted to devote more time to her new marriage. With her White House experience and television celebrity, Furness would have been perfect for the job. No one at the meeting could think of anyone who could match her credentials and charisma.

Then Robert Blum, an assistant to the mayor, wondered aloud why they had even considered Furness, a "Johnson castoff," when they should have been thinking about appointing a "Lindsay original." At that point Sweet challenged Blum to come up with a "Lindsay original" within twenty-four hours.

By the end of the day Blum still had not thought of a single person for the job. When he arrived home, he asked his wife, Barbara, for suggestions.

" 'What should the person be?' " Blum said his wife asked.

"I said, 'First of all, it ought to be a woman. I think the public interest in consumerism is going to call for a woman. Secondly, I think she should be Jewish.' We were coming up to an election in 1969. Lindsay had enjoyed the support by and large of Jewish organizations, and Jewish groups in the city were an important part of his constituency. I thought a highly visible appointment of someone who was Jewish would be more attractive politically, other things being equal.

"Then she said, 'You know who might be interesting? Bess Myerson.'

"I said, 'Gee, she would be terrific. Do you think she would do this?' "

73

The Blums had met Bess three or four times over the years at fund-raisers and meetings for the League School in Brooklyn, a private school for autistic children, where Bess was on the board of directors. "We were impressed by her commitment," said Blum, who, with his wife, was a founding parent of the Association for Autistic Children. "Here was a person who was willing to give her time and her heart and her talent to a relatively obscure organization because she thought it was good."

The next morning Blum walked into Deputy Mayor Sweet's office and recommended Bess Myerson for the job. Sweet approved of the idea and immediately took the suggestion into Lindsay's office.

"He came right back out and said, 'Gee, do you think she'd serve?'" Blum recalled.

After Lindsay offered Bess the position, she asked him to give her forty-eight hours to think it over. Bored with her appearances on daytime television game shows, she was intrigued by the offer. "She told me she was tired of the artificial world," recalled Lenora Slaughter, who was still running the Miss America pageant at the time. "She said, 'Lenora, I am sick and tired of cosmetics and phony new dresses and always having to be on a show. I want to be me.'"

Although Bess was interested, she hesitated. The pay was $75,000 less than her previous income, and her marriage to Arnold was unstable. "When you were brought up the way we were brought up, and you saw what happened to evicted people, you were always concerned about having financial security," she explained later.

But Arnold surprised her with his encouragement and support and promises to tutor her in government, politics, and law. In fact it seemed as if her appointment had rekindled their relationship, which had suffered tremendously since their dispute over having a child. "He said, 'You don't need the security of the earning power,'" Bess remembered years later.

The next day Bess called Lindsay and told him she would accept the job. "I thought it would be a fantastic chance to put myself on the line and see if I could deliver," she said later.

On February 3, 1969, Lindsay publicly announced her appointment, describing her as a "charming and committed citizen of New York." Bess needed no introduction to New Yorkers. Almost everyone knew the homegrown beauty queen.

When reporters questioned her qualifications for the job, Bess turned to her childhood in the Bronx. Growing up during the Depression, the daughter of working-class Jewish immigrants, she explained, made it "simple to identify with people who create a quality of life for themselves with pennies, nickels and dimes."

Her appointment came at the height of the consumer movement that was sweeping the country. Prices were rising with inflation, and the public was growing increasingly dissatisfied with the quality of goods and services. With the dollar worth only 77¢ of what it was in 1959, the public was no longer willing to pay for shoddy merchandise.

Fueled by the populism of the 1960s, the movement had become increasingly aggressive and militant. As individuals became aware of the power of the purse, politicians and businesspeople recognized they could no longer ignore consumers' demands. In 1968 Councilman Ed Sadowsky led the fight to combine New York City's Department of Markets with the Department of Licenses to create the Department of Consumer Affairs.

It was the only municipal agency in the country with the power to issue regulations and impose fines on fraudulent merchants. With a $3 million budget the agency was responsible for licensing more than a hundred types of businesses, ranging from sidewalk cafés to locksmiths. The inspectional force examined thousands of scales every year, checked the flow of gasoline pumps, and enforced city regulations governing price posting and the sale of products.

Sadowsky was distressed when he first learned that Lindsay was appointing a former beauty queen–turned–television personality to head the new agency. "I made some noise about it: 'Hey, this is too important to leave to a beauty queen,'" he said. "And hell hath no fury like Bess Myerson scorned. She descended upon me with her then-lawyer, Howard Squadron. They took me out to lunch. It was intended to win me over and explain that despite the fact that she was a beauty queen, she was a woman who had considerable skills and could do this job just fine. It was a pleasant enough experience for me to withdraw any objection. Thereafter, she did get to work at getting a very good comprehensive consumer protection law passed."

Bess was very much aware that some people at City Hall and in the press corps did not think she was qualified for the job. "Whipped cream" and "window dressing" and "What does an ex–beauty queen know about consumer affairs?" were among the comments that filtered down to her in the weeks after her appointment. To her dismay, almost all of the newspaper stories about her appointment began with the phrase "Bess Myerson, Miss America 1945." Accompanying the stories in a couple of newspapers were photographs of her in a bathing suit when she was crowned. Even the august *New York Times* reported that Bess, during a visit to a city council meeting, "was paid all the honors appropriate to a Miss America."

Bess had expected to encounter some difficulty in shattering her beauty queen image. "See, the Miss America title became part of my name. My name was Bess Myerson, former Miss America. . . . And I thought, well, here we go again. We're just going to have to dispel that, and we're going to have to drop 'former Miss America.' It had to become Bess Myerson, Commissioner of Consumer Affairs."

Soon after her appointment was announced, Bess learned that she would immediately have to establish herself as one tough customer with the mayor's senior staff. Although Lindsay told Bess that she could hire whomever she wanted without regard to the job candidate's political party, a top mayoral aide tried to break that promise within weeks of her appointment. The mayoral aide wanted Bess to demand that Simon Lazarus, whom she had just hired as her counsel, change his registration from Democrat to Republican. She refused. "She was very tough," Lazarus recalled. "He collapsed immediately. It was very clear that she was being tested."

In most cases, though, Bess used her charm before displaying the tough, aggressive side of her personality. Sid Davidoff, then a special assistant to the mayor, remembered the first day Bess turned the charm on him. He suspected that she knew he had opposed her hiring, and he expected her to be somewhat hostile to him during their first meeting. Instead Bess caught him off balance by oozing all over him: "'Oh, you're Sid Davidoff. Oh, I just didn't expect anyone so young. I will just adore working with you.'

"What are you going to do when a former Miss America is standing there telling you that?" Davidoff said. "I was twenty-seven years old. She got me with two blows before I had a chance to respond. She had her agenda. She did not use a club, but she was not afraid to use a club."

In the weeks between her appointment on February 3, 1969, and her swearing-in ceremony a month later, Bess immersed herself in consumer protection issues. Victor Marrero, a special assistant to the mayor, put together a three-ring binder that contained detailed explanations about consumer regulations, the organization of the department, and what issues the mayor would like to see pursued. "She mastered it very quickly," Marrero said. "At no point did we have any doubt about her intelligence and her ability to master the intricacies of the job and the content."

Arnold, too, fulfilled his promise to help coach Bess. He suggested they leave New York for Palm Springs, where they could spend a few days free of distractions, studying consumer law and the ways of government. She packed her three-ring binder in a suitcase, along with other reports and papers from the department and a few books, including David Caplovitz's _The Poor Pay More_, which detailed abuses in the urban marketplace. Inside her purse was her horoscope, which she had cut out of the paper a few days before: "Come through with what you have promised where your vocation is concerned, and do nothing that jeopardizes your reputation."

After a few days, however, she concluded that Arnold was more interested in dominating and controlling her than in helping her become acquainted with consumer law. As they sat by the pool, baking in the hot desert sun with their books and papers, she later complained, he relentlessly drilled her on points of law, consumer issues, and the structure of city government. He gave Bess long lectures and insisted that she take notes so he could later test her recall. She said he also demanded that she keep notes and records of all her daily activities once she took over the agency so that he could review them when she got home.

By the time of her swearing-in ceremony at City Hall on March 4, 1969, Bess was prepared to deliver an acceptance speech that would erase any doubts about her convictions and ability to defend consumers. Her family and friends squeezed into the Blue Room at City Hall, which was already packed with Lindsay administration officials, reporters, photographers, and television crews. With John Lindsay at her side she opened her speech: "As a native New Yorker, I declare with pride and conviction that this is the greatest city in the United States. It can also be the most difficult.

"Right, Mayor Lindsay?" She turned to him and smiled. "In my innocence and in this difficult city, I accept the responsibility and the exciting challenge to protect and defend the consumers of the city of New York. I do so with a sense of dedication and the determination to succeed. . . ."

She promised to move quickly on consumers' complaints, seek new laws that would give consumers additional protection in the marketplace, and "identify the culprits and their illegal methods to all the people in the city."

Her lengthy remarks, interrupted by several bursts of applause, won over some skeptical members of the City Hall press corps. The *New York Daily News* City Hall bureau chief, Edward O'Neill, described her in the next day's paper as the city's "new—and tough—commissioner of consumer affairs."

Following a small reception held in her honor, Bess left City Hall to begin her first day on the job in the agency's dingy offices, ten blocks north of City Hall, at 80 Lafayette Street. She sat down with her counsel, Simon Lazarus, and together they went through her mail. Among the piles of letters and invitations was a request from the Better Business Bureau that she speak at an upcoming luncheon. To establish a reputation as a tough defender of consumers, Lazarus suggested that Bess accept the invitation and deliver a speech attacking the Better Business Bureau for "misleading consumers into a false sense of security that prompts them not to demand strong government protection." By immediately creating an adversarial relationship with the business community, he contended, Bess would ensure that no one would be able to question her commitment to consumers. Bess agreed, and the speech was drafted that week. "Her willingness to do it, I thought, was remarkable," Lazarus said later.

Nine days after Bess took office she accompanied Lindsay to the Better Business Bureau's luncheon at the elegant Plaza Hotel on the southern edge of Central Park. Almost two hundred men filled the room. After the luncheon Lindsay made a few brief remarks, saying that "improving the consumer's plight is essentially a matter of communications."

Then Bess strode up to the podium in a flowing white dress. A hush fell over the room as she opened her speech with a few pleasant remarks and then suddenly changed the tone of her voice. Always the passionate speaker, Bess exhorted her hosts to protect the "fed-up" consumer and to publicize the names of stores that generated "an unusually high proportion of valid complaints." As she had planned earlier with Lazarus, Bess criticized the bureau for not supporting new consumer protection laws and asked it to work with her to "attack those areas where criminals monopolize and rig the market."

"The audience was stunned," Lazarus said. "Lindsay was sitting next to her. He did not expect it. He was so embarrassed. He was really upset. The reporters were amazed. It made her a fascinating public figure. I've worked for politicians who were better on substance than Bess, and I have also worked for politicians who are not as good. There were few who understood and had the guts to do what it took to create a public persona that was respected for leadership, courage, toughness, and so forth. That speech to the Better Business Bureau took a lot of courage. She was taking on significant people."

In a single speech Bess had dismissed any speculation that she would be a pushover or a figurehead. A few weeks later she reinforced her position in another speech to a group of industry executives: "You will find that I am tough enough and that my staff is tough enough and that the consumer is going to be even tougher than we are." She warned that the New York City Department of Consumer Affairs would be "acting as the people's lobby."

Within months Bess became an urban folk hero. The public loved to hear her rail against shoddy merchandise and unscrupulous merchants. Storekeepers were terrified that she would show up unannounced at their stores. They knew that television cameras and reporters would be following right behind her. "She turned out to have this incredible charismatic power," Lazarus said. "You would get out of the car with her, and mobs were just drawn to her like a magnet. People were fascinated with her."

"Her work was brilliant," said another close aide, Henry J. Stern, who was then a thirty-four-year-old Harvard Law School graduate and assistant city administrator sent over by City Hall to help Bess reorganize the agency and run the department. "She transformed a sleepy agency into a national model of consumer effectiveness. It led to the establishment of dozens of others. She was extraordinary."

At the agency Bess surrounded herself with a dedicated, bright young legal staff. Heads rolled within weeks after her arrival at the agency as she fired veteran city employees to make way for the graduates of the country's best law schools. Working with Stern, Lazarus, and, later, Philip Schrag, a young lawyer who was the chairman of the Mayor's Advisory Council on Consumer Affairs, she mapped out a strategy to impose some of the toughest consumer protection regulations in the nation and persuade the New York City Council to increase the agency's enforcement powers. The department's unofficial motto tacked on her door read: "The impossible we do today. The totally impossible we do tomorrow."

Bess realized that she could not fully understand the problems shoppers encountered in the supermarket when a French couple handled all of her grocery shopping and cooking. And so, on some mornings, on her way into the office, she would instruct her driver, Joseph Baum, to stop outside of supermarkets so that she could run inside and inspect the supermarket shelves and the dairy and meat cases. Then she would return to her office full of questions and concerns for Henry Stern, whom she appointed as her first deputy commissioner. "She would find the injustice, and we would find a way to deal with it," explained Stern, who became the city's parks commissioner during the Koch administration. "It was a synergistic combination of a real, commanding public figure with devoted lawyers with the technical ability. And people really liked each other's company and worked late in the evenings. It was like the New Deal in the beginning. The first hundred days of 1933 were like what we did in 1969 with all of these consumer regulations."

Bess's decision to hire bright young lawyers disturbed some veteran employees who thought the "youngsters," as they called them, were cocky and did not have the experience ultimately to get things accomplished within a huge government bureaucracy. "They were mostly young kids fresh out of college, very well educated, and they looked upon the civil service people as peons," remembered a former deputy commissioner who was at the department when Bess arrived. "But those were the people who made the department run. They were the heart and soul. They were too old to be insulted by a group of kids. I can't tell you how many good people packed their bags and left."

Moe Greenspan, a retired chief inspector who worked with the agency for more than thirty years, also recalled a schism between the new employees and the old. "There was a tremendous amount of resentment because they came in with the attitude that civil servants were all a lazy bunch of do-nothings and that they knew everything and they were going to run the show. The morale was destroyed. The inspectors did their jobs as professionals, but there wasn't that little extra."

Over the objections of veteran employees, Bess dramatically expanded the public relations staff soon after her arrival. "She kept taking my lines [jobs] for inspectors and hiring people for the public relations office," said the former deputy commissioner who was at the agency when Bess arrived. "I went into her office and told her that I needed inspectors. She said, 'I can run this job right from my office with the newspapers and television stations. I don't need inspectors.'

"I couldn't take it," he said. "I packed it in and left."

Others thought Bess was brilliant to use the media to educate the public about the agency's work and consumer issues. "I think she gave the Department of Consumer Affairs a fantastic reputation," acknowledged another former top official in the agency who was there when Bess arrived. "Something we couldn't do. She put us on the map. She gave consumerism a big push."

Almost everything Bess did was noted and distributed to reporters. Press releases were cranked out almost daily. Bess had no trouble grabbing headlines or getting invitations to appear on talk shows. She was soon getting as many television and radio appearances as consumer affairs commissioner as she had while working as a full-time television personality. "Whenever she scheduled something, everyone would go," remembered Rita Delfiner, who covered Bess as a consumer reporter for the *New York Post*. "You knew that if you covered it, you would get a story. She was really enthusiastic about it. When consumers got mad at their butcher, they would say, 'I'm going to tell Bess Myerson on you.' Merchants were terrified that they would be reported, because she had such clout. That was the kind of mood. She was like everyone's Molly Goldberg. She was like every consumer's guardian angel."

Within six months of taking office Bess was entreating the state legislature to defeat a bill that would overturn a city law requiring meat to be packaged in transparent wrap. She traveled to Washington to urge Congress to create a federal department of consumer affairs. And she had publicly criticized a toy manufacturer for marketing a pink plastic baby rattle that contained sharp pieces of shrapnel.

She had sent inspectors into 421 restaurants to investigate whether they were serving "shamburgers," burgers that were not 100 percent beef. She had launched campaigns against phony veal cutlets, "paper" furniture, and supermarkets that used red lights to make bad meat look red and yellow cellophane to hide spoilage in chickens. She also attacked unlicensed auto mechanics, excessive hospitalization rates, and "fresh" fish that had actually been frozen.

At Bess's first public hearing, less than three months after she was sworn into office, she introduced a proposal to impose "unit pricing," which gives shoppers the item's price per pound, per ounce, or per foot. And she did it with such drama and entertainment that the newspapers compared the event to an "audience participation show."

Flanked by floodlights and twenty-eight boxes of detergent, cans of tuna, and bottles of soda, Bess proceeded to demonstrate the difficulty shoppers faced in choosing the best bargain from a dazzling array of packages and products. She placed three bottles of Mr. Clean on a table and then turned to the audience. "Most people believe that the larger the package, the more economical it is," she said in her melodic voice, looking directly into the television news cameras. "But often this is not true. Often larger packages cost just as much on a per-ounce basis as the smaller ones. Sometimes they cost more."

Then she announced the contents and prices of each of the three bottles and called for a show of hands from the fifty people seated in the audience to indicate which they thought was the best value. After most people chose the largest bottle, Bess paused dramatically and then revealed that the midsized bottle was the best bargain. Similar demonstrations followed.

Among the speakers who came to testify in favor of the proposed regulation that morning was Ed Koch, the brash, newly elected congressman from Greenwich Village who would later become mayor of New York. Koch and Myerson had met through her top aide, Henry Stern. Koch and Myerson soon came to admire each other's political style.

At the hearing Koch urged Bess to move ahead with unit pricing and let "New York City lead the way in consumer protection and give us in Congress an example for the nation. . . ." He continued, "I would like, also, to commend Commissioner Bess Myerson Grant for her initiative and her enthusiasm. She is devoting herself without reservation and without fear to the consumer interest."

It was Bess Myerson's devotion "without reservation and without fear" that troubled some prominent businesspeople and industry groups. Unit pricing was the first of her initiatives to come under attack. Food merchants' associations threatened to bring a lawsuit should the regulation take effect. And Irving Stern, a member of the Mayor's Advisory Council on Consumer Affairs, publicly criticized Bess for failing to do her homework. Stern, who was also a vice president of the Amalgamated Meat Cutters Union, scolded her for not learning how much it would cost storekeepers to comply with the regulation and what impact the compliance would have on shopping bills. The industry estimated the proposal would cost $50 million to implement.

Instead of waiting for the city council to pass legislation requiring unit pricing, Bess decided to go ahead and issue a regulation that imposed it citywide. The supermarket and food industry responded with a lawsuit that prevented the city from enforcing it. But Bess had raised public consciousness about the issue, so there was enough political pressure on the council to get unit pricing legislation approved. Unit pricing soon became New York City law and a model for cities and states around the country.

The city council was reluctant to move forward on other pieces of consumer legislation in 1969, but Bess's popularity had made her a formidable adversary; it was almost impossible for the council to ignore her requests.

Working with Philip Schrag, Bess achieved her biggest victory with the city council during her first year in office. The Consumer Protection Act of 1969 was the most important legislation created during her tenure. Without the law the department could only impose a fine against swindlers. Moreover, the city could neither recover money for consumers nor stop the swindlers from continuing their unlawful methods. The legislation would outlaw all "deceptive" and "unconscionable" transactions and enable the city to seek civil penalties, criminal fines, and mass restitution on behalf of all victims of fraud in the city.

After intensive lobbying efforts, the bill was approved and signed into law on December 30, 1969. A single sentence—"No person shall engage in any deceptive or unconscionable trade practice in the sale, lease, rental or loan or in the offering for sale, lease, rental or loan of any consumer goods or services or in the collection of debts"—made it the toughest consumer legislation in the land.

Bess worked long, hard hours that first year in office, remembered her driver, Joseph Baum: "The hours were ridiculous. It never stopped. It went into the night."

She gave away her season tickets to the Metropolitan Opera and the New York Philharmonic. All she wanted to do when she returned home late in the evening was to play her baby grand piano or curl up with a book from their "Kennedy library," which she contended held "every book ever written about the Kennedy family."

She was so wrapped up in her job that she did not have the time to worry about her deteriorating relationship with Arnold. Even so, she could not completely block out Arnold's constant complaints that she was never available to accompany him to parties and events. She said he would lash out at her by questioning her decisions at work and criticizing her public statements. She did, however, occasionally try to accede to her husband's wishes that she be by his side at public events. Joseph Baum remembered the night Arnold Grant wanted Bess to join him at the Waldorf-Astoria Hotel for a dinner—the same night as the department's annual retirement dinner in Queens. Bess told Baum she thought it was important that she, as the new commissioner, make an appearance at her department's event. On her way home from the office she asked him for advice, and he told her not to worry about the retirement dinner. He suggested that she send a telegram.

After they swung by Arnold's office and picked him up, Bess decided to mention the Queens retirement dinner to him and explain why she felt she should go. When they pulled up at 25 Sutton Place, Arnold told Baum to wait outside. "We're going to talk this thing over," Baum said Grant told him.

Baum waited outside Sutton Place for almost an hour. Then Bess emerged wearing an evening dress. Arnold was in a tuxedo. They got into the car, and Arnold directed Baum to take them to the Waldorf. "And then he said to me in the car, 'Look, Joe, you come back to the Waldorf at nine o'clock. Pick up the commissioner and take her to this retirement dinner, but I want her back at ten o'clock.'"

Baum picked up Bess at nine. He raced her over the 59th Street Bridge to the retirement dinner in Queens. "Then I got her out of there, and I raced her back to the Waldorf, and just before we got there, she said, 'Joe, you have to see what I walked out of. Come up to the ballroom.'

"So I did. You know what it was? It was the Friars, and they were honoring Barbra Streisand. I stood against the wall because there were no seats at any of the tables. I stayed just a short time. It just didn't look right, my standing there. When I saw her the next day, she said to me, 'Do you know what you did?' I said, 'What?' She said, 'You walked out on Streisand. She sang, "People."'"

When Bess learned a few weeks later that Streisand was to perform at a fund-raiser for Lindsay, she arranged for Baum to have a front-row seat. Baum said it wasn't the only kindness Bess showed him and his family. Years later, after she left the Department of Consumer Affairs, she called Baum when she heard Pope John Paul I was to visit New York. "She knew that my wife was Polish Catholic. She said to me, 'Joe, Olga has to see the pope.' She arranged it, and we went to the Mass at Yankee Stadium. It was very nice. These are the things she would do. She was that way."

"She did an enormous amount of good for people along the way," said Henry Stern, who was her closest aide and who has remained a close and loyal friend over the years. "All kinds of minor kindnesses and interventions in people's personal lives that nobody else does. This was a person who went out of her way to perform an extraordinary number of kindnesses for people from different walks of life."

Not everyone who worked with her at the Department of Consumer Affairs would agree. Some staff members saw her efforts to be nice as calculating and manipulative. Others remember her as demanding, imperious, and arrogant, with little regard for other people's schedules and feelings. They say she was chronically late for appointments and could often be heard screaming at typists and clerks.

One former deputy commissioner remembers the time he tried to explain to Bess that she could not go ahead and order thousands of buttons with the agency's new logo—"Wise Up!"—without getting the expenditure approved through the proper budgetary channels. He said he was shocked at her reaction: "She called up Mayor Lindsay, right in front of me, and said, 'Who do I have to lay to get these buttons paid for?'

"This is my great commissioner," said the former aide in disgust. "Anyway, Mayor Lindsay got the money for her."

Within months after she had arrived, her popularity with the public and the press enabled her to get almost anything that she wanted from City Hall. "She was clearly independent. There were no reins on her," recalled Sid Davidoff, who helped manage Lindsay's 1969 reelection campaign. "She didn't always carry the political message we would have liked. But when the chips were down, when John needed her, she was there."

In the fall of 1969 Bess had decided to campaign on Lindsay's behalf. Together out on the hustings, they were a campaign manager's dream, Davidoff said. "No negatives at all. He had that star quality, and Bess Myerson shared the spotlight. She was just spectacular out there. She was the fighter for the little guy, the little person buying in that supermarket. A former Miss America. Everyone wanted to see her and touch her. It was an exciting thing to see."

A few days after the November general election Bess flew alone to London, England, to visit her daughter, Barra, who had left Bryn Mawr to study acting at the Royal Academy of Dramatic Arts. Arnold was funding her training over Bess's objections to Barra's decision to pursue an acting career.

In London, away from Arnold, Bess told a close friend that she was hoping to be able to reach a decision about her marriage. Her husband's earlier involvement in her job as commissioner had seemed to alleviate some of their personal problems, but the tension at Sutton Place had increased in the seven months since her appointment. Her feeling a year ago that remarrying Arnold had been a terrible mistake was now a strong conviction. Maybe, when she returned from London, Bess would summon her courage to ask him for a divorce and leave the financial security that he represented behind.

14
For Love and Money

On the afternoon of November 12, 1969, Bess went shopping alone along London's fashionable New Bond Street. She was in town to visit her daughter, and she looked smart in her trench coat over black pants and a black sweater as she ducked in and out of the trendy shops. In one of the boutiques she lingered at a display counter, admiring a sweater. Apparently thinking that no one was watching her, she slipped the sweater into a shopping bag and walked past the cash register and out the door.

One of the store clerks, though, had been eyeing her and followed her out to the sidewalk, where he confronted her and demanded that she surrender the shopping bag. Bess implored him to let her pay for the sweater and go, but the clerk insisted that she remain inside the store while he contacted London's Metropolitan Police Department. Minutes later Constable Moya Woodheath arrived to make the arrest.

Bess begged Woodheath to let her pay for the sweater and pulled out cash from her wallet to show that she had more than enough money to cover the cost. But Woodheath ignored Bess's pleas and placed her under arrest for "theft from a shop." She then escorted Bess out of the store and onto the sidewalk to wait for a police van to take them to the West End Central Division station house.

As they were standing outside, Woodheath recalled, Bess suddenly bolted away and began running down the street. She covered almost two blocks before Woodheath was able to catch up and force her back to the store where the police van was to pull up.

Luckily for Bess, the police were unaware that their shoplifting suspect was a former Miss America and a high-ranking official of the city of New York. And Bess wasn't about to let them in on those facts. Knowing that her arrest would be a huge embarrassment that could cost her her job as consumer affairs commissioner, Bess kept her public position to herself when questioned by London's metropolitan police.

According to Woodheath's police report, Bess gave the police her married name, Bess M. Grant, and said she had been married to an

Arnold Grant since 1946. She claimed that she was "unemployed" until February 1968, when she took a job as a "research worker with a home economics firm, Consumer Affairs, in New York."

She went on to explain that she earned approximately $400 each week and that her husband provided her with an additional $800, perhaps in hope that the police, knowing of her substantial income, would conclude her shoplifting arrest was really just a terrible mistake. After all, why would a woman of her means try to steal a sweater? She was unable to convince them, however, and after about three hours in custody she was released and ordered to appear the next morning before Sir Aubrey Fletcher in Marlborough Magistrate Court for a hearing. According to records, however, she never showed up.

Bess did not tell anyone of the arrest until years later. Looking back on her life, her longtime friends say they believe the shoplifting incident was the beginning of a pattern of erratic behavior that she was able to hide from the public for almost two more decades. She waited eighteen years before finally pleading guilty and paying the fine. Yet even when her secret was revealed to the public at that time, no one could believe that Bess Myerson was capable of shoplifting—until she did it again.

The Sutton Place apartment became a marital battlefield after Bess returned that November. Unable to bring herself to ask Arnold for a divorce, she focused all of her attention on her job and spent as little time as possible at home with her husband.

Exacerbating their marital difficulties that fall, Bess told Arnold that she no longer needed his advice on how to run her agency. She later said he was annoyed that she had stopped taking home the notes of her daily activities that she had been showing him.

But the fact was that she didn't need him to tell her what to do. After seven months on the job, she now had confidence in herself and her bright young staff of lawyers educated at Columbia, Harvard, and Yale. She was also no longer interested in listening to Arnold's long lectures on how to handle her job, and she told friends that she was weary of listening to Arnold demean her.

After all, Bess was a big hit with the press and the public and seemed to be making great progress in a very short period of time. The mayor was more than pleased. To Bess, Arnold's harangues were a sign that he was once again attempting to dominate her and control her life, just as he had done in their first marriage.

By January 1970 they had virtually ceased talking to each other. Arnold had come to regard their marriage as a nightmare. Bess was given to coming home extremely late and sometimes not at all. She would depart for entire weekends without telling him where she was going; nor would she tell him where she had been when she returned.

It wasn't long before Bess took to sleeping in the guest room.

Disgusted with his wife, Arnold began taking his meals in the library to avoid her. Most of the spacious apartment that he had spent so much time and money renovating during their first marriage went unused during this war of nerves.

It was sometime in March 1970—about the time Bess entered the hospital for cosmetic surgery to remove the wrinkles around her eyes—that Arnold discovered her diary in their bedroom. Bess had been a diligent recorder of her own life for a long time, having written down her thoughts and observations about her life and the people in her life in sometimes brutally frank fashion since 1945. What Arnold read in her diary had a devastating effect on him and convinced him that Bess had been an unfaithful and conniving wife who was interested in only one thing—his money.

Leafing through the pages of Bess's diary, Arnold concluded that she had had affairs with two and possibly three men since they had remarried in 1968. Tucked inside the pages of the diary he found a passionate love letter to Bess from one of these men, which said in part: "I have little or no illusions about you, Bess, for I know you more than in the biblical sense. There is nothing delusionary in my love for you."

In the diary Arnold also came across a passage that suggested he might have been right about Bess's wanting another child so that she could obtain a bigger chunk of his fortune in the event of a divorce. He concluded, moreover, that Bess would rather have had him dead than alive, for Bess had written several weeks after her 1968 surgery that "if A [Arnold] would die, I would have the safety + security of a house, a place to exist. . . . I would then reach out to new experiences and have people around me."

Another entry made a few days later referred to him as "more like a thing. I must manipulate. I must make him conscious of me every moment, become completely dependent on him."

"With his ego, it just blew his mind," remembered someone who knew Arnold well during this time. "He kept saying Bess was an evil woman. He became obsessed. He was furious. It was the only thing on his mind. All he talked about was how horrible Bess was and that she was awful, disgusting, but he was never specific. We thought it was just him being obnoxious, until later, when we learned what was going on."

When Bess left the hospital following her cosmetic surgery, she arrived home with a friend to find Arnold furious. Demanding a divorce, he ordered her to leave the apartment immediately, taking just her clothes. He did not mention that he had read her diaries. He just insisted that she go *now*. To make his point Arnold reminded her of the prenuptial agreement she had signed, in which she had promised to leave the Sutton Place apartment if either of them concluded that the marriage was over.

Arnold's demand that she leave their home forced Bess to confront contradictory impulses. On the one hand, despite all of the tension and acrimony that now consumed their marriage, Bess still worried about making it on her own financially and living alone. On the other hand, Bess knew that if she capitulated and moved out, she would probably forfeit any chance to win the apartment in a divorce battle. At first she considered leaving and even looked around Manhattan for an apartment. After a time, however, Bess concluded that she was once again allowing Arnold to dominate her and dictate what she should do. She decided to stay.

In May Bess contacted a lawyer to help her stand up for herself against her husband's unilateral demands that she move out. This marked the beginning of a period in which they communicated with each other through their lawyers, even though they continued to live in the same apartment. It was marital cold war.

Arnold, meanwhile, was taking steps of his own to escalate the battle. He cut off her $3,000-a-month household and personal allowance and wrote letters to the upscale Manhattan department stores she frequented notifying them that he would no longer be responsible for her bills. He also began putting some of her personal possessions—trivial things like her records, hair dryer, and books—into locked closets for which only he had the keys.

In early June Bess's lawyer notified Arnold that she had retained counsel, which drew a retort from Arnold's lawyers that simply reiterated his demand to Bess months before: that she move out and live up to the terms of the prenuptial agreement she had signed willingly at the time of their remarriage in May 1968.

Her lawyer then came back to Arnold with a proposal that Bess would leave their Sutton Place apartment and agree to a divorce forthwith if he would pay her $250,000 up front and agree to provide her with another $17,500 annually.

On June 19 Arnold struck back by changing all the locks at Sutton Place and having the telephone lines disconnected. He refused to provide Bess with a set of keys to the apartment, telling her that she was now a guest in his house and would be let in and out by the servants— just as any other guest coming to call.

Bess held firm, however, and still refused to move out of the apartment. On July 13 a now-enraged Arnold went to court seeking a formal separation. On the same day he changed the locks on the apartment a second time and then sent his servants away on vacation. He made a reservation for Bess at the Hampshire House hotel on Central Park South and sent a suitcase containing some of her clothes to her attorney's office.

Bess was at a meeting in City Hall while all this was happening and learned of Arnold's latest move when a messenger interrupted the session with a court summons and a letter from Arnold explaining once again why he wanted a formal separation.

Dear Bess:

Months ago I told you that I intended to terminate our occupancy of the apartment at 25 Sutton Place. Constantly eating alone, isolated in one room without companionship, conversation or company of any sort has become unbearable, intolerable and senseless. You then stated that you would look for your own home and move shortly. You have not done so.

I have therefore closed the apartment, terminated the help and moved into a hotel. At the same time, I have reserved accommodations for you at the Hampshire House. A bag has been packed for a few days, and sent to your lawyers. If there are any other of your clothes or possessions which you desire, have your attorneys advise my attorneys thereof and it will be properly arranged. Any possession of yours that you do not now desire will be sent to storage in your name and a detailed list thereof sent to your attorneys. I have made these arrangements for us to move into separate premises since by statements and actions you have, as you intended, succeeded in bringing our marriage to an end for all practical purposes.

Arnold

Bess was furious. As it turned out, her current husband had done to her exactly what she had done to Allan Wayne during their divorce fight: changed the locks on their apartment and sent the separation papers to the office.

That night, at Bess's instructions, her city driver called a locksmith to the Sutton Place apartment, where the new locks were opened, allowing Bess to get back into the apartment. Her driver then broke the locks Arnold had placed on closets so she could get her belongings.

The following morning Bess sent word to Arnold, who was living in a hotel, that she intended to remain in the apartment but that she was not treating the apartment as hers exclusively and that he could return or visit the apartment at any time. The siege of Sutton Place continued.

Arnold was by now nearly beside himself with rage. He confronted Bess at their apartment a few days later and angrily demanded that she vacate the apartment within twenty-four hours because he intended to sell it immediately. He told her that he would keep her in court until she spent her last dime and that he was perfectly willing to spend all of his time presiding over her demise. Despite Arnold's threats, however, Bess stayed put at the Sutton Place apartment and showed no inclination to move out.

On July 31 Arnold offered a hint of the until-now secret weapon he hoped to use to force Bess out of the apartment and out of his life. Court papers that he filed seeking Bess's ouster from the apartment contained a brief mention of her diaries. Though newspapers reported the filing, they gave few details. Arnold's reference to her diaries caused Bess great concern—concern that she soon would learn was entirely warranted.

Four days later the attorneys representing Bess and Arnold met in yet another attempt to hammer out a settlement. It was at this meeting that Arnold indicated he was in possession of pages from Bess's diaries that could cause her great embarrassment if they were ever made public in a divorce trial. "He blackmailed her with the diaries. He threatened to destroy her," said a friend of Bess's.

Faced with this new information, Bess said she would move out of the Sutton Place apartment and sign a formal separation agreement in return for a modest financial settlement. Arnold's lawyers insisted that she leave the apartment first. While she was packing, they said, they would put the finishing touches on a separation agreement and work out the details of a financial settlement with Arnold.

On August 6 Bess left the Sutton Place apartment. With nowhere else to go, she sought refuge with Lilly Bruck, her close friend and volunteer coordinator at the Department of Consumer Affairs, who had a large home in nearby Scarsdale. Bess's driver, Joseph Baum, helped her haul boxes of possessions up to Scarsdale, where she planned to remain for the rest of the summer while looking for an apartment in Manhattan.

As in the case of so many bad marriages that crumble into bitterness and recrimination, the Grants' impending divorce had reached the stage where they began battling over the most inconsequential possessions. Arnold followed Bess to Scarsdale the next day and insisted on inspecting the boxes of belongings that Bess had removed from Sutton Place and was storing in Lilly Bruck's attic. Arnold spent three hours rummaging through the boxes in stifling, ninety-degree-plus heat. Occasionally he would come down the stairs and warn Bruck that she was an accomplice to a crime by allowing Bess to store items of his that his wife had pilfered from his apartment. While he claimed that most of the items in the boxes belonged to him, he left that Saturday afternoon with only a Japanese screen.

At this point Arnold was worth at least $7 million. Bess was worth roughly $1 million. And they were fighting over household items like a Pyrex double boiler, a potato baker, a marble cheese tray, and a fondue set that were stored in Bruck's attic. Arnold was claiming, moreover, that Bess had taken twelve crystal corn-on-the-cob dishes from Sutton Place and replaced them with six cheap ones.

Having agreed to move out of the apartment, Bess was expecting Arnold to present her with the separation agreement and the terms of a financial settlement forthwith. But Arnold, pointing to the boxes in Bruck's attic, refused to proceed on any settlement until Bess prepared a detailed accounting of all the property she had removed from their

Sutton Place apartment. Bess supplied him with the accounting two weeks later, around August 17.

Arnold still did not come up with the separation agreement. Instead, on August 24 Arnold, who was again living at the Sutton Place apartment now that Bess was gone, went to court seeking exclusive occupancy of the apartment. With the detailed accounting of all of the property Bess had removed in hand, he also asked the court to order Bess to return to him everything she had taken from the house. "She has taken many, many items from their home," Arnold's attorney, Morris Abrams, told the *New York Post* at the time.

A hearing on Arnold's request for exclusive occupancy was scheduled for September 8 in Manhattan Supreme Court. On that day lawyers representing both Arnold and Bess asked for a postponement. They said they were trying to work out a solution.

Just before the hearing Bess's daughter, Barra, who was then twenty-two, had attempted to intercede on her mother's behalf while in New York on vacation from London. Barra called Arnold, and he told her that he would agree to a settlement provided that Bess return the items in Bruck's attic.

On September 10 Bess returned some, but not all, of the boxes. This wasn't enough to satisfy Arnold, however, who began complaining that Bess had also removed some of his furniture from Sutton Place. Bess tried to schedule meetings with his lawyers in the hope of getting a settlement, but nothing was forthcoming.

By late October it became apparent to Bess that Arnold wasn't interested in offering her a settlement at all. He had achieved his goals: she was out of the apartment and had returned to him most of the household items from Bruck's attic that he had wanted. And so there was no incentive for him to offer her a dime.

On October 26 he filed a suit for divorce in Manhattan Supreme Court. He was moving toward a full-scale—and very public—divorce trial. Unless she agreed to walk away without a dime, he intended to expose her diaries. He told a friend that he wanted people to know what Bess Myerson was really like.

Faced with a divorce action, Bess asked the court to prohibit the press and the public from attending her divorce proceedings, and then she asked that her husband be required to provide her with temporary alimony. Bess wanted $3,500 a month from her husband as well as exclusive occupancy of their Sutton Place apartment, pending the outcome of the divorce proceedings.

Arnold told the court that Bess didn't need temporary alimony, claiming that $400,000 in deferred income from her television career and stock holdings of about $600,000 made her a wealthy woman. He pointed out that she still had the $95,000 that he had given her during their first divorce settlement. He argued further that she earned approximately $50,000 a year from her salary as a city commissioner and from interest and dividends on her investments.

The court agreed with Arnold. On February 22, 1971, Manhattan Supreme Court justice Margaret Mangan denied Bess's requests for temporary alimony and exclusive possession of 25 Sutton Place. She also refused to grant Bess's request to seal the record. In her ruling Judge Mangan wrote: "To qualify for financial relief, a wife must demonstrate she is unable to adequately support herself from her own funds during the pendency of the action. There appears to be no demonstrative necessity of temporary alimony, and moreover the trial is imminent."

The judge's decision did not bode well for Bess's hopes of winning alimony on a permanent basis, particularly since Bess had signed a prenuptial agreement waiving any right to alimony. With her prospects for postdivorce financial support from Arnold looking gloomy, and Arnold threatening to expose the intimate secrets she had confided in the pages of her diaries, Bess decided to give up any claims on his money or the Sutton Place apartment.

On April 28, 1971, after a private meeting in the judge's chambers, Manhattan Supreme Court justice Morris Spector awarded Arnold the divorce decree. The grounds for the action were not disclosed, and the proceedings were closed to the public. According to a statement released by Arnold's lawyers that afternoon, Bess had withdrawn her defense to the divorce actions and her claims for "separation, alimony, counsel fees and a property settlement."

Bess nevertheless left the marriage far wealthier than she had entered it. She had been able to invest most of her earnings from her television days because Arnold paid most of the bills. Worth a little more than $100,000 when she first married Arnold in 1962, she had increased that figure nearly tenfold.

The meeting in Judge Spector's chambers was possibly the last time Bess and Arnold ever saw each other. Six years later, in 1977, he was hospitalized in Westchester County for Alzheimer's disease. He died in the hospital three years later, on November 15, 1980.

After his death, recalling her years with Arnold during an interview with *New York* magazine, Bess said: "If I had known he was sick, I would never have left him. That's the type of person I am."

15
"Bess Myerson for Mayor"

On a Sunday afternoon in March 1971 Bess rode downtown in the front seat of her chauffeur-driven Chrysler sedan to a new neighborhood consumer complaint center at 147 Delancey Street on Manhattan's Lower East Side. She had scheduled a press conference to announce the center's opening so that she could draw attention to her efforts to reach out to the city's low-income neighborhoods. Area residents would now be able to walk in off the street and register their consumer complaints in person.

Bess also wanted to use the forum to announce that her divorce from Arnold was about to be finalized. "The first thing I want to make clear is that from now on you may call me Bess Myerson," she told reporters. "I am no longer Mrs. Grant, and that will become official very soon."

Bess would say no more about the divorce and quickly changed the subject to the newly opened neighborhood center, which she hoped would "change the feeling of hopelessness that people have about getting action from governmental agencies, by providing face-to-face action on their complaints."

With the divorce and Arnold's threats soon to be put behind her, Bess found herself spending more of her evenings and weekends with the young people she worked with at the agency as well as her first deputy, Henry Stern, and some of his friends, including Congressman Edward I. Koch, then forty-three. Talking about that period, she said a few years later, "I moved from one space to another space. I found that I enjoyed talking and arguing about politics and government."

Spending evenings in Chinatown and Greenwich Village with her politically oriented new friends, Bess found that she did not miss Sutton Place or the glittering social life she had left behind. "I've had the Norell dresses and the opening nights, and none of it seems so important anymore," she said.

Although Bess still worried about her financial situation, she was beginning to lose her fear of being alone. She filled many of her empty nights with work, sometimes returning to the office in a sweater and jeans to read letters from people who believed they had been swindled. She traveled frequently to Albany and Washington, D.C., to testify for consumers and kept herself so busy in the months following her divorce that she couldn't find time to furnish the spacious two-bedroom apartment on the ninth floor of a prestigious postwar building on East 71st Street, just off Fifth Avenue, which she had bought for $114,000 following her divorce.

By 1971 the woman who had been arrested for shoplifting only two years before had added significantly to her list of accomplishments in consumer protection. *Life* magazine put her on the cover that July with the headline "A Consumer's Best Friend, Bess Myerson on the prowl for stores that cheat us." She had dramatically changed the way people shopped in supermarkets, following up her unit pricing legislation with "open dating," signed into law by Mayor Lindsay on April 23. The open dating law, which was adopted by other cities, states, and counties around the country, required grocers and food companies to stamp a final date of sale on perishable foods, such as meat, poultry, fish, dairy products, eggs, fruit, vegetables, and baked goods.

Six months after the *Life* cover story, while still commissioner, Bess returned to television to host a syndicated, five-day-a-week talk show on consumer issues. Called "What Every Woman Wants to Know," it aired on Channel 7, WABC-TV, in New York. Soon after production began, however, it became apparent that Bess was unable to meet the demands of the heavy production schedule while working for the city of New York. One of the show's producers described her as "a horror," saying, "She had no regard for other people's schedules and lives. Thousands and thousands of dollars were lost because she was always late. . . . Usually you would look forward to tape day, but we used to cringe and talk about 'What is she going to do to us today?'" The program was canceled after only a few months on the air.

Bess's demeanor in the television studio underscored a side of her personality that was not seen by the public. To the television audience Bess was a bold, outspoken fighter for the little guy. At the office, however, her impetuous insistence that every problem be solved at once often caused confusion and tension among her staff.

One woman who worked closely with Bess at the Department of Consumer Affairs recalled that Bess was "very condescending with people. She would yell and put people down. She knew she could be an intimidating presence. If she came in contact with anyone who showed weakness, she would use that weakness to bolster herself."

At the same time, Bess could be charming and considerate with employees on whom she depended daily. She would ask about their families and offer to use her clout to help their relatives find jobs. She would recommend doctors and was willing to cut through red tape for her close associates and friends. When one of her staff members once complained to Bess that her husband had to wait for a bed in a New York hospital, Bess got on the phone to the hospital's top administrator, and a bed was made available immediately.

In return for such treatment Bess expected her employees to be faithful and tolerant, and her solicitousness did engender powerful loyalty among many. One former high-ranking official in her agency remembered some secretaries who "voluntarily became her slaves." Bess's friend and co-worker Lilly Bruck said that Bess had a "charm, a warmth that's irresistible. She enveloped people in her warmth. When she dropped them, they fell hard."

Howard Tisch, a deputy commissioner under Bess, recalled, "She could turn on you very quickly. She wasn't close to anybody except for Henry Stern. My feeling was always that she was somewhat a loner."

Stern was in charge of the agency's day-to-day operation, but no one doubted that it was Bess who was really in charge. "Bess was the boss," Tisch said. "Nobody ever challenged that. She is probably the strongest-willed person I have ever met. I had great admiration for her. She knew exactly what she wanted, and she knew how to get it, and you did not want to be in her way when she went to do it."

Bess's conquering-hero image in the press began to worry some of Lindsay's top aides, who thought she was becoming too independent and who found her increasingly difficult to deal with on some issues. One mayoral aide said, "She was a publicity saint, and she realized that she was popular with the press, and she became a little difficult to manage. She took on many things that were over her head, but the press never caught on. They never looked into the details. They never analyzed the merits. The press just loved her. She had that weapon over City Hall. You had to go slow in handling Bess because she had the press bamboozled."

Her attacks on the business community had some Lindsay aides worried that the mayor would have trouble raising funds for a possible presidential campaign. "She did not always carry the message that the political people wanted," recalled Sid Davidoff, one of the mayor's aides at the time. "[Lindsay] was much more tolerant. He felt it was her department, her area. She could do no wrong. She was unimpeachable."

Bess and the mayor became something of an item in the City Hall gossip mill as catty rumors circulated that there was more than just a professional relationship between the handsome mayor and his beautiful commissioner. At one point Bess felt compelled to walk up to Lindsay's wife, Mary, and put the rumors to rest. As Bess recalled, at a party in 1972, "I said to Mary, the rumor about my having an affair with John was, unfortunately, not true. If you knew my mother, I said, you'd know this was one Jewish girl from the Bronx who would never dare take home a shagetz [a gentile boy]."

Since Lindsay had been so supportive of her efforts, his top aides were surprised and angered in the spring of 1972 when Bess declined a request from them to campaign for Lindsay in Florida, where he was running in the Democratic presidential primary. Bess might have been enormously helpful to Lindsay in Florida, particularly in Miami Beach and its surrounding environs, where there was a large Jewish population. She told one of the mayor's campaign aides, however, that she didn't want to mix politics with consumerism. "She said it was not in keeping with 'my image,'" recalled the aide. "I was livid. To me it was the final straw. She had been given a great appointment, and she owed it all to John Lindsay. I considered her ungrateful and told her so. I told her to get the hell out of my office."

Bess returned to her own office from that meeting and drafted a letter of resignation. But the mayor refused to accept it and asked Bess to remain at her post until the end of his administration.

Lindsay returned to New York from his failed presidential campaign to find himself fighting the image of a lame-duck mayor. With only about a year left in his second term, some of his aides began to depart the administration. Those departures fueled speculation that Lindsay would not seek a third term and led to considerable political jockeying among Democrats and Republicans interested in succeeding him.

Bess found herself being mentioned frequently in the newspapers as a possible successor. May Okon, a reporter for the *New York Daily News*, spent time with Bess in the fall of 1972 while working on a profile for the newspaper's Sunday magazine. Okon found Bess vacillating between "wide-eyed innocence and embarrassment at her name being linked with the mayoralty."

Bess insisted in a lengthy interview with Okon that she had no interest in running for elective office. The very night following that interview, however, Bess called Okon at her home and asked her to serve as her campaign manager.

"What are you going to run for?" Okon asked.

"I don't know yet," Bess replied. "I'm trying not to think about it."

"Why? Are you afraid if you run you'll lose?"

"No," Bess said. "I'm afraid I'll win."

Exhausted from working ten-hour days for almost four years, Bess, it turns out, was not interested in running for mayor. She wanted to step down as commissioner and parlay her celebrity as a consumer advocate into a high-paying job in the private sector. "I wanted to put my life together," she explained several years later. "I couldn't afford to run. I had this apartment which had been unfurnished for three years."

Nevertheless, she was so popular that people walked up to her on the street and asked her to run for mayor. One night in early 1973, while she sat on a crowded dais during a banquet, the headwaiter approached her and whispered in her ear, "I'm here to tell you that I represent all the waiters at the Hilton, and if you run, we'll all vote for you." In February matchboxes imprinted with "Bess Myerson for Mayor" mysteriously appeared around town.

On the first Saturday of March 1973 she called Lindsay at Gracie Mansion and told him she intended to resign before the end of his term later that year. Lindsay asked her to postpone her resignation until after he made his own intentions public the following week. She agreed, and a day after he announced he would not seek a third term Bess submitted her resignation, effective March 31.

Her decision to resign angered some of Lindsay's aides, who felt she should have remained until the end of the mayor's term. Henry Stern, however, would later say, "She had done four years, and four years is what she promised herself. It was the right time. If she stayed through the end of Lindsay's term, it would have looked as if she were holding on to the job."

The timing of her resignation announcement created a political firestorm of rumors and speculation that she was running for public office. On the night of her announcement the telephone rang incessantly in her apartment as friends called to ask about her plans. Rita Delfiner, a reporter for the *New York Post*, spent three hours with Bess that night in Bess's apartment. Claiming she was under "overwhelming pressure" to run for office, Bess told Delfiner: "I know people want me to run for mayor, but it's just not for me. I am not going to run for any public office in the foreseeable future. I want to take what I've done and learned, and move it forward."

For all of her public disavowals, Bess, a liberal Democrat, nonetheless agreed to meet with Republican governor Nelson Rockefeller the next day about running for mayor, possibly on the Liberal and Republican lines. The governor had conducted a secret poll in the last days of February to find the most electable candidate and to help the city's Republican leaders decide whether to form an alliance with the Liberal party in the mayoral election. He wanted to talk with Bess about the results. Bess took Max Kampelman, who later became the chief U.S. arms negotiator during the Reagan administration, with her to the meeting for a steadying hand. She was dating Kampelman at the time, and she trusted his advice.

Rockefeller's poll showed that Bess had been rated as the strongest potential candidate among six mayoral possibilities: Lindsay, who had already ruled out a third term; Abe Beame, the city's comptroller; Congressmen Mario Biaggi and Herman Badillo; and former mayor

Robert Wagner. Forty-nine percent of the 406 registered voters polled
believed that Bess would make an "excellent or good" mayor. Beame was
a distant second with 39 percent. Lindsay was last.

It was an impressive showing, and Rockefeller offered to support Bess
in a citywide campaign under a joint Republican–Liberal party banner.
The poll and the governor's support put heavy pressure on Bess to run.
Ever since she was a young girl, she had been instilled with ambition by
her mother and had been driven all of her life to achieve. How could she
say no to the governor of the state of New York?

"I'm very moved by this show of confidence," Bess told reporters
after the meeting. "My immediate reaction is that it's fantastic and
incredible. It's a great honor to have the confidence of the people. It's
extremely flattering. A very wise person who once offered counsel said,
'Keep your options open.' "

Amid all the speculation about her political plans Bess resigned as
planned at the end of March. At a final press conference as consumer
affairs commissioner on March 30, tears welled in her eyes as she talked
about her "mixed emotions" about stepping down. She listed the thirty-
five consumer laws and regulations enacted during her tenure but said
the task of defending consumers would never be finished. "You helped
me get our message across," she told the reporters who crowded into
the Blue Room. "You made us happen." Bess made a final plea to
President Richard Nixon to "freeze all foods at the present prices" and
begged the public to be "alert shoppers and be aware of the consumer
protection laws which exist."

Bess refused to talk about her own political plans, but in response to a
question about whether a woman could govern a city she replied that a
woman can and should be mayor of a major city. "I think one day a
woman will be mayor, possibly even in New York," she said.

In the weeks that followed her resignation the newspapers were filled
with speculation about a possible bid by Bess to become mayor. Judith
Michaelson of the *New York Post* asked prominent New Yorkers whether
they thought Bess would make a good mayoral candidate. Former mayor
Robert Wagner, Congresswoman Shirley Chisholm, and Eleanor
Holmes Norton, then head of the city's Commission on Human Rights,
thought Bess would be a formidable candidate.

On April 3 the *New York Post* ran an editorial suggesting a Myerson-
for-mayor campaign. In a highly complimentary commentary the paper
said: "In a time of deepening cynicism about government, she had
obviously established her credentials as a public servant who can be
trusted—whose independence, concern and dedication are recognized
and appreciated. She had simultaneously shown the capacity to adminis-
ter a vital department effectively and tough-mindedly to evoke the
intense loyalty. . . . We do not disparage some earnest contestants now in

the field. But we believe Bess Myerson's advent would impart freshness, spirit and hope to the city's political landscape."

Others, however, questioned whether Bess had enough experience to run New York City. One of them was Brooklyn Democratic boss Meade Esposito, who said, "As consumer affairs commissioner, she alerted a lot of people to what it's all about. My wife loves her. But as far as the mayoralty is concerned, I don't know. Bess lacks the experience. We're dealing with a $10 billion budget."

Despite her strong showing in Rockefeller's poll, Bess had no illusions about the hard realities of running for office in New York City and knew a citywide campaign would be a tough and possibly ugly battle. She was also aware that breaking the gender barrier that had kept women out of high political office would be no easy task. One veteran operative of New York City politics recalled, "In 1973 and 1974 it was not easy for a woman to run for citywide or statewide office. People just didn't think a woman in New York, anyway, could win. Yet her name always came up among insiders as the first woman because she was so well known as a consumer advocate and a beauty queen. She was Jewish. She had everything going for her."

Bess also knew how dirty political campaigns could get in New York, and she must have worried that her arrest on shoplifting charges in London might be discovered and that excerpts from her diaries, now kept from the public in sealed divorce papers, might be leaked to the press.

Within a month of stepping down from her consumer affairs post Bess ended the speculation and said that she would not run for mayor— that year. She was careful not to rule out a future campaign for political office. Then she flew off to Los Angeles for a visit with her daughter, Barra, who had left London to try to make it in Hollywood.

Bess continued to date Max Kampelman but, according to a close friend who had urged Bess to marry him, did not take the relationship that seriously. Bess was also dating another man who was in the broadcasting industry. And she found time to date a very rich young businessman in the shipping industry whom she had been seeing off and on since 1968, when she was still married to Arnold Grant.

None of the relationships were serious. It would be several years before she would fall passionately in love with a man.

Bess also turned her attention to buying works of art and furnishing her two-bedroom apartment off Fifth Avenue. The apartment was virtually bare but for a piano, a bed, a tree, a small table, and a few chairs. She redecorated it, painting it beige and emphasizing the soft hues of the desert, which she loved. She purchased a large beige velvet sofa for the living room and chrome and glass end tables. She filled the apartment with Greek, Roman, and Coptic treasures and a newly bought Byzantine mosaic from the fifth century.

During this time she was approached by several magazines to write about consumer issues and soon was earning considerably more than she had in the Lindsay administration. She wrote a column called "Buying Time" for *Vogue*. She also joined *Redbook* magazine's staff as a contributing editor but hired her old friend and speech writer, Walter Canter, to actually write the articles.

By the end of the summer new responsibilities crowded Bess's schedule. She was writing a nationally syndicated newspaper column that ran twice a week in the *New York Daily News* and other papers around the country called "Listen, Bess." Readers would write in with their consumer-related problems, and Bess would respond with practical answers. She also joined Hunter College's political science department as a visiting professor to work with students on a guidebook for local government officials interested in establishing consumer agencies in their communities.

Six months after leaving city government she returned to television in September as the narrator of an ABC special, "A Woman's Place," in which she examined the role of women in society. She said she turned down several opportunities to make television commercials that would have paid her six-figure sums, including an offer of $350,000 to spend six days shooting commercials for an auto manufacturer. She wanted to earn money, but she had promised herself that she would not trade her name for the money she could earn doing television commercials.

For all that high-mindedness, however, she went to work in November 1973 for Citibank as a $100,000-a-year consumer affairs consultant, at the same time that the bank was under attack by Ralph Nader for being more concerned with its well-heeled customers than its small depositors. Bess defended taking the job by saying she intended to help the bank adopt pro-consumer policies. "I wanted to work for companies where I could make changes," she explained later to the *New York Times*. Citibank, she went on to say, was more responsive than the city council had been when she first approached it with the Consumer Protection Act.

But Bess's decision to work at a major bank surprised and disappointed some consumer advocates who had regarded Bess as a strong and powerful voice in the consumer movement. They saw her move to the private sector as a sellout.

Meanwhile politicians were eyeing Bess in early 1974 as a potential candidate for another contest: the U.S. Senate race. Brooklyn Democratic boss Meade Esposito, who had publicly questioned whether she was qualified to be mayor only a year earlier, approached Bess about running. He thought she might be an effective senator, but more importantly, she was a Democrat who the polls said could beat the Republican incumbent.

Bess did not even flirt with the idea that March of 1974. "At the moment, I'm not running and I'm not interested because I don't see how it would be feasible," she told a reporter. She did not, however, tell the reporter why.

16

The Struggle Against Cancer

As Bess was beginning her career as a highly paid consultant for Citibank in late 1973, she felt tired and run-down and told friends that she thought she was anemic. She was also running a low-grade fever that she couldn't seem to shake and had a slight pain in her side. Finally she went to see a doctor. He told her not to worry and suggested she return for another checkup in six months.

Sensing that something was wrong, however, Bess sought an opinion from another doctor, who sent her to the radiology department at Mount Sinai Medical Center. X-rays indicated that Bess had a growth of some kind on one of her ovaries. Years later Bess would remember the call from her doctor: "He said, 'You are going to have to come into the hospital right away, and if there are no beds, then we will make up a bed for you.'"

Bess checked into the hospital the next day and underwent surgery to determine the extent and seriousness of the problem detected by the x-ray. Surgeons removed what she would later describe as a tumor on her ovary. She felt a tremendous sense of relief when her doctors came to her hospital room after she had awakened from the anesthesia and told her that the tumor was benign and posed no health risk. "I was on my way down in the elevator to go home when they told me they were wrong. It was not benign. It was malignant," Bess remembered.

She returned to her hospital room, and that afternoon her doctors gathered around her bed and told her that she had ovarian cancer, a particularly deadly malignancy that kills roughly 65 percent of the women it strikes because it has usually spread too far by the time it is detected. "I wanted to know exactly what the prognosis was," she recalled. "They wanted me to undergo more surgery at that point, and I said, 'I can't do it. I just cannot assault my body again that way.'"

Her doctors believed they had caught the cancer early enough and agreed to postpone surgery for a hysterectomy for a few months, though they insisted that she immediately begin a rigorous eighteen-month-long regime of chemotherapy.

The news that she was stricken with cancer stunned and terrified Bess. She was forty-nine years old, single, and alone, and she had been looking forward to a new life of freedom after her time-consuming and demanding job as a top city official. If the cancer wasn't bad enough, Bess also found herself facing a costly operation and prolonged chemotherapy with no health insurance. She had inadvertently allowed her insurance to lapse after leaving the city government. Deluged with medical bills, she worried whether she would have enough money to pay for continuing medical care.

Bess was frantic that Citibank would cancel her contract upon learning she had cancer, then a misunderstood disease. "The big C was much more scary," she remembered. "People would say, 'How could you work with anybody who has that?' People were afraid to invite you to dinner." So she kept it to herself, telling only her closest friends, and continued to go to work each day holding her terror inside. "I didn't tell anybody then. I was determined not to talk about it," she recalled. She also worried that her elderly parents would be devastated if they knew she was ill.

Five months after the cancer diagnosis, in April of 1974, Bess was scheduled to undergo a hysterectomy. On the night before she was to go into the hospital she hosted a CBS television special, "Women of the Year," broadcast live from Lincoln Center. Advance publicity had generated a lot of interest in Bess and the show. The *Chicago Sun-Times*, for instance, said that it was "unlikely that any of the recipients will be more deserving of that title than the woman presiding at the awards program."

Although she had already started her chemotherapy treatments, no one watching her on television that night would have guessed that she was ill. She looked vibrant and glamorous, as always, standing onstage in a flowing evening gown with Billie Jean King, Barbara Walters, Patricia Harris, and other prominent women.

The next morning Bess checked herself into Mount Sinai and underwent surgery. Doctors found no other trace of the disease. Awakening from the anesthesia that afternoon, she felt tremendous comfort when she learned that her daughter, Barra, had returned home from California to be with her. "I sort of felt this body lying next to me. There was Barra, sort of stretched out. When I came to, she said, 'You're fine. You're fine, Mom.'"

Although her doctors were optimistic about her chances, Bess was nonetheless aware that in ninety-seven out of every hundred cases ovarian cancer resurfaces within two years. Her doctors told her that it would be five years before she could feel confident that she had beaten the odds and had overcome the disease. For the next five years, she would later recall, the fear that the cancer would return was an almost constant preoccupation: "To know the statistics as I did. To know the possibility of it happening. To be so shocked and shattered when it happened. When you don't even have a history of that happening to you in branches and branches of the family."

Having come face to face with her own mortality, Bess seemed to undergo a dramatic change in her personality, close friends recalled. "She became hard," said a man who was dating her at the time she learned she was ill. "She was fighting with everyone. She became defensive and tough. When you have something that you cannot control, you lose your self-confidence, and she lost her self-confidence. She changed overnight. She was no longer invincible. The world had been her oyster, and now she could lose everything."

Bess acknowledged years later that her struggle against cancer conferred a cynicism and bitterness on her. When she remembers overcoming cancer, she speaks in terms of waging battles, gathering all of her forces together: "This was the priority. No matter what else happens, no matter what else they throw at you—the fears of other people—you do what you have to do. I did what needed to be done. I knew I had to be strong. If you have to win a battle, whether it is to maintain the position of working or whatever, you have to hold on to it; you fight."

While Bess had always been concerned about her financial security, she was now committed to earning and saving as much money as possible. She wanted to have enough money to provide herself with the very best in medical care. Two months after her surgery she signed a $150,000-a-year contract with Bristol-Myers to work as a consumer consultant. And despite her illness and the chemotherapy, she continued her $100,000-a-year job at Citibank and her columns for the *New York Daily News* and *Redbook*. "I felt that because I was ill I would need to be very independent, financially independent, so that should anything happen, I would be able to treat myself well," she remembered. "Would you have done anything differently? You would have made sure that you worked and that you made sufficient money so that you could invest in your illness if you had to or in your health."

Not until five years later, in 1979, would she publicly disclose her battle with the disease. The occasion was a conference she attended for women with breast cancer at the Waldorf-Astoria in Manhattan. After a doctor on the panel told the audience that eating the right foods, quitting smoking, and reducing alcohol intake could help reduce the chance of cancer, Bess stood up and announced that she had followed a proper diet, rarely took a drink, and never smoked and still got cancer.

The chemotherapy continued for the entire eighteen months that her doctors had first recommended. Although she didn't suffer the hair loss associated with some rigorous chemotherapy treatments, Bess sometimes became nauseated. But she said that she tried to overcome those side effects by never giving in to the treatments. She continued with her daily routine, even scheduling appointments and forcing herself to attend meetings after her chemotherapy sessions.

Yet friends remember that her moods seemed to change in the days immediately following a treatment. "There was this really bizarre behavior," said a close friend of Bess's at the time. "She would be very erratic, short-tempered, just strange. She would lash out at people in a vindictive way, become very cold and mean-spirited. It was just bizarre, and the explanation was that it would be the effects of the chemotherapy."

Within months of her surgery Bess forced herself to return to the social circuit and a regular television show. In June she attended a dinner dance for Nancy and Henry Kissinger hosted by former governor Nelson Rockefeller and his wife, Happy. By the fall of 1974 she was the host of a new monthly show for public television called "In the Public Interest." It was critically acclaimed and was nominated for an Emmy award.

She resumed her political activities as well, campaigning that September for Brooklyn congressman Hugh Carey, the Democratic candidate for governor that fall. She appeared side by side with Carey at rallies and made a television commercial endorsing him. Carey won the election and appointed Bess to head a statewide task force on consumer protection that he charged with recommending what new laws would be put on the books to protect consumers. He also wanted Bess to join his administration as the state's commerce commissioner and made an appointment to discuss it with her at her Manhattan apartment.

When Carey and an aide arrived, however, Bess was sick in bed from her chemotherapy. Olga Baum, her maid and wife of her former driver, Joseph Baum, served the governor-elect and his aide tea while Bess tried to get dressed for the meeting. With Olga's help she was finally able to dress and emerge from her bedroom to speak with Carey about the job. She told him she was not interested in returning to government at this time. Her priority was to get well and make money.

Within months of her meeting with Carey in the spring of 1975, Bess's name once again surfaced as a potential candidate for the Democratic nomination to the U.S. Senate.

The pressures on her to run were enormous. David Garth, the New York political wunderkind who had scored victories for Lindsay, Carey, and New Jersey governor Brendan Byrne, believed the Democratic nomination was hers for the asking. "There was no doubt about it. She would have had all the money. She would have had both lines starting off," said Garth, referring to the Democratic and Liberal parties' support.

In November 1975, however, Bess ruled out a campaign. Since she was still keeping her cancer a secret, some people in politics and in the press speculated that she wanted the nomination on a silver platter. She had recently completed her chemotherapy, but she was reluctant to give up her high-paying consulting jobs and television appearances and make a commitment to politics until November 1978—which would mark five years since her cancer had been discovered. By then she could feel confident that she had won her battle with the disease.

Determined not to disappear completely from the public and political landscape, however, she attended political doings and lent her support to certain candidates seeking citywide and statewide offices. Though another woman, Bella Abzug, was running in the primary, Bess chose to throw her support to former United Nations ambassador Daniel Patrick Moynihan instead.

Speculation is the fuel that drives politics, and it was not long after Moynihan's victory over Buckley in the 1976 Senate race that Bess was being mentioned by politicians as a possible New York City mayoral candidate for 1977. Once again the polls showed her leading a pack of City Hall hopefuls, including incumbent mayor Abraham Beame. She also was shown running ahead of her close friend, Ed Koch, the tall, plain-speaking congressman serving his fifth term from the East Side's affluent "silk stocking district."

Even so, Bess still wasn't interested. She told one reporter back then: "It's an extremely harsh experience for any candidate. I am not addicted to the limelight. Right now I like to have the choice of when I want to be public and when I don't. Let's face it, I'm not the same 21-year-old girl whom everyone remembers from Atlantic City."

Ed Koch was interested in running, though, and had been seeking Bess's support for almost a year. To Bess, Koch was *auf den tisch*, a Yiddish expression meaning that the vocal, candid Koch was on the table, on the level. She liked his style. They were from similar backgrounds: they had both grown up during the Depression and were both children of hardworking Jewish immigrants.

Koch had entered the mayoral race briefly in 1973 but withdrew when it became clear he did not have the money or the support he would need to win. This time, however, with Bess's backing, he stood a chance of winning.

17
First Lady Bess

In September 1976 Bess invited Ed Koch and David Garth to her Upper East Side apartment for a dinner party. Koch had asked Bess to arrange the gathering so he could meet Garth, the media wizard he was hoping to persuade to mastermind his impending mayoral campaign. "I knew him by reputation," Koch said later. "I hoped that when I ran, he would be willing to become my media consultant and run the campaign."

Bess had known Garth since 1969, when he had put together the package of television commercials that helped John Lindsay win reelection as mayor. Garth had the reputation of being a kingmaker, and he charged fees commensurate with that stature—upward of $15,000 a month. Few disputed that he was worth the money. Garth had transformed Hugh Carey from a little-known Brooklyn congressman into New York's governor in 1974. Now Bess was hoping that he would work the same magic for Koch, another little-known congressman, and make him the mayor of New York City.

Garth, however, didn't hold out much hope that Koch could win. What persuaded Garth to take Koch on as a client was Bess, who believed Koch could win and pressed Garth to go with her good friend. "She liked him very much," Garth recalled. "She was very supportive of him. She was the best name. She was the only name that was supporting Ed."

With her celebrity status and charisma, Bess brought star power to the campaign of a man whose own early polls showed him to be known by only about 6 percent of the city's population outside his congressional district. Her support and Garth's decision to join his campaign gave Koch immediate credibility with the city's major political contributors. Raising money was essential to a candidate running in the high-priced New York media market, and Bess worked hard for Koch in those early days of 1977, speaking at political fund-raisers and drawing audiences for him to make his pitch.

One looming problem, however, threatened to derail Koch's campaign. As a middle-aged bachelor from Greenwich Village, he had endured rumors about his sexual orientation since his first political battle in 1963 against Tammany Hall boss Carmine DeSapio, whom he had defeated for the Village's Democratic leadership post. A homosexual becoming mayor—even of New York City—was considered impossible.

Before taking on Koch, Garth had confronted the congressman with these rumors and asked him point-blank whether they were true. Koch assured Garth that there was nothing to the talk. But convincing his consultant and convincing the public were two different matters. Garth worried that a cleverly orchestrated whisper campaign of innuendo might be enough to destroy Koch's chances.

The solution Garth came up with was to link Koch and Bess so closely together in the minds of New Yorkers that the public would fully expect her to become the city's first lady at the conclusion of the campaign. *Village Voice* writers Jack Newfield and Wayne Barrett would later call this strategy "the immaculate deception."

On Friday, March 4, 1977, Koch rented a room at the New York Hilton Hotel and formally announced his candidacy for the Democratic mayoral nomination. Bess, now the chairman of his campaign, stood next to him at the podium and appeared with him in most of the newspaper photographs the next day. Over the next few months Bess divided her time between the Koch campaign and her own business affairs. She would hit the big political events with Koch and spend the rest of the time during the late spring and summer of 1977 tending to her consulting jobs at Citibank and Bristol-Myers. Just a week after Koch's announcement, for example, Bess held her own press conference for Bristol-Myers at the St. Regis Hotel to unveil the *Consumer Guide to Product Information*, a 129-page booklet that Bristol-Myers ultimately distributed free to more than a million people and that was later criticized because it failed to warn consumers of possible cancer-causing ingredients in hair dyes made by the company's Clairol division.

Through the spring and summer Koch gradually inched up in the polls. His campaign slogan, an attack on the administrations of Lindsay and Beame, who was seeking reelection, was catchy and succinct: "After eight years of charisma and four years of the clubhouse, why not try competence?"

Koch also seized on the crime issue at the right time. The public was horrified by the looting in the city's poor neighborhoods during the Consolidated Edison power outage in July and terrified by Son of Sam, a serial killer who had shot thirteen young men and women. It was in this atmosphere that Koch began calling for restoration of the death penalty for certain crimes. By doing so, he was shedding his liberal

Greenwich Village image and striking a chord with many more conservative New Yorkers, particularly those in the city's vote-rich outer boroughs. Television commercials created by Garth portrayed Koch as the tough-on-crime candidate New Yorkers were looking for.

"We had the blackout and the looting, and right after that the city went crazy," recalled former congresswoman Bella Abzug, who was running against Koch in the primary and had been leading him in the polls. "And then he campaigned on the death penalty. . . . He turned the whole race around."

Koch's message caught the attention of Rupert Murdoch, the owner of the *New York Post*. On August 19, three weeks before the primary, Koch got his biggest boost when Murdoch delivered an extraordinary front-page endorsement. A few days later the *New York Daily News* followed with its support. Suddenly big contributions began filling Koch's campaign coffers, which allowed him to continue airing his television commercials. By late summer Koch had received endorsements from the *New York Post* and *New York Daily News*. An unlikely victor six months ago, he now stood a chance of winning the September 8 primary.

As primary day closed in, Bess was in Aspen, Colorado, on vacation. Koch and Garth wanted her back in New York to help with the campaign, and she arrived home at the end of August, ready to pitch in.

Bess proved to be a formidable street campaigner as she traveled with Koch around the city, greeting voters at subway stops and street corners and standing at his side at rallies in the Bronx and street festivals in Little Italy. She was a big celebrity who the public remembered had fought passionately for their interests as commissioner of consumer affairs. She exuded warmth and charm on the street and in front of the television cameras. "More people knew her than me," Koch said. "She walked with me, and people said, 'There's Bess.' "

Around the campaign office she could be everybody's mother. She instructed campaign volunteers to take vitamins and warned them against eating junk food. She always seemed to be touching people, straightening their ties, tucking in their shirts, or pushing their hair back behind their ears.

Bess could also be difficult, if not impossible, to handle. "She was a prima donna," said one aide, who was shocked when he saw Bess hand her sneakers to a campaign staff member and ask that they be polished white.

Until she grew to trust the campaign aides who had been assigned to work with her, Bess sometimes would call ahead to scheduled events to make sure that the directions for getting to the site were accurate and that the event had been planned properly. "She could be a nightmare," said another campaign worker. "She went through people. She could be very tough. She gets angry and she blows up. You have to ignore her, though. . . . She has to have trust in somebody."

In those final days before the primary Bess went everywhere with Koch. It was Ed and Bess, Bess and Ed. Koch told voters that, if elected, he would make Bess deputy mayor for economic development. At rallies he would ask the crowd: "Wouldn't she make a great first lady of Gracie Mansion?"

They held hands and smiled for the television cameras, looking as if they were very much in love. The gossip columnists began to speculate about a romance between the former beauty queen and the unattached bachelor. Voters no longer wondered whether Koch was gay. They wanted to know when Ed and Bess were getting married. "He needed her desperately," said Abzug. "She went around with Koch holding his hand as if they were going to get married. That was what her role was. It seemed to me she was always with him."

Garth, in effect, was offering voters a package deal: they would get not only competent Ed Koch but beautiful Bess too. Garth reinforced what he would later call this "subliminal message" by putting both of them on a campaign poster, the only poster in recent memory, he noted, that featured someone in addition to the candidate.

On the night of September 8 Koch watched the primary returns with Bess and about fifty other supporters at his Madison Avenue headquarters. It was almost eleven o'clock when they made their way to the upstairs room at Charley O's for a victory party. Ed Koch, who only three months before had not been taken seriously as a mayoral candidate, had won, capturing 180,914 votes.

He beamed as he strolled with Bess into the room packed with more than four hundred cheering campaign workers and friends chanting, "Eddie, Eddie, Eddie." At the microphones he warmly embraced Bess and introduced her to the crowd as "the most important person of the campaign." When they held their arms aloft, the crowd started yelling, "First Lady Bess."

The race for the Democratic nomination was not over, however. With seven candidates in the race, Koch had come out on top but had still won only 20 percent of the vote. This meant that eleven days later he would face a runoff election with Mario Cuomo, who had finished second to Koch, trailing him by about 10,000 votes. The other mayoral opponents—Bella Abzug, Abe Beame, Joel Hartnett, Percy Sutton, and Herman Badillo—had been eliminated from the contest.

In those eleven days Koch and Cuomo took to the streets and the television airwaves to battle for the thousands of votes that had gone to their defeated challengers. The pace was frenetic. Bess continued campaigning for Koch, joining him at rallies everywhere he went. She was a bold and passionate speaker and sometimes a little too fearless. During a rally at Arthur Avenue in the Bronx, Koch encountered a hostile crowd of Cuomo supporters who hurled anti-Semitic insults and called him a "fag." The crowd frightened members of the campaign, who wanted to leave, but Bess refused. Pam Chanin, a campaign aide and friend of Bess's who was at the scene that day, remembered that Bess insisted on staying. "She grabbed Ed with one hand, and she started to walk through the crowd. She began shaking hands with people, and the crowd parted like the Red Sea. She completely broke the crowd's anger. It was amazing," Chanin said.

Much of the battle was being waged on television. Koch had already spent close to $500,000 on television advertising. Now he and Cuomo were each spending $50,000 a day on dueling television commercials. Cuomo launched the first attack with a TV spot that showed Koch's face disappearing into Lindsay's, the man many voters blamed for the city's fiscal crisis. Cuomo followed up that commercial with another suggesting that Koch was the kind of candidate who would change his position when it was politically expedient. To make his point Cuomo showed a weather vane spinning in the wind.

The Koch camp was furious. Garth retaliated with a final commercial that featured Bess in a powerful thirty-second spot. Staring directly into the camera, a serious-looking Bess asked: "What ever happened to character, Mr. Cuomo? We thought your campaign would do better than that." It was played on every available commercial television slot in the final weekend of the runoff campaign.

Bess said later that she agonized over whether to do the commercial. "But then I figured that if I didn't, it would be cowardly. So I asked Cuomo, in our commercial, 'What has happened to character?' I thought it was time that Cuomo, this knight in shining armor, should be unhorsed," she said.

With the help of the Brooklyn and Bronx Democratic party bosses, hundreds of loyal party workers turned out the vote for Koch on September 19, 1977. He beat Cuomo in the runoff election by capturing 55 percent of the vote and became the Democratic candidate for mayor. Once again he stood at the podium celebrating his election-night victory with Bess at his side. "My role from the start of the campaign was to help Ed as much as I could. It's been a long, hard road to victory," she told the crowd of supporters.

Ordinarily the winner of the Democratic mayoral nomination would not have to worry about an opponent in New York City's general election. The Republican candidate that year, state senator Roy Goodman of Manhattan's Upper East Side, was given little chance of winning. But Mario Cuomo refused to give up the fight and entered the general election race as the Liberal party's candidate. Ed Koch would have to keep on running hard.

During those two months Bess continued to appear regularly at
Koch's side. Susan Berman, writing a profile on Bess for *New York*
magazine, joined Bess and Ed on the campaign trail in October. (Bess
told Berman that she was glad to see that Berman was attractive. "I have
had such trouble with fat, ugly reporters. They hate me," Bess told her.)
On the way to the Columbus Day parade, Berman wrote, the limousine
carrying Bess, Koch, and other campaign aides kept turning up the
wrong streets. Koch was worried that the parade up Fifth Avenue would
be over before he arrived. Everyone in the car offered an opinion about
what to do next.

"Suddenly," wrote Berman, "a tightly controlled melodious voice
rises from the backseat above the din. An imperious voice. It is a 'take
charge' voice that speaks in well-defined capital letters. The Voice says,
'Ed, Get Out. I'll Take Care of It. Just Make Like the Mouse That
Roared.'" Bess then stepped out of the car, got directions from a nearby
policeman, and navigated Koch to the head of the parade in what
seemed like a matter of seconds.

As Bess and Koch marched down Fifth Avenue together with big
crowds lining both sides of the street, two little girls were overheard by
a *New York Times* reporter.

"See? That's Bess Myerson," said one of the girls to the other as they
watched the parade pass them at 53rd Street.

"Gee," said the other.

"And her husband is running for mayor," the other added knowingly.

Speculation about a wedding between Ed and Bess had moved off the
gossip pages onto the news pages. A *New York Daily News* headline
asked in late September, "Will Bess Be First Lady Come November?" In
the story Bess played coy, telling the newspaper, "I have enormous
respect and deep affection for Ed, but my private life has always been
private and I have never talked about it."

Koch, for his part, encouraged the speculation. In a television interview that fall he was asked about the possibility of marrying Bess. "It's
always a possibility," he said, "but I don't want to talk about it. She's an
incredible person—a warm human being that I really adore."

Behind the scenes at campaign headquarters, however, no one on
Koch's staff ever believed there was a romantic relationship between Ed
and Bess. Bernie Rome, the campaign treasurer, remembered bringing
up the subject of wedding bells to Koch while the two were having
dinner at Rome's vacation house in Westhampton, Long Island. "I said
to him that my mother-in-law had said that it would be a fine thing for
his career to marry Bess Myerson. He didn't look up. He didn't answer.
Nothing. There was a very awkward silence," recalled Rome, who never
again brought up the subject.

Ten years later Koch would still deny that he had purposely encouraged speculation about a romance with Bess. He acknowledged, however, that the perception of such a relationship helped his campaign: "I didn't hold press conferences denying the substance of that fantasy, but we didn't create it. It was not a strategy on my part."

In late October, with Election Day fast approaching, Garth's worst fears began to materialize. Rumors about Koch's sexual orientation were beginning to swirl. Hints that Cuomo's campaign workers had hired a private detective to find out whether Koch had any "boyfriends" had reached the Koch campaign. And in Queens, posters had been plastered on telephone poles urging voters to "Vote for Cuomo, Not the Homo." There were also rumors that sound trucks were driving through Queens, blasting a similar message. Reporters began to question among themselves whether Bess's very public role in the campaign was a strategy by Garth to head off these rumors early in the campaign.

The first time the issue appeared in print was on October 30 in the *New York Times Magazine*. Reporter John Corry addressed the question of Bess's role in the campaign head-on and added, "There is not the slightest evidence to suggest that Koch is now, or ever was, a homosexual or that his deepest passions have ever been engaged by anything other than politics." Corry asserted, however, that one of Myerson's functions in the campaign was to dispel rumors that Koch was gay.

The same day, Koch and Cuomo appeared together on a television news program in which WABC-TV's Peter Bannon asked Koch if his frequent appearances with Bess Myerson were made to "dispel rumors of any hint of homosexuality." Koch replied in a calm voice that Bess was not a foil and that it was "crude to use false innuendo." As Koch left the studio, radio reporters were waiting to ask him to elaborate on his answer, and in the course of being interviewed he flatly denied he was homosexual but added that, if he was, he would hope that he would not be ashamed of it. Radio programs reprised his comments throughout the day, and the story was carried on the local television news broadcasts that night. The newspapers that appeared the next morning, however, either had buried the issue deep in their campaign stories or had chosen not to mention it at all.

With all these rumors flying about in the week before Election Day, Koch did his best to maintain a cool exterior. Bess, however, was livid. She called the rumors the Big Lie—a not-so-subtle reference to Nazi propaganda techniques. On the Sunday before the election she told a Sheridan Square rally that there was an "ugly, scurrilous and deliberate attempt to deny a man his potential because of a big lie."

When a *New York Post* reporter covering the event called in the story and told Joyce Purnick, the paper's leading political reporter, about Bess's comments, she realized that the issue was gathering momentum and that the newspaper would have to make a decision about how to handle this delicate and, for Koch, potentially damaging story. Bess's comments to that rally marked the first time anyone in the Koch campaign had suggested publicly that the Cuomo camp was mounting a smear campaign against Koch. Purnick, now an editorial writer for the *New York Times*, checked the Koch campaign's schedule and saw that she could catch Bess at a rally that night at Fordham University's campus next to Lincoln Center.

Purnick pulled Bess aside just outside the entrance of the university's auditorium. "I said, 'Listen, I understand that you said something, that you are upset,'" Purnick recalled. "She proceeded to unload on me. She was very upset. 'This man has worked all of his life. How dare anyone try to impugn his integrity!' she said. She put the entire issue on the public record. She was very emotional and very excited."

Word reached Koch campaign headquarters that Bess was going public with her accusations and raising the very issue that Garth had worked so hard to defuse since first signing on with Koch. As Bess and Purnick continued their conversation in Bess's car, a call came over the car phone from the Koch campaign. "Whoever was on the other end was giving her hell," Purnick recalled.

"Why shouldn't I talk about it?" Bess demanded of the caller. "Why should he get away with it?"

Purnick returned to the *Post*'s newsroom that night with Bess's comments in her notebook. Purnick recalled being "very troubled. I really agonized, given the timing, over what to do."

She talked it over with fellow reporter Michael Rosenbaum, and together they decided it wasn't fair to raise this issue with only one day left before the election. Had the story appeared on election eve, there would not have been enough time for Koch to adequately discuss the issue and for Cuomo to respond to the charges made by Bess. After conferring with an editor, they decided instead to spell out all the details in a lengthy piece to run right after the election.

On Tuesday, November 8, the voters once again went to the polls. Ed Koch was elected the city's 105th mayor, getting 713,000 votes, or 50 percent, to Cuomo's 587,000, or 42 percent. Goodman, the Republican, ended up with only 60,000 votes. At 11:30 that night Ed and Bess stood together at the victory podium and held their arms aloft in triumph. As the band played "Happy Days Are Here Again," the crowd chanted, "First Lady Bess."

The next day, however, for the first time since the campaign had begun that spring Bess made it clear that she had no intention of becoming New York's first lady or returning to government as a member of the Koch administration. "I must have my privacy," she told a reporter. "I don't want to go back into government. I want . . . to have my freedom. I don't want to be devoured by the administration of an office again. . . . I served my four years. I don't like repetition."

It was difficult, though, to destroy the political fantasy created by David Garth that fall. The gossip pages continued to speculate on wedding plans at Gracie Mansion. Even the mayor's seventy-four-year-old father, Louis, said he expected a wedding announcement before the mayoral inauguration.

But Bess, wise to the way of city politics, wasted little time trying to arrange for a city job for her brother-in-law. Koch sent him over to Bernie Rome, who was now heading the city's Off-Track Betting Corporation. Rome interviewed Bess's brother-in-law but was unable to offer him a job because none were available. Calls soon started coming in from City Hall. "Bess is coming back from vacation, and I know that she is going to ask about her brother-in-law," one mayoral aide told Rome. "It was her understanding that he was going to have a job at OTB."

Rome was furious. He was trying to fire people to meet fiscal constraints, and now Koch's aides were telling him to come up with a patronage job for Bess's relative. "Have Bess call me," Rome said. A few days later, she did.

"Why don't you hire my brother-in-law?" he said she asked.

"We don't have any jobs here, Bess. We are overstaffed, and we are not hiring anyone," Rome replied.

"Oh, I was in government. I know how that works. You fire someone's ass out of there and hire my brother-in-law."

"I can't do that, Bess," Rome said.

"Well," Bess replied, according to Rome, "you will hear from the mayor." Then she hung up.

Koch himself called Rome the next day.

"He said to me, 'Bernie, why can't you hire Bess's brother-in-law?'" Rome recalled. At the mayor's insistence, Rome finally offered Bess's brother-in-law a job—as a $12,000-a-year clerk. Bess's brother-in-law, hoping to earn at least $25,000 a year, turned it down.

Bess and Ed continued to see each other occasionally after the election. They went to the movies and to dinner in Chinatown, and in December they attended the glittering ball for the Council for a Beautiful Israel at the Plaza Hotel.

By the time Ed Koch was sworn into office on January 1, 1978, Bess had another man on her mind. Within months, he would become an obsession.

18
Obsession

On a Saturday night in October 1977, near the end of Ed Koch's mayoral campaign, Bess arrived alone at a formal dinner party at a friend's huge Park Avenue duplex apartment. About thirty guests—most of them wealthy real estate developers and investment bankers who sat on the boards of the city's leading cultural institutions—were already sipping cocktails in the wood-paneled study. At a few minutes after eight they were ushered into a dining room where place cards guided them to their chairs. Bess was seated next to a wealthy private investor named J. Gordon Marcus.*

At forty-eight, Gordon owned a seat on the New York Stock Exchange and lived in his own apartment in the Carlyle, the city's only five-star hotel. His family had grown rich through New York real estate, but Gordon, armed with an MBA from Harvard, had set out on his own and made a fortune through savvy investing in the stock market.

Gordon could be a charming dinner companion. He spoke rapidly, and jokes and funny stories seemed to tumble out of him. He cut an impressive figure as well. A stylish dresser, Gordon was tall and angular, with broad shoulders, wavy brown hair, and intense green eyes behind horn-rimmed glasses.

Gordon had arrived at the party that night with Charlotte Ames,* a beautiful, blond, vivacious thirty-four-year-old writer who had grown up outside of Boston and later married a wealthy theatrical producer who was much older than she. They had recently been divorced, and she was living on upper Park Avenue with their seven-year-old daughter. Gordon was in the midst of a divorce himself after almost twenty-five years, and now Charlotte was hoping to marry him once his divorce became final.

Gordon was usually attentive to Charlotte at the dinner parties they often attended, but on that night he became so engrossed in conversa-

*J. Gordon Marcus is a pseudonym.
*Charlotte Ames is a pseudonym.

tion with Bess that he virtually forgot about Charlotte. Bess, who was then fifty-three years old, was regaling him with stories about the campaign trail and turning on her considerable charm, telling him, "I should have married someone like you at twenty-four and moved to Scarsdale." After dinner they moved to the living room and sat together on a couch, talking for another couple of hours until Charlotte finally approached them and suggested quietly to Gordon that it was time to leave.

A few days later Bess left a message at the Carlyle that she was looking for him. He had enjoyed their dinner party conversation and called her back to ask her to dinner. Soon they were seeing each other regularly. Bess began telling her friends that she was in love and that Gordon seemed to be everything she was looking for. "Here was someone who was Jewish, who was younger than she, and who was also presentable," said a woman who knew Bess at the time. "She was completely captivated by this man. He was the first man since her divorce from Arnold whom she said she could marry."

Gordon was taken with Bess as well and began juggling his relationship with Charlotte to make time for Bess. For a while Charlotte had no idea there was another woman in Gordon's life. Then, in late January 1978, during a week-long vacation with Gordon in Jamaica, she began to suspect he was seeing someone else because he frequently made telephone calls from a phone booth instead of from their hotel room.

When they returned to New York, Charlotte confronted him with her suspicions. At first denying there was another woman, eventually he acknowledged that he had been seeing Bess. Moreover, he said he wanted to continue to see her. Charlotte was shocked that Gordon was throwing her aside for a woman who was twenty years older than she.

With Charlotte out of the picture, Bess and Gordon began seeing each other almost every night and were practically living together at his apartment in the Carlyle. They enjoyed doing the town together. They went to Harry and Leona Helmsley's "I'm Wild About Harry" birthday party. They were also seen at Elaine's, the popular East Side restaurant, at Broadway openings, and at Studio 54, where they watched the Academy Awards on television that spring with actor Yul Brynner.

Bess was often on Gordon's arm at political functions and dinners at Gracie Mansion. She introduced him to Governor Carey and Mayor Koch. That spring they traveled together to Arizona and spent a few days at tennis pro John Gardner's tennis ranch. By the spring of 1978 New York's gossip columnists were no longer speculating about wedding bells for Bess and the mayor. They were now writing about Bess and Gordon. The *Daily News* reported they were "very much in love."

By late summer, though, Gordon had started seeing Charlotte Ames again, behind Bess's back. He also dated other women. Apparently Bess "was a little bit too crazy for him." After having dinner together a few times, Gordon and Charlotte traveled to the Maine coast for a long weekend.

It didn't take Bess long to suspect that Gordon might be seeing someone else. By the end of the summer she was questioning him intensely about his schedule. According to a source close to Gordon, she took to taping their telephone conversations so that she could study his voice inflections for any hint of deceit. Bess would then play back tapes for Gordon and suggest that his tone of voice revealed betrayal. "He appeared to be really enamored with Bess," Marilyn Funt, one of Bess's closest friends, said later. "When she found out about the other women, she was shocked."

After Bess learned he was again seeing Charlotte, she angrily confronted him. "If I were twenty years younger, this never would have happened. I could have kept you," she was said to have told him. Bess was unaccustomed to having a man leave her, for as she once explained, "Men go after me, and I choose among them."

For all her anger, however, Bess was not ready to walk out on the relationship. And Gordon could not bring himself to tell Bess that he no longer loved her. He agreed to continue seeing her, and over the next year they met occasionally for a drink or dinner. Still in the middle of his divorce, Gordon was dating lots of women and not ready to settle down with any one woman at that time. Perhaps Bess thought she could still win his heart. Her chances, however, were slim as long as Charlotte Ames remained in the picture. Gordon always seemed to return to his earlier love.

A few weeks after Bess first challenged Gordon about his relationship with Charlotte, he ran into her unexpectedly—in his own apartment. As Charlotte remembers it, he had been having brunch downstairs in the Carlyle's dining room with Charlotte and her daughter when he discovered a hole in his sock and returned to his apartment for a new pair. Walking into his bedroom, he discovered Bess, in jeans and an old sweater, standing on a stool and rummaging through boxes on the top shelf of his closet.

"What are you doing?" he demanded. "How did you get in here?"

Bess told him that a chambermaid had let her in. Then she hurried past him and out the door without an explanation or apology. That very night Gordon and Charlotte were watching the eleven o'clock news when Bess appeared on the screen at a political fund-raiser, looking stunning in a chiffon Stavropolos gown. "I couldn't believe this was the same person that Gordon had described standing on a stool, going through his bedroom closet," Charlotte later recalled.

Within a few days Gordon and Charlotte began to be plagued by a mysterious caller who would telephone them repeatedly and then hang up when they answered. Sometimes the caller would pause long enough to breathe into the phone. Other times Charlotte would hear music on the other end. The identity of the caller was a mystery. "I would get about thirty calls a day. It went on for months. It drove me crazy," Charlotte said.

Gordon also began receiving strange messages on his answering machine. The first was left while Gordon and Charlotte attended a party and then went to dinner at a midtown Manhattan restaurant. When Gordon played back the tape that night, he heard a deep male voice describe precisely where he and Charlotte had gone that evening. "We knew we were being followed because we didn't decide until we were walking up Fifth Avenue to go to a party on upper Fifth Avenue," Charlotte remembered. "And then while we were at the party, we decided where to go for dinner. Then, after we got home, there was this tape recording saying where we had been."

The anonymous telephone calls persisted. A few weeks after getting the message on his answering machine Gordon returned home to find a piece of paper slipped under his apartment door listing the names of restaurants he had been to with Charlotte in the preceding few days.

Several weeks later, on October 14, 1978, Gordon and Charlotte boarded an Eastern shuttle for Washington, D.C., to visit her mother for the day. They met her in the lobby of the Madison Hotel and then went to Sans Souci for dinner. When they returned to New York the following day, another taped message was waiting for them at Gordon's Carlyle apartment.

The same male voice described in detail their movements in Washington the previous day. Whoever he was, he knew they had boarded the Eastern shuttle, had seen them meet an "unidentified woman" at the Madison Hotel, and knew they had gone to dinner at Sans Souci. Charlotte, already on edge because of the phone calls and the earlier taped message, now became terrified that a stranger had intimate knowledge of her life. She worried about her mother, who lived alone in Virginia, and about herself and her eight-year-old daughter living alone in New York City. Shouldn't they go to the police? Gordon said no. He dismissed it as a lot of nonsense.

What Charlotte did not know at the time was that Gordon was still seeing Bess occasionally and that Gordon suspected Bess was responsible for having them followed. Bess could always tell him where he had been, what he had been wearing, and whom he had been with. He knew that she was furious that he continued to see Charlotte Ames.

Three weeks after Gordon and Charlotte returned from Washington, on November 5, 1978, they were attending a political fund-raiser at the El Morocco nightclub for their close friend New York City councilman

Carter Burden, who was running for the U.S. Congress. With only a few days left before the election, Burden's credibility had been dealt a hard blow. Bess, who had promised her political support months earlier, withdrew her endorsement of Burden that very afternoon. She accused him of using her endorsement in radio commercials and on door-to-door fliers without her permission. Bess aired her complaint in the newspapers, a move the Burden campaign feared would hurt his effort to unseat Republican congressman William Green.

Those in the Burden campaign who knew about Bess's failed relationship with Gordon believed that her action was triggered by the fact that Gordon was Burden's close friend and chief fund-raiser. But Bess told reporters that it was "ludicrous" to suggest she would have withdrawn her endorsement because of her problems with Gordon. "I have never confused my personal life with my political integrity," she told the *New York Daily News*. "Nobody delivers me. I deliver me."

Just before the November election, which Burden was to lose, the mystery caller stopped leaving taped messages on Gordon's answering machine, though the hang-up calls continued. Meanwhile, Bess had started to date other men. Over the next year she was seen in the company of former New York State Supreme Court judge Jerry Becker; Edward Klein, then the editor of the *New York Times Magazine*; millionaire businessman Mort Hyman; investment banker and former commerce secretary Peter Peterson; and shoe manufacturer Jeffrey Endervelt.

Bess also ended up on the gossip page of the *New York Post* when she was accused by a prominent divorce attorney of adultery with millionaire businessman Benjamin Lambert, who was separated from his wife at the time he was seeing Bess. "We have absolute evidence of adultery. We have absolute evidence that she was overnight at his house," attorney Raoul Lionel Felder, who would later represent Nancy Capasso, told the *New York Post* in March 1979.

Denying the allegations, Bess told the newspapers that she and Lambert were "just friends . . . [he was] one of my many friends." As for the adultery charge, Bess said, "My God, of course it's not true. Poor Ben. And that poor lady. I have no personal relationship with Mr. Lambert. I just think the lady is obviously very upset and very angry." Bess recalled for the *Post* that the last time she saw Lambert "was at a meeting at his house about rehabilitating slum areas. We're both interested in that. He's a very pro-bono-minded gentleman."

Though Bess was seen about town with other men, she continued to see Gordon once in a while in 1979 and in the early months of 1980, unbeknownst to Charlotte. One morning before dawn in late 1979,

Charlotte was awakened in her apartment by the ringing of a telephone. A woman was on the other end of the line.

"Is Gordon there?" the woman asked.

Charlotte was half asleep, yet she recognized Bess's distinctive low voice.

"Who is this?" Charlotte demanded.

"Elizabeth Rubin," the caller replied.

"He's sleeping. I don't want to wake him."

"It's urgent," the caller insisted. "It's about his children."

Charlotte leaned over and woke Gordon. "It's Bess," she said and handed him the phone.

Gordon took the call in another room. When he returned to bed, he told Charlotte that it had, in fact, been Bess. She had said she was calling from a gurney in a Miami hospital, where she was about to undergo surgery for cancer. Bess told Gordon that she had gone to Miami for the surgery because she feared that word about her illness would leak out if she had gone to a New York hospital and that it would jeopardize her chances of winning the 1980 Democratic nomination for the United States Senate. She pleaded with Gordon to get on the next plane to Florida to be with her when she came out of surgery that afternoon.

Gordon was shocked at the news, and he left Charlotte's apartment to continue the telephone conversation in the privacy of his own home. He considered going to Florida that morning, but after talking to a close friend of Bess's, he believed it would give Bess false hope that he was interested in reviving their relationship. As it turned out, Bess was not in the hospital for cancer surgery. She has since told friends that she went to Miami for cosmetic surgery to remove scars left from her 1974 hysterectomy.

The hang-up phone calls to Gordon and Charlotte—mostly to Charlotte—continued sporadically through the spring, summer, and fall of 1979. Charlotte finally became completely fed up with the harassment and contacted the telephone company for help early that fall. The company agreed to attempt to trace the phone calls, and after several weeks of trying to pinpoint the origin of the calls, a pattern emerged.

According to Charlotte, the phone company told her that the majority of the calls were coming from three pay telephones in Manhattan. One of the telephone booths was on the corner of East 71st Street and Madison Avenue, and the other two were on East End Avenue. Charlotte asked Gordon if he knew anyone who might live or work near those phone booths. Bess, he replied.

Bess lived on East 71st Street, just a block from Madison Avenue. Her ghostwriter, whom she would meet with frequently to discuss her book on consumerism and her articles for *Redbook*, lived on East End Avenue, across the street from one of the phone booths. The other booth, at the corner of East End Avenue and East 88th Street, was across the street from Gracie Mansion, the home of Mayor Ed Koch, whom she had been seeing more of that fall as she considered entering the U.S. Senate race the next year.

Armed with this information, Gordon confronted Bess and asked whether she was the one making the calls. Bess adamantly denied it.

Soon afterward Charlotte and Gordon stopped getting calls. Then, a few months later, in the spring of 1980, after Gordon had finally stopped seeing Bess, anonymous letters began to arrive. The first one was addressed to Gordon at the Carlyle. "Dear Nothing," the letter began. "You should be hearing from some of the girls you laid and screwed. You will be sorry for what you have done to one of them. You will be punished in ways you don't know."

The letter ended with this promise: "More follows."

19

"Too Tall, Too Beautiful, Too Rich"

In the months after her relationship with J. Gordon Marcus cooled in August 1978, Bess began sounding out friends and political cohorts about her idea of seeking the Democratic nomination for the United States Senate in 1980. After nearly a decade of campaigning on behalf of others, Bess was finally ready to become a political candidate herself.

Her doctor had given her a clean bill of health that November. She had passed the magic five-year mark for patients with ovarian cancer with no sign that the disease would recur. She also had saved about $4 million from her salary and investments, though she sometimes confounded her friends by living as if she were on the brink of bankruptcy. There was no one man in her life. What's more, Bess was bored with her high-paying jobs as a consumer consultant for big business and eager to do something different, try something new.

In February 1979 Bess invited some of her closest friends to her apartment for a tuna lunch to discuss her political ambitions. A friend remembers that Bess said, "I don't have anything more to do in life. I have to do something now. It's my time."

Bess's sights were set on a formidable goal—unseating Senator Jacob Javits, the popular liberal Republican who after twenty-four years in the U.S. Senate was planning to run for his fifth term. The idea of Bess as a candidate was attractive to some Democratic strategists, who theorized that she could win back some of the Jewish Democratic voters who had supported Javits in the past.

Before worrying about Javits, however, Bess would have to win the Democratic primary in September 1980, and that would be no easy task. Her principal challenger was expected to be Elizabeth Holtzman, the no-nonsense Brooklyn congresswoman and graduate of Harvard Law School whose aggressive questioning during the impeachment hearings of former president Richard Nixon had attracted national attention. Others considering running in the primary included Bess's former boss, John Lindsay, who was attempting a political comeback, and John Santucci, the Queens district attorney.

123

Through the spring, summer, and fall of 1979 Bess moved deliberately to lay the foundation for a 1980 Senate race. Like many would-be
candidates, she was coy with the press, refusing to say explicitly that she
was planning to run for Javits's seat. Yet she was doing everything that a
potential candidate should have been doing.

As early as the spring of 1979 Bess began calling in the political chits
she had accumulated from her years of campaigning for others. Within
the first few months of the year Senator Moynihan promised to help
and Governor Carey put her in touch with his major fund-raisers. Her
biggest ally, of course, was her old friend, Mayor Ed Koch, who told
listeners of WMCA-AM's Barry Gray radio talk show that spring, "If
she runs, she'll wipe the floor with all the other people. She would walk
away with the race."

That summer Bess spent hours on the telephone seeking contributions from wealthy or influential friends and acquaintances. By the end
of 1979 she had more than $200,000 in the bank and her list of
contributors looked like a "who's who" of the rich and famous: movie
producer and director John Avildsen, actress Greer Garson, television
game show creator Mark Goodson, hotel owners Leona and Harry
Helmsley, television producer Norman Lear, attorney Arthur Liman,
chicken king Frank Perdue, financial columnist Sylvia Porter, and
model Christina Ferrare, who was then married to maverick auto
producer John DeLorean.

Bess also began making the obligatory rounds of the city's various
Democratic clubs and ventured into upstate New York to make speeches
and oil her rusty campaign skills. She sought support from prominent
Democrats, but not all of them were in her camp. Her biggest rebuff
came from Gloria Steinem, who complained that Bess had not staked
out positions on many important issues. Steinem called this "unacceptable" and urged Bess to abandon her candidacy and support Holtzman.

Steinem's criticism underscored one of the problems of Bess's early
campaign. While she spoke knowledgeably and at length about consumer questions and the importance of supporting Israel, she appeared
to know little about many of the major issues confronting the country.
She made the mistake of telling reporters that she intended to learn the
issues as her campaign progressed, a remark that drew a laugh from
Andrew Stein, then Manhattan borough president, who suggested that
Bess was "trying to beauty queen her way to the nomination."

Stein's comment struck at the very heart of what Bess had been trying
to overcome since the day she was crowned Miss America in 1945. Even
her years as the city's feared and celebrated consumer affairs commissioner had failed to transform her celebrity image as a beauty queen and
television's "Lady in Mink" into the persona she had long sought for
herself: that of a serious and hardworking woman who had overcome the

odds and made something of herself. The Miss America title seemed to be linked inextricably to her name: "I've always been Queen Bess," she said at the time. "It's a theme that runs through my life. It colors everything I do."

Her own private poll, taken in the fall of 1979, reflected her image problem with voters. "Everyone in New York state knew who Bess Myerson was and liked her, but hardly anyone was convinced that she had the experience to be a U.S. senator," recalled Bess's campaign manager, Dick Eaton, then a thirty-year-old lawyer and political veteran who had worked on U.S. senator Moynihan's campaign.

What she had to do to win in 1980 was shatter her beauty queen image and remind voters that she had been in government and in business. However, her one major public service credential—her impressive record as the city's consumer affairs commissioner in the early 1970s—now had a serious downside. After leaving the Lindsay administration, Bess had gone through the revolving door of the business-government complex and had gone to work as a consumer consultant for Citibank and Bristol-Myers, two companies that came under criticism from consumer advocates for some of their policies.

Out on the hustings in those early days of the campaign—in cities like Buffalo, Syracuse, Rochester, and Binghamton, where she was giving her stump speech a dry run before facing the aggressive New York City press corps—she got off to a weak start. Instead of talking about issues, she sought to "emotionally bind" herself with her audiences by telling them stories about her early life. She recounted her upbringing in a working-class Bronx family during the Depression, describing her parents as "boat people" from Europe. She told Jewish audiences stories about never being good enough to please her mother, and she talked about facing discrimination while Miss America.

She was relying on what she described at the time as her "special magic." As she explained to a reporter during the campaign, "I have a history of really impacting on audiences, of getting standing ovations and having people embrace my concepts, and it's a very powerful feeling, and it must be used very carefully as well, you know. I feel people, and they feel me. And I think that is an enormous responsibility. I felt it all through my life, and I feel it doubly now in terms of the Senate. They're waiting for something to happen, and I really think I can make the difference for them and make something happen and give them hope, which is something they haven't had for a long time."

The question remained, though, whether Bess, with all her charisma and persuasive powers, was talking about the concerns that would win her votes at the polls.

In January 1980 Bess rolled up the Bedouin rug in her living room and took down the Picasso and the fifth-century Byzantine mosaic from her walls. The clay pot that had been a gift from Moshe Dayan was packed up. So was the sculpture of horses from the kingdom of Amenhotep that graced the refectory table in her living room. Her black Steinway grand piano was covered and moved into a corner.

As she set up temporary campaign headquarters in her apartment to save money for the summer and fall, it soon became clear that Bess was going to have her work cut out for her. Liz Holtzman, in the days after declaring her candidacy that January and unveiling an issue-oriented campaign that stressed her eight years of experience in the U.S. Congress, began surging ahead in the polls. Bess, meanwhile, wanted to hold off for as long as possible before formally declaring her candidacy so she could hold on to the consulting and writing jobs that had paid her nearly $493,000 in 1979.

Bess bided her time, studying hard and cramming onto three-by-five index cards facts and figures about the MX missile system, the B-1 bomber, federal mass-transit aid, and the state's balance of payments crisis. "Bess had amazing dedication to put all of this stuff in her head. For the most part, she was diligent," Dick Eaton recalled. Positioning herself as the moderate-to-conservative candidate, Bess prepared to attack Holtzman's liberal congressional record and consistent votes against defense appropriations. It was the only chink in Holtzman's armor, the Myerson camp concluded, and they intended to link a strong American defense to the integrity of Israel.

With her artworks stored away and her piano shoved into a corner, Bess's apartment was transformed into a suite of offices that buzzed with activity. The dining room was the nerve center. Files filled the drawers of her buffet. Position papers and fund-raising lists were strewn across Bess's heavy chrome and glass dining table. Eaton, her campaign manager, worked out of her second bedroom. Another campaign aide was assigned work space in the kitchen and told to use the kitchen counter as her desk.

In those early days of the campaign Bess was preoccupied by money. She wanted to cut as many corners as possible to save for an upcoming television advertising blitz. She typed letters herself and hopped onto the Fifth Avenue bus to go to a campaign event. "Bess had no concept of money," one campaign aide recalled. "The woman had a lot of neurotic tendencies. She once asked me, 'How do I know if I have enough money to buy a car?' I was astonished. When you have four million dollars, you have enough money to go out and buy a car."

One of Bess's worries during the spring of 1980 concerned who was eating the Schrafft's chocolate candies she kept in the crystal bowl on her living room coffee table. "She thought that the volunteers who came to work at the apartment were helping themselves to things. She would always ask two things. She would want to know the latest jokes, and is anybody out there taking those chocolate candies?" recalled a volunteer in the campaign.

One night Bess's parsimonious ways led her on a raiding party to her office at Citibank. The incident would become known within the campaign as the "liberation of the typewriter." After delivering a speech about the history of women at the Marble Collegiate Church on Fifth Avenue, Bess directed her driver to pull up outside of Citibank's midtown Manhattan headquarters. It was approaching midnight.

"She knew the doorman," recalled one of the two campaign aides who accompanied Bess inside. "He waved us all through, and we went up. She took a typewriter. She also happened to have in her bag a couple of garbage bags, which she filled with file folders, Scotch tape dispensers, notebooks, pens, and paper. She was going to use their supplies. She felt that maybe Citibank owed it to her."

As they followed Bess's instructions and carried the garbage bags and typewriter out of the building, one of the campaign aides turned to the other, rolled her eyes, and whispered, "Can you believe we are doing this?"

Like many candidates caught up in a high-stakes campaign, Bess was a demanding boss whose moods could swing widely and unpredictably. "If you want to work on the campaign, call so-and-so right now, raise some money, or leave," Bess would shout to volunteers working on weekends. Then, in the next breath, she would offer to fix dinner for everyone or suggest they all go to a movie.

She also promised to help her volunteers find jobs once the campaign was over. One volunteer recalled, "Her favorite thing to say was 'We are going to find you a great job where you can make piles of money.' She was very good at opening doors, and then she expected you to make the most of that opportunity."

Again Bess fell into the role of being everybody's mother, scolding her staff for eating junk food and for failing to take vitamins and for not getting enough exercise. Bess herself gulped a myriad of vitamins several times a day without the benefit of water and tried to find time to keep in shape by pedaling her bicycle around Central Park or jumping rope.

"She showed many sides of her personality," recalled a former longtime friend who worked on the campaign. "She could be very sweet and giving. She really tried to extend herself in certain ways, but she used to take her pound of flesh in return. She would treat me very badly at times. Then she would be very contrite and loving."

A senior staff member encountered few problems with Bess, which he attributed to his senior position in the campaign: "She is a very smart, very shrewd person who was nice to people when she needed to be nice to people, and if she sized them up and realized that she didn't have to be nice, she wasn't nice. If you were a peer, she didn't give you problems. If you were a worker, she could be pretty tough."

Bess, it struck some of her campaign workers, had a powerful need to be in control. On the way to campaign events she invariably complained that her driver wasn't driving fast enough and threatened to drive herself.

"In the campaign she always had to be in control," recalled the former longtime friend who worked on the campaign. "She couldn't let go. But then again, there was no one to let go to. It was amateur night at the races. With all of her contacts, all of her money, there was no organization. When Ed Koch ran, there was a real organization around him. Bess didn't have that."

Bess had been trying to persuade her old friend David Garth, the political media wizard, to oversee her campaign. But for all she had done for two of his major candidates, Governor Carey and Mayor Koch, Garth was playing hard to get. As early as the spring of 1979 Garth told her he wasn't interested. "I told her I want to stay out of the Senate race in New York. It's just a pain in the ass," Garth said at the time.

But Bess persisted and finally convinced Garth to help. Garth's reluctance was based on his belief that Bess would lose the Democratic primary. After Holtzman's announcement in January private polls showed that Bess would have great difficulty beating the Brooklyn congresswoman. As Garth later recalled, "There was no way that Bess was going to beat that. We advised Bess not to run. The poll was that strong. I wanted to let her know what she was in for."

Despite the strong possibility of defeat and the likelihood that she would have to use almost $1 million out of her $4 million in savings to mount an effective media campaign, Bess insisted on running. She was convinced that 1980 was her year. "She said she still wanted to do it," Garth recalled. "I told her, 'If you want to do it, we'll do it.'"

Garth put his top associate, Maureen Connelly, in charge of the campaign. At thirty-one, Connelly was a veteran of a dozen political campaigns, a smart, savvy political professional who had been Koch's press secretary at City Hall after working at Garth's side in the 1977 mayoral campaign. Her first challenge was to help Bess shed her celebrity image and show voters that Bess was a serious candidate who would bring her experience in government and business to Washington. On the biographical sheet handed out to reporters by the campaign there was no mention of the Miss America contest that had first brought Bess to public attention.

The campaign message was virtually a carbon copy of the one that had worked so well for Senator Moynihan in his 1976 campaign. The plan was for Bess to take a hard line on defense, a risky move in a primary that attracted many liberal voters, and to complain that the state of New York was not getting back as many federal dollars each year in services and aid as its citizens were paying into the government in taxes.

On May 6 Bess returned to the Sholem Aleichem Cooperative Houses in the Bronx with her ninety-year-old father, Louis, to officially open her campaign. Her mother, Bella, then eighty-eight, was confined to a bed in a Bronx nursing home and unable to accompany them. Although most of the working-class Jewish families from the original cooperative had moved out years ago, a few old neighbors remained, and they greeted Bess warmly and led her to the basement, where they had put out a punch bowl and plates of cookies in celebration of her return. Her father said at the time, "I'm very proud of her. There is only one Bess."

As the Senate campaign got under way, Bess saw J. Gordon Marcus less frequently, but she remained obsessed with him and would later be accused of engaging in a harassment campaign against him and his girlfriend. It had finally become apparent to her that he had no intention of giving up Charlotte Ames and his other girlfriends to have a serious relationship with her. That spring she began to focus most of her attention on another man, Jeffrey Endervelt, a rich, successful shoe manufacturer who was in his thirties and who would later marry Polly Bergen. Endervelt took an active role in the campaign and often accompanied Bess to fund-raisers. "We liked him," said a member of the campaign staff. "He was tall, good-looking, and even-tempered. He put up with a lot of nonsense from her." Bess was seen on his arm at political fund-raisers and other affairs until another younger man attracted her attention at the annual Queens County Democratic party dinner.

Unlike Democratic dinners held in Manhattan hotel ballrooms, the Queens annual bash at Antun's, a huge catering hall on Springfield Boulevard, was an informal affair. There was no dais or long-winded political speeches. The buffet-style dinner tables were lined up against the wall with chafing dishes filled with heaping piles of roast beef, ham, and lobster. With almost six hundred people milling around the room, it was the perfect setting for Bess to mingle with scores of loyal party workers, city contractors, and potential campaign contributors.

Bess made her entrance shortly after 9:00 P.M., looking like a movie star in her white dress. Donald Manes greeted her warmly. As borough president and Queens Democratic county leader, Manes was widely considered to be the second most powerful politician in New York. A strapping, bulky, gregarious man in his late forties with short brown hair, pasty skin, and a big smile, he called himself the "King of Queens." He led Bess through the crowd, introducing her to party workers from his large and disciplined party machine and to city contractors who often made big political contributions. Toward the end of the night Manes introduced Bess to his old friends, Carl Andy Capasso and his wife, Nancy, as they were about to walk out the door.

Andy Capasso was a thirty-five-year-old multimillionaire, a big-time city contractor who laid sewer pipes for a living. His grandfather and father had been in the sewer construction business, and he had started his own company from scratch in 1968, not long after he met his wife, Nancy. Funny and charming, he is somewhat handsome when he smiles. As a city contractor, he understood the importance of knowing the pols, attending fund-raisers, and contributing to their campaigns. Andy was usually generous with candidates, giving them huge donations.

From the first night he met Bess, he was taken with her, his then-wife Nancy recalled. "He fell for her hook, line, and sinker," she said. A few days after the fund-raiser Andy called Bess at her campaign headquarters and offered to do whatever he could to help her raise money. Bess was grateful for his support and invited him to a fund-raiser that Ben Heller, a New York art dealer, was throwing for her at his summer home in the Hamptons.

Andy accepted the invitation and showed up with Nancy. Bess was accompanied to the party by Jeffrey Endervelt. A campaign worker remembers that Endervelt was miffed that Bess seemed to be paying most of her attention to Andy that day. "Andy Capasso was really putting on the moves," a campaign aide said. "He was jumping around her, and she was jumping around him. I was really pissed that she was going for this guy over Endervelt."

After the fund-raiser Bess began to talk regularly with Andy on the telephone. He amused her with his one-liners, and she found his lack of airs refreshing. He was smart and down to earth. That summer he collected thousands of dollars on her behalf from his friends in the sewer and construction business.

Bess needed all of the campaign contributions she could get as she began a series of television commercials that would ultimately cost her campaign about $800,000, much of it her own money. The strategy was to build up Bess as someone experienced in the world of business and government, someone voters could imagine as a United States senator. The commercials all closed with the same tag line: "She knows government. She knows business. She knows how to get things done . . . for New York."

Koch lent his support to the effort and taped a commercial in which he told viewers, "She's a fighter. . . . She's effective." So did Senator Moynihan, who said, "Bess and I can work together effectively."

Anyone who spent a day on the sweat-and-shoe-leather circuit with Bess that summer would have found it hard to conceive of her losing. "Everybody knew her by first name," recalled her campaign director,

Ken Lerer. "She was everybody's daughter or everybody's mother. She was terrific."

Though Bess knew her campaign stump speech by heart, she was unsure of herself when forced to discuss issues off the top of her head. Candy Jones, the former model whose late husband, Harry Conover, had been one of the judges in the 1945 Miss America contest, recalled being "shocked" by Bess's performance when Bess appeared on her radio talk show on WMCA-AM. "She was not together at all. She was not well versed in the issues. Whenever I would ask her a question, she would fumble through this big fat binder, looking for the answer," Jones said.

This spelled trouble for the impending debates. As Lerer later recalled, "I think she has a large intellectual capacity. But she wasn't comfortable in the debate format. She had never done it before. . . . This was her first campaign, and Liz Holtzman was a tough character. In the debates she always had Bess off balance."

As the summer progressed, the fighting got rougher on the campaign trail and in the debates. Holtzman went after Bess in radio ads in early August for her role as chairman of the board of a community-based, nonprofit consumer counseling service that had been accused of engaging in deceptive practices by the very agency Bess once headed—the city's consumer affairs department.

As the front-runner, she was also the target of attacks by Lindsay. In one radio debate Lindsay accused her of selling out consumers by leaving her job as the city's consumer affairs commissioner and going to work for Citibank and Bristol-Myers as a highly paid consumer consultant. "When you left my administration, you traded that experience for protecting the interests of banks and corporations," John Lindsay said. "You just went to the other side. You made a hell of a lot of money, and a lot of that income was sheltered." He went on to charge that Bess's heavy television spending—which Lindsay could not hope to match—was being underwritten by anticonsumer "special interests."

At a loss for an effective comeback, Bess stumbled, saying merely, "I have no question about my loyalty to consumers at all."

Despite her lackluster performance in debates, newspaper polls published in early September gave Bess hope. On September 1 the *New York Daily News* published a poll that showed that residents of the New York City metropolitan area, by a two-to-one margin, believed Bess would win the Democratic primary. Her closest rival was Holtzman, followed by Lindsay and then Santucci.

The next day a *New York Times* poll also showed Bess leading the field. Among Democrats likely to vote in the primary, Bess led Holtzman 38 percent to 27 percent. Lindsay had 15 percent, and Santucci, who had been a late entry in the race, had 8 percent. The *Times* noted, however, that the sampling for the poll had ended on August 28, just as Holtzman's television campaign was about to begin.

While the polls must have been encouraging to Bess and others in the campaign, Maureen Connelly, who was heading the campaign effort for Garth, was unimpressed. In New York Democratic primaries the liberal vote is heavy, and liberal voters in most campaigns do not start thinking about a race until after Labor Day. "If you are the moderate candidate in the Democratic primary, you have to be pretty far ahead by Labor Day," Connelly said. And Bess was not. She also had to face her opponents in yet another debate.

On the day the *Times* poll was published Bess headed over to an auditorium at 823 United Nations Plaza for a debate sponsored by the Anti-Defamation League of B'nai B'rith, the same organization that had launched her career making speeches against racism and anti-Semitism during her 1945 Miss America reign. Almost three hundred people, most of them Jewish, attended. Lindsay, Santucci, and Holtzman were all there. Soon after their opening statements, however, it became clear it would be a contest between Bess and Liz.

The *Times* polls worried members of Holtzman's staff, and a campaign aide told a *New York Times* reporter that day that Holtzman intended to get tough with Bess. She fulfilled her promise. Minutes into the debate that night, Holtzman launched her harshest attack on Bess's integrity, accusing her of failing to stand up to the president of Citibank when the bank had bowed to the Arab boycott of Israel. "You had a choice of resigning in public protest or staying on and drawing a paycheck," Holtzman said. "You chose to stay on. I couldn't have stayed on and drawn a paycheck. That is the difference between us."

Bess looked stunned, according to the coverage of the debate in the *New York Times* and the *New York Daily News* the following day. Her jaw tightened as she chewed on the end of her glasses. Unable to come up with a sharp retort, Bess repeated her well-rehearsed campaign theme that the federal government was shortchanging New York. Then she paused. "Let me take a few seconds to respond to a woman who questions my loyalty to the Jewish community and the state of Israel." Bess argued that she had tried to persuade the bank to change its policy but was unsuccessful. "But I don't quit. I stay and work from the inside."

Bess struck back at Holtzman the following morning. Furious that Holtzman had questioned her loyalty to Israel, Bess replaced the commercials emphasizing her business and government experience with one attacking Holtzman's congressional votes "against every defense appropriation, every defense authorization."

Acting against the advice of her top campaign aides, Bess insisted that the commercial against Holtzman run up until the September 9 primary. Some strategists believe she hurt herself with the party's heavy liberal vote by emphasizing her hawkish position on defense.

In the closing days of the campaign Bess was exhausted, but she kept her sense of humor with members of the press. While waiting for a radio debate to begin, Bess told Maurice Carroll, then working for the *New York Times*, that she intended to have Bert Parks as her emcee on election night. "If I win, he can sing 'Here she comes, the next United States senator,'" Bess told Carroll. "And if I lose, he can sing 'There she goes.'"

The strain of campaigning for months, however, was evident to some members of her staff. "She was yelling and screaming at everybody," said a former friend who was a campaign aide. "She said to me, 'I can't stand you anymore. Go home.' And so I never came back to the campaign. I shouldn't have paid any attention to her. Emotionally, I was wrung out. She was losing, and I was sad about it."

On her way home on the Sunday night before election day Bess stopped by her daughter Barra's apartment on the Upper East Side. Bess was with two of her closest friends, Marilyn Funt, a writer, and Pam Chanin, who worked at City Hall. As they were about to leave, there was a phone call for Chanin. It was campaign headquarters with bad news. The *New York Post* was running the results of its latest poll in the next day's newspaper. The survey showed that Bess would lose.

Holtzman's television campaign, combined with her attack on Bess for not leaving Citibank, had turned the election around.

Now Bess was ten points behind Holtzman, according to the *Post* poll. Pam Chanin hung up the phone and wondered how she was going to break the news to Bess.

They went downstairs and got into the car. Bess wanted to stop at her health club before going home. As they headed to the club, Bess began wondering aloud about the possibility of losing the race. "Imagine all of this time, all of this energy, and my money," Chanin recalled Bess said at the time.

"Stop imagining, Bess," Chanin said and then told Bess that she was trailing Holtzman by ten points.

"Oh," Bess replied in a calm voice. "That's what you were talking about on the phone upstairs."

"She was very quiet, very calm," Chanin recalled.

On Election Day, September 9, more than eight hundred thousand voters went to the polls throughout New York state. Bess was hoping for a heavy turnout to offset the effectiveness of Holtzman's statewide organization. While Holtzman had five thousand volunteers distributing leaflets throughout the state, Bess was relying heavily on her $800,000 television campaign.

At around three o'clock that afternoon Bess was in her apartment when she got a call from her campaign director, Ken Lerer. The exit polls confirmed what the *New York Post* had reported the day before. Holtzman looked like the winner. She thanked him for calling and then hung up. "Bess was really devastated by losing the race," Marilyn Funt later told *New York* magazine. "When she heard the news, she just broke down and cried like a child."

Bess would later say she lost the race because she was "too tall, too beautiful, too rich."

After the polls closed at 8:00 P.M., Bess went over to the Sheraton Centre on Seventh Avenue and spent the next couple of hours cloistered in a hotel suite waiting for the numbers with Koch, Garth, Connelly, her daughter, and a few close campaign aides and friends. The exit polls were accurate. Holtzman had captured 41 percent of the votes to Bess's 31 percent. Lindsay got 16 percent, and Santucci won 12 percent. Santucci's late entrance into the race had hurt Bess. He had won the moderate-to-conservative ethnic votes that might have gone to Bess.

Holtzman had won the Democratic nomination with overwhelming margins in Queens, Brooklyn, Manhattan, and suburban Westchester County. Bess won the Bronx, Staten Island, and upstate New York by a small margin. The Jewish vote that Bess had thought was hers also went to Liz Holtzman. Her loss among Jewish voters was particularly devastating to Bess, the self-proclaimed "Queen of the Jews."

The telephone rang nonstop in the hotel suite as people called to offer their regrets. Garth took most of the calls. "She was in another world," recalled Ken Lerer. At around eleven o'clock Bess went downstairs to make her concession speech in a hotel ballroom that held more than two hundred disappointed supporters.

There was no trace of disappointment on her face, no tears in her eyes when she strode into the ballroom, smiling, with a bouquet of American Beauty roses in her arms. With Barra and Mayor Koch at her side, Bess delivered what Maureen Connelly would remember as the best speech of the campaign. She thanked her campaign workers for their effort and told them she was proud of the campaign. Gracious in defeat, she promised to support the Democratic ticket, although she added with a laugh that she would first try to convince Liz Holtzman that she was "not accurate in her appraisals of the reality of what is going on."

Then, still smiling as if she had won, she threw her American Beauty roses one by one to the crowd.

20
The Letters

As Bess's Senate campaign progressed through the spring and summer months of 1980, the harassment of J. Gordon Marcus and Charlotte Ames not only continued but escalated. The anonymous threatening letter that had been left for Gordon at the desk of the Carlyle that spring had proven right on one point: more was to follow.

In March 1980 Charlotte Ames also began receiving crude and obscene letters filled with anti-Semitic references and details about Gordon's alleged affairs with a multitude of other women. A few months later Gordon learned that four other women he had dated in recent months were receiving similar anonymous letters. After the hang-up telephone calls in 1979, Gordon had immediately suspected that Bess might be responsible for the harassment. She had been furious with him when he finally ended their relationship in the spring of 1980, asking him to explain why he no longer loved her at a joint meeting with her psychiatrist and friend, Dr. Theodore Isaac Rubin. He went to the meeting hoping that he might persuade Bess to accept his decision. She said she did.

Gordon was convinced Bess was responsible for the letters that summer until she called him in July and complained that she too was receiving anonymous letters, warning of a plot to undermine her Senate candidacy. She was only two months away from the September 9 Democratic primary, and the letters, Bess told Gordon, alleged that he and Charlotte were masterminding a campaign of rumor and innuendo to ruin her.

Gordon told Bess that he had no such plans. Bess angrily suggested to Gordon that Charlotte might be writing the letters and covering up her role by sending some to herself. "Call off your girlfriend," Bess warned Gordon.

When Gordon later told Charlotte of his conversation with Bess, Charlotte said that she would like to talk to Bess directly and compare their letters. Working together, perhaps they could figure out who was harassing them.

Charlotte's first letter had been hand-delivered to her doorman that March by a taxi driver. It was typed on white stationery with a sketch of a cat at the top. "Do you know that Gordon has another woman?" the letter inquired. "She's beautiful and bright. They carry on at the Carlyle and at her place in Scarsdale. They're in constant touch with each other. Check his phone bills. Nick and Barbara introduced them and are delighted it took. Don't think you're good enough for their buddy. Are these pimps your friends? More follows."

More did follow. Over the next few months a succession of similar letters arrived at Charlotte's apartment typed on the same stationery as the first. One of the letters suggested that Gordon was carrying on affairs with Bess and a prominent New York socialite at the same time Charlotte was seeing him. The letter, signed "a friend," said that Charlotte's own friends thought Gordon was treating her like a "doormat" and that "He wipes his feet and his penis on you when he is finished with his other ladies. He is a male whore."

Charlotte didn't believe the allegations, but the letters frightened her. She worried that whoever was writing them was so unbalanced or obsessed that he or she might try to harm Charlotte or her daughter. "I used to be so scared I would go to a friend's apartment to open them. It was just awful," she recalled. But Charlotte did not go to the police with her concerns. She figured the letters would be of no concern to police in a city that has up to ten homicides a day.

When a letter arrived naming her own mother as one of the women Gordon was supposed to be having an affair with, Charlotte's concerns eased. "It was the happiest day of my life," she said, having concluded that the letter writer had somehow seen Gordon's address book and was simply pulling out women's names and including them in the letters.

On July 15, a few days after Charlotte learned from Gordon that Bess too was getting threatening letters, she put in a telephone call to Bess at her Senate campaign headquarters. Charlotte recalled that a secretary answered the telephone and said Bess was unavailable.

"Who's calling?" the secretary asked.

"Charlotte Ames."

"Charlotte Ames," the secretary repeated. "Mmmm. Your name sounds familiar. I think I just put something in the mail to you."

Charlotte left her telephone number and hung up, wondering what Bess's secretary possibly could have mailed to her.

Later that night, Charlotte said, Bess returned her call. They talked for almost an hour about Gordon and the letters. Bess told Charlotte that she had received three or four letters filled with threats and that she had been shaken by them.

Charlotte suggested to Bess that they bring the matter to the attention of the police. But, Charlotte recalled, Bess asked her not to go to the police: "She said that she thought the letters might fall into the hands of the press and ruin her campaign." Instead Bess asked Charlotte to turn over the letters to her. She said she would show them to a close friend who was a lawyer and ask for his advice. Charlotte agreed and said she would leave her letters with Bess's doorman.

Before Charlotte hung up, she remembered to ask Bess what her secretary had put in the mail to her. Probably some campaign literature or an invitation to a fund-raiser, Bess replied.

Charlotte thanked Bess, but after the conversation she couldn't imagine why Bess would invite her to a campaign function. After all, Gordon had finally ended his relationship with Bess because of her, and she had heard from Gordon that Bess was unhappy about being thrown over for a younger woman.

The next morning Charlotte received another vulgar, anonymous letter in the mail. The following day an invitation to attend one of Bess's campaign events arrived in the mail. That sequence led Charlotte to wonder whether Bess had sent the anonymous letter and then sent her the invitation to mask her possible involvement. But after thinking about it, Charlotte couldn't imagine Bess taking the time or the risk to write such vile, anonymous letters while at the same time campaigning for the U.S. Senate.

In the days following her conversation with Bess, the letters continued. At the end of July Charlotte's mother received one at her home in Virginia, about Charlotte and J. Gordon Marcus. A magazine headline, "Get Rich Quick," was pasted on the top of the letter and was followed by this message:

> J. is the way. Have your say and Charlotte will play. Come today then J. will pay. He may seem gay but he makes hay. Tell him what you may. A girl he'll lay, not always Charlotte A. So what you'll say is buy. We hear you say J. will pay. Be nice and play the game your way. It will pay. Your Jew for Charlotte you'll have one day.

A few days later Charlotte got another letter. This one was typed on the torn-out cover of a recent issue of *New York* magazine with the headline "Perfect Weekends." Typed directly on the page below the headline was this message, which referred to friends of Gordon's:

> Perfect weekends can be yours if you spend them with a nice man. When will you have yours? Only if you find out the truth. Why don't you call Ron or Anna or Bess or Pat? Because you are chicken and J. is a shit, which makes you chicken shit. Call Kay and she will show you evidence of times spent together. Better to find out now than to live more days and months and years in sadness. Be smart. We are your friends. The only ones you have.

Charlotte had sought to escape the harassment that summer by moving with her daughter into Gordon's rented house in the Hamptons, which had an unlisted telephone number. But whoever was writing her letters and making occasional hang-up phone calls to her apartment in the city had managed to track her down at the rented house on Montrose Avenue in Watermill. One night in early August, only a few days after she had received the "Perfect Weekends" magazine cover, a woman called and asked, "Is this the Montrose Avenue jewelry store?" There were no jewelry stores or commercial businesses on Montrose Avenue. The next day the phone calls started up at the rented house. "I really thought that whoever it was wanted me to know that they knew where my house was," Charlotte said. "I was terrified. I would be there alone at night with my daughter, while Gordon was in the city, and I was scared. It was a big house with lots of windows. I packed up my stuff, put Katherine into the car, and drove back to my apartment in the city. The number had been unlisted. Now that she had it, I knew that it would just never stop."

The telephone call to the Hamptons that August was the last straw. Sick and tired of strange phone calls and bizarre letters because of her relationship with Gordon, she told him she wanted to break up. They agreed not to see each other for a few months. "I didn't see him again until the fall," Charlotte said.

Whoever was writing the anonymous letters, however, apparently did not know that Charlotte Ames was no longer seeing Gordon. The letters continued in August, with many having an anti-Semitic tone. One arrived in the form of a ditty:

> He conned her. He donned her in clothes. He brought her a jewel and a rose. She cried that's a sin. He lied and he'd win. Then a new cunt felt his Jewish nose. He came from the family of wealth. She was after this Jew for his gelt. But he wouldn't commit. He chased every tit, and he cared not a shit how she felt.
>   The end of the saga. More follows.

A few days later, perhaps the most vulgar and obscene of the letters arrived at Charlotte Ames's apartment:

> We now know that with Kay he has been ruthless. Her daily calls to him are fruitless. He played her all summer. Took his piece from her. One weekend he fucked her cunt juiceless. . . .

Charlotte stopped reading and threw down the letter in disgust. She decided to go to the police. It was late August, almost a month had passed since she had turned her letters over to Bess, and still she had not heard anything.

Charlotte called Bess and asked whether her lawyer had reached any conclusions about the letters. According to Charlotte, Bess told her the lawyer was still reviewing them. Exasperated and tired of waiting, Charlotte told Bess that she wanted her letters back and planned to take them to the police. But Charlotte said that Bess again pleaded with her not to go to the police. With only a few weeks until the Democratic primary, Bess reiterated her worries that word of the letters would leak to the press and hurt her campaign. Charlotte reluctantly agreed to wait until the campaign was over.

On September 23, two weeks after Bess lost the primary to Liz Holtzman, Charlotte got another anonymous and obscene letter in the mail. She called Bess again and asked Bess to return the letters she had given her two months before. Once again, Charlotte recalled, Bess said that her lawyer friend was still investigating. This time Charlotte insisted on getting the letters back. A week later Bess finally sent a package containing the letters to Charlotte's apartment. Included in the package were a few letters that Bess claimed she had received threatening her campaign. One said:

Dear Loser,
   Read Suzy's column, Tuesday of next week. The story about your illness will appear. She will not reveal your cancer to begin with. A drop of news at a time until it spreads. You will be sorry you played around with Gordon. You took him away from Charlotte. As it always happens another woman took him away from you. More follows.

Yet another suggested that Charlotte was behind a countercampaign:

Dear Miss America,
   The story in the *New York Times* was just what you deserved. You are an empty clown and you should retire from life before you mess up everyone else by embarrassing yourself and New York by representing us. You are being asked now to return to Charlotte Ames, all the notes and gifts in your possession that you ever received from Gordon. She has a right to them and you don't. If you contact Gordon instead of Charlotte, you will be doing the wrong thing. Believe us. Charlotte knows about this request and she is expecting them. Gordon has told her about the gifts he has given you. You are to return them as soon as possible. You are to drop them off at her house. . . . A marriage is pending. Mrs. Marcus is going to give Gordon the divorce he has been waiting for. She knows that Charlotte took him away from her. She is afraid not to follow Gordon's demand because he will cut her off. He will cut her off anyway because that is what he plans. He will have as little to do with their children because he wants to give Charlotte's daughter all of his attention and really take her own father's place.
   You will try to see him again. It is when you try to see him again she

will know about it. If he tries to stick his Jewish nose in your cunt make
sure it is wiped off. He will probably be coming from another woman. He
will always be coming from another woman. How does he rate you on
blow jobs? He has some expert blowers and you rate pretty low. He has
talked about you making love and your body. What laughs he provides you
better know it. He is moving ahead with the counter campaign. It may not
appear in the newspapers, but you should know that he is helping
Holtzman's campaign through a good friend of his and hers. That is the
latest tactic. You had better believe what we are telling you. We are in
touch with a very good friend of Charlotte's they tell us all. Watch for the
announcement of their marriage in the newspaper. Keep away. He may
keep calling you as he is calling the others. We know of two others he is
seeing in addition to Charlotte. Remember there are twenty-four hours in
a day and he lives it to a hilt. He is a phony and a liar. Whatever he tells you
is a lie. He will deny what he is doing. We do not believe him. Return all
notes. That is very important. Return all gifts. That is very urgent. Keep
away from him. That is a must or you will suffer. God gives us roles to
play. Watch and do not wonder how and why. More follows.

Another letter warned Bess:

One day soon you will know why you should not be doing what you are
doing. There is no way you will win this election. Not even if you try to
buy it with your money. There is a real movement going on being led by
Charlotte Ames to stop you. She and J. Gordon Marcus will do everything in their power to see that you don't. That fuck-face son of a bitch
thinks he is God's gift to women is bad mouthing you anytime he can.
Charlotte Ames has gathered together her troops and he is going to give
her the money to start the campaign. In the end you will know who is
responsible. You will be smeared in the press. There is no way you can stop
this. There is no way she will be stopped. There is no way he will be
stopped.
    That will be your end for moving in on her. If J does not see you it will
be because he feels guilty about what they are doing and he doesn't want
you to suspect them. You will not be able to stop this not even if you agree
never to speak or stop. He is hers forever. Keep out.

Armed with the letters, Charlotte contacted a friend who was a lawyer
and asked for advice. He recommended that she hire a private investigator to look into the matter immediately.

Meanwhile, Gordon was spending most of his time with a young
woman who worked as a producer at a local television station. They had
been dating since Charlotte had ended her relationship with Gordon
that summer. In October the producer began getting hang-up telephone
calls at her apartment. Then, on Friday, October 31, a woman identify-
ing herself as "Andrea" called her office and asked to speak with her.

The producer's secretary told the caller that she was in Boston and was not expected back until that night.

The same day, an anonymous message was left for Gordon at the Carlyle informing him that the producer's flight from Boston would be an hour late. But Gordon was not picking her up from the airport that night. He was on his way to Boston to join her there for the weekend.

When Gordon returned home to the Carlyle on Monday, a Bergdorf Goodman shopping bag was hanging on his outside doorknob. Under layers of tissue paper was what police later determined to be human excrement. Gordon immediately suspected Bess had sent him the package out of anger that he was seeing the producer. He had had enough.

He first talked with Charlotte, who he knew had hired a private investigator. When Gordon called the investigator and told him about the package left outside his door, the investigator said it was a matter for the police.

On Tuesday, November 4, the day after he returned from Boston, Gordon called Bess and told her that he was going to the police. Bess told him there was no need to contact the police because they were already investigating the letters she had received during the campaign that said he had tried to undermine her campaign and ruin her.

In fact Bess had not gone to the police at that point. The next day she called New York police commissioner Robert McGuire directly at One Police Plaza and told him that she was receiving annoying telephone calls and bizarre letters from a former lover, J. Gordon Marcus. She asked him to have a detective look into it.

McGuire turned the case over to the department's Intelligence Division, and Detective Gloria O'Meara was assigned the case. Over the next few days O'Meara interviewed Bess, Charlotte, the television producer, and Gordon, who had not yet contacted the police. From interviewing Gordon, O'Meara learned that at least seven other women had received anonymous letters similar to those sent to Charlotte during the last nine months. All but one of the women had one thing in common; with the exception of Charlotte's mother, all had dated Gordon within the last two years.

Charlotte recounted for O'Meara the history of the harassment dating back to the hang-up phone calls that had begun in late 1978 and the strange taped messages from the man who had been able to recount her movements and Gordon's. Charlotte also turned over the twenty-six anonymous letters she had received between March and September 23, 1980.

Even though the police were now involved, the television producer continued to be harassed by hang-up telephone calls. About a week after O'Meara began her investigation the woman who had identified herself as "Andrea" called the producer's office again. Pretending to be her own secretary, the producer tried to engage "Andrea" in conversation to find out more about her. But "Andrea" would say only that she was a friend and needed to speak to her directly. When the producer said that she was speaking with her directly, the caller promptly hung up.

That night the producer called Gordon and told him about the call. Gordon said he suspected "Andrea" might actually be Bess. To test his suspicions he took a tape of Bess's voice over to her apartment. After listening to the tape, she concluded "Andrea" and Bess were the same person. Gordon called O'Meara with the information.

On Friday, November 14, Bess called Detective Gloria O'Meara twice about the case. She wanted to know what Gordon Marcus had told her about his love affairs. O'Meara told Bess that it was a confidential police matter and she could not discuss it. Bess countered by saying that it was her understanding from the police commissioner that she would be kept apprised of the results of the investigation. But O'Meara held firm and refused to discuss her investigation with Bess.

A few days later Gordon got a mysterious call from a man who identified himself as "Tony" and said that he was the television producer's ex-lover. "Tony" warned Gordon to stay away from her. "Tony" said that "Andrea" was his secretary and that he was the one who had left the misleading message at the Carlyle about the producer's flight from Boston being late. Gordon suggested a meeting, and he arranged to meet "Tony" that weekend at the Museum Cafe, a restaurant on Columbus Avenue. Gordon alerted O'Meara, who arranged for detectives to stake out the restaurant. But "Tony" never appeared.

By November 19 the police had installed a special device on the producer's telephone that allowed them to trace the anonymous calls she had been getting. Over the next three days there were three such calls. All were traced to Bess's apartment.

At the end of November O'Meara submitted a confidential report of her findings and conclusions to her superiors, and the report was forwarded to the police commissioner. O'Meara's report concluded that Bess was behind the harassment campaign and had filed the complaint as a diversionary tactic. According to Detective O'Meara's report, Bess was responsible for about fifty anonymous letters and telephone calls to Charlotte, Gordon, and his other female friends. The report also concluded that Bess had written the threatening letters to herself. No conclusion was reached, however, about who may have left the excrement for Gordon outside his hotel apartment door.

Years later Bess refused to discuss her relationship with Gordon, saying only that he was "a juggler." She also refused to talk about the police allegations against her. "I don't even want to talk about it," she said. "It is obscene because no one has really bothered to tell the truth. . . . I got too involved in his life, with his children and their problems. I tend to do that. And then there is a need for denial, accusations, and counterclaims. All the things they mention and accuse me of were not true."

When Charlotte and Gordon asked the police about prosecuting the case, Charlotte, who married Gordon in 1983, said they were told there was not enough evidence. "I was told it was a misdemeanor and that there wasn't enough evidence to convict anyone of any crime," Charlotte said.

That November the police commissioner took O'Meara's findings directly to Mayor Koch and briefed him on the investigation. McGuire recalled telling Koch that Bess might be "acting out" because of her devastating loss at the polls. McGuire also said later that a high-ranking official in the department told him he would warn Bess to stop the harassment. The matter went no further.

Koch acknowledges that McGuire told him about the telephone calls, but he does not recall McGuire's mentioning the letters or the package left outside of J. Gordon Marcus's hotel door. Koch said he did not ask to see a copy of O'Meara's report and never asked the police for elaboration. As he later recalled, he dismissed the situation "as a matter involving jilted lovers" and said that he considered it an "aberration."

Koch knew that Bess had been going through a difficult time since losing the Democratic primary. She had asked him to appoint her the city's deputy mayor for economic development, even offering to do the job for one dollar a year, but he had refused her request even though he had told cheering crowds during the 1977 mayoral campaign that she would be a great choice for precisely that position. "I said no. I did not think she was qualified for that," Koch later said.

The fall of 1980 was one of the worst times in Bess's life. She had been rejected at the polls. She had been discarded by J. Gordon Marcus. She had spent almost $800,000 of her own money on a losing campaign. And her old friend, Ed Koch, had declined her post-campaign request to join his administration. If all that wasn't bad enough, Bess's ninety-year-old father, Louis, had died that fall, not long after she had lost the primary. She had always been much closer to him than to her mother, and his death caused her tremendous pain. "It was a very low time, a very low time," she said later. "Then he passed away after the primary. It was a very hard time for me. I was really depressed."

During this intensely painful period in Bess's life Andy Capasso could not have been more kind and generous. What had started as a "telephone relationship" during her campaign had evolved into an affair in the fall of 1980. Bess desperately needed someone to help her get on with her life.

"When she lost that campaign, she felt deserted and abandoned by everyone," said a close friend of Bess's at the time. "Normally when you lose a campaign you have a fund-raiser to pay off your debt. Nobody ever got one together for her. When she lost, Jewish café society moved away from her. She kind of lost her cachet. Then he pursued her. He really pursued her."

Andy Capasso was unlike any other man she had been involved with, but she was attracted to him. "He is a stand-up guy," said another friend. "He is street-smart. I think that is one of the things that she liked about him. He's real smart."

Andy treated Bessie—as he called her—like a queen. He put his chauffeur at her disposal, allowed her to use company office space and staff to tend to the final details of closing down her Senate campaign, and called on his contractor friends to kick in some more money to help Bess erase her big campaign debt.

"After the election was over, everybody in my campaign ran to the other candidate," Bess told writer Patricia Morrisroe. "When you lose, people don't know what to say to you, they don't call you. This man was the only person who picked up the phone."

After having been rejected by J. Gordon Marcus for a younger woman, Bess must have been happy that she now had a much younger man—twenty-one years her junior—to tell her repeatedly that she was beautiful and sexy.

There was something else, too, that pulled Bess toward Andy. He reminded her of her father. She didn't realize it until she accompanied Andy to one of his construction sites one afternoon. As she watched him crouch on his hands and knees and touch one of his sewer pipes and explain with pride how he did the best work in the city, she thought of her father. "I watched him, and my memory came back to my father, who used to take me on the job," she said. "He would say, 'Just feel that wall. It feels like glass. You don't see a piece of the brush. You don't see a bump.' The way that he touched it. It is comparable to someone holding a palette and a paintbrush or somebody holding their own canvas or an instrument. That is the way Andy felt about his work."

By December Bess had moved all of her files from her closed campaign headquarters over to the offices of Nanco, Andy's company, in the Long Island City section of Queens. She spent several days a week there that fall as she worked to close down her campaign. At first she sat at a desk in the engineering department; later she took over the conference room next to his office. None of the other employees were allowed into that room while Bess and her belongings were there.

Andy and Bess would often talk during the day and work out together in the company gym. So that he could spend evenings with Bess, Andy would tell his wife he had to attend late-night meetings with union officials, engineers, or mobster Matthew "Matty the Horse" Ianniello.

At Christmas, however, Andy went to Palm Beach with his wife and family to spend a week in his condominium there. Bess remained in New York and continued working at his office.

On Tuesday, December 30, 1980, Bess was standing at the office's copy machine when suddenly she felt very warm. She dropped a pile of papers she was carrying. "Sweat came pouring down my face like a waterfall," Bess said a few months later. "I was scared stiff." She was reaching for a chair to sit down when she collapsed.

"She was completely disoriented and perspiring," recalled an office worker at Nanco. "We sat her down in the engineering department, and there was mass confusion."

Andy was still in Palm Beach. As one of the engineers went through Bess's wallet looking for the name and telephone number of her daughter or a doctor, Andy's secretary dialed his number at his Florida condominium. He told her to call the Astoria Volunteer Ambulance squad immediately and tell them to rush Bess to Lenox Hill Hospital. He instructed her not to give Bess's real name to the ambulance squad.

Nancy Capasso later remembered that her husband was very upset that day: "There were these frantic calls back and forth, but I didn't know what it was all about. He was hiding it. You can imagine the tension he was under. So he was screaming all the time, but I didn't know why. He was taking it all out on me, and I didn't even know what was happening."

Bess was taken to the emergency room and admitted to Lenox Hill Hospital's intensive care unit at 8:00 P.M. She had suffered a stroke.

21
Andy and Nancy

In the days following Bess's mild stroke, the press offered varying reasons for her hospitalization. On January 1, two days after Bess entered the hospital, the *New York Post* reported she was hospitalized following an attack of hypoglycemia. The following day, January 2, the *New York Times*, quoting a close friend, said that she had sustained a back injury when she fell from a ladder while redecorating her apartment. A hospital spokesman told the *Times*, "I've received a press release from her press agent saying she has a slipped disc. That's our version then."

Bess was fortunate in that the burst blood vessel damaged only a tiny bit of brain tissue. Although she had difficulty speaking immediately following the stroke, she did not lose any feeling in her arms and legs. She remained in the hospital for almost three weeks until she recovered completely.

As soon as Andy returned home from Palm Beach, he hurried over to Lenox Hill Hospital to see her. He visited almost every day. It was at the hospital where some of Bess's friends met Andy for the first time. "She would call him Mr. Capasso," said a former friend who was introduced to Andy in Bess's hospital room. "I thought she had exercised bad judgment with men in the past, but I thought this guy was the pits."

To some of Bess's friends Andy spelled trouble. He was married, with two young children, and after her disastrous relationship with J. Gordon Marcus, they worried about Bess getting deeply involved with another unavailable man. One of her friends told Herb Rickman, special assistant to the mayor, who was close to Bess at the time, that she thought Andy was "sleazy" and urged Rickman to use whatever influence he had with Bess to get Andy away from her.

In Bess's circles there seemed to be no room for a multimillionaire sewer contractor who lacked a college education. No matter how much money he had.

Carl Andy Capasso was born in New York City on September 10,

1945, two days after Bess was crowned Miss America in Atlantic City. His parents, Michael and Josephine Capasso, named their only son after his paternal grandfather, who had started a sewer and construction business in Brooklyn.

Andy's father had also gone into the business, but with mixed success. Andy still remembers the electric company turning off the lights because his father was unable to pay the bill. The constant flux in his father's fortunes created tension in his parents' marriage, and Andy usually found himself taking his mother's side during heated arguments. Years later Andy vowed never to reprise his father's financial mistakes.

As a young boy growing up in Brooklyn, he was instilled with the work ethic, spending his Saturday mornings shining shoes in a local barbershop. By the time he reached high school, his father had moved the family into a new house in Old Westbury, an affluent suburb on Long Island. Andy attended the local high school, Wheatley High. A classmate, Allyn Kandel, recalled that he was a gregarious teenager with lots of friends. "He was extremely bright, possessing a certain intelligence and maturity that went beyond his years," she said.

By Andy's senior year in high school his father was so deeply in debt that he lost the house to the mortgage company, forcing the family to move into a rented house in nearby Roslyn. When Andy graduated in 1963, he immediately went to work for his father's company, called M.C. & Son, arriving on the job at 6:00 most mornings. At night he worked with his father on the books and on drawing up bids for other jobs. They were lean years for the family business, recalled childhood friend Richard Haas, now an airplane pilot, who worked alongside Andy in the company. "Typically we would work six or seven days a week if the work was available. . . . To say Andy learned the construction business from the bottom up is an understatement."

Two years after Andy graduated from high school, he started work on a sewer project for a developer in the Jamaica Estates section of Queens. The developer had knocked down an old mansion to build four big homes on the property at Somerset Street and Grand Central Parkway. They blended nicely into the old, established neighborhood of expensive Tudor and brick homes.

On the job that spring of 1965, Andy, then nineteen, met Nancy Roth Herbert, a pretty twenty-six-year-old housewife. She had moved into one of the big new houses the year before with her husband and three small children. Andy introduced himself one morning when he asked if she would mind moving a car parked in front of her house because it was blocking his backhoe.

Nancy still remembers how handsome Andy looked that day as he stood in her doorway in his dusty work clothes. He was just slightly taller than she, but he had a powerfully built body and jet-black curly hair, long dark eyelashes, and a disarming smile. She followed him outside with the car keys, and they chatted a little. "There was instant chemistry," she later said.

At 5'9" tall, Nancy was a striking beauty with green eyes and long chestnut-brown hair that fell to her waist. She had a great sense of style, and she must have struck Andy at the time as being very rich and sophisticated. Jamaica Estates was one of the wealthiest sections of the city, home to doctors, lawyers, and corporate executives.

Nancy grew up as an only child in nearby Hollis Hills, a middle-class Jewish neighborhood. Her father ran a company that manufactured notions for chain stores. A graduate of Skidmore College, she received a degree in nursing, but she worked only briefly as a nurse. Soon after her graduation she married Howard Herbert, the handsome son of a successful clothing manufacturer, whom she had dated steadily while in college. Both sets of parents approved the match. A graduate of Exeter and Dartmouth, her husband had been the president of his college fraternity. Marrying him seemed quite a sensible thing to do at the time. "He was every girl's dream," Nancy said.

Within five years they had three children: two girls and a boy. She thought she should be happy, living in her brand-new home with her husband and her babies, but she was miserable. Her husband worked long hours for his parents' company and frequently traveled, selling coats and suits all over the country. He sometimes stayed away from home for months at a time.

Bored and lonely, at age twenty-six Nancy was tired of shopping, vacuuming, and attending PTA meetings and lunches with "the girls" in the neighborhood. One of "the girls" at the time was Marlene Manes, whose husband, Donald, was spending long hours away from home, too, building his political career, which eventually led him to Queens Borough Hall, where as borough president and head of the Queens Democratic party he became one of the most powerful political figures in New York.

As spring turned into summer in 1965, Nancy found herself talking almost every day with Andy Capasso, the young ditchdigger working outside her house. By the middle of the summer it was obvious to both of them that there was a strong physical attraction, she said. They would "eyeball" each other as they stood together on the sidewalk. Finally, one morning, he asked her, "So when are you going to invite me in for a cup of coffee?"

At first a little nervous about having a strange man in her house, Nancy asked a neighbor to join them. Seated around her kitchen table, sipping coffee, they joked and laughed for almost an hour. "He was very likable," said Nancy. "He was funny, charming, and very bright. There was lots of chemistry."

They began having an affair almost immediately, secretly meeting at his tiny apartment in the Forest Hills Inn. From the beginning, she said, Andy begged her to leave her husband for him. Finally, about a year and a half later, Nancy asked her husband for a legal separation. Howard Herbert moved out of the house.

Nancy's closest friends were stunned when she broke the news. "He was a kid, and all of us had graduate degrees," said Judith Yeager, Nancy's next-door neighbor and good friend, referring to the circle of friends she shared with Nancy. "He was very different from what we were used to. He was definitely blue-collar. That was just not our world. It just wasn't done. You are dealing with a social group of doctors, lawyers, and accountants, and here is Andy, the ditchdigger. He just didn't fit in."

Nancy's mother couldn't believe that her daughter was leaving her Ivy League husband for a laborer, either. What did Andy Capasso have to offer? "Her mother used to call me and beg me to talk her out of it," Yeager said.

Nancy didn't care what her parents or anyone else thought. She moved ahead with a divorce. While Andy may not have been as sophisticated or as well educated as Howard Herbert, Nancy could not deny her passionate feelings for him.

And Andy apparently felt the same about her. "He was madly in love," Yeager said. "I thought he was in awe of her. He was entering, what looked to me, like a new world to him, into the world of the Jewish American princess. . . . He was a charming, bashful young man overwhelmed by Nancy and her world."

Nancy saw in Andy a determination and ambition that persuaded her that he would make something of himself. She encouraged him to leave his father's company and start his own business. At the end of 1967, at age twenty-two, Andy left his father's business and went to work for another construction company as a bulldozer operator. His plan was to put some money aside and eventually start his own construction company. Within months he had turned his apartment at the Forest Hills Inn into an office. He leased construction equipment and managed to convince a few builders to hire him as a subcontractor.

Andy called his new company Nanco Contracting Corporation, which, according to Nancy, was named for her. "He painted NANCY on the nose of his equipment," Yeager said. "She wasn't even embarrassed." During their bitter divorce years later, however, Andy insisted that he had named the company after himself. He claimed the *N* in Nanco stood for Naples, the place of his family's origins, the *an* was for Andy, and the *co* represented the first and last letters of his surname.

In the early years of the business Andy worked between fourteen and eighteen hours a day. Nancy insists that she helped him get started by keeping the books, signing checks, doing the payroll, and dropping off bids at municipal offices. By early 1970 Andy's company was finally able to obtain bonds and bid on big city contracts. In March of that year Andy was awarded his first job with the city's Department of Environmental Protection, a $26,835 contract to build storm and sanitary sewers on Union Turnpike in Queens. He quickly built a reputation in the city for doing good work and getting it done on time.

By late 1970, five years after Nancy and Andy first met, she was finally free to marry him. Her bitter divorce from Howard Herbert was about to become final, so she was deeply distressed when she learned Andy had been seeing another woman, a pretty stewardess who lived in Louisville, Kentucky.

Finally Nancy gave Andy an ultimatum: dump the stewardess or she would never see him again. Andy agreed to break off his relationship with the stewardess and marry Nancy. In December 1970 they bought a small colonial house together for $51,000 in Greenvale, just outside of New York City in Nassau County on Long Island. They planned to marry the following spring, as soon as her divorce was final.

On March 28, 1971, they were married in a civil ceremony at Yeager's home. Nancy was thirty-two. Andy was twenty-five. Only family members and a few close friends were there. Donald Manes had provided the judge but was unable to attend the wedding. In a photograph taken outside Yeager's home that afternoon, Andy is beaming as he stands next to his new wife, with his hand on her shoulder. Nancy is smiling, too, looking like a happy bride in a cocktail-length brown and white dress, holding a small bouquet of flowers in her right hand.

During their marriage Andy could not have been a better stepfather to Nancy's three young children—Helené, who was eleven when Andy and Nancy married, nine-year-old Steven, and six-year-old Debbie. Both Nancy and her three children agree that he was a loving and caring father, treating the children as if they were his own.

"He was very good with the children," Nancy said. "And he supported the fact that we were all Jewish." Andy, baptized a Catholic, sent one of his stepdaughters to Israel so that she could learn more about her Jewish heritage. At Steven's bar mitzvah Andy took over the role of Steven's real father during the ceremony. Instead of saying the prayers in English, Andy, a former altar boy, studied Hebrew so that he could stand by his stepson's side and recite the prayers in Hebrew.

A year after Andy and Nancy were married, Nancy gave birth to their first child, a boy. A daughter was born two years later. The house in Greenvale no longer seemed big enough for their family, so they decided to move. In the early 1970s Andy's business was doing well enough for them to be able to afford a Georgian colonial mansion with a circular driveway in Old Westbury, the Long Island suburb where Andy had spent his teenage years. Surrounded by almost three acres of land, the seven-bedroom house had a swimming pool and a tennis court. Andy and Nancy had come a long way since the day she found him digging a sewer line outside her home.

Just a year after they moved to Old Westbury, though, New York City was confronted with a fiscal crisis that resulted in deep cuts in the city's budget and a sharp reduction in the number of city contracts awarded for street improvements and sewer connections. Determined not to end up like his father and lose his beautiful new home, Andy scrambled for work, taking jobs in Connecticut and New Jersey to keep his new business going. Once he got through those difficult years, the company grew rapidly in the late 1970s as New York City began to recover and resume its construction projects. He added more and more people to his payroll, including his struggling father, to save him from financial ruin.

By 1976 Andy owned his own office building for his company headquarters in the Long Island City section of Queens. He had twenty-five employees and more than $4 million in contracts. Within six years, by 1982, he had $32 million in contracts and employed more than 400 people. By 1986 Andy held ninety-seven city contracts worth $200 million for a variety of projects ranging from street paving to sewers and water pollution control.

To succeed in the construction business in New York, Andy cultivated relationships with politicians, city engineers, and powerful union officials. He even entertained people with ties to organized crime, which dominated the cement industry and other aspects of the construction business. During the mid-1970s, in Palm Beach, the Capassos played host to former Teamster boss John Cody, who controlled almost every truck that moved in the New York metropolitan area. Cody, regarded by law enforcement officials at one time as an associate of the Gambino organized crime family in New York, was later convicted on federal charges for evading taxes on kickbacks.

Several nights a week Andy would return home late, telling Nancy he had meetings with "Matty and the guys." "Matty" was Matthew "Matty the Horse" Ianniello, the Capassos' friend and neighbor. He was a captain in New York's Genovese organized crime family who was later convicted of racketeering. "There isn't a person who is using cement or in construction that doesn't have to deal with the Mafia, day in and day out," Nancy once said. "Sure, we knew them. Sure, we would have dinner with them. But what does that mean? You have to do business with these people. That doesn't mean you are one of them."

As Andy's sewer contracting business expanded during the late 1970s, Andy and Nancy began to lead a lavish lifestyle. They bought an oceanfront condominium on Dune Road in Westhampton Beach. In 1978 they bought two condominiums on Sunrise Avenue in Palm

Beach. They traveled to Europe on the *Concorde*, spent Christmas in Palm Beach, and took February school vacations in Aspen or the Caribbean. "We had a lot of fun," Nancy said. "It certainly wasn't dull. We were energetic people.... The company was really growing. We did a lot of traveling. Things seemed very good."

Andy seemed to like the idea that his wife's statuesque beauty attracted the attention of other men. He liked to "decorate" her, Nancy recalled, with the finest clothes and jewels. During a trip to Italy they attended a party where most of the other women were dressed in couturier clothes and expensive jewelry. After they left the party that night, Andy told Nancy he wanted his wife too to have nice things, and when they returned to New York he bought her an expensive Hermès handbag. He was also extremely generous with jewelry during their marriage, giving her thousands of dollars' worth of jewels, including a diamond necklace and huge ruby and diamond earrings from David Webb. "Everything was wonderful. There was enough for everything," Nancy said.

Although Andy was now earning millions of dollars, the Capassos were not members of New York's wealthy social set. There were no invitations to attend glittering charity balls in Manhattan or fancy Park Avenue dinner parties. They were living in what *Vanity Fair* writer Marie Brenner called a "social Sahara."

Other than Andy's "business associates," they socialized most often with their family and Nancy's old friends and former neighbors in Queens, including Marlene and Donald Manes, who was now Queens borough president and Democratic party leader. "We weren't in any kind of social circles," Nancy said. "It was just our plain old friends. I think that's what he didn't like. I wasn't into social climbing. It wasn't my thing. I didn't think about it."

But, she said, Andy would talk about it all the time. "I think he was a real poor boy from Brooklyn from way back, even though he did live in Old Westbury at one time. He just wanted all of these things. First he wanted things. Then he wanted status."

At the end of 1979 Andy suggested they move into Manhattan. Nancy believes that a palatial Manhattan apartment symbolized wealth and privilege to him. It was as if a move to Manhattan would bestow on Andy the social respectability that he so badly wanted and an entrée into the fast-paced, jet-set social world that had eluded him.

Nancy agreed to leave Old Westbury, thinking she might see more of her husband if he did not have to commute. Like Nancy's first husband, Andy spent much of his time away from home—on business, he would tell her—and Nancy was growing increasingly frustrated spending her evenings alone. They started to argue about his long hours at work and his late-night meetings with "the guys." "Things were bad before Bess,"

Steven Herbert Capasso, Nancy's son from her first marriage, later told columnist Cindy Adams. "There was always fire and tumult in our house."

But Nancy remembered passionate reconciliations following their explosive arguments. Although there were difficult times, overall she thought her marriage was good. "It had its ups and downs. But it was okay. I thought it was fine, and I think he did, too. I just wanted to see him more."

After looking at dozens of apartments on Manhattan's exclusive Upper East Side, Nancy and Andy found what they were looking for at 990 Fifth Avenue in a prestigious prewar building with only six apartments, across the street from the Metropolitan Museum of Art. It was a thirteen-room duplex apartment with eleven-foot ceilings and panoramic views of Central Park. There were five bedrooms, four bathrooms, and wood-burning fireplaces in the living room, dining room, and master bedroom. On April 14, 1980, they bought it for $764,897 in cash. The monthly maintenance fee was $5,914.07.

Hoping to create a showplace, the Capassos paid architect Robert A. M. Stern another $1.5 million to design extensive renovations that would take almost a year to complete. With its combination of modern and classical architectural elements, the apartment was later featured on the cover of *Architectural Digest* magazine. No expense was spared. Each room was equipped with its own built-in stereo system. Stern imported marble from Italy for the bathrooms and for the spectacular marble staircase with curvilinear brass handrailings leading up to the second floor. In the living room, using floor-to-ceiling windows framed by heavy pilasters, he gave the room what the magazine described as the "light and space of an Italian piazza."

Overseeing the renovations and furnishing of the apartment kept Nancy Capasso busy during the fall of 1980 and much of 1981. She would spend almost $1 million on antiques and paintings. Working closely with Stern, she chose large, comfortable chesterfield sofas covered in Rose Cummings chintz for the living room. For the dining room she spent $200,000 on an early Victorian mahogany table on scroll-carved lion's-paw feet and a set of six George II carved mahogany chairs. To the master bedroom she added an antique camelback mahogany loveseat covered in striped satin and a Chippendale walnut writing desk. She also purchased several paintings, including an untitled Cy Twombly for $192,500 and a Jean Dubuffet for $75,000.

During this time Andy seemed preoccupied and did not take as much interest as Nancy had anticipated in choosing the expensive furnishings and paintings for their new apartment. And although they were now living in Manhattan, only minutes from his company headquarters in Queens, Nancy saw even less of him in the evenings: "He was always disappearing. He was never around. He said he was meeting Matty all the time. He'd go out in the evenings, and he wouldn't come home till three or four in the morning. It was awful. When he came home, he was horrible. He was cold and emotionally removed. I didn't know what it was. I was totally cut off. I was a mess, and I didn't know why."

Here she was, living in a fabulous Fifth Avenue apartment, able to buy virtually anything she wanted. She had two full-time maids. The family had a fleet of seven cars at its disposal, including a 1979 Mercedes with Nancy's name in brass affixed to the dashboard. She also had her own limousine and driver to take her and the children to appointments around town and out to the Hamptons, shopping on Madison Avenue, and once a week to Balducci's, a gourmet grocery store in Greenwich Village. She had unlimited credit at Saks Fifth Avenue, Bloomingdale's, Martha's, Henri Bendel, and Bergdorf Goodman, where she spent $25,000 that winter on a sable jacket. "I had everything I wanted— materially, that is," said Nancy. "He would give me anything I wanted, just to keep me quiet. If I wanted a pretty dress, I got a pretty dress. There was no question of money."

Why then, she wondered, did she feel so sad? Why did she one day find herself sobbing uncontrollably as she sat in the back of her limousine, wearing a $5,000 dress from Martha's? "I sensed something was wrong with us, but I couldn't put my finger on it. I was going crazy."

One night she met her old friend, Judith Yeager, for drinks at the Stanhope Hotel on Fifth Avenue, just a few blocks from her apartment. "She started telling me that she didn't know what was happening to her life," Yeager recalled. "Andy was never home. They had bought this gorgeous apartment, and she couldn't even have company because she never knew whether he would show up. She never knew where he was and thought that he was hanging out with the guys at night doing deals. At that point she didn't think there was another woman."

And Nancy did not suspect anything that weekday afternoon in January 1981 when she spotted Andy's limousine and driver parked outside of Lenox Hill Hospital.

"What are you doing here?" she asked one of her husband's drivers, James White.

He said, "I don't know. You better ask him."

Just then Andy walked out of the hospital toward the waiting car.

"Who were you visiting?" she asked.

"A sick friend" is all she remembers he replied.

At the time, Nancy said, she didn't think much of his vague response. She assumed his "sick friend" was one of his numerous business associates. She never would have guessed that he was visiting Bess Myerson, much less having an affair with her.

22
The Other Woman

Two weeks after Bess was released from Lenox Hill Hospital, Mayor Koch invited her to Gracie Mansion to celebrate her recovery. For whatever reason, Bess continued to lie to the press about her hospitalization. "I had a bad fall," she told a *New York Daily News* reporter that night. "I fell off a painter's ladder, my late father's ladder, in fact, and hit my head on a table. I had a concussion and injured my back. It was all a lot worse than people thought."

She apparently did not want anyone to know that she had suffered a stroke or that she was rushed to the hospital, not from her apartment, but from her married lover's company headquarters in Queens.

According to a former friend who knew about the relationship at the time, Bess seemed to become even more dependent on Andy's attention and generosity during the months following her stroke. With the stroke coming on top of her deep depression, she was very vulnerable. Andy was ready to meet her every need.

Now that Andy was living in Manhattan and no longer had to commute, he could get together with Bess more easily. His new Fifth Avenue apartment was only ten blocks from her apartment building. He saw her several nights a week and sometimes early in the morning before he went to work, according to his driver, who remembered picking him up outside his home around 5:00 A.M. and dropping him off at Bess's apartment.

"I think he was in total awe of her," said a former close friend of Bess's. "He told her that he had been in love with her for years and that she was his ideal."

Andy was not always Bess's ideal. Bess once said to a friend who had known her for years, "You think I don't want to go out with someone who is my age, successful, and Jewish?" And to other friends, Bess would complain about Andy's drinking and his "table manners." Bess's disparaging comments about Andy disturbed a former friend whose home Bess and Andy visited frequently during their secret affair. "He seemed like such a nice man, but he couldn't do anything to please her. She would talk on the phone to him for hours and berate him. My mother was visiting once, and Bess was at my house, talking to him on the phone. My mother said to me, 'Why does he put up with such things?' It was unbelievable."

While Andy appeared to Bess's friends to be very much in love with Bess at the time, he may also have been trading up, replacing his princess with a queen.

"Money. Power. Social status," said Judith Yeager, Nancy's longtime friend. "Andy is always climbing a ladder, and he made his first step with Nancy, and then he saw national fame and political power, and that's Bess.

"Here is a guy approaching his forties who is a very appealing person. He is a helluva lot of fun, and he has the same charm that he has had since he was nineteen years old. And he is looking to run around. What would you have expected him to do? Well, all of us would have expected him to find a showgirl, some young actress, someone twenty years younger than he. Who does he pick? He picks a woman who is twenty years older than he, who may look good for a sixty-year-old—but why?"

Another former friend of Andy's also saw his relationship with Bess as part of his continuing quest for social respectability and political power. Nancy agreed. She believed Andy might have been seeking the one thing that had eluded him despite all of his hard work, determination, and millions of dollars: entrée into Manhattan's powerful and political social circles. "Bess gave him all of that," Nancy said. "I guess, with her, that's where he could get into a new circle."

In return, "Mr. Capasso" gave Bess almost anything she wanted. To some of Bess's friends the key to the relationship seemed to be money. Although Bess was worth millions, she constantly complained to Andy that she did not have any money because of her staggering campaign debt and medical bills.

Andy paid for virtually all of her expenses, from her dry cleaning to her groceries. He gave her credit cards and use of his limousine. His driver picked Bess up regularly and drove her to Rhode Island, Connecticut, and southern New Jersey, where she delivered speeches to women's groups and Jewish organizations, usually for a $5,000 fee. Andy also later gave Bess a fur coat and expensive jewelry. He once said to his other chauffeur, Tony Bailey, "The best is for Bess because she is 'Queen of the Jews.'"

Within months after getting out of the hospital, Bess started work on a diet book with literary agent and writer Bill Adler, based on diets developed by the New York City Department of Health's Bureau of Nutrition. It was her second book. She had published a guide for consumers in 1979 that did not sell as well as she had hoped. But the diet book became an overnight success with its catchy title, *I Love New York Diet*, and its promise that dieters could lose ten pounds in seven days. The book was panned, though, by Jane Brody in the *New York Times*. In her "Personal Health" column she quoted experts who complained Bess "took the whole diet out of context" and "makes promises the average person can't possibly hope for."

In 1981 Bess also started work with her good friend and psychiatrist, Dr. Ted Rubin, on a cable television show called "Please Make Me Happy." Bess and Rubin were cohosts of the show in which guests were invited to discuss their problems. "It was a curiosity. In a strange way, she needed that therapy herself. She needed to be made happy," said a woman who worked on the show, which aired only a few times before it was canceled.

After "Please Make Me Happy" went off the air, Bess found another television opportunity, this time as a consumer reporter. It made perfect sense for Bess to combine her two most successful careers: television and consumerism. That November of 1981, almost a year after she had suffered her stroke, Bess signed a six-figure contract with WCBS, the CBS network affiliate in New York, to report consumer news. She started working the following February when the station started its "News at Five" show, appearing on the air three or four times a week with consumer-oriented reports.

Television news producer Mort Fleischner was lured away from WABC to work with Bess at WCBS. "She was the selling point," said Fleischner, who grew up in New York and had always admired Bess. "At that point in her life she was still Queen Bess. She was perceived to be the most powerful woman in the city. When she walked into City Hall, the waters would part. Television crews don't ordinarily get that kind of reception."

Fleischner remembered, "Being her producer was wonderful in the terms she made my life very easy." She was a natural with the camera, and she made up for her lack of experience in daily news reporting with her expertise on consumer issues and by calling on her powerful and influential friends for stories. She carried a fat address book filled with names and telephone numbers. "She was capable of calling up anyone at anytime and getting them on the telephone," added Fleischner. "Her phone book was enormous, and from the standpoint of CBS that made her invaluable."

Fleischner recalled the day they were doing a story on IRAs. As they approached their deadline for getting the story on the air, they did not have a bank official willing to go on camera. "We were stuck, so Bess picks up the phone and says, 'Walter, I need your help.'" By airtime they had Walter Wriston, then the chairman of Citicorp and one of New

York's most powerful corporate executives, on camera to answer all of her questions about IRAs.

Fleischner said that overall he found Bess professional and easy to work with. Despite her stardom at the station, he described her as a "hard worker" who "took direction well."

"She is the type of woman who is capable of being tough. No bullshit. At times she came down very hard on me. She was at the same time capable of being a Jewish mother."

Reporting a consumer story out on the street must have reminded Bess of her days as consumer affairs commissioner. While visiting a video arcade for one story, Bess noticed violations of city regulations. She walked outside, found the nearest pay phone, and reported the arcade to the city's commissioner of consumer affairs. City inspectors were immediately dispatched to the arcade, and summonses were issued.

In late 1981, almost a year after her husband had become deeply involved with Bess, Nancy Capasso still did not know that her husband was having an affair. But tired of his never spending any time at home, she decided to take a full-time job as a realtor for Sotheby's International Realty, one of Manhattan's most prestigious real estate firms. Through her new job, she had heard about a waterfront estate in Westhampton Beach on the market for almost $1 million. It was a huge, wood-shingled, five-bedroom house built in 1920, with a swimming pool and a small cottage on the property. Ever since she had moved from Old Westbury into Manhattan, Nancy had missed not having a house. "I thought maybe that was the problem. I thought I needed a house." Andy seemed enthusiastic about the idea, she said. He later said he saw investment potential in the property, which was located on almost two acres of land, overlooking Quantuck Bay.

Any hopes that Nancy had about the new house bringing them closer together were dashed just before the closing. "He said, 'You don't have to be at the closing.' I said to myself, something is fishy here, because he had never said anything like that before when we purchased something."

Her name did not appear on the deed. "He wouldn't put anything in my name," she said.

Nancy decided it was time to consult a lawyer, who assured her that in the event of a divorce the Westhampton Beach house would be considered marital property whether or not she had her name on the deed.

Then the lawyer asked her what she wanted to do. Proceed with a divorce?

"No," Nancy told him. She decided to wait.

All during their courtship Andy and Bess had been discreet about appearing together in public. One night in early 1982, however, Andy made the mistake of taking Bess to a popular Chinese restaurant, Fortune Garden, where he had often taken his wife.

Nancy happened to be having dinner with a friend in the restaurant's front room when Andy walked in alone and headed toward the back room. She caught a glimpse of him out of the corner of her eye just as she was preparing to leave. After paying the check and putting on her fur coat, she walked to the rear of the restaurant to see whom he was with. He had told her earlier that evening that he had a "business meeting." As she walked into the restaurant's back room, she could hear her heart pound under her coat. What if he was with another woman? What would she do? What would he say?

She spotted him at their favorite table, partially hidden behind a column, having dinner with Bess Myerson. "I was stunned. He said he had just got there, and they were having a business meeting."

Bess looked up at her and smiled sweetly. "Oh," Nancy remembered Bess said to her. "Andy tells me you're so successful as a real estate broker. Maybe I should be a broker, too."

Nancy left the restaurant completely confused. If Andy were having an affair, she told herself, it would not be with a woman "old enough to be his mother." She didn't see Bess Myerson as heavy competition.

When Andy returned home late that night, she asked him about his relationship with Bess Myerson. He told her they were "just friends."

She didn't think much more about it until a few months later, when she and Andy were invited to the wedding of Bess's daughter, Barra. She couldn't understand how they had come to be invited. How close were Bess and Andy, anyway?

Barra, then working as a screenwriter, was marrying Brian Reilly, who was also a writer. Bess was not thrilled that her daughter was marrying a Roman Catholic, and before the wedding she told Brian that she had made sure he would not see a penny of her money. The wedding was held at the Harkness House in Manhattan, which Bess arranged at a reduced rate. (When she was preparing her federal income taxes the following year, she returned to the Harkness House and asked the rabbi to write her a letter saying that the fee she had paid for her daughter's wedding ceremony was a charitable contribution.)

Nancy was surprised that she and her husband were among the small group of guests. She thought it was strange, too, that Andy seemed to know so many of Bess's friends. "How could this be?" Nancy recalled saying to herself. "I don't know these people. It didn't add up, but I wasn't making it add up. Everybody knew but me."

At the reception Bess whispered to some of her friends, "Be nice to Nancy." Some of Bess's friends were appalled that she had invited Nancy to the wedding, particularly when so many people were aware of Bess and Andy's affair. One friend of Bess's was so disgusted that he walked up to Nancy in the middle of the reception and said to her: "Hey, can't you see what is going on?"

Nancy gave him a puzzled look. "What are you talking about?"

He would not say more. Startled by the stranger's comments, Nancy walked over to Andy and insisted they go home.

Finally Nancy was convinced her husband was having an affair, though she still did not suspect fifty-seven-year-old Bess. When they returned home that night, they argued bitterly. She said Andy told her she was paranoid.

Despite his disavowals, Nancy became even more doubtful of his fidelity during a family vacation that spring at their Palm Beach condominium. "He used to go wandering off to the Breakers Hotel to 'important business meetings' and not let me go," she said. Only later did Nancy learn that Bess was staying at the nearby Breakers Hotel at the same time.

It was during Bess's visit to Palm Beach that she learned that her mother had died in a Bronx nursing home at the age of ninety. Bess flew back to New York and was met at the airport by Andy's driver, Tony Bailey, who took her to the funeral service. Bailey later said that he was surprised by Bess's lack of emotion over her mother's death. Instead of driving out to the cemetery for her mother's burial, Bailey said that Bess wanted to go back to the airport so she could catch a flight back to Florida. But Bailey claims he persuaded Bess to go to the cemetery and that she finally agreed. He drove the Nanco limousine carrying Bess in the funeral procession.

Nancy had hoped that she and Andy would spend more time together now that they had a house in Westhampton Beach. But she was wrong. Although Andy came out to the Hamptons on weekends during the summer of 1982, he rarely spent time with her.

Bess made elaborate arrangements to meet secretly with Andy in the Hamptons at homes owned or rented by her friends. One of Bess's friends remembered leaving the back door open on Friday nights for Andy, who usually arrived at her home about 3:00 A.M. to slip into bed with Bess. "I never knew whether he was going to be there at breakfast or not," said the hostess. But she never considered Andy a freeloader. "He would get up early and get bagels and lots of stuff to pay the rent on his end of the table."

On weekend afternoons Andy would often tell his wife he was going to play tennis with a friend and then drive over to see Bess at her friend's house. He usually parked his Mercedes in the garage just in case his wife or a friend drove past the house and wondered what he was doing there. Andy and Bess usually sat around the pool, soaking up the sun. The hostess remembered thinking at the time that there seemed to be an intense physical attraction between them. One weekday afternoon, the hostess said, she looked out the window to see Bess and Andy swimming together nude.

By that summer of 1982 Andy no longer bothered apologizing to Nancy for his absences. "He would just do whatever he wanted," Nancy said. "He offered no explanations. The whole thing was a nightmare."

Finally, as autumn approached, Nancy was enlightened. A good friend who worked with her at Sotheby's International Realty had heard about the long-running affair during a party that weekend in the Hamptons. On Monday morning the friend approached Nancy and told her, "Someone says that something is happening there. . . ."

"What? Who is she?" Nancy demanded.

"Bess Myerson," Nancy recalled her friend said.

"I was stunned for a minute and then relieved that I wasn't crazy," Nancy said.

Another friend then acknowledged that she had heard that Andy had bought Bess a midnight-blue Mercedes 380 SL. Determined to find out whether the rumor was true, Nancy took a couple of hours off from her job that afternoon and went over to the Mercedes dealership where Andy usually bought and leased his cars. Pretending to be her husband's secretary, she told the dealership that she needed a copy of the bill of sale for a midnight-blue Mercedes 380 SL purchased earlier that summer. "Tears were running down my face," Nancy recalled. "I went through this whole spiel about how I was his secretary and how I was going to get fired because I lost that bill of sale."

The dealership finally handed her the bill of sale. It said that on July 22, 1982, Nanco had paid $41,000 for the car, with a company check, and that Bess Myerson had picked it up.

Nancy was in a state of shock. The rumor was now confirmed. She returned home and waited up until the early morning hours for Andy to walk into the apartment so she could confront him with the bill of sale. Angrily denying her accusations, he insisted that he and Bess "were just friends."

Unconvinced, Nancy retained the well-known and flamboyant New York divorce lawyer Raoul Lionel Felder for advice in the event that she decided to proceed with a divorce. She also began checking out all of her husband's excuses for his late nights. One of the people she called was their former neighbor in Old Westbury, "Matty the Horse" Ianniello.

"Andy goes every evening to see you?" she asked.

"Nobody sees Matty every night," Nancy said he replied.

"Did you know about Bess?"

"I can't explain what Andy is doing with that old bag," Nancy said Ianniello told her.

Not long afterward, Nancy learned that Andy's relationship with Bess was not the first extramarital affair he had had during their marriage. Maybe Bess was just a fling, she thought. Then she listened to a cassette tape that a maid who worked at the Capassos' Westhampton Beach estate had turned over to her. Andy had apparently installed recording devices on the telephones in Westhampton Beach, Nancy believed, to find out how much she knew and if she were consulting a divorce lawyer. Inadvertently he had taped himself one Friday night when he left a touching message for Bess on her answering machine in New York:

"Hi, baby. How are you? It's ten after seven. I'm sorry, I didn't have any opportunity to call you sooner. I just tried the office and there was no one there and, uh, I'm home, here in Westhampton, and I expect to be here. I will be here tonight and, uh, I'll try you a little later. I love you. I miss you. And I'll try you until I get you. I'm sorry I couldn't call you before, baby, but I just didn't have the opportunity. Think of me. I miss you. Hope everything is okay with you. I've been thinking about you, your situation, the problem, and everything that goes with it, and I'm concerned about it, baby. I hope everything is okay for you, for me, and for us, and I'll speak to you later, dear."

He made kissing noises into the phone before hanging up.

Nancy was devastated. She told Felder to go ahead and tell her husband that she wanted to start negotiations for a divorce. On October 20, 1982, Felder wrote Andy a letter saying that he was representing Nancy. Andy hired his own lawyer, Sam Fredman, and letters flew back and forth between the attorneys. Millions of dollars were at stake: the Fifth Avenue apartment, the Westhampton Beach waterfront estate, the Palm Beach condominiums, and his company, Nanco Contracting Corp., which Nancy would later claim in court she helped build.

As the lawyers attempted to work out a settlement, Nancy and Andy continued to live together in the apartment with their two children and Nancy's twenty-two-year-old daughter, Helené. They argued constantly. Andy later said Nancy told him during this time to be careful about what he ate because she had put cyanide in his food. Another time, he said, Nancy told him: "You just worry about making money, I'll spend it. I know what to do about it. There isn't a diamond big enough to pay me for the way I have suffered in my life with you."

Nancy confided in her old friend, Judith Yeager, about her marital troubles and asked her to come to the Manhattan apartment one night for dinner. Yeager arrived at about 7:00 P.M. on Friday, November 5, 1982. She didn't expect Andy to be there, so she was surprised to find him in the kitchen, making spaghetti and chicken for them. Shortly after she arrived, Yeager joined him in the kitchen. She remembered that Andy had tried to talk to her ex-husband during her divorce years earlier. "Andy really tried to help me," she said. "And I felt I wanted to do the same thing in this situation. Having known them as young people, newlyweds, I could not believe that they were still not in love with each other."

In the kitchen, Yeager said, Andy was drinking wine steadily and rebuffing any attempt she made to discuss the situation. "I couldn't get to first base with him. If I would ask him a question, he would either be nonresponsive or he would tell me, 'None of it is true.' He kept saying over and over again to me, 'My wife is telling the world stories about a very dear friend of mine. She is slandering us. Bess is just a very good friend of mine, and Nancy is lying to everybody about us.'

"Whatever I said to him, he would say, 'It isn't true.' Then I asked him, 'How come, Andy, you are out all night?' He wouldn't respond to that. He would just again go through the rehearsed remarks: 'Bess is my dearest friend, and it is not right that Nancy is lying about it.'

"I could not get anywhere with him. He wasn't talking to me heart to heart. I was wasting my breath."

Dinner was surreal. There they were, Nancy and Andy, in the midst of divorce negotiations, having dinner with their children and an old friend in whose living room they had been married. Over dinner, Yeager said, no one talked about the marital problems. In fact, she remembered that Andy had tried to be charming.

Then, at about 9:00 P.M., after the dishes were cleared away from the table, Andy went upstairs. Nancy assumed that he was going to "freshen up" for his evening "appointment" with Bess.

She followed him upstairs with the children to get them ready for bed. A few minutes later, Judy Yeager and Helené heard Nancy scream.

Andy later said that as he was washing up in the upstairs bathroom, his eight-year-old daughter came in and asked, "Where are you going? Out with your girlfriend?"

"Where did you hear that?" Andy asked.

"Mommy," Andy later said the child replied.

Andy was enraged. He tore out of the room, past his daughter, shouting obscenities at his wife. "He must have thought that I put her up to that," Nancy said later. "I didn't even know what was happening. I had come upstairs to check on the kids, to see if they had taken their showers and had gotten ready for bed, and there he was, hurtling at me out of nowhere. He was screaming I don't know what, and then he flung me over a glass table, and I ended up on my back like a turtle. Then he started stomping on me."

Still wearing his heavy black dress shoes, he kicked her repeatedly, leaving at least six large bruises on her thighs, buttocks, and back. Her screams alerted Judy and Helené, who bounded up the marble staircase. The two younger children were crying in their bedrooms. Helené started screaming at Andy as she tried to pull him off her mother.

Yeager yelled that she was calling the police, but Nancy screamed, "No. Get the doorman."

Yeager ran downstairs and called the doorman. "By the time the doorman came up, things were pretty quiet," she said. "I went upstairs again, and Andy was in his daughter's room, muttering over and over to himself, 'She tells my daughter that I am going to see my girlfriend. How does she do such a terrible thing? She tells my daughter that I am going to see my girlfriend.'

"He was absolutely out of control, and he was drunk, and he was unwilling to deal straight. He was taking the offensive, saying to Nancy, 'You are imagining this, and because you are imagining this, you are hurting me.' Not vice versa. 'You dare to tell my child that I have to go because I have to go visit my girlfriend.' The truth is that *is* where he was going."

Shortly after the incident Andy left the house. Badly bruised and shaken by the beating, Nancy went into the bathroom to inspect her wounds. Then she went downstairs with her friend and the children. Yeager tried to calm Nancy down by reminiscing about their lives twenty years before in Jamaica Estates. Nancy pulled out a photo album, and they flipped through the pages, looking at photographs of their children going off to camp together. A few hours later Andy returned home. When he saw that Yeager was still there, he left again for the night.

Andy later said that he apologized to his wife for the incident and expressed to her that the beating had made him feel "seriously depressed, anxious, embarrassed, [and] upset. . . ." He was so troubled that he sought help from Bess's therapist and good friend, Ted Rubin. When asked years later about Andy's having beaten his wife, Bess said the same thing that some people had said about her and her first husband, Allan Wayne: "Mr. Capasso is the sweetest, gentlest of men. She obviously provoked him."

The next day Nancy contacted her attorney and told him what had happened. He told her to take photographs of her bruises. Within two days they filed a petition on her behalf in family court, seeking an order of protection. A hearing was scheduled for December.

Andy was furious. Nancy said that he told her, "If I dared to take him to 'nigger court,' which is what he called family court, I would pay for it the rest of my life."

Andy and Nancy continued to live together in the Fifth Avenue apartment, and their constant sniping at each other must have seemed unbearable. She accused him of stealing her jewelry, and he accused her of trying to poison their children against him.

On the day of the family court hearing Andy took the stand. Nancy's lawyer asked him to remove one of his size twelve, triple E black leather dress shoes and hold it up so the judge could see how heavy a weapon it was. After hearing testimony and reviewing the photographs of six large contusions on Nancy's body, Judge Bruce Kaplan issued a six-month protection order, restraining Andy from any further violence. "There is no dispute as to whether Mr. Capasso threw Mrs. Capasso over a coffee table and then kicked her a number of times," Kaplan said. "Observing the documentary evidence, photographs, I can see at least six different extremely large bruised areas. This for the purposes of the Family Court Act establishes that Mr. Capasso did assault Mrs. Capasso on the evening of November 5, 1982."

Kaplan concluded that while the daughter's remark may have provoked Andy, "it most assuredly does not justify admission of a vicious beating, and I must characterize, based on the testimony and the photographic evidence, that what happened was a vicious beating."

On December 20, 1982, Andy struck back. He filed for a divorce on the grounds of "cruel and inhuman treatment." In his divorce papers he accused Nancy of calling him a "dumb guinea" in front of the children and charged her with telling him, "These kids have to know you are a piece of shit." In asking the court for a divorce, Andy sought custody of their two children and sole and exclusive use of the Fifth Avenue apartment, Palm Beach condominiums, and Westhampton Beach estate.

Nancy was on her way out the door to meet a friend and see the hit Broadway musical *Cats* when a stranger handed her a summons and the divorce papers. Despite everything that had happened between them in the previous months, she was surprised that Andy had moved ahead to end their marriage. She had been thinking in terms of a separation.

Capasso v. *Capasso* was now in New York State Supreme Court.

Toward the end of the summer of 1982, just before Nancy discovered that Bess and Andy were having an affair, Bess confided in a close friend that she was thinking about dumping Andy. She had been with Andy for almost two years and, her friend said, was tired of being the "other woman." What's more, Andy was beginning to bore her. She no longer found his savvy street sense appealing. She told one friend that his "coarse manners" embarrassed her.

"She was ready to get rid of him," said the friend, who was close to Bess at the time. "She had had enough of his money. She didn't need it anymore. She used him for what he was to be used for, and she was ready to move on. She didn't like to stay with anybody too long anyway.

"But then the shit hit the fan about Nancy knowing. She felt that she could not abandon him at that point."

How could she walk out on Andy after he had stood by her in the agonizing months following her failed campaign for the United States Senate? How could she break off her relationship with a man who had visited her every day at Lenox Hill Hospital? How could she leave him as he proceeded with a messy divorce?

She decided to stay.

As things would turn out, sticking by Andy Capasso during his bitter divorce might have been one of the biggest mistakes she had ever made.

If Bess had walked away that fall of 1982, and cut Andy Capasso out of her life, she might never have ended up five years later on the steps of the U.S. Federal Courthouse in Manhattan with her reputation besmirched and her life in tatters.

23
Cultural Affairs

After spending almost a year in television news, Bess wanted out. She had expected to have lots of time to probe consumer-related stories. Instead she found herself frequently called on to cover daily news stories on a variety of subjects, a situation that she thought did not provide her with enough time to do the consumer stories.

In February 1983 she sent word to her old friend, Mayor Koch, that she would like to come back to government and head the city's Department of Cultural Affairs. With a $46 million budget in 1983, the department had the second-largest arts budget in the country, smaller only than the National Endowment for the Arts and Humanities. Some money was distributed to neighborhood arts groups and used to fund a variety of public programs and services, but almost 90 percent of it went to support the city's thirty major cultural institutions, such as the Metropolitan Museum of Art and the American Museum of Natural History.

More than thirty people had been interviewed for the $62,000-a-year job since the former commissioner, Henry Geldzahler, had resigned in October. No one candidate with all of the qualifications that Koch was looking for had emerged—except for Beverly Sills and Jacqueline Kennedy Onassis, and they had both turned him down. Koch wanted someone with "superstar status" to head the agency, someone who could bring visibility to the department and help raise millions of dollars from the private sector to help fund arts programs.

While Koch had ruled out Bess in the fall of 1980 for the job she had wanted then—deputy mayor for economic development—because he thought she didn't have the experience for the post, he thought that she would make a superb commissioner of cultural affairs. Bess's celebrity not only would bring visibility to the arts, but she had government experience, political skills, and a demonstrated ability to raise money.

Heading a municipal agency for cultural affairs might not seem like an important post in many cities, but the arts in New York, as Bess once said, "is as important a commodity as wheat is in Kansas and steel in

Pittsburgh." On any given weekend at least two hundred music, dance, and theater performances are given, and more than 150 museums and public exhibition spaces are open. In 1983 a government report concluded the arts pumped an estimated $5.62 billion a year into the city's economy.

On Monday, February 21, Bess and Mayor Koch met for lunch at a Columbus Avenue restaurant to talk about the job. Bess accepted but told him she did not want to begin work for about two months. She wanted to finish some of the stories she had been working on at WCBS-TV, and she intended to take a vacation. She seemed enthusiastic about her return to government, even though it meant taking an enormous cut in pay. She later said she saw her life coming full circle as the city's cultural czar. Once again she would be immersed in the arts, just as she had been as a young girl, studying the piano with Mrs. LaFollette and music at the High School of Music and Art.

Planning to depart on a trip to Jerusalem later that week, Mayor Koch wasted no time in announcing Bess's decision to join his administration. Two days later, at an eleven o'clock City Hall press conference, they appeared together in the same room where Mayor John Lindsay had introduced Bess fourteen years earlier as his commissioner of consumer affairs.

"It took me five years to get her into government, and I'm delighted," Koch said disingenuously, making no reference to the fact that he had rejected her request for a post two years earlier.

"It's a great way to continue my love affair with the city," Bess told reporters.

How did she intend to obtain more private funds from corporations when the federal government's own budgetary "tight squeeze" might make it difficult for her agency to seek outside funding? a reporter asked.

"They haven't been squeezed by me," she answered, a broad smile crossing her face.

"And that's a pleasure," Koch chimed in.

Bess later explained to a reporter that she wanted to raise more money for the arts from small businesses. "Community leaders and shopkeepers will come out to see Bess Myerson," she said, adding with a laugh, "if only to see what I look like now."

On the press release distributed to reporters that day the last sentence said Bess's appointment was subject to the usual "city clearances." But the background check conducted by the city's Department of Investigation did not turn up Bess's 1969 shoplifting arrest in London or the results of the New York City Police Department's November 1980 investigation into charges of harassment.

Koch, who had been briefed about the harassment campaign in 1980, said later that he had not considered the police department's findings when he asked her to join his administration in 1983. "Between the time I knew of it and [the time] I appointed her, I had seen her many times and didn't see anything unusual or bizarre in her behavior. I assumed it was an affair of the heart and not a consideration for me."

The week before Mayor Koch announced her appointment, Bess had been in Aspen, Colorado, with Andy and his children. She stayed with friends while Andy and the children stayed in a rented condominium nearby. She had flown back to New York alone when Andy first got word from his attorney that Nancy had obtained a court order evicting him from their Fifth Avenue apartment. He was furious, not only about being thrown out of his own home but also about being accused of having beaten his wife a second time.

In attempting to convince the court that she should have exclusive occupancy of the Fifth Avenue apartment during the divorce proceedings, Nancy reported that Andy had attacked her again, a charge that her husband denied adamantly. She said the second beating had occurred just before he left for Aspen during an argument over her decision to return a $10 toothbrush he had purchased at a local drugstore. She said he first threw a scotch and water in her face, then grabbed her by the shoulders and banged her head against a wall. Her attorneys argued the attack was a violation of the order of protection issued by family court judge Bruce Kaplan two months earlier and that he should be barred from ever entering the apartment again.

On February 16 the motion came before state supreme court justice Hortense W. Gabel, who had been assigned jurisdiction over the *Capasso* v. *Capasso* divorce case. She ruled in favor of Nancy and ordered Andy to vacate the apartment immediately. "Serious allegations have been made by the defendant [Nancy] that the plaintiff [Andy] has engaged in various acts of violence against her," her decision said. Gabel did, however, grant Andy exclusive use of the couple's waterfront estate in Westhampton Beach.

Four days later Andy returned from Aspen with the children. On his way home from the airport he stopped by his office and called Nancy to ask about the judge's order granting her exclusive occupancy. He said she told him on the telephone: "That's right. I told you I was going to have you thrown out of here."

When Andy asked to pick up some clothes and personal things that night, he said she objected but changed her mind and told him it would be okay.

Nancy denied ever giving him permission to come into the apartment and said she asked him to leave the children downstairs with the doorman and come back the next day with his attorney. So she was shocked when he stepped off the elevator into their grand marble foyer that night. "He was angry, and he went into the closets and pulled out all of our luggage and started filling them with everything possible, including my Frank Sinatra records from college," she said. "I was terrified. I called the police and locked myself in the bathroom. When the police got to the building, they called up on the intercom, and he answered it. 'There's a mistake,' he told them. 'Nobody called the police.'"

Based on Andy's statements, the police left. Nancy remained in the bathroom. As Andy continued to pack some things, Nancy could hear him shout repeatedly that she would pay for the rest of her life. His last words were "You will get nothing," which he shouted before disappearing behind the elevator's closing doors.

Waiting outside the apartment on Fifth Avenue was his chauffeur, Tony Bailey, who put the suitcases and bags in the trunk. "He was fuming," Bailey remembered. They drove first to a drugstore, where Andy picked up a few things, and then to four or five luxury hotels before Andy found a vacancy at the Westbury Hotel on East 68th Street, just three blocks from Bess's apartment.

Within two weeks Bess and Andy no longer had to worry about being discreet about their relationship. On March 7 their long-held secret affair had made its way onto the front page of the *New York Post*. Next to Bess's picture ran the headline "Irate Wife Evicts Escort of Bess Myerson." On the paper's widely read gossip page, "Page Six," the article began: "Newly named Cultural Affairs Commissioner Bess Myerson, whose frequent escort around town has been her former campaign advisor Andy Capasso, has lost one social friend, Andy's wife, Nancy. . . ."

Nancy took the opportunity to deliver a few potshots at Andy and Bess, telling the *Post* that she had never known her husband liked older women, "although he always liked my mother."

About Bess she said: "She's been around more years than a normal mortal. It's disgusting. If it was a 28-year-old blond I wouldn't be so insulted."

Bess would later tell writer Patricia Morrisroe that the article, which Bess believed was planted by Nancy, drew her even closer to Andy. "It made me more supportive of him, because I'm supportive of friends," she explained. "She just threw us to the wolves. But I'm used to that. Women take their vengeance out on me because they think I have it all."

Before beginning her new job at the Department of Cultural Affairs on April 26, Bess finished up her work at WCBS-TV and flew with Andy to Caneel Bay, on St. John in the Caribbean, to celebrate her city appointment and to help him celebrate a $53.6 million contract that he had just won to build a sludge-processing complex at the Owls Head sewage treatment plant in Brooklyn. Although he had never done such work before, he had won the contract after submitting the lowest bid. Years later the city contract would become the focus of numerous inquiries as investigators attempted to determine what role his friendships with former Democratic political bosses Stanley Friedman and Donald Manes had played in the selection process.

Despite his tremendous business success that spring, Andy had become preoccupied, almost obsessed, by his divorce. He was enraged that Nancy had evicted him from the apartment. Drinking heavily and losing nights of sleep, he sometimes took out his frustration and anger on his employees, accusing some of them of betrayal and giving information to Nancy. He was always looking over his shoulder, because he suspected that Nancy had hired a private investigator to follow him. He worried too that she was tapping his telephones, and he had the office phones repeatedly swept for bugs. "The divorce was getting the best of him," Andy's former secretary said.

Andy spent weekdays at a suite in the Westbury Hotel and weekends with Bess at his Westhampton Beach home. During their first weekend alone at the house, Bess brought out a suitcase full of clothes and other belongings and hung her clothes in a guest bedroom. By the following weekend she had moved all of her things into the master bedroom.

In March they began interviewing live-in servants to care for the waterfront estate. They decided on Shirley and Ray Harrod, a British couple who had worked in various homes for more than twenty years in the United States. The couple was paid $2,300 per month. Bess gave the Harrods specific instructions about what to do should Nancy Capasso or her children from her previous marriage ever appear at the door.

"She said Mr. Capasso was going through a very messy divorce, and the security had to be very strict, for they didn't want any of Mrs. Capasso's children to come into the house or Mrs. Capasso," Shirley Harrod later said.

At the five-bedroom home in Westhampton Beach on Quantuck Bay, Shirley Harrod recalled, Bess quickly established her position as the lady of the house. She rearranged the furniture, brought out some of her own china, and instructed Harrod to get rid of all of Nancy's potted plants, telling her that she didn't like "living in a jungle." She also asked her not to answer the phone with "Capasso residence." "Hello" would do.

After Bess began working at the Department of Cultural Affairs in late April, Andy's driver often picked her up outside of her office at 2 Columbus Circle on Thursday or Friday afternoon to take her to the 23rd Street heliport, where she would meet Andy and board a seaplane for the twenty-minute trip to Westhampton Beach. They would be delivered almost to the back door, landing in the bay behind his house.

That spring and summer of 1983 Andy and Bess frequently entertained. Bess's longtime friend Herb Rickman, a special assistant to the
mayor, stayed with them several weekends that summer, sometimes
taking the seaplane with them on Friday afternoon. Federal investigators would later contend that Bess and Andy were using Rickman to
draw them closer to the mayor because Andy might have been worried
that his connections with organized crime were too close. He wanted
desperately to move in the right circles, the investigators argued, so that
he could cloak himself with respectability.

On Memorial Day weekend Bess and Andy invited Mayor Koch,
along with his good friends Bobbie and David Margolis, who own a
home nearby, to Westhampton Beach for a barbecue.

Although most of Andy and Bess's friends knew they were an item,
Bess apparently did not want everyone to know she was sleeping there.
One afternoon, Shirley Harrod said, as a group of guests was arriving at
the house, Bess "walked out the kitchen door and came in the front door
as if she had just arrived."

A frequent topic of conversation among Bess, Andy, and their close
friends that summer was Andy's divorce. Both Bess and Andy constantly railed against his estranged wife. Andy once explained to a
houseguest that Nancy put him down all the time and had loved only his
money. "The official version was that their marriage had been troubled
long before Bess arrived on the scene," the guest recalled. "He said that
she had been fooling around with a tennis pro. And he said she was
embarrassed by him and never liked to entertain his friends."

Even so, Andy felt ambivalent about ending his marriage. "I'm an
Italian man," the houseguest remembered Andy saying. "I get married
until death. There is no divorce in my family."

But Andy felt that Nancy had left him no choice when she threw him
out of his Fifth Avenue apartment and splashed their marital troubles on
the front page of the *New York Post*. And for that Nancy would have to
pay. "I'm not giving her a dime," chauffeur Tony Bailey later recalled he
said.

In March Andy fulfilled his promise by refusing to pay the $5,914.07
monthly maintenance charges on the Fifth Avenue apartment and
virtually all of the household bills. While he promised to continue
paying all of the children's expenses, he insisted that Nancy pick up the
rest of the expenses herself using her income from Sotheby's International Realty and the interest she was earning from thousands of dollars
he claimed she had stashed away in certificates of deposit during their
marriage.

Claiming that under state law he was obligated to pick up the tab,
Nancy struck back in court. Her lawyers requested that Judge Gabel
award Nancy temporary alimony and child support payments. Since it

takes almost two years for many divorces to go to trial in New York, state law requires that a spouse, most often the wife, receive temporary alimony and temporary child support until the divorce has been granted and the division of marital properties and assets has been made. Temporary alimony and child support payments are intended to meet the spouse's reasonable needs and essentially maintain the lifestyle the spouse had known before the marriage broke up. A number of different factors are considered when a judge determines how much temporary alimony to award a wife, such as whether the wife earns a sufficient income to support herself.

Temporary alimony can also be a major factor in determining strategy in a bitter divorce. For example, if a spouse receives a substantial temporary alimony award, there is less incentive to settle the divorce quickly or bring on a speedy divorce trial, because the permanent alimony award could be lower. On the other hand, if a wife receives a small temporary alimony award, the husband might try to drag his heels in bringing the divorce to trial out of concern that he might end up having to pay more.

In order to maintain the lavish lifestyle Nancy enjoyed before Andy filed for divorce, she claimed in an affidavit on April 29, 1983, that she needed $6,060.13 a week in temporary alimony and $1,933.17 a week in child support. Her attorney, Raoul Lionel Felder, had a reputation for overstating his request in order to get as much money as possible for his client.

In addition, Nancy asked the court to compel Andy to pay the $5,914.07 monthly maintenance on the Fifth Avenue apartment, the $1,669 monthly mortgage and maintenance fee on their Palm Beach condominium, and $9,665.18 in household bills that included virtually everything from her $308-a-month dry-cleaning bill to the cost of getting the vacuum repaired.

"He has cut me off without a cent," she stated in the affidavit. "He has done this to get even with me because of my application to this court for exclusive occupancy of our Fifth Avenue apartment and to force me to settle this case on his terms. . . . He knows that there is no way in the slightest that I can afford to maintain, even remotely, the lifestyle to which he has accustomed us over the years. He has acted out of pure vengeance."

Andy and Bess worked together with his lawyers to prepare a response to Nancy's request. Andy's chauffeur remembers frequent trips to pick up divorce papers from Andy's office and drop them off at Bess's house. In Westhampton Andy and Bess spent hours at the dining room table, discussing strategy and making notes in the margins. They talked about the divorce incessantly, recalled the maid, Shirley Harrod: "They were so very upset about the whole thing. Mostly about the payments."

One afternoon, she said, Andy threw the papers on the table and said to Bess, "Isn't there something you can do about this?"

Harrod said she did not hear Bess's reply.

On May 17 Andy submitted his response to the courts on Nancy's request for temporary alimony. In his affidavit Andy charged that Nancy had "wildly exaggerated" her need for temporary alimony and child support. He claimed that her request would cost him $515,488.44 a year, five times more than what he had spent on the family when they had all lived together in 1982. He claimed that Nancy had "artificially inflated her expenses to the financial frontiers of the imagination."

He also stated in the affidavit that he would continue, however, to pay for all of his children's expenses. "Frankly, I do not need my wife, her lawyer, or anyone else to remind me of my obligations towards my children. I have gladly and willingly paid all of their expenses, every single one . . . and I continue to pay for those expenses on a current basis because I love my children and care for them very much. My cultural heritage dictates that I have a sacred obligation to support my children and a court order is simply unnecessary because I would not dishonor myself by not doing so."

By May 24 both sides in *Capasso* v. *Capasso* had submitted their arguments in motions before Judge Hortense W. Gabel. As the judge assigned to rule on divorce motions, she would determine how much, if any, temporary alimony and child support Nancy Capasso would receive.

Nancy took comfort in knowing that Judge Gabel was making the decisions in the case. It had been Judge Gabel who had granted exclusive occupancy of the Fifth Avenue apartment to her in February. And she had heard that Judge Gabel was a veteran public servant with a sterling reputation who was generous to women in divorce cases. Once, after learning that musical composer Alan Jay Lerner was $12,000 behind in his alimony payments, Judge Gabel had placed his property in receivership and named his ex-wife as the receiver.

What Nancy did not know that spring of 1983 is that Judge Gabel and Bess Myerson had been acquainted for fifteen years. And that on Wednesday, May 25, the day after she had filed a motion requesting Judge Gabel to grant her temporary alimony, Bess Myerson and Judge Gabel were on their way to Gracie Mansion in Bess's chauffeur-driven city car.

24
Mother and Daughter

S eventy years old in 1983 and nearly blind, Hortense Gabel—
Horty to her friends—was considered "one of the grandes dames"
of the courts and a legend in legal and government circles for her
skirmishes with the city's legendary city planner and power broker
Robert Moses. As a small, frail-looking woman who peers out from
thick glasses, her appearance gives little indication of the toughness and
determination that helped her overcome her poor eyesight and break
down gender barriers to reach the highest levels of city and state
government.

In the 1950s and early 1960s, while Bess was modeling minks on
television game shows, Hortense Gabel was regarded as one of the most
powerful women in New York. As head of Mayor Robert F. Wagner's
campaign against "slumlords," she was a highly visible public figure
who captured the press's attention in much the same way Bess did years
later as Mayor Lindsay's commissioner of consumer affairs. She battled
landlords at every turn, staging well-publicized "raids" on their buildings, where she would decry the poor conditions, demand immediate
improvements, and seek large fines against building owners. The *New
York Times* called her the "lady against the slums."

Hortense Wittstein Gabel was born in the Bronx on December 16,
1912, to a comfortable, middle-class Jewish family. Her father, Ruben
Wittstein, was a politically active lawyer whose friends included the
powerful Bronx state supreme court judge Al Cohn, father of the well-
known New York attorney the late Roy Cohn. "Government was always a
topic for table conversation," she once said. "I was very lucky in my
choice of parents."

Her mother taught her to read and write at home because she was so
nearsighted that the family doctor did not think she could learn much in
a classroom. When she did finally enter the local public school at around
age eight, she excelled and skipped several grades. She went on to
Hunter College and then followed her father's footsteps, entering

Columbia University Law School in 1932. "It was a complete case of father identification," she once said. She was one of five women in her class.

When Hortense graduated from law school, the country was in the midst of the Great Depression and there were few job opportunities, particularly for a young female lawyer. She finally found a position at Stern & Rubens, a small firm that specialized in copyright law. She was fired after a few months on the job, however, when her poor eyesight made it impossible for her to work the switchboard while the telephone operator and the male lawyers were at lunch. She eventually ended up working at her father's firm, where she remained until a friend suggested in 1941 that she interview for a job with the city as an assistant corporation counsel under Mayor Fiorello La Guardia. "The situation was so bad with men going off to the war, maybe they might have to take a woman," she recalled a friend telling her at the time.

The importance of politics in getting a city job was explained to her during her job interview. After impressing the corporation counsel with her credentials, she was told to return with an "endorsement" from a local political leader. She picked up her "endorsement" from her father's good friend, Judge Al Cohn, and soon started work for the city. She remained with the office of the city's corporation counsel, writing mostly appeals, until 1944.

It was then, at age thirty-two, that she married Dr. Milton Gabel, a gentle and soft-spoken army dentist who was thirty-seven years old. Throughout her marriage he would be supportive of her political ambitions and her career.

Soon after their wedding the Gabels left New York for Camp Hood in Texas. Not one to sit around as an army wife, Hortense got a $60-a-week job as a reporter on the local paper, only to end up getting fired, she later said, after revealing a tax scandal involving some prominent members of the community. She then took a position doing public relations work at the army base.

When they returned to New York after the war and moved into a modest apartment on the Upper East Side, Hortense once again found it difficult to persuade law firms to hire her. "Since I had a good record I thought I would have no trouble, [but] I was told, oh, no, only male veterans were allowed. . . ."

Instead she became a volunteer for the American Jewish Congress, and at a dinner party in 1948 she met the group's founder, Rabbi Stephen S. Wise, who talked about having recently formed an organization called the New York State Committee on Discrimination in Housing. A liberal Democrat, she flung herself into the cause, ultimately becoming the housing organization's executive director. "It was such a breathtaking thing that you could dream that some day Negroes might have the chance to live wherever they wanted to," she later told Robert Caro, the Pulitzer Prize-winning author of *The Power Broker*, a biography of Robert Moses. Moses was the powerful city official whose controversial public works projects over the years helped change the face of New York.

Soon after she took over the organization, in 1949, she gave birth, at age thirty-seven, to her only child, a daughter the Gabels named Julie Bess—Julie after the character in *Showboat* and Bess after Hortense's mother. Unlike most women during the early 1950s, Hortense continued to work outside the home as the executive director of the state Committee on Discrimination in Housing. As she became increasingly involved in local Democratic politics, she hired a full-time nanny and cook to help her care for her baby daughter and look after the apartment.

In 1955, when Julie was six years old, Hortense entered state government, working under former governor W. Averell Harriman as general counsel to the New York State Rent Commission—the highest legal post in state government then held by a woman. Later that year she was promoted to deputy state rent administrator.

Highly regarded as a housing expert, she was invited by Mayor Robert F. Wagner to join his administration in 1959 as an assistant to the deputy mayor on housing issues. When she was appointed, her daughter's fourth-grade class wrote letters of congratulations, and Julie accompanied her mother and father to City Hall for the swearing-in ceremony. Julie Bess, who would later change her name to Sukhreet, was beginning to show signs of an independent nature. "She's proud of me," her mother said at the time, "but she also expresses her own individuality. I remember that during the Ives campaign for governor she came to me and said, 'Mother, I have to tell you I'm a Republican.'"

It was during the Wagner administration that Judge Gabel became known for her efforts to expose abuses of the urban renewal plans under Moses' direction. She helped to preserve city neighborhoods and improve the quality of existing housing. During her tenure she was credited with preserving more than two hundred city blocks in six neighborhoods and saving the homes of some 150,000 residents.

Robert Caro called Hortense Gabel the only city official who would listen to the poor at the time and said, "I also found that she herself, at a time when it was really dangerous to do so, went all alone to some of these urban renewal sites which were then called the worst slums in the world to investigate for herself the living conditions there."

Her political instincts were strong. When it looked as if a split in the city's Democratic party might cost Wagner reelection, she reached out to party "reformers" and set up a group known as the New York Forum, designed to bridge the gap between reformers and regulars and help provide Wagner with sufficient political support to be reelected in

November 1961 despite a divisive Democratic primary.

A few months later, on April 2, 1962, Mayor Wagner appointed Gabel to a $22,500-a-year job as head of the city's new Rent and Rehabilitation Administration, where she was responsible for regulating the city's 1.7 million rent-controlled apartments. With a staff of seven thousand inspectors, she was supposed to keep the city's five million tenants of rent-controlled housing and their landlords happy, an almost impossible task. "I don't know why I'm looking forward to this job—I wouldn't wish it on my worst enemy," she said at the time. "It's probably the most devilish job in the world."

In a "Woman in the News" profile in the next day's *New York Times*, she was described as a "many-sided woman, with a gentle, maternal concern for friends and associates; an almost wistful idealism that neatly balances the desirable with the possible, a shrewd, tough political sense, and a driving ambition."

The article said she seldom left those who came in contact with her indifferent. Either people liked her or they did not. "She is accused by those who dislike her as being too ambitious, too much the behind-the-scenes operator, too concerned with publicity."

Most of the newspaper stories in those years were flattering pieces, the most glowing account appearing in the *New York Times Magazine* on August 12, 1962, titled "Lady Against the Slums." Writer Gertrude Samuels depicted Hortense Gabel as a tireless crusader who dreamed of a "slumless New York" and expected her staff to be equally committed. "No one who meets Horty . . . can long remain unmoved by her personality, humor and convictions," Samuels wrote. "Her detractors (and they are, not unnaturally, legion) are outraged by her political maneuverings. Her supporters point to her devotion to ordinary folk and to her practical idealism."

The article made mention of Gabel's family: her supportive husband and "their precocious brown-haired daughter Julie, who, says Horty, 'is 13 years old going on 20.'"

At the end of 1965, when Mayor Wagner left office, Gabel left city government, spending the next several years as a housing consultant, lecturer, and member of various civic organizations. She remained politically active, however, and worked in 1969 for Mayor John Lindsay's reelection campaign. The following year she did consulting work for the Lindsay administration, and in August Lindsay appointed her to a vacancy on the civil court in Manhattan.

She remained on the civil court until 1975, when Governor Hugh Carey appointed her at the age of sixty-three to fill a vacancy on the state supreme court. Her sponsor with Governor Carey was none other than former mayor Wagner, who had headed an independent judicial screening panel that the governor had set up. She retained the seat in the next election.

The Sholem Aleichem Cooperative Houses in the Bronx today.

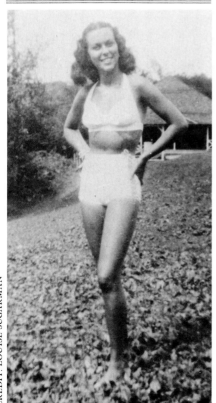

Bess at the Birchwood Camp
in Brandon, Vermont, where
she worked as a camp counselor
during the summer of 1945.

Bess playing the piano during the Miss New York City contest in August 1945.

Bess wearing the white bathing suit that her sister, Sylvia, sewed her into before the swimsuit competition at the Miss America pageant in September 1945.

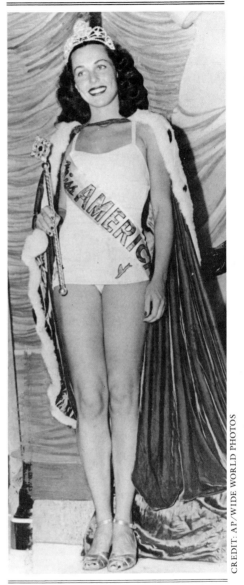

Moments after Bess is crowned Miss America in 1945.

The contestants in their Catalina swimsuits line up on the bleachers during the Miss America contest in September 1945. Bess is in the top row, center.

Bess returns to Atlantic City in 1946 to turn over her scepter and crown.

Bess and her two sisters, Helen (left) and Sylvia, the day after she won the title.

Bess and Allan Wayne on their
honeymoon at Grossinger's,
three days after they were
married on October 19, 1946.

Bess signs autographs for
students at a Philadelphia high
school, where she spoke out
against bigotry and hate for the
Anti-Defamation League of
B'nai B'rith during her
Miss America reign.

Bess and her daughter Barbara, who
later changed her name to Barra,
return to Atlantic City for a visit.

Bess as the "Lady in Mink" on "The Big Payoff."

Bess and Allan Wayne leave the courthouse with their nine-year-old daughter Barbara, during a custody battle in 1956.

A publicity shot of Bess distributed in 1959 after she joined the panel of "I've Got a Secret."

Bess as hostess of Macy's Thanksgiving Day Parade.

Bess clowns around with Betsy Palmer, Tom Poston, and Garry Moore on the set of "I've Got a Secret."

Bess and Arnold Grant
as they depart on their
honeymoon in
May 1962.

Mayor John Lindsay administers the oath of office to Bess on the
day she is sworn in as commissioner of New York City's Department of Consumer Affairs.

The night before Bess underwent surgery for ovarian cancer in April 1974, she was the moderator of a nationally televised show broadcast from New York's Lincoln Center, honoring "Women of the Year" named by the readers of *Ladies' Home Journal*. Bess, seated at center, is flanked by Martha Griffiths (left) and Dorothy Height, right, two of the women honored. Standing are other winners (from left): Patricia Harris, Barbara Walters, Billie Jean King, Barbara McDonald, and Dixy Lee Ray.

While consumer affairs commissioner, Bess drops in at a New York City supermarket and uses her own weights to check a scale.

Ed Koch kisses Bess Myerson, his campaign chairperson, on September 19, 1977, the night he won the Democratic nomination for mayor.

At a debate during the 1980 Democratic primary for the United States Senate, Bess is seated next to John Santucci, Elizabeth Holtzman, and John Lindsay.

Bess with daughter, Barra, and Mayor Edward I. Koch on the night she lost the Democratic nomination for the U.S. Senate.

Bess at her swearing-in ceremony in 1983 as New York City's commissioner of cultural affairs.

Bess and Andy Capasso pose at Maxim's in December 1986.

Nancy Capasso reads about the indictment in the *New York Daily News*.

Bess and Andy Capasso at his waterfront estate in Westhampton Beach, Long Island.

Hortense Gabel is sworn in as special assistant for housing in 1959 by Mayor Robert Wagner, as her husband, Dr. Milton Gabel, and their daughter, Julie Bess, who later changed her name to Sukhreet, look on.

Sukhreet Gabel and retired state supreme court judge Hortense Gabel today.

Bess removes andirons from
Andy Capasso's Westhampton
Beach estate in October 1987.
After the photo appeared
on the front page of the
New York Post, Nancy accused
Bess of stealing the andirons.

Bess arrives at the courthouse for her arraignment on federal
charges in October 1987.

Just a few hours after her arraignment, Bess meets with the author in the office of Bess's publisher, Esther Margolis, who is seated behind the table.

Bess leaves the district magistrate's office in May 1988, where she was released on $150 bail after being arrested for shoplifting nail polish, earrings, and batteries from a Hill's department store in South Williamsport, Pennsylvania.

Outside of the federal courthouse on December 22, 1988, after Bess learns the jury has acquitted her of all charges.

On the supreme court Judge Gabel built a record marked by compassion and progressivism. She also devoted much time to acting as a mentor for young female lawyers, encouraging them to climb the judicial ladder, and helped found the National Association of Women Judges.

In April 1982, at age sixty-nine, Judge Gabel was assigned to oversee matrimonial cases in the state supreme court in Manhattan, one of the busiest jobs in the courthouse but something of a step down for someone who had been so feared and revered in the past. She was a motion judge who ruled on matters—such as temporary alimony and child support—that needed to be resolved before a divorce case was settled or went to trial.

At about the same time that Judge Gabel began presiding over divorce matters, her daughter, Sukhreet, announced to her parents that she was returning home from the University of Chicago.

After three years in the prestigious university's Ph.D. program in sociology, Sukhreet had decided to drop out and turn her attention to finding a job that might put her on the path toward a career. Having failed to find a job in the Midwest, she was returning to New York for the first time in seven years to start what she hoped would be a new life.

Before Sukhreet even arrived home, Judge Gabel had immersed herself in a job search for her daughter, drawing up a list of prominent people she knew in government and big business to contact on Sukhreet's behalf. While Judge Gabel and Sukhreet had had a difficult relationship over the years, Judge Gabel had the highest respect for her daughter's intelligence. She made phone calls and wrote letters to virtually everyone she knew in a position of power and influence in New York to introduce "my interesting daughter, Sukhreet."

Sukhreet's life stood in sharp contrast to her mother's. While the judge had made her way through a man's world with a combination of brains, pluck, and determination, Sukhreet seemed to run into difficulties at every turn. While she was articulate, exceptionally bright, and well read, she had led a troubled life, marred by chronic depression and a divorce, and never seemed able to finish what she had started.

An only child, Sukhreet had grown up in the care of nannies while her mother was off fighting her battles with the city bureaucracy and her father was tending his dentistry practice. It was a lonely childhood in which Sukhreet felt excluded from her parents' busy lives, unloved and unwanted. She tried hard to be "a good little girl," as she described it, "but no matter how hard I tried, I didn't feel lovable. It wasn't that I wasn't given love. It was just not in the form my mind could use."

From the time she was five years old, she moved in the company of adults, and she learned how to attract their attention by being precocious. At her parents' dinner parties she played the role of the "world's littlest cocktail waitress" to the prominent politicians and public officials who were their guests. "There's Carmine the Sap," she piped up in her little-girl voice the first time she was introduced to Tammany Hall Democratic kingpin Carmine DeSapio. "I was considered a tiny adult rather than a child myself," Sukhreet remembered.

"She was very precocious," says a longtime family friend whose daughter was a close friend of Sukhreet's. "Too smart, actually, for her own good. I think children should grow up gradually, and Julie grew up too fast. She did not have a proper childhood."

Dinnertime was especially trying for her as she sat through her mother's long monologues about the latest skirmishes in city government. "My mother would ask, 'Julie, how was your day?' I would reply, 'Hmpf.' Then she would ask my father, 'How was your day?' My father would say, 'Oh well, so-and-so was in the office. It was nice.' And then he would say, 'Dear, how was your day?' And that was an excuse for Mother to launch into an hour-long diatribe about her day. My mother was a real natural political animal. She loves a good fight. There's nothing she likes better. 'And I said to him, and he said to me, and I said to him.' It was this pitch-battle war over the dinner table, this intolerable battle. . . . And he could listen to it for a steady hour.

"Now that I can look back at it, I felt like a kid in a custody battle. There was a battle raging around me at all times. She was fighting with Robert Moses. She believed that she was on the side of the angels. It was a nightly struggle. It was so upsetting to my poor stomach that I would eat two candy bars and gobble up cookies after school so I would not be hungry and have to sit at that goddamn table. It was very tough for me. I had a hard life, truthfully."

Invariably Sukhreet's memories of her growing-up years are dark ones. When she was eleven, for instance, her parents moved to her mother's sister's house in Scarsdale for more than a year. Sukhreet's young cousin had recently drowned, and eleven days later her uncle had dropped dead of a heart attack. Her mother nursed her aunt through these tragedies, taking her husband and daughter in tow. Sukhreet would later remember her aunt's house as "the house of death."

"When my aunt and my mother would cry," Sukhreet later recalled, "I thought maybe they were wishing it had been me instead."

For Sukhreet, being Horty Gabel's daughter was not easy. There were enormous pressures to succeed. "You couldn't just do something well. You had to do it better than anyone else." As a teenager, Sukhreet had once mentioned to her mother that she was thinking of becoming an occupational therapist. "Maybe you could be the president of the hospital," her mother suggested instead.

In school, however, Sukhreet had trouble following rules and finishing her work. By her own description she was "exponentially bright."

But her fourth-grade teacher recalled that Sukhreet didn't perform up to her potential: "She was always daydreaming, fooling around. She never did her homework. She would apple-polish, bring in small gifts for the teacher to make up for not doing her work." The teacher said she once brought up her concerns about Sukhreet to Hortense and Milton Gabel at a parent-teacher conference. "I remember telling Judge Gabel that there was some imbalance, something was wrong."

Sukhreet believes that she suffered from depression as a child and that by the time she reached early adolescence her parents knew something was wrong. "People thought I was crazy. That it was all in my head. Depression makes you sad, and I was always sad. And my parents agonized over it. They didn't know what to do with me."

They sent her to psychiatrists, but a talking cure did not help, Sukhreet said. Then her parents enrolled her in the private United Nations School, attended by the sons and daughters of diplomats, hoping that Sukhreet might find the international flavor of the school stimulating and exciting. Instead Sukhreet found that she was "bored to tears." Concluding that she was sufficiently self-educated and a "rather gifted child," she dropped out in the middle of the tenth grade at age fifteen.

It was a rebellious step for the daughter of ambitious professionals. She said, though, that her parents didn't argue with her decision. "My father was great about it. This was the mid-sixties, when everyone was doing his own thing. He said he had no choice. My mother was even more understanding. I think she understood that when I was good and ready I would go back. They did not know how to react to this strange bird who was their daughter. I wasn't this conventional American teenager. I am sure that it was kind of disconcerting."

In the spring of 1965 Sukhreet took a full-time job at the World's Fair, manning a booth at the Indian Pavilion. She happily exchanged her skirts and dresses for saris, dyed her long hair black, painted a red dot on her forehead, and changed her name to Sukhreet, which means "one with the tradition of happiness."

For the next few years she immersed herself in Indian culture, wearing saris as a symbol of her rebellion against her parents. She later said her Indian costumes allowed her to express her independence and yet maintain a relationship with her parents at that time. "I was an unsure adolescent who had been raised with a mixture of too much independence and too much overinvolvement. I look back on that period, which lasted about seven or eight years, and it was a perfectly logical way to meet my particular needs as an adolescent female."

When Sukhreet was seventeen, with the World's Fair over, she worked as a ward clerk in a hospital. The depressions she believed had troubled her periodically even as a child grew worse. She recalls being so deeply depressed at one point that she suffered what she called hallucinations. One image that repeatedly entered her mind was of falling on her face and breaking her teeth. After she told her parents that she was experiencing hallucinations, they once again sought professional help for her. "My parents wanted to commit me to a mental hospital," she said. "But I thought that if I went in there, I would start screaming and never stop."

The depression gradually lifted, and Sukhreet went on to take a high school equivalency exam and study nursing at Bronx Community College. She tried her hand as a nurse for a few years but found that she didn't like the job and quit.

During this time she always seemed to have a boyfriend and dated a lot of men, including two older men who later rose to political prominence in New York—state attorney general Robert Abrams and Mayor David Dinkins, who was elected on November 7, 1989.

Sukhreet says that she dated Dinkins, who was forty years old and married at the time, once or twice. Dinkins behaved like a "perfect gentleman," although she admitted that they "kissed passionately one night in a doorway."

Uncertain of what she wanted to do with her life, Sukhreet decided that she would like to spend some time traveling around the world and set her mind on saving money. For several years she worked as a tour guide at the United Nations. She even worked for a time at a massage parlor on New York's West 57th Street until, she said, her mother found out what she was doing and insisted that she quit.

By her twenty-second birthday she had managed to save $6,000, and she departed on a tour that would take her to more than sixty countries in two years.

When she returned home, she decided she was ready for a formal education, and after passing college proficiency exams, she enrolled in New York University's School Without Walls program. Two years later, in May 1974, she emerged with a bachelor of science degree after studying international affairs, languages, art, and political science.

Sukhreet then spent the summer at Oxford University in England, studying British politics and society. That fall she continued her studies at Johns Hopkins School of Advanced International Studies, first in Bologna, Italy, and then in Maryland. She dropped out of Johns Hopkins before earning a master's degree, however, complaining that the program was too oriented toward international business.

At the same time, she was romantically involved with a handsome young Dutch diplomat, Jan Revis, whom she had met at a party in New York. The romance flowered, and on June 8, 1975, they were married. Two hundred guests attended the reception, which was held in the New York mansion of socialite Marietta Tree, an old friend of Sukhreet's mother's. Tulips from Holland were flown in for the occasion. In their wedding picture Sukhreet is slim and beautiful in a flowing white wedding gown.

Thirteen days later Sukhreet and her new husband left for the Dutch Embassy in Suriname in South America, where they lived for two years. "It was hotter than hell," she recalled, "and it was very hard to be a person from one culture living in the middle of another culture in the midst of another culture."

Dutch Embassy policy prohibited her from working, so she had little to do other than to visit the local public works projects, entertain other diplomats, and become acquainted with local customs. "I was lonely, alone with my books and no one to talk to. My husband was a very nice man, but dull, very dull."

By 1977, when her husband was transferred from Suriname to Brussels, Sukhreet was beginning to wonder if her marriage had been a mistake. She had become weary of cocktail parties and playing the role of diplomat's wife.

To escape the drudgery of her marriage, Sukhreet decided to enroll as a part-time student at the University of Chicago under an arrangement that required her to travel to Chicago to attend classes for one semester each year. Her husband didn't take kindly to Sukhreet's decision. "He was very resentful. He was much more jealous than if I had had another man."

The marriage continued nonetheless, but after moving with her husband to Beirut in 1979, Sukhreet decided to enroll at the University of Chicago that fall as a full-time student to fulfill the requirements for a Ph.D. in sociology. Six months later Sukhreet and Jan were divorced. They split the $34,000 they had in savings, and she used her half to help fund her tuition. Her parents and student loans paid the rest of her bill. "He [Jan Revis] married his former secretary as soon as the ink was dry on the divorce papers," said Sukhreet. "I married the University of Chicago."

She concentrated on her studies, taking lots of courses on race relations, and found a new boyfriend, Tony Babinec, a sociology major in his early twenties from a working-class Polish Catholic family. He was taken with this exotic thirty-year-old woman from New York and moved into a condominium she had bought near the university in Chicago's Hyde Park neighborhood with monetary help from her parents.

The University of Chicago was rigorous, and Sukhreet found herself having to study hard for the first time in her academic career. She did not do as well in her classes as she would have liked and flunked the first series of major exams.

By early 1982 she had decided to leave the university. She said she did not think the Ph.D. was worth another two years writing a dissertation. She was also running out of money from the divorce settlement and was tired of living the life of a graduate student. She expected her academic credentials and her experience living and traveling abroad to enable her to walk into any Fortune 500 company and get a high-paying, glamorous job right away.

But she soon found out she was wrong. She first tried to get a job in Chicago and had no luck, so she returned to New York. At least in New York she could rely on her mother's connections.

When she returned to New York in early spring of 1982, her mother presented her with a list of contacts. She had helped so many young women get into law schools and climb the judicial ladder over the years that it must have seemed perfectly natural to "network" on behalf of her daughter.

As Sukhreet remembers it, her mother would get on the telephone to her prominent friends and say: "I have an interesting daughter who has just come back from many years abroad and Chicago, and she is looking for some advice as to the future direction of her career and for some help on her résumé. Would you be good enough, Mr. or Ms. whoever, to spend some time, maybe fifteen minutes, with Sukhreet and give her some good advice?"

Then her mother would follow up the phone call with a note, attaching a copy of Sukhreet's résumé. Among the thirty to forty letters that Judge Gabel sent out were letters to Herb Rickman, special assistant to Mayor Edward I. Koch; Brendan Sexton, the city's sanitation commissioner; Joseph Christian, then head of the New York City Public Housing Authority; William Passannante, New York state assemblyman; Barbara Cohen, deputy city personnel director; Fabian Palomino, a top aide to Governor Mario Cuomo; Mark Siegel, New York state assemblyman; Edward Costikyan, former Manhattan Democratic leader and a prominent lawyer; and Milton Gould, partner in the large Manhattan law firm of Shea & Gould.

Her mother's phone calls and letters opened up doors all over New York, and Sukhreet says she was attending up to four or five meetings a day in 1982. But after interviewing for jobs for a year and writing three hundred letters to the presidents of major corporations, job counselors, and headhunters, emphasizing her research skills and international background, she was still without full-time employment. She received only two solid job offers, and she turned both of them down. One job was working as a paralegal at Shea & Gould. The other job was working for the city's housing authority as a building supervisor in a city housing project. Sukhreet did not see how either job would put her on a career path.

In March of 1983, as she approached the first anniversary of her job search, Sukhreet found herself once again deeply depressed. She had run out of money and was living in a back room in her parents' apartment. The pressure to find a job, particularly from her father, was overwhelming, she said.

Desperately needing a change of scenery, she got into her 1982 Toyota one morning and headed for Chicago to visit Tony Babinec. They had tried to maintain a long-distance relationship over the past year. By the time she reached Ohio, she had worked herself into such a state that she found herself speeding at ninety miles per hour during a driving rainstorm, hoping for an "unfortunate accident."

But all she got was a speeding ticket. She arrived safely at the apartment she had shared with Babinec. Any hope she had of finding solace in their relationship was dashed when she found two unwashed wineglasses at the foot of the bed. "He denied it outright," Sukhreet recalled. "It was the straw that broke the camel's back." She spent the next two weeks crying in bed in Chicago and contemplating suicide. Nothing Babinec said or did could console her.

She had known depression all of her life, but never before had she felt such despair. When she returned to New York, she walked into Payne Whitney Psychiatric Clinic on East 68th Street in Manhattan. A doctor suggested she voluntarily admit herself for examination and review. She said the doctor told her she was suffering from severe clinical depression.

That afternoon she called her parents from the hospital and told them she would be out of town for a few days. She did not want them to know what was happening to her until she felt better.

A week or so later she called her parents again and told them she was at Payne Whitney. Her mother and father immediately came to visit. During the next six weeks her mother visited as often as Sukhreet would permit, often bringing her flowers and packing a nice lunch for them to share. Tony Babinec flew in from Chicago and also visited with her.

Not long after Sukhreet checked herself out of the hospital, she accompanied Babinec on a business trip to Italy and the Netherlands. Her parents thought a trip to Europe might be good for her. They paid for her trip and all of Babinec's travel expenses that were unrelated to his business.

Horty and Milton Gabel were hoping that Sukhreet would return from Europe in better spirits and have better luck in finding a job.

25
Seduction

On Wednesday, May 25, 1983, Bess ordered her new city driver to swing by Judge Gabel's apartment building to pick up the judge for that night's gala at Gracie Mansion. The affair was a celebration of Bess's appointment as the city's new commissioner of cultural affairs, and she had invited Judge Gabel a few days earlier—an invitation that had surprised and flattered the judge, who had not been to Gracie Mansion in years.

Judge Gabel had known Bess for fifteen years, having met her at a Hunter College alumni meeting, but she did not know Bess well. Though they had a mutual friend in Herb Rickman, they almost never socialized together and were little more than acquaintances, running into each other at parties or political gatherings or meetings of the Women's Forum, an organization of New York's most prominent women. As Judge Gabel once put it, "We were friendly, rather than friends. We liked each other, but we were not close."

That's why Rickman, a special assistant to the mayor, was surprised to see Judge Gabel at Gracie Mansion as Bess's guest. Rickman had helped organize the gala to introduce Bess to the city's arts community, and he knew that almost all of the two hundred guests were leaders of the city's many cultural institutions. Only a few of Bess's close friends had been asked to attend, including Andy, who had arrived early to help his nephew, Michael, set up the sound system for the party.

The case of *Capasso* v. *Capasso* had been in the judge's hands for three months at the time of the gala. Rickman would later remember that the judge was curious that night about whether Andy was at the party. "Is what's-his-name here?" Rickman recalled the judge asked him at one point during the night.

"You mean Andy Capasso?" Rickman said.

"Yes," he said she replied.

He looked around the room to point out Andy but couldn't spot him at that moment.

Rickman's recollection would later clash with the judge's insistence that she didn't even know that Bess and Andy were a couple at that time.

It was on this festive night of May 25, 1983, federal prosecutors would later allege, that Bess's seduction of Hortense Gabel began.

The next evening, at Bess's invitation, Judge Gabel and her husband, Milton, attended the opening of the Department of Cultural Affairs' art gallery. The two women continued to talk on the phone over the next few weeks as Bess called the judge frequently to seek advice on a Koch proposal to collect property taxes on many cultural institutions—a proposal that was ultimately dropped.

A few weeks later, Sukhreet said she learned for the first time about her mother's relationship with Bess, when her mother called to ask her if she would attend a dinner party she was throwing on June 17.

"Who's going to be there?" Sukhreet recalled asking her mother.

"Well, Bess Myerson, for one," she said her mother replied.

"That's interesting. Aren't we coming up in the world? How did you come to be inviting Bess Myerson?"

"I was standing at a cocktail party and ran into my friend Herb Rickman, and Bess was standing next to him, and she rather invited herself," Sukhreet remembered her mother said. "Well, are you coming?"

"Maybe I'll be there," Sukhreet said.

By the time Sukhreet arrived that night, almost all of the ten or twelve guests were present, seated in a circle in the living room. She greeted her parents with a kiss and smiled broadly as they introduced her to Bess, Herb Rickman, and the few other guests she had not met in the past. Seeing her lovely smile and charming manners, no one would have guessed that only a few weeks before Sukhreet had been hospitalized for severe depression.

Most of the guests were old friends of her parents, some of whom she had known since she was a child. Sukhreet was delighted to find herself seated next to Bess, who struck up a friendly conversation, asking all about her studies at the University of Chicago and her experiences as a diplomat's wife living abroad. Embarrassed about her lack of employment, Sukhreet did not mention that she was looking for a job. "I didn't want to meet Bess Myerson with my hand out, begging," she later said. "It seemed that she was holding a social conversation with me, and I didn't want to talk business, and my business, at that time, was jobs."

Deeply immersed in conversation, they joined the line at the buffet table, filled their plates, and returned to their chairs, seemingly oblivious of the other guests. Sukhreet was flattered that "a celebrity" was paying her so much attention, particularly since her long job search had left her with little self-confidence. The two talked about how they both enjoyed taking long walks and going to the movies. "She seemed like a very nice person," Sukhreet said. "I thought that she seemed to have a real interest in me. How refreshing! How very nice!"

As Bess was about to mingle with the other guests, Sukhreet said, Bess asked for her telephone number. "I'll call you sometime. If you ever feel like getting together, it would be fun," Sukhreet remembered Bess said at the time.

Judge Gabel was delighted that Bess was paying so much attention to her daughter that night. "Bess told me she liked Sukhreet very much and she would see what she could do for her, and of course I was pleased," Judge Gabel recalled years later. "She was impressed with Sukhreet's knowledge of languages and her knowledge of art. Sukhreet is a cultivated woman . . . more than her mother, I must say, and Bess was impressed. I was tickled pink."

On Thursday, June 23, 1983, less than a week after Bess met Sukhreet at the dinner party, Judge Gabel signed an order granting Nancy Capasso temporary alimony and child support. With more than eighteen hundred motions passing through her chambers a year, including almost five hundred requests for temporary alimony and child support alone, Judge Gabel could not possibly personally examine every motion. She was assisted by her top aide and law secretary, Howard Leventhal, and a pool of law assistants who wrote most of the decisions. In fact virtually all of the requests for temporary alimony were first reviewed by Leventhal and a law assistant from the pool.

In *Capasso* v. *Capasso* the assignment fell to a highly respected law assistant, Les Lowenstein, who, after studying the papers submitted in May by both sides, concluded that Nancy should receive $2,000 a week in temporary alimony and $500 a week in child support from Andy. Lowenstein also believed that Andy should pay the mortgages, maintenance, and household expenses on all of the couple's properties.

He turned over his recommendation to Howard Leventhal, who agreed with his findings after carefully examining the proposal. Leventhal took the recommendation into Judge Gabel's chambers and left it on her desk for her review and signature.

A few days later, on June 23, Judge Gabel called Leventhal into her chambers to discuss the proposed $2,000-a-week alimony in the Capasso case. "I think that the award is a little on the high side and that it ought to be reduced somewhat," Leventhal later recalled Judge Gabel told him.

She crossed out the $2,000-a-week figure and changed it to $1,500. Then she lowered the child support payment from $500 a week to $250.

"Judge, this is support for the children," Leventhal said. "You have got to give them more money than that. Look at all the money this guy has. He can support his children."

Judge Gabel crossed out $250 a week and made it $350. Then she signed the order, one of the highest awards for temporary alimony and child support that she had ever approved.

Although Nancy Capasso had originally requested $6,060.13 a week, she was pleased with the judge's decision granting her $1,500 a week, which totaled $78,000 a year in temporary alimony, plus the $18,200 in child support. The order also specified that Andy pay $5,000 for an accountant to help her untangle his complicated financial dealings so she could determine his net worth before going to trial.

In addition, she no longer had to worry about paying the hefty maintenance and utility bills on the Fifth Avenue apartment. Judge Gabel's order required that Andy pick up those bills, along with the mortgages, maintenance, taxes, and utilities on their other properties in Palm Beach and Westhampton Beach.

Andy was outraged by the order, calculating that the financial responsibilities imposed by the judge would cost him more than $250,000 a year. "He was angry as all get-out," recalled Rickman. "He felt he was being taken for every penny by her."

Before Andy sent his first alimony check, he asked his lawyers to challenge the decision. Within two weeks, on the afternoon of July 5, one of his lawyers, Alton Abramowitz, appeared in Judge Gabel's chambers on the sixth floor of the courthouse with a formal written request for a temporary restraining order and an opportunity to reargue her decision.

In the court papers Andy's lawyers contended that Judge Gabel "obviously overlooked and or misapprehended material facts. . . ." They argued that Andy could not possibly afford to pay Nancy $1,500 a week in temporary alimony and $350 a week in child support along with all of the other expenses. Abramowitz requested that Judge Gabel stop all temporary alimony payments until after Andy's defense team had been able to make its case.

Howard Leventhal was in the outer office when Abramowitz arrived. Abramowitz handed him the request, and Leventhal quickly read over the court papers. He later said that he told Abramowitz that he doubted the judge would agree to the request to reargue the motion unless Andy agreed to pay some support to Nancy until the judge reconsidered the alimony and child support issue.

"How much are you prepared to pay?" Leventhal asked.

"Well, my client isn't prepared to pay anything," Leventhal remembered Abramowitz told him.

"Well, I will take it in to the judge," Leventhal replied.

While Abramowitz waited in the anteroom, Leventhal took the request into Judge Gabel's chambers and told her that Al Abramowitz wanted to reargue the Capasso decision. "He thinks it's too much," Leventhal told the judge.

"Well, let me see the papers," he recalled the judge replied.

Leventhal handed over the documents and waited while she read them.

As he remembered it, a few minutes later she looked up and said, "Well, I think perhaps we were a little too generous with Mr. Capasso's money, and we should reduce it a bit."

Over Leventhal's protest, Judge Gabel granted Andy Capasso's request to reargue the case and, pending the outcome, slashed the alimony payments in half, from $1,500 a week to $750 a week. She also reduced the child support payments by another $100 a week to $250.

By the middle of July both sides in *Capasso* v. *Capasso* had submitted their arguments to Judge Gabel in writing. Andy's lawyers contended that Andy could not afford to pay the alimony as well as pick up all of the other bills. While his annual income approached $1 million a year, his attorneys argued that most of that income was already committed to pay income taxes and debt service on money he had borrowed for real estate and tax shelters. They contended, too, that Nancy was earning a substantial salary as a real estate broker and that she had access to about $200,000 in savings accounts.

Nancy disputed her husband's claim that he couldn't afford to pay her. "He has substantial monies which will enable him to continue his luxurious life style," she claimed in court papers. "If I do not receive relief from the court, then my husband will be able to force me to use up my limited resources in order to attempt to get me to settle this case on his terms."

Departing from the usual practice of referring all motions to the pool of law assistants for review, Judge Gabel decided to handle the *Capasso* v. *Capasso* case herself that July. "I think I will do this one myself, Howie," Leventhal recalled the judge told him.

Of the thirty-seven hundred motions that passed through her chambers during the entire twenty-seven-month period she presided over the matrimonial division, the Capasso case was the only one she handled alone. She explained years later that she wanted to handle it herself because it was "one of the biggest, if not the biggest, income-type cases that I had."

On July 21 the lawyers in *Capasso* v. *Capasso* appeared in her courtroom to make their arguments over how much Andy should pay. His lawyers called Nancy's request for $1,500 a week "unfair." Nancy's lawyers retorted that Andy wanted Nancy to "starve" out of "vengeance" for having been thrown out of their Fifth Avenue home.

Although Judge Gabel was more impressed with the arguments made by Andy's lawyers than Nancy's that day, she reserved her final decision in the case. In fact, she did not reveal her decision for almost two more months. By the time she did, Bess Myerson had given the judge's daughter a city job.

Just a few days after the two had met at the dinner party on that Friday night in June, Bess called and invited Sukhreet to the opening of Joseph Papp's New York Shakespeare Festival in Central Park and to the dinner Papp was giving for VIP guests before the performance. Sukhreet was delighted to accept and happy about making a new friend.

Bess later said she found Sukhreet to be charming and bright that summer. So did Bess's close friend, Sandy Stern, who attended the performance in the park with them that night. "And Sandy is not impressed by anyone," Bess said later.

Sukhreet got another call from Bess a few days later, suggesting they meet for dinner at the Chinese restaurant Foo Chow on Third Avenue, just a few blocks from Bess's apartment. Over dinner, Sukhreet recalls, Bess appeared to be intensely interested in what she had to say.

Sukhreet remembers telling Bess how she became interested in the sociology of culture at the University of Chicago and how she had always been intrigued by museum administration. She said Bess told her that her background might possibly qualify her for a job at the Department of Cultural Affairs. "We can certainly find you something to do with museums," Sukhreet recalls Bess said that night.

"She also suggested that I should go to law school," Sukhreet said. "I told her, 'I've just come from a Ph.D. program, a pretty tough place. I don't know if I'm prepared for law school and to start a whole other career.'

"And she said, 'You could go to Fordham,'" referring to Fordham University Law School. "It's right next to the Department of Cultural Affairs. I can fix it so that if you have classes during the day or if you have to study, your hours can be arranged so that you can work and go to law school together.'"

As they were talking about Sukhreet's future, Sukhreet remembers, a dark-haired, heavyset man in his late thirties wearing an expensive suit approached their table, came up behind Bess, and put his arm around her. "C'mon, Bess, let's go," Sukhreet remembers the man said. "My friends are waiting for us at Abe's Steak House next door, and we're all waiting for you, Bessie. C'mon."

"Really, I'm here with Sukhreet," Bess replied, according to Sukhreet. "I'd much rather finish my dinner and be with Sukhreet for the time being. I'll join you when I'm done."

From the proprietary way he put his arm on her shoulder, Sukhreet assumed the man was a romantic friend, but Bess did not identify him, and Sukhreet thought it would be impolite to ask who he was.

Over the next few weeks, Sukhreet said, Bess called her several more times, inviting her to go with her to the movies, to join her on long walks, and to meet her for dinner or visit her at her apartment.

Sukhreet was delighted with her new friendship. Bess was helping her with all areas of her life, promising to help fix her up with men, to put her on a diet, and to advise her on subjects ranging from what makeup she should wear to what quality of paper her résumé should be typed on. Bess even gave the résumé to a professional writer on her staff to jazz it up.

Sometime in the middle of July, Sukhreet remembers, Bess suggested that she consider joining the Department of Cultural Affairs staff as a volunteer until a full-time position became available. Sukhreet said she was told that she could begin the job as soon as Bess returned from her two-week trip to Europe. Sukhreet agreed in the hope that it might turn into a full-time position.

She recalled telling her mother that summer about all of the wonderful things Bess was doing for her and about the possibility of a job at the Department of Cultural Affairs.

Judge Gabel did not let on that she already knew about her blossoming friendship—from Bess. "Sometime in July, if I'm not mistaken," said the judge, "Bess called me up and told me that she was taking Sukhreet on as a volunteer, a full-time volunteer, and then later on she told me that she was trying to get her put on the payroll but didn't know how successful she would be, and then eventually she did."

What Sukhreet, and, for that matter, Nancy Capasso and her lawyers, did not know that summer of 1983 is that Judge Gabel and Bess were communicating regularly. They had at least five face-to-face meetings according to a specially commissioned mayoral report, and they frequently left messages for each other at their offices, usually on their private lines, according to telephone logs. Judge Gabel's secretary and top aide remembered answering the judge's private line on several occasions that summer and taking messages from Bess, who usually identified herself as "the commissioner."

Other times, in an apparent attempt to disguise her identity, Bess left messages under assumed names: Barbara Goodman or Mrs. Robinson. Once when Howard Leventhal asked Judge Gabel about the Mrs. Robinson who left frequent messages, he said that she told him: "Oh, that's Bess. She's byzantine. . . . "

Remembering those phone conversations, Judge Gabel later said they usually spoke about Sukhreet. "I was very eager for Sukhreet to find this kind of interesting work, and I wanted her to be in public life. I was certainly being nice to Bess, not only because I liked her, but because Bess showed an interest in my daughter. . . ."

On July 22, the day after Andy Capasso's lawyers made an oral presentation before Judge Gabel on why he could not afford to pay $78,000 a year in alimony, Andy and Bess departed for a trip to Europe. "Mr. Capasso was extremely distressed by the divorce," Bess later said. "All these reports that I stole this man—I was appalled by it. I could just see the tension in his face. So I said, 'I'm going to Europe. Would you like to come?'" They spent a few days on a yacht in the Mediterranean and then a few more days in the south of France.

If Andy was hoping to escape his marital troubles and his ex-wife, he was to be disappointed.

At the elegant Hôtel du Cap in Cap d'Antibes, where Bess and Andy were staying, they ran right into Nancy in the lobby. "I guess the world isn't big enough for both of us," Nancy remembers telling her husband. She was staying with a girlfriend at a nearby Monte Carlo hotel, and they were going to have lunch at the Hôtel du Cap, but they decided to leave.

Although Bess was convinced that Nancy was following them, Nancy later claimed she had no idea Andy and Bess were staying at the hotel and called the episode an "unfortunate coincidence." "I thought I was hallucinating. It was freaky. Halfway around the world, at the same moment, at the same place. It was just awful. I've never been back to the south of France."

Shortly after Bess and Andy returned from their European vacation, Bess invited Sukhreet out to Andy's Westhampton Beach house for the weekend. Sukhreet was grateful for an opportunity to escape the scorching summer heat of the city, and she drove out to eastern Long Island on the first weekend in August.

Soon after she arrived and found Bess sitting by the pool, Bess led her on a tour of the house, which included a stop inside a small room used as a walk-in closet. Sukhreet watched as Bess bent down and opened a chest of drawers, revealing a drawer full of bikini tops and bottoms. "She pointed them out to me and mentioned that they were not hers, but that they were her friend's ex-wife's." Bess must have been obsessed with Nancy's bikinis. The maid once recalled Bess trying on Nancy's swimsuits and modeling them for Andy.

After the house tour, Sukhreet was introduced to Andy. She found Andy to be "polite but distant."

Over the weekend Sukhreet spent time beside the pool, watched Andy and Bess play tennis, and joined them for dinner at a seafood restaurant. She met Bess's daughter, Barra, who had rented a house nearby for the summer with her husband, Brian, and daughter, Samantha. At one point that weekend Bess and Andy went off to a party and left Sukhreet at the house. She was livid. "I was shocked. I thought this was incredibly rude. . . . I felt, gee, if I ever had a houseguest, I would take them along. But again, I didn't have the assertive skills that I have now, and I didn't know what was going on. What could you say? I put up with it."

Bess did invite her, however, to accompany them to a gathering at the home of her close friend, Dr. Ted Rubin, and his wife, Eleanor. As Bess was getting dressed, Sukhreet said Bess started thinking aloud: "I don't know whether I ought to be doing this, whether I should bring you or not, and Andy is not in favor of it, but I am going to do it. Oh, by the way, what was your married name?"

"I told her that my married name was Revis," Sukhreet later said.

"Well, I want you to use that name at the party. If you tell anyone your name, you tell them your name as being Revis," Sukhreet remembered Bess told her.

Sukhreet thought Bess's request was peculiar, but she agreed to go along with the plan. As it turned out, she didn't have to identify herself as Miss Revis. "No one asked. No one cared," she said, adding that Andy and Bess did not introduce her to anyone at the party, not even to the host and hostess who greeted them at the front door when they all arrived.

Before Sukhreet left the next afternoon for the long drive back to New York, Bess said she expected to see her in the office at the Department of Cultural Affairs the following morning to begin work as a volunteer. Sukhreet said Bess had told her that she wanted her senior staff to get to know her so they would help find room in the budget to hire her.

As a volunteer, Sukhreet accompanied Bess to performances of the New York Philharmonic and board meetings at the Henry Street Settlement House. She also accompanied Bess one night that August to the Jamaica Arts Center in Queens, where Bess had been asked to deliver a speech. As they walked into the building, Sukhreet said, they spotted a photographer from the *New York Daily News*. Bess told Sukhreet not to stand next to her: "It's too early for us to be seen next to each other. My staff won't like it," Sukhreet remembers Bess saying. It seemed plausible to Sukhreet, and she stepped back. After the speech Bess instructed Sukhreet "to work the room" and introduce herself as Bess's assistant. "I was a diplomat's wife and a politician's kid. It was standard operating procedure for me.

"I thought that Bess was, in a sense, you know, giving me a chance to strut my stuff to see if I could try and do these things. I thought that I had a very thorough interview process. I mean, I couldn't have been more thoroughly looked over."

On the weekend of August 20 Sukhreet returned to Westhampton Beach for another visit with Bess and Andy. This time they spent more time together. On Saturday afternoon they drove to nearby Mattituck to spend an hour visiting with her mother, who was staying with friends. Sukhreet said she felt close enough to Bess that summer that she asked for advice as a friend, not as her boss. "I am not your boss. I am not your friend. You are my child," she said Bess told her at the time.

Until that weekend in Westhampton Beach, Sukhreet said, she had no idea her mother was ruling on the Capasso divorce case. She found out on Sunday morning from Bess and Andy's maid.

Sukhreet awakened at around 9:00, got dressed, and walked across the lawn from the guest cottage to the main house for breakfast. In the kitchen she found Shirley Harrod peeling vegetables at the kitchen sink. As Harrod fixed her toast and tea, it occurred to Sukhreet that she had never formally introduced herself, so she stuck out her hand and said, "Oh, by the way, my name is Sukhreet Gabel."

"Oh, hello. I'm Shirley Harrod," the maid said, and then she began thinking aloud. "Gabel? Gabel is a very familiar name. Isn't there a Judge Gabel?"

"Yes," Sukhreet replied.

"Oh, you know there is a judge—isn't Judge Gabel presiding over Mr. Capasso's divorce?"

Sukhreet said she was stunned. "Secretly, silently, internally, I went, oh my God. It had never occurred to me in a million years. I knew that my mother was a judge. I knew that she was in Part V, which was divorce court. I knew that Andy Capasso was getting a divorce, but I never put it together. It never entered my mind. So I was absolutely taken aback, but I didn't think that it was appropriate to show that feeling to the maid, so I quickly changed the subject to the most bland thing I could think of. As I recollect, I was talking about the swimming pool. I wanted to talk about anything under the sun but that."

When Andy and Bess finally came downstairs for breakfast around 10:00 or 11:00, Sukhreet said, she did not bring up her conversation with the maid. "I mentioned absolutely not a word of it. I was their houseguest. If they hadn't mentioned it to me and hadn't hinted to me, . . . it was simply good manners not to bring it up."

That afternoon she sat by the pool and then walked over to the court to watch Andy and Bess play tennis. Before leaving for the drive back to the city, Sukhreet said, Bess told her that she might be able to go on the payroll that week.

On the three-hour drive back into the city, Sukhreet thought about what the maid had said about her mother ruling on Andy's divorce. She later said she suspected it "wasn't kosher" for her mother to be ruling on the case while Bess was trying to find her a full-time job. But what bothered her even more was that she thought that her mother was once again intervening in her life. "I felt, oh, for Christ's sake. I am thirty-four. Am I ever going to escape my mother? Can't I have my own friends and my own relationships without my mother getting involved?"

When she arrived home at about 5:30 P.M., she called her parents in Mattituck, where they were staying for another week. As she remembered it, her father answered the phone.

"Hi, Dad. How are you? How's your weekend? I was out at Bess Myerson's place in the Hamptons—you know she stays out there with her boyfriend, Andy Capasso . . . and I learned that mother is presiding over Andy's divorce case. What in the hell is going on?"

"Never mind. Don't get involved. Your mother knows all about this," is what Sukhreet later recalled her father said. "Let her handle it. You keep looking for a job. Just don't get involved."

Years later her father would not remember that conversation at all.

Following her father's advice not to get involved, Sukhreet did not mention anything to Bess at the Department of Cultural Affairs the next day, when she resumed her responsibilities as a full-time volunteer. She was close to getting a job. That afternoon Bess sent Sukhreet downstairs to the agency's personnel director to fill out a job application form so all of the paperwork would be ready for Sukhreet to go on the payroll as soon as a "budget line" could be found.

Two days later, on Wednesday, August 24, Bess called Sukhreet into her office. It was Sukhreet's thirty-fourth birthday.

"Happy birthday," she said Bess told her. "How about the title of special assistant to the commissioner?"

After eighteen months Sukhreet finally had a job. She called up her parents, who were still vacationing in Mattituck, and told them the good news. "My mother was delighted," Sukhreet said.

On the following Monday, August 29, Sukhreet went on the payroll. The same day, her mother returned from Mattituck and was back on the bench at the state supreme court in Manhattan. After having been away for almost two weeks, Judge Gabel faced a crowded calendar and a stack of papers to go through on her first day back in the office. One of the cases on her calendar that afternoon was *Capasso* v. *Capasso*. The lawyers from both sides were scheduled to be in her chambers at two o'clock that afternoon.

Before leaving on vacation, Judge Gabel had drawn up a draft of her final decision in the case and had turned it over to her law secretary, Howard Leventhal, telling him to make it more "legalistic." After looking over the judge's draft and seeing that the judge had decided to cut Nancy's alimony from $1,500 a week to $500 a week, he told her that he thought she had reduced it too much.

"Well, this is what I think is appropriate," he said she replied at the time.

Although Judge Gabel had already drafted a decision in the Capasso case, she asked the lawyers involved to appear in her chambers once again to make their arguments in person. Leventhal later said he thought it strange that the judge was requesting to see the attorneys again, but she told him she wanted to question the lawyers on certain minor points before making her final decision.

That afternoon Judge Gabel asked the lawyers for Nancy and Andy to provide her with additional information on several issues, including how much electricity Nancy used at the Fifth Avenue apartment, so she could figure out how much of the utility bill Andy should be expected to pay.

She did not indicate to them that she had drafted an order lowering Andy's alimony and child support payments.

The next night, on August 30, Judge Gabel walked a few blocks with her husband, Sukhreet, and Sukhreet's friend Tony Babinec to a Chinese restaurant to celebrate their daughter's birthday and new job. Bess met them there for dinner and toasted Sukhreet's future. She picked up the $66 tab, paying for it with Andy's Diners Club card.

Two weeks later Judge Gabel issued her final decision in the case, slashing Nancy Capasso's temporary alimony payments from $1,500 a week to $500 a week and the child support payments from $350 a week to $180 a week. The judge also decided not to require Andy to pay $5,000 to Nancy for an accountant to examine his business records. The decision, however, continued to require Andy to pay the mortgages and maintenance on the couple's properties, although Judge Gabel said he no longer had to pay the more than $300 a month for utilities in the Fifth Avenue apartment.

While the new decision cut Andy's child support payments, he was still responsible for paying for the children's tuition, religious education, camp, and clothes. But this provision was never included by the judge in the final court order issued two weeks later.

Not surprisingly, Nancy was unhappy when her lawyers called her with the news. They told her not to worry. They intended to appeal Judge Gabel's decision, and they were confident it would be overturned.

On the day the judge issued her decision, the *New York Post* ran another story about Bess and Andy, along with a photograph of them standing together on the steps outside City Hall. Judge Gabel later said that was the first time she knew there was a connection between Bess Myerson and the *Capasso* v. *Capasso* divorce matter.

Her secretary, Brenda Shrobe, remembered walking into the judge's office that morning with a copy of the article. She had taken numerous messages from Bess Myerson on the judge's private telephone line that summer, and she knew that it was Bess Myerson who had finally hired Sukhreet.

"Did you know anything about this?" she asked angrily.

"No," Judge Gabel replied.

That weekend Andy and Bess celebrated with champagne and chocolate cake at the estate in Westhampton Beach.

And within a few weeks, Bess's driver, Nelson Pagan, later said, he was in Bess's office one afternoon when she asked him to deliver a bouquet of flowers to Judge Gabel. The flowers actually had been sent to Bess, but she inserted a new card, rewrapped them, and sent them off with Pagan, who delivered them to the judge's apartment building.

Andy's celebration of the judge's decision was short-lived, however, because less than two weeks later Nancy renewed her offensive against her husband in court. Her lawyers submitted a motion to the judge asking that Andy be barred from keeping his two children overnight at his Westhampton Beach home while Bess was there. The motion marked the first time that Bess's name showed up in the *Capasso* v. *Capasso* divorce papers.

Gabel asked Howard Leventhal to handle Nancy's motion. Since there were no allegations that Bess and Andy were engaging in indiscreet conduct while his children were visiting, Leventhal recommended that Nancy's request be denied.

"Is this a correct decision?" Judge Gabel asked him.

"Yes," he replied.

26
"Tough Love"

From the moment she took office at the Department of Cultural Affairs, Bess encountered hostility from some members of the senior staff. For one thing, the acting commissioner, Randall Bourscheidt, was bitterly disappointed that he had not been made commissioner. Bourscheidt, a tall, blond, cool-headed administrator, had been at the agency for some time as the former commissioner's top deputy. According to other high-ranking agency officials, he had a difficult time hiding his disdain for Bess's cultural credentials.

To many people in the arts community and within the agency, Bess was not considered to be "of the arts." As one former senior staff member explained, "Maybe she sat on the stage and played the piano at Carnegie Hall, but she wasn't of the arts. She was of politics."

Bess's "tough love" management style also did not endear her to the staff. She shocked some employees when she announced during her first staff meeting that she "knew all about city employees" and that they didn't like to work. According to one staff member, Bess told of her decision while commissioner of consumer affairs to send an employee to the basement and that that employee was never heard from again.

Soon after she arrived at the agency on April 24, 1983, senior staff members inquired as to whether she intended to hire a special assistant. Bess told them she felt that her secretary could take care of whatever a special assistant might do and that she didn't need or want an amanuensis. So when Bess announced later that summer that she planned to hire Sukhreet Gabel as a special assistant, some members of her staff were surprised that she had changed her mind. At first no one knew that Sukhreet's mother was Judge Gabel. "Nobody had a clue about any connection at all," a senior staff member said.

Sukhreet, however, was not as discreet about her family connections as Bess might have liked her to be. Shortly after she was put on the payroll she mentioned to Judith Gray, a friend of Bess's who had recently been hired as a publicity director for the agency, that her mother was presiding over the Capasso divorce.

Gray was stunned. She later told investigators that she confronted Bess and asked her how she could hire Sukhreet in light of Judge Gabel's role in the divorce case. Gray said Bess told her it was not a "big deal" because Sukhreet would fill a role in the agency. She also said that she felt sorry for Sukhreet because she had a difficult relationship with her mother.

"What am I going to do with you?" Sukhreet said Bess asked her when she found out that Sukhreet was telling people in the office that her mother was ruling on the Capasso divorce.

Soon afterward she found herself spending less time in Bess's company either as her friend or as her special assistant. Bess did not ask her to accompany her to evening performances and board meetings as frequently as she had in the past.

Sukhreet was also assigned to work for other supervisors on a variety of projects, such as distributing Carnegie Hall concert tickets to senior citizens' organizations and school groups. Other assignments included making a borough-by-borough breakdown of arts groups funded by the agency.

Sukhreet brought all of her research skills to bear on the project. She spent days on it, dramatically expanding the project's scope as she came up with nearly a dozen variables by which to examine the agency's programs, including breakdowns of cultural institutions visited by adults versus children, by minority groups versus nonminority groups, by out-of-state versus local visitors. It was an earnest effort, but she missed her deadline. "It did not make a good political impression to do more than what was assigned," she said later.

By early October, just a little more than a month after she began working full-time, senior staff members were in Bess's office complaining that Sukhreet's job performance was unsatisfactory. She was missing the thrust of assignments. She was taking too long to complete projects. She couldn't seem to focus on her work.

What further annoyed the senior staff members was the way Sukhreet "acted as though the commissioner could not do anything to her because she knew something." One former cultural affairs staff member said Sukhreet once told her that she was concerned about what might happen "if it ever came out that my mother is a judge and if the papers ever found out."

The papers did find out. On October 17 Susan Mulcahy, then editor of the *New York Post*'s "Page Six," got a tip that Bess had hired the daughter of a judge ruling on her boyfriend's divorce case. Mulcahy remembered that her source told her that "it was no coincidence." She assigned reporter Richard Johnson to the story, and he started making phone calls that day.

All inquiries from the press for Bess were directed routinely to her press secretary, Richard Bruno, and Johnson's was no exception. Bruno took down Johnson's questions and told him he would get back to him shortly with a response from the commissioner. Bruno went straight into Bess's office to tell her that the *New York Post* wanted to know whether Sukhreet was Judge Gabel's daughter and how she had come to be hired at the agency.

Bess was furious. She was convinced that Nancy Capasso and her lawyers had gone to the press. She told Bruno that Sukhreet was, in fact, the daughter of Judge Gabel, but that everything, except for a few housekeeping matters in the divorce, had been decided before Sukhreet had been hired.

For "damage control," she instructed Bruno to tell the reporter that she had had nothing to do with Sukhreet's hiring and that Sukhreet had been referred to the agency by Herbert Rickman of the mayor's office. Bess also pointedly reminded Bruno that he too had interviewed Sukhreet for the position.

Following Bess's instructions, Bruno returned Richard Johnson's call and told him what he later acknowledged was a series of lies and misleading statements about Sukhreet's hiring that were reported as facts in the next day's paper.

Minutes after Bruno left her office, Bess walked over to Sukhreet's desk to ask if she had received a call from Johnson. Sukhreet replied that she just got a message that he had called and she was about to call him back. "Well, Bess at that point was beside herself with anxiety, and she began fluttering around," Sukhreet said.

Bess instructed her instead to wait until after lunch to return Johnson's call. The plan was that Bess and Bruno would listen in on the conversation over their extensions. "And whenever Mr. Johnson would ask me a question, I was to pause, and after being fed the appropriate answer, I was to respond," Sukhreet said.

Resentful of the way she was being treated, Sukhreet returned from lunch five minutes early and called Johnson herself. "I figured, I'm an adult, and I'll answer these questions as honestly as I can. And I finally said, he's calling me. He's calling me, goddamn it. I'm a thirty-four-year-old woman, for goodness' sake, so stop treating me as though I were seventeen, which some people seem to have this enormous tendency to do."

She dialed Johnson's number: "Hello, my name is Sukhreet Gabel, from the Department of Cultural Affairs, and I understand that you've been trying to get in touch with me.

"And he said, 'Yes, Miss Gabel. Is it true that your mother is Judge Gabel?'

"Yes, it is."

Just then Bess stepped off the elevator and walked past Sukhreet's desk. Her face darkened when she saw Sukhreet on the phone. "Is that Richard Johnson?" she whispered. Sukhreet nodded. Bess drew a slashing line with her finger across her neck to indicate Sukhreet was to hang up. But Sukhreet ignored her and resumed her conversation, lying to Johnson that she knew nothing about the divorce or Bess's involvement with Andy.

As soon as she hung up, Bess summoned her into her office and angrily told her that she did not expect her employees to disobey her orders. "Now, what did you tell Mr. Johnson?"

Sukhreet recounted the conversation, expecting Bess to be pleased that she had misled Johnson. But Bess remained cold and distant and sent her back to her desk, where Sukhreet called her mother to see if Johnson had interviewed her as well.

He had, and the judge told Sukhreet that she was worried. "I hope it blows over. I'm really nervous about the press picking it up," she remembered her mother telling her over the phone.

With a newspaper reporter now on her trail, Sukhreet sat at her desk and began to daydream about being swept up in a public scandal, the object of intense press scrutiny and public curiosity. The image of Megan Marshak, the woman who was with Nelson Rockefeller when he died, popped into her mind: "Do you remember that all of a sudden she would have her picture taken every time she would leave her apartment? Well, I imagined myself as Megan Marshak, another homely photo girl."

The next morning, across the top of the *New York Post*'s "Page Six" ran the headline "Small World: Bess hires kin of divorce judge."

> New York is a big city—but it can be a small world. That's the way the folks at the Department of Cultural Affairs explain the hiring of the daughter of the judge who's handling the divorce of Bess Myerson's boyfriend. . . .
>
> The connection appeared to be a surprise to everyone, including the judge, who told Page Six's Richard Johnson, "I didn't even know Bess Myerson was involved in this [divorce case] until I saw a piece on Page Six a few weeks ago. . . ."
>
> The official word from the department came from Assistant Commissioner Richard Bruno: "I interviewed her [Sukhreet] and I hired her. She was among a number of applicants and she was the outstanding candidate. . . ."

Judge Gabel picked up a copy of the *New York Post* on her way into the courthouse that morning and read the article alone in her chambers. She was deeply troubled. She thought that maybe she should recuse herself from the case. "I felt, when I saw the clipping, it seemed to me maybe it might be considered to be in bad taste or wrong somehow for me to represent them," she said later.

Walking out of her chambers, clutching a copy of the *New York Post* in her hand, she asked her secretary and top aide, "Did you people see this story? Do you think in view of this article that I should offer to recuse myself from sitting on the Capasso case?"

"I think it would be a good idea, Judge," Leventhal replied.

By coincidence, the lawyers involved in the *Capasso* v. *Capasso* case were scheduled to appear before her that morning on another matter that needed to be resolved right away, before the divorce went to trial: Andy's request that the court allow him to remove a $192,500 Cy Twombly painting from the living room of the Fifth Avenue apartment so he could sell it and use the proceeds to obtain a bond for a major sewer construction job.

At 11:55 A.M. that day the lawyers and Judge Gabel met in her robing room to discuss the *Post* article and whether she would continue to preside over the case.

Nancy's lawyer, Raoul Lionel Felder, insisted that Judge Gabel stay on the case. "I think we have been dealt with squarely here," said Felder. "I think you win some, you lose some. I have some decisions in this case I am happy with, I have some decisions in this case I am unhappy with. I'd be very surprised if it were otherwise. I am perfectly satisfied. If I have problems, I appeal. I think I got a fair shake, my client got a fair shake here. I have no motions to make."

"That's fair," Judge Gabel replied.

Andy's lawyer, Alton Abramowitz, said that he was also "perfectly satisfied to keep the case here."

"I will accept this acknowledgment with considerable appreciation," Judge Gabel said. "As all of you know, my pride in my reputation for calling the shots as I see them is supported now by the statements that you and Mr. Abramowitz have made, and under the circumstances I shall proceed to hear argument on this pending motion."

Raoul Lionel Felder would say later that he might have asked Judge Gabel to recuse herself from the case if he had known then about the extent of her relationship with Bess during the spring and summer of 1983 and the circumstances surrounding Sukhreet's hiring. He said Judge Gabel did not disclose all of the facts to him that afternoon and said nothing to clear up the impression in the *New York Post* that Bess had had nothing to do with getting Sukhreet her job.

As Herb Rickman read the *New York Post* that morning in his tiny City Hall office, he was deeply distressed to find his name in "Page Six." He couldn't believe the paper had been told that "the official

word" from the Department of Cultural Affairs was that *he* had referred
Sukhreet to the agency and that Bess had had nothing to do with
Sukhreet's hiring.

Just a month before the article appeared, Rickman later testified, he
had warned both Bess and Judge Gabel that it was a big mistake for
Bess to hire Sukhreet Gabel while the judge was presiding over the
Capasso divorce case. Hadn't they considered the blatant appearance of
a conflict of interest that her hiring suggested?

But Rickman said Judge Gabel told him she didn't want to talk about
it. And Bess had assured him that Sukhreet's hiring had been "cleared"
through City Hall. For that reason, Rickman said, he did not mention
the situation at the time to his longtime friend and boss, Mayor Ed
Koch, whose office was just down the corridor from his at City Hall.

But now that his name was being dragged into a mess, Rickman said,
he told the mayor that he had had nothing to do with Bess's decision to
hire Sukhreet Gabel. According to Rickman's recollection, Koch told
him not to worry about the "Page Six" article because Bess had called
and said she was sending him a letter with a full explanation.

Relieved, Rickman called Richard Bruno and Bess to tell them that he
never wanted to hear his name linked with Sukhreet Gabel again.

At the Department of Cultural Affairs that morning copies of the
New York Post article had made their way onto virtually everyone's desk.

Bess called a senior staff meeting to discuss how she should respond.
Sukhreet was not invited. She was busy following Bess's orders to make
a list of everything she had done since she arrived at the agency and to
put together a package of letters of recommendation and references so
that Bess could have them on file.

According to Richard Bruno, who attended the meeting, Bess wanted
to send a letter to Mayor Koch that would cast the most favorable light
on Sukhreet Gabel's hiring. The task of writing the letter fell to Bruno.
Bess dictated the key points she wanted him to make. The letter was sent
to City Hall in the hands of her city driver the following day. Bess also
had her driver drop off a copy at Judge Gabel's home.

Dated October 19, 1983, the letter read:

Dear Ed:
Because of yesterday's incomplete and misleading article in the *New York
Post* about my hiring of Sukhreet Gabel, I felt that I should provide you
with a succinct and thorough outline of the facts and sequence of events.

Through July and the beginning of August, Richard Bruno, whom I
had recently appointed Assistant Commissioner in charge of public
affairs and development, began to organize this new unit, reassigning
people already on staff and interviewing them for one actual and several
possible openings. Among the two dozen people that he interviewed was

Sukhreet Gabel. She had originally applied to the Office of Economic Development, to staff the international business development desk. At that time, no position was available at OED, and she was advised to investigate possibilities at other city agencies. She sent her résumé to the Department of Cultural Affairs, and an interview was arranged.

Both Assistant Commissioner Bruno and Deputy Commissioner Randy Bourscheidt recommended her to me as a bright, enthusiastic, articulate and a potentially valuable employee. Several projects that suited her skills emerged almost at once. . . .

I made this decision in the context of having known her mother, Judge Hortense Gabel, for many years, as a judge of the highest integrity whose reputation is impeccable, and in light of the fact that the matrimonial actions involving Mr. and Mrs. Capasso had been in the courts since February. Most of what was to be decided had already been decided in the first six months, a major part of it in favor of Mrs. Capasso. Thus it seemed to me that not only was there in fact nothing improper in this action, but any basis for inferring or attributing the appearance of impropriety was absent. In fact, I have just learned that lawyers for both sides requested Tuesday morning (the day the article appeared) that Judge Gabel continue with one piece of unfinished business which was before her on that day.

During the past six weeks, Sukhreet has worked diligently, expanding the ticket distribution program so that it encompasses an ongoing collaboration with the Department for the Aging, meeting with foreign visitors, and doing important research and writing for both my Deputy and Assistant Commissioner. Her performance has been excellent. She represents the Department and the city well. I do not regret my decision. A person who is that highly qualified should not be discriminated against because her mother is a public figure. I regret only any embarrassment or concern that the *Post*'s interpretation of the situation may have caused you or the Department.

As always, I look to you for wisdom and advice.

Sincerely,
Bess

Bess's old friend, the mayor, had no reason not to believe her detailed account, and after reviewing it with his chief of staff, Diane Coffey, he sent Bess a note on October 21, 1983, expressing confidence in her decision to hire Sukhreet:

I have your note of October 19 commenting on the hiring of Sukhreet Gabel. While your note wasn't necessary, I do appreciate your having thought to write it. Based on the recommendations made to you, her talent and your own appraisal, you did exactly the right thing in filling an open job with an able person.

Soon after Bess sent her October 19 letter to Koch, Sukhreet said,

Bess told her to go and thank Richard Bruno for "getting her off the hook."

Although her title was special assistant to the commissioner, Sukhreet found herself virtually isolated from Bess after the *New York Post* article appeared. The invitations to accompany Bess to evening performances or to meetings outside the office, which had slowed down when Sukhreet began telling department employees who her mother was, became even rarer. And now Sukhreet spent most of her time working under other supervisors.

As part of being pushed aside, Sukhreet said, she was given such assignments as coming up with a cleaning contract for the building.

Then, she said, Bess asked if she had any business cards with her title as special assistant to the commissioner. When Sukhreet showed her a box of four hundred cards, she said, Bess took them from her and dumped them into the trash as she watched.

"Do you have any others on you? How many have you handed out?" Bess demanded.

"Only a few," Sukhreet replied.

Sometime later, Sukhreet said, while she was attending a function for foreign diplomats, Bess noticed her collecting business cards. "She walked up to me, and she said, 'You weren't giving out any business cards, were you?'

"And I said, 'No. These are simply ones that I have received.'

"'What have you got there? I want to see what's in your pocket,'" Bess said as she reached into the pockets of Sukhreet's blazer to see if she was telling the truth.

The clearest message, Sukhreet says, was the assignment of her desk under a reorganization. She had expected to be moved to a desk right outside of Bess's office, but instead she was given a desk on the same floor next to the lavatory in what she called "Siberia." "While I normally don't care very much about the size of my desk or whether or not I have a window, I felt that there was a message in being put next to the lavatory. I was very upset."

As soon as she found out where her desk had been placed, she went into the ladies' room, turned on the water, and began to sob. A few minutes later she heard a knock on the door and a voice saying, "Who's in there?"

It was Bess.

"It's me, Bess, Sukhreet."

"Open up," Bess ordered.

Bess walked past Sukhreet, who was standing at the sink, and used the facilities behind another door. When she emerged, she must have noticed Sukhreet's red eyes and swollen face.

"Well," she said, putting her hand on Sukhreet's shoulder, "you've just got to learn to roll with the punches, kid." Then she walked out the door.

Another time that fall, Sukhreet said, Bess suggested she visit a psychiatrist at a clinic that offered prospective patients an evaluation for $50. Sukhreet said she agreed to go and visited a doctor there for two months before deciding it wasn't doing her any good.

Sukhreet complained to her mother about the harsh treatment she was getting, and her mother called Bess and asked why Sukhreet could not have a desk outside of her office. Sukhreet said her mother told her that Bess intended to give her more interesting assignments, such as drafting legislation to be presented to the city council, but that assignment never came to pass.

Although Sukhreet's relationship with Bess had cooled noticeably since the *New York Post* article, she decided to host a small dinner party for Bess in her studio apartment that December, following the diplomatic custom of entertaining your boss. Among the people she invited were Bess, Herb Rickman, her parents, and Bob Vanni, the counsel for the department. Sukhreet said she was seated only a few feet away from Bess in the one-room apartment when she overheard Bess talking about her to Bob Vanni. "I can't understand Sukhreet. She makes me crazy. I just don't know what I'm going to do about her," she heard Bess say.

Sukhreet was astonished. Didn't Bess know she could hear what she was saying? And how could she say such things at a party Sukhreet was giving in Bess's honor? Struggling to fight back her tears, Sukhreet went into the kitchen and started washing the dishes.

It was then that Sukhreet realized she had to start looking for another job, and the following week she began making inquiries at other city agencies. Judge Gabel started calling on her friends again as well. She contacted the director of the state's women's division on Sukhreet's behalf and wrote a letter to a prominent attorney, saying that she believed "Sukhreet's international and language skills are excellent and that she has excellent administrative and negotiating abilities." But no interesting job offers came her way.

Meanwhile, her job performance at the Department of Cultural Affairs declined in the eyes of her superiors. In early 1984 Deputy Commissioner Randy Bourscheidt complained in writing to Richard Bruno about Sukhreet's job performance. Bourscheidt's note, labeled "For your eyes only," included a copy of a memo written by Sukhreet. Bourscheidt evidently thought Sukhreet's memo was so bad that it required no other explanation from him than "This is the quality of work I get from Sukhreet."

Her memo concerned comments Bourscheidt might make when introducing author John Updike at a February 1984 dinner in Updike's honor:

To: Randy
From: Sukhreet
Date: 24 February 84
Subject: John Updike Dinner
I have spoken to Mrs. Zwicker, Zwick and others. All they want you to do is to stand up and say "Welcome to the city of New York" and sit back down, in two or three minutes.
You might want to say:
"New York, as the great metropolitan center of culture for the region, for the country, and for the world is a large factor in any writer's experience. I would, however, like to digress and spend just a moment discussing the economic and social impact of John Updike's work on the city of New York. We, New Yorkers, spend a good deal of money and expend a lot of emotion on writers. Mr. Updike's work has provided the grist for the mills of countless animated cocktail and dinner conversations and those are, of course, a major New York industry. John Updike's work has been the subject of scholarly treatises and has provided employment for many of our resident professors and concomitantly keeps our students off the streets and home instead with a good book. New York newspapers are filled with reviews and bestseller list notations. John Updike, of course, is a main stay. Perhaps Mr. Updike's most important economic contribution to the city of New York is to its very large publishing industry. Thank you, John Updike for helping the city of New York to stay financially and emotionally afloat and welcome."

The quality of her work became the talk of the senior staff. Richard Bruno decided to bring it to Bess's attention after he claimed Sukhreet failed to complete an assignment properly for him. He had asked her to obtain some biographical material on some well-known people for a project he was working on. When she told him she was unable to find material on some of the people, he noted that he found the information himself in *Who's Who*. In a nasty letter to Sukhreet, Bruno wrote, "I feel that you performed a barely adequate job on what for you should have been a routine assignment."

In a meeting with Bess, Bruno told her that there was "universal dissatisfaction" in the agency with Sukhreet's performance. He said Bess told him she was surprised to hear that, but if he felt that way, he should put it in writing.

On May 8, 1984, Bruno sent Bess a memo outlining Sukhreet's failings. "Too many days just show too little activity, or at least the work is not sufficiently documented," he wrote. "Although she is not without talents and abilities, after some ten months, it is my opinion that her particular skills do not match with any current needs here at DCA. I feel that given other critical personnel needs, keeping Sukhreet on staff is a luxury that we can no longer afford."

After Bess received the memo, she called Sukhreet into her office and told her the senior staff wanted to have her fired. "She said that I shouldn't worry, that she was going to protect me," Sukhreet said later.

Sukhreet was now just biding her time, preparing to leave the Department of Cultural Affairs as soon as she could get another job somewhere else. Her mother continued to look for her as well and, in early June 1984, finally interested one of her friends, Marcella Maxwell, in hiring Sukhreet.

Maxwell, formerly the dean of Medgar Evers Community College in Brooklyn, considered Horty Gabel a mentor and a friend. She had called the judge for her advice when she sought Koch's appointment to become the city's commissioner of human rights. Judge Gabel had sent a letter of recommendation on her behalf. On May 19, 1984, Maxwell was appointed to the post.

A few days later Maxwell and her husband were having dinner with Judge Gabel and her husband at the Gabels' apartment when the judge suggested that her daughter, Sukhreet, might be an asset to the commission. She explained that Sukhreet was having some personality problems with Bess and that she was looking for another job. The judge thought Sukhreet might make a terrific executive assistant because of her background in sociology and race relations at the University of Chicago and her knowledge of languages.

Maxwell was intrigued, and she told the judge that she would call Bess and ask permission to hire Sukhreet away from cultural affairs. "And Judge Gabel said, 'I have her telephone number. Why don't you make a call?'"

Maxwell dialed Bess's home telephone number from the judge's apartment and got Bess on the phone. "Bess, you know I am going to be heading the human rights commission, and I am going to be building a staff, and I would like for you to consider letting Sukhreet come and work with me because of her background. I'd like her to serve as my executive assistant," Maxwell explained.

"You need a black executive assistant," she said Bess replied.

"Is there anything wrong with her work or any reason you wouldn't want to let her go?" Maxwell asked. "And the only thing she said was that she was 'a little pretentious.'"

Maxwell asked Bess to think about it, and then she rejoined the Gabels. Judge Gabel naturally wanted to know what Bess had said, but Maxwell was too embarrassed to repeat Bess's comment that Sukhreet was pretentious. She told Judge Gabel only that Bess was reluctant to let Sukhreet go.

Within a few weeks Maxwell interviewed Sukhreet for the position, and after reading a letter Sukhreet wrote detailing her academic studies and interest in race relations, she decided she would hire her for a $40,000-a-year position as deputy executive director.

Determined not to let Bess block her way, Sukhreet submitted her resignation on Friday, June 15, 1984. She said Bess was furious. "She no longer had control over me," Sukhreet said. The following Monday she started work in her new job as deputy executive director for the city's Commission on Human Rights.

It immediately became apparent, however, that Sukhreet would not fit into the organization well. "Sukhreet came in with a lot of very strange notions about how a professional person acts, dresses, and behaves," said one senior-level staff member. "She came sashaying into the dingy, dirty offices, wearing flowing white outfits and little hats. She looked like she was going to a tea party."

Sukhreet did not seem to be able to function in her new role. "She saw the world in a way that no one else did," said the senior-level staff member. "She could not follow through on substantive material. She made up stories about why she couldn't get things done. She would take two- and three-hour lunches, telling us she was 'networking.' I could not think of allowing her to address a group."

"I would say, 'I need this,'" said the senior staff member, "and she would put on a smile, make excuses, and attempt to be cute. She was a darling child who never grew up."

One of Sukhreet's first assignments was to help organize Marcella Maxwell's July 14 swearing-in ceremony at City Hall. As the event drew near, Maxwell and her staff discovered that Sukhreet had failed to accomplish virtually all of her assigned tasks. When they asked to see a sample of the invitation, Sukhreet told them she had not yet designed it. Then, just before the ceremony, she finished writing the speech for Maxwell to deliver at the event. By the end of July Maxwell concluded she had to fire Sukhreet.

Before telling Sukhreet, Maxwell thought it would be best to explain to her old friend, Judge Gabel, why she felt she had to fire her daughter. She suggested they meet for lunch at a Greek restaurant across the street from the courthouse.

Over lunch Maxwell explained that Sukhreet was "unable to function within the framework of the new direction the agency is taking, and I am going to have to let her go."

"She will kill herself," Judge Gabel said.

"What are you talking about?" Maxwell asked.

"She's in deep therapy," Judge Gabel replied.

"I was very upset," remembered Maxwell. She agreed to permit Sukhreet to resign from the agency "in order not to destroy her."

Two or three days later Maxwell received a phone call from Bess

Myerson, whom she barely knew, inviting her to come to the Department of Cultural Affairs for lunch. They agreed to meet on August 7.

Over lunch that day Bess talked about herself and her accomplishments as cultural affairs commissioner and offered Maxwell tips on how to persuade the city's Office of Management and Budget to increase her agency's budget. In the middle of describing her own "excellent presentation" to the city's budget director, Bess blurted out without explanation: "You have to fire Sukhreet Gabel."

Maxwell was shocked. She did not ask Bess to elaborate. She had not mentioned to anyone except Judge Gabel that she was unhappy with Sukhreet's work and that she was thinking of letting Sukhreet go. She was surprised that Bess would tell her to fire Sukhreet when Bess had never indicated during their earlier telephone conversation that there had been anything wrong with Sukhreet's work at the Department of Cultural Affairs.

Three days later, on August 10, Maxwell asked Sukhreet to resign from the agency. Sukhreet was deeply disappointed that her new job had not worked out.

Having no idea that Bess had suggested to Marcella Maxwell that she should be fired, Sukhreet accepted an invitation from Bess to attend a party that weekend. She now thinks that Bess was kind to her so that she could extend control over her.

Unemployed once again, Sukhreet started writing more letters and going to more interviews. Her mother once again joined in the job search, writing on her behalf to Nat Leventhal, the president of Lincoln Center, and also to a theatrical producer she knew.

What made that summer bearable for Sukhreet, however, was a young Englishman, John Levinson, who was working as a consultant for a management consulting firm in Manhattan. They met one warm summer night in August through mutual friends at a concert in Central Park. She fell deeply in love. He was tall, charming, and well educated, having attended Oxford, Cambridge, and Harvard. And he must have been taken with Sukhreet's considerable charm and impressed by her international background. Within two months she had moved into his apartment and they were engaged to be married.

That October they planned a trip to England so she could meet his mother before the wedding. On the night before they were supposed to leave, Levinson told her he didn't want to see her anymore and asked her to move out of his apartment. She said he didn't explain why he wanted to end the relationship.

Sukhreet was devastated. Not only had she lost her job; she had also lost the first man she had loved since Jan Revis. Once again sadness overwhelmed her and she plunged deeper and deeper into another severe depression that left her unable to get out of bed in the morning.

Out of desperation her father called Tony Babinec, her old boyfriend in Chicago, and asked him to come to New York to visit Sukhreet. "She was in pretty bad straits when I visited in October," Babinec later said. "When I [lived with] her, she could never sit still and be idle, she was usually shining shoes, polishing shoes, doing things around the house.

"But she didn't want to deal with the outside world. She just wanted to spend time around the apartment. She had no interest in pounding the pavement for a job. That seemed to last. There was no visible difference for months. In February or March '85 when we expected her to have shaken all that, she hadn't really changed. That's when they started to talk about electroshock for the first time."

Sukhreet agreed to the electroshock therapy and underwent twelve to fifteen sessions at a doctor's office before the depression lifted.

She resumed her job search, but she felt that her eleven-month stint in city government was an unexplainable blemish on her résumé. She blamed Bess for her failures and grew angry at what she saw as her mother's constant meddling in her efforts to find a job. A few years later, her resentment would explode.

27
Capasso *v.* Capasso

On the scorching-hot summer morning of July 31, 1984, Nancy Capasso waited for the movers to take her belongings out of the two-bedroom condominium in Westhampton Beach and move them into the basement of her mother's condo in the next town. She was furious that she had to leave and turn over her keys to Andy under the terms of the separation agreement dictated months earlier by Judge Gabel.

It didn't seem fair to Nancy that she should have to give up the oceanfront condominium every other month when Andy had been granted exclusive use of their nearby $3.5 million waterfront estate. Why did he need a two-bedroom condo at the beach when he had a five-bedroom house down the road to entertain Bess, Mayor Koch, and his other new friends? But none of Judge Gabel's rulings had seemed fair to Nancy ever since she found out Bess had hired the judge's daughter at the same time the judge cut her substantial alimony and child support payments by more than half.

It seemed to Nancy that virtually every ruling favored her estranged husband. Over Nancy's strong objections, Judge Gabel had granted Andy permission for Bess to be an overnight guest while the children were visiting. Judge Gabel had granted Andy's motion to sell the couple's $192,500 Cy Twombly painting so that he could obtain bonds for his sewer business and improve his cash flow. And Judge Gabel had ignored Nancy's request that she reconsider her decision after Nancy discovered that Andy had bought a $1.6 million Park Avenue apartment, which indicated that he was hardly suffering financially.

Nancy was surprised that no one else saw, at the very least, an appearance of impropriety with Sukhreet Gabel working for her husband's girlfriend. She had expected the gossip item in the *New York Post* to result in city and court officials calling for full-scale investigations. But nothing happened at all. None of the other newspapers had picked it up. No one had bothered to check out Bess's version of the circumstances surrounding Sukhreet's hiring.

The city and state investigative bodies, including the state Commission on Judicial Conduct and the state special prosecutor for the court system, failed to pursue it. The city's own Department of Investigation, which investigates misconduct in city government, did not look into the matter even after department officials received an unsigned letter spelling out further how Sukhreet had been hired.

Not even Nancy's lawyer, Raoul Lionel Felder, thought the gossip page item offered enough evidence to request that Judge Gabel remove herself from the case.

When she asked him in January 1984 to submit a motion that Judge Gabel recuse herself, Felder responded in a letter, stating that he could not make such a motion "in my professional judgment." He said he thought the best strategy was to appeal any decision that she did not like to the higher courts. "I have seen absolutely no evidence, nor have I been presented with any evidence, of any impropriety or anything of that nature concerning the judge," he wrote in the letter. "I hardly think an item in a gossip column qualifies as grounds for making such a serious motion. . . . Therefore, since as you indicate the making of this motion is of powerful and extreme importance to you, the choices are quite simple: substitute a lawyer who will feel he can make this motion commensurate with his professional responsibility, or continue with this office without the motion having been made. . . ."

Before hiring another lawyer to represent her, Nancy agreed to wait and see how the Appellate Division would rule on her appeal of Judge Gabel's decision reducing her temporary alimony payments from $1,500 a week to $500 a week and child support payments from $350 a week to $180 a week.

Felder proved to be right. On March 1, 1984, the Appellate Division voted five to zero to reverse Judge Gabel's September 30, 1983, order, calling her original decision to grant Nancy $1,500 a week "realistic and just in terms of the financial situation of the parties. . . ."

The Appellate Division also suggested that if Andy was worried about the hefty alimony payments he now had to pay until the divorce was final, he should cooperate with Nancy by turning over his business records for her lawyers and accountants to review, so they could all "proceed expeditiously to trial."

Andy was reluctant to have Nancy and her band of lawyers and accountants rummaging through his business records. For one thing, it was his position that Nancy did not have a stake in his sewer and construction business. In his mind, it was not a marital asset to be carved up under the state's equitable distribution laws.

He also did not want her lawyers examining his checks and receipts, because he knew he had something to hide.

Although she had won on appeal, Nancy decided to change lawyers.

She was still unhappy that Felder had not asked Judge Gabel to step down. She hired a new lawyer, Herman Tarnow, to handle her upcoming divorce trial.

To avoid disclosing his business records and paying thousands of dollars in attorney fees at a divorce trial, Andy agreed to meet with Tarnow over breakfast in June 1984 to discuss settling the case out of court. It soon became clear, however, that Andy and Nancy were millions of dollars apart at the bargaining table.

Estimating that Andy's net worth, including his business, totaled $15 million, Tarnow told Andy that he was looking for $7.5 million for Nancy to settle the case. But Andy insisted that Nanco was not part of the equation and that he didn't have that kind of money. He offered to give Nancy $1.5 million to $2 million and to sign a judgment for divorce right away.

Nancy turned the offer down. As a real estate broker in Manhattan, she knew what apartments cost on the Upper East Side, and she did not think that was enough money for her to buy a fancy apartment, furnish it, and live comfortably for the rest of her days. She told him she would take her chances at a trial.

In late June and July Tarnow scheduled depositions with Andy, one of the first steps in gathering information about his finances for trial. A tough-talking, street-smart divorce lawyer who goes for the jugular, Tarnow spent much of his time at the first depositions questioning Andy about how much money he spent on his mistress, Bess. Ostensibly he was trying to determine Andy's income and expenses during the marriage, but what he was really doing was showing that settling the case on Nancy's terms might be easier than having to answer his questions and dragging Bess's name through a divorce trial.

But Tarnow was wrong. His questions only made Andy angrier and more determined not to give in to Tarnow's demands for $7.5 million.

In July Nancy gave Andy another reason to consider settling the case. From one of Andy's former employees she had heard that he was involved in a scheme that could get him into trouble with the Internal Revenue Service and possibly put him in jail.

Over the years he had developed a scam that generated $1.5 million in cash for him through the creation of phony liability claims. He randomly selected dozens of people's names from the Coles directory (which lists people by their street address) who lived near ongoing Nanco construction projects. He made out corporate checks to them, but, of course, none of the individuals named as payees on the checks had ever filed claims against Nanco, nor did they ever receive the proceeds of the checks. Instead Andy directed his employees to endorse the checks fraudulently, cash them at the European American Bank, and then turn the nontaxable cash income over to Andy. It paid for the seaplanes, European vacations, and lavish lifestyle he enjoyed with Bess.

On July 25, 1984, at an all-day pretrial deposition with Tarnow, Andy became worried that Nancy might have found out about his scheme and that she might try to blackmail him into giving her a large divorce settlement. Andy figured that was the only reason Tarnow was pressuring him during the deposition to turn over "insurance claims."

Tarnow did not know the extent of the scheme, but he sensed that Andy was extremely sensitive about his "insurance claims," so he pushed him on the issue by requesting that Andy bring copies of the in-house claims with him to the next deposition on August 2.

The request for the in-house insurance claims worried Andy. He tried to call Nancy several times over the next few days but was unable to reach her. Finally he contacted her by phone at the condominium in Westhampton Beach on the morning of July 31. He wanted to ask her to tell Tarnow not to request the insurance claims or ask him any more questions about them. When the telephone rang that morning, Nancy was waiting for the movers to arrive.

As soon as she recognized Andy's voice, she switched on a tape-recording device that she had bought after Tarnow advised her to tape her conversations with Andy. That way, she could play them back to Tarnow and they could discuss negotiating strategy.

Andy got right to the point. "I want to talk to you about an issue that is obviously rather sensitive, which is this line of questioning which your attorney is on," he began. "I want to know what you have in your mind."

"In regards to what?" asked Nancy, playing dumb.

"What are these insurance claims he is asking about and the things he is looking for?" Andy asked.

"I am not quite sure," Nancy replied.

"You're not sure?" Andy said in disbelief.

"No."

"Well, obviously you told him something. You must know something that I did, and you obviously told him, and that is what he is pursuing."

Nancy paused. "I would rather not talk on the phone. I would rather come and see you over the weekend or next week and we'll talk."

"I don't want to wait until the weekend," Andy said. "Thursday is the day he intends to ask me these questions, and I want you to tell him not to. If you care to tell him not to and if you don't care to tell him not to— you know, I would like to know that too. . . . If you want to take something and go to the authorities with the hopes of having me put in jail, I suppose I'd like to know that."

"I would never do that," Nancy insisted. "Okay? I would never do that. . . . You are the father of my children. I care about you, unfortunately. And I will not ever pursue jail, nor will I ever get you in trouble. You have my word."

But Andy continued to ask about her intentions and Nancy reiterated her promise, until finally she said she might be interested in a "trade-off."

"Tell me what a trade-off means," Andy said.

"I don't know. The beauty queen," she said.

"Who is the beauty queen?" Andy asked.

"I have enough on her."

"You have enough on who?" Andy asked.

"The beauty queen," Nancy replied, referring to Bess.

"What does enough mean, that you have enough on her in what regard?" he asked. "In what regard do you have anything on her? Do you think because I bought her a lunch it is in conflict of interest with the city? He wasted four days on lunch and dinner with her and twenty minutes on my financial statement. Your interest is in my financial statement. In case you're interested, that is where your interest lies, not who I had lunch with."

"Your lunch comes out of my money," she said.

"My income isn't your money," he said angrily.

Nancy tried to get off the phone, but Andy refused to end the conversation until she promised to tell her lawyer not to ask for the insurance claims.

"I will call you back," Nancy promised. When she hung up the phone, she realized that his concerns over the insurance claims had dramatically changed the balance of power in their negotiations for a settlement. She decided to play hardball.

That night she called Andy and told him she would instruct her lawyer not to ask any more questions about insurance claims if he agreed to return her jewelry, which she contended he stole from her at the beginning of their divorce action, and if he made her a "fair and generous settlement." Andy told her that he did not have the $7.5 million that she was looking for, and he again offered to settle the case for $1.5 million to $2 million.

Nancy found that figure unacceptable. But when they tried to negotiate, they both found they could not get past their bitterness. Though Nancy had known about Bess for almost two years now, she could not let go of her anger over being rejected for an older woman. And Andy would not let her forget that she had had him kicked out of their Fifth Avenue apartment.

"You are going to pay," Andy told her that night on the phone. "You're going to pay for throwing me out of that apartment. You're going to pay."

"We can't negotiate," Nancy said finally.

"When I finally settle with you, if the number is twenty dollars, then I am going to say you are going to get nineteen dollars, because the dollar

I want for throwing me out of the apartment. Okay? You're going to pay for throwing me out of that apartment. I'm telling you that now. I told it to Tom. I told it to Felder. And I'm telling it to you. You're going to pay for throwing me out of that apartment. . . ."

"And you are going to pay for your girlfriend."

Finally, after more than an hour on the phone, Nancy again promised to call him back the following day to tell him what she would do about the insurance claims.

Before calling Andy, Nancy told Tarnow how worried Andy had sounded about turning over his insurance claims. They agreed that Tarnow should take over the negotiations.

She called Andy the following morning and told him that she had authorized her attorney to negotiate on her behalf. She also reassured him that she did not want to put him in jail and that she had asked Tarnow not to request the insurance claims until after Andy had proposed a settlement.

After feeling utterly powerless in Judge Gabel's courtroom, Nancy felt that she now stood a chance to get a fair settlement from her husband. She not only had the insurance claims; she had him on tape virtually admitting that he had committed a crime.

A few days later Andy met with Tarnow to discuss a settlement. According to Andy, Tarnow opened the conversation by calling him an "asshole" and telling him that he had to agree to a $7.5 million settlement or he would be going to "Danbury" (federal prison). Andy said Tarnow also told him, "Bess Myerson goes down the drain next week."

Andy was disgusted. "You know, like I should shudder and maybe pay 7.5 million dollars for that," he later told Nancy. He despised people who did not treat him with respect, and he deeply resented anyone who backed him up against a wall.

Unable to negotiate with her lawyer, Andy tried to explain his situation to Nancy. He wanted to sit down with her and show her the numbers, but she declined. She did not want him to confuse her with explanations of his complicated business deals. She just wanted him to come up with a dollar figure close to $7.5 million. And unless he did, she told him, she would just as soon go to court and have a judge determine the worth of their marital assets, including Nanco.

When Andy said that she could never prove in court that Nanco was a marital asset, Nancy exploded in anger. "Don't worry about what I prove when I go to court," she yelled into the phone. "Right now you don't have to worry. Till then you can just run around . . . and you can flash your lights with your flashy sixty-year-old broad and look like the asshole of New York. Okay? It's almost embarrassing that you were my husband. Okay? That you look like such an asshole to the world . . . because she buried bigger and better than you, kiddo, and she'll bury you too. Or maybe she won't bother burying you. She's too old. . . ."

Andy tried to steer the conversation away from Bess, but it was impossible once Nancy got going.

"I'm not the Nancy you once knew," she told him, her voice rising. "I got real smart. I was a real asshole. Okay, I'm not an asshole anymore. That I promise you. Somebody said, 'Boy, they'll feel sorry when Nancy gets back on her feet' when I was having a nervous breakdown at our fancy beach house two summers ago and crying in a limousine. You know, 'cause I was a dope and I didn't want to believe what was happening, okay? Well, I'm on my feet now, okay? And I'm on them square. . . ."

Andy insisted that she would not receive a penny more from him after a court battle and that she would have to end up paying $100,000 to $150,000 in attorney fees.

"I don't know if I can afford to go to court," he said. "I may go broke."

"So go broke," Nancy said angrily. "I don't give a shit. Go broke. Go drop dead. I don't care what you do. Take Bess. . . . She's almost a senior citizen. Fucking asshole that you are. You're going with a fucking senior citizen with liver spots. So gross. You fucking putz, what's she doing to you? . . . You chucked your whole life for her. What an asshole you are. People laugh behind your back. . . . She did you real good. Breaking up the home of five children."

"Nobody can break up a home, Nancy," Andy interrupted. "You know that. You lost me, okay? You lost me. . . . No woman stole me from you. No woman's capable."

Their conversation ended once again with no progress having been made toward settlement. They tried again over the next few months to negotiate but to no avail. Any hope Nancy had of prodding him into offering a better settlement by threatening to expose his insurance claims did not materialize.

By the fall of 1984 Nancy was looking for a trial date. Still Andy refused to provide access to his financial records, which her lawyers needed to build her case. Meanwhile other issues, which needed to be resolved before their divorce was settled, continued to crop up, such as who would pay for repairs at the Fifth Avenue apartment building.

Even though Judge Gabel left the court's matrimonial division in June and was no longer ruling on divorce cases, Nancy discovered in December 1984 that Andy's lawyers were trying to have Judge Gabel continue to make rulings in her divorce case.

Without her attorney's knowledge, Nancy wrote to Judge Gabel asking that the judge voluntarily remove herself from the case. The letter, dated December 22, 1984, began:

Dear Justice Gabel:

I am the plaintiff in this action. My attorney, Herman Tarnow, did not participate in the preparation of this letter, and does not even know that I am writing it.

I am appealing to you directly to disqualify yourself from my case because I have no other alternative. Since the inception of this case, your decisions have endangered my ability and that of my two small children to subsist pending the ultimate trial of this matter. And I have recently learned that motions in our case made after you left the matrimonial part will be referred back to you.

I do not mean this letter to be accusatory, but I think a review of your prior decisions will raise in your own mind the possibility that something might have interfered with your sense of justice and fair play.

(As you know, the *New York Post* reported on October 18, 1983, that your daughter was employed by Bess Myerson, who is my husband's acknowledged paramour in this case. I want to believe that this fact did not interfere with your decisions. Miss Myerson was later named the co-respondent in this case.)

I will briefly refresh your recollection of the standard of living enjoyed by Mr. Capasso, and myself, and our two children prior to our separation. . . .

Nancy then proceeded to enumerate in her letter the costly trappings of the lifestyle to which she and the five children had become accustomed—the fleet of cars, expensive vacations, and a huge summer home. She complained that Judge Gabel's decisions caused hardships for her family. The letter concluded:

That we are surviving this ordeal at all is due entirely to the Appellate Division's reversal of your decisions. Because we have heard of your fine reputation for protecting women in my circumstances, your decisions in my case are inconsistent with your rulings in other cases, and are inexplicable. I am sure that you can see this.

In sum, the only appropriate action you can now take is to remove yourself from my case. For the record plainly represents, at the least, an appearance of impropriety.

Respectfully yours,
Nancy Capasso

Nancy said she never received a reply.

Judge Gabel later acknowledged that she read the letter and threw it away. It was found years later crumpled up in the file.

She made no other rulings in *Capasso* v. *Capasso*.

Over the next few months, through the spring of 1985, Andy made several more attempts to settle the divorce before going to trial. As he had feared, Tarnow and Nancy had finally been given permission by the courts to go through his business records.

All of the records were spread out on a table in a conference room in Andy's Long Island City company headquarters. Nancy worked with Tarnow and an accountant to try to piece together Andy's complicated business dealings. Among the documents they found a bundle of mysterious checks made out to cash to dozens of individuals. While they did not know the full extent of Andy's scheme, Tarnow and Nancy made copies of the checks. In any event, Tarnow thought, the checks would help prove his case that Andy was worth much more than he claimed. As it turned out, the checks were eventually linked to Andy's insurance claims scheme.

The trial date was finally set for July 8. A few weeks before that day Andy made one last attempt to settle the case. He called Nancy and doubled his original offer to almost $4 million. He wanted the divorce out of his life, he said, so he could get his mind back on his business and get on with his life.

"I wouldn't make the same mistake of marrying her like you," Andy said.

"So what do you get out of her?" Nancy asked.

"What do I get out of her? I get peace and tranquillity, because I'm not married to her."

"She doesn't look like the type to give peace and tranquillity," Nancy said.

"Maybe not. But at least I'm not married to her. If I was, it would be worse than with you. . . . Where's she going to go? I'm her only outlet."

"Oh," Nancy said. "She doesn't have any other beaux?"

"Maybe she does. Who gives a fuck? She does me a favor."

"Oh? What favor?"

"I don't have to see her every night. That's the favor."

They talked for another half hour but still were unable to reach a settlement.

In the days before the trial, Tarnow attempted to increase the pressure on Andy by going over to City Hall and meeting with Mayor Koch's top counsel, Patrick Mulhearn, about calling the mayor and special mayoral assistant Herb Rickman to testify that their good friend, cultural affairs commissioner Bess Myerson, had committed adultery. Tarnow knew that both Koch and Rickman had visited Andy's Westhampton Beach home while Bess was living there, and he knew that Andy and Bess would not want Mayor Koch called to testify at Andy's messy divorce trial.

During their meeting, Tarnow said later, he told Mulhearn he considered it improper that Bess had accepted gifts from Andy, since he was a city contractor. But Mulhearn said the gifts were not unethical because "they are good friends." Tarnow also later said that he brought up the fact that Sukhreet Gabel was hired by Bess while Judge Gabel was presiding over the case. Mulhearn insists, however, that Tarnow did not discuss Sukhreet's hiring with him at all.

On July 8, 1985, the divorce trial *Capasso* v. *Capasso* opened in the Manhattan courtroom of state supreme court justice Andrew R. Tyler, who did not have a reputation for distinction on the bench. In November 1977 Tyler had been convicted of committing perjury for lying to a grand jury about meeting with a convicted gambler. The jury's verdict, however, had been overturned without an order for a retrial. Later Tyler was indicted on another charge for improperly granting bail to a defendant, but that charge was dismissed before trial.

Nancy was worried about Judge Tyler's well-known friendship and political connection to Stanley Friedman, the powerful Bronx Democratic party boss, who was a close friend of her husband's. Andy had hired Friedman on a few occasions to represent him on various matters. Friedman was a powerful figure in city government at the time. He was said to control dozens of key jobs in the city's Department of Environmental Protection, the city agency that awarded Andy his multimillion-dollar sewer contracts.

Nancy recalls feeling as if she wanted to turn on her heel and walk out the door. Once again she was up against the city's powerful pols and judges, and after her experience with Judge Gabel, she thought she would have no chance of getting a fair trial. She told Tarnow that she wanted to request that another judge handle their case, but Tarnow explained that they had insufficient grounds on which to ask Tyler to recuse himself. "Let's make a record, and we'll win on appeal," he told her.

Since the most important issue in the case was money, the lawyers agreed to get some other issues out of the way, such as to whom the divorce should be granted. Both Andy and Nancy were accusing each other of adultery, and neither wanted to waste days proving the other's allegations, so Nancy abandoned her plan to call Bess Myerson and Mayor Koch to the witness stand to prove that Andy had committed adultery. In exchange for her not pursuing that tack, Andy agreed to give her the divorce on the grounds of cruel and inhuman treatment.

With the first phase of the divorce case now over, the lawyers began the fight over Nanco and the couple's extensive real estate holdings, property that was worth millions of dollars.

Andy took the stand first. Adamant that Nancy should not be awarded any portion of his sewer business under the state's equitable distribution law, he denied that she had played any role whatever in the - forming of the company. He also claimed that she did not entertain his business associates, like other wives, and that she did not contribute much to the household because they had had full-time servants for years. He did acknowledge, however, under cross-examination, that he had made Nancy an officer in the company. "But she was only a figurehead," he insisted. "She never did anything for the company, Mr. Tarnow. If she ever did anything for me, it was in the form of a favor, but she did not work for the company, and even when she was on the payroll for the company, it was in a no-show position. . . ."

While Nancy decided against using the incriminating tape recordings in which Andy pleaded with her not to go to the authorities, Tarnow cross-examined Andy on the stand about the dozens of mysterious checks used in his insurance claim scheme. Andy's lawyer did not let Tarnow go very far before objecting on relevancy grounds. Judge Tyler agreed.

The twenty-one-day trial extended over four months. In the middle of August Tarnow tried his next tactic—Bess Myerson. He sent a subpoena requesting that she appear in court to testify at the trial and that she bring along with her "all records of expenses paid on your behalf." Tarnow contended that Andy had squandered at least $100,000 in "marital assets" on Bess and that that money should be added to the pot, to be divided in half.

On August 28, the day she was to show up in court, a lawyer, Leonard Shalleck, appeared on Bess's behalf and requested that Judge Tyler quash the subpoena, arguing that her testimony and the documents sought were not "relevant or material to any of the issues here."

But Tarnow said that he needed her testimony to prove "the wasteful dissipation of marital assets" on an "adulteress" and gave as examples Bess's use of the Capasso family car and Nanco limousines, Andy and Bess's seaplane hops, and their trips together, all of which Andy had paid for.

Andy's attorney, Sam Fredman, argued that all Tarnow wanted to do was embarrass Bess and use her because she was a public figure.

Judge Tyler agreed to quash the subpoena. Bess did not have to appear in court at all.

Even though he did not have Bess's testimony, Tarnow continued to hammer away at Andy on the issue, asking him to detail his expenses and his business and real estate holdings.

Then, after Andy's testimony, accountants for both sides took the stand with their varying estimates of Andy's net worth, followed by real estate brokers who testified about the value of the Capasso properties and antique dealers who offered estimates on the value of the paintings and furniture in the Fifth Avenue apartment.

On September 11 Nancy finally got her chance to tell her side of the story. She painted a much different picture of the early days of Nanco, which she insisted was named after her. She described doing the payroll, dropping off bids, and handling the books. "I was very involved, always," she said.

By the middle of October both sides had completed their testimony and Judge Tyler asked the lawyers to present him with "findings of fact and conclusions of law," which would set forth what each side wanted in the divorce case and why. Tarnow was still looking for $7.5 million. Andy's attorney claimed that Nancy should get no more than $2 million, based on dividing up some of the real estate they owned together. He also claimed that Nanco was not part of the pie.

After almost two months of deliberation Judge Tyler issued his final decision on December 18, 1985. Although Nancy had been skeptical from the beginning because of Tyler's political connections with her husband's pal, Stanley Friedman, she was unprepared for his final judgment of divorce.

Judge Tyler had virtually lifted word for word the findings and conclusions proposed by Andy's lawyers at the end of the trial. Accepting Andy's contention that Nancy had made absolutely no contribution to the marriage as a wife, mother, or business associate, Judge Tyler concluded that she had no claim to Nanco and that she should not receive a penny more in alimony or child support payments. He granted her some of the proceeds of the sale of the Fifth Avenue apartment, along with the $200,000 two-bedroom condo in Westhampton Beach. The number added up to about $2 million, the same figure that Andy had offered her as a settlement a year before.

Andy got everything else.

Nancy was stunned. She couldn't believe it. Judge Tyler had granted every single one of Andy's wishes, down to the pieces of antique furniture and Royal Copenhagen china that he had asked to take from the Fifth Avenue apartment. Andy got the $1.9 million five-bedroom house on three acres in Westhampton Beach and both Palm Beach condos. Tyler also accepted Andy's assessment that his property in Long Island City was worth $268,000, even though Nancy's lawyer presented evidence that it was, in fact, valued at $4 million.

Most of the $2 million Nancy was awarded was to come from the sale of the Fifth Avenue apartment. And this was $1 million less than half of the apartment's appraised market value of $6 million in 1985. Tyler ruled that she receive only half of the market value in 1983, at the beginning of the divorce action, when it was valued at $3 million.

Just days after Tyler issued his decision Nancy called her original lawyer, Raoul Lionel Felder, and asked him if his office would handle her appeal. Felder's wife, Myrna, the former head of the New York State Women's Bar Association, is legendary in matrimonial circles for arguing appeals effectively.

At first Raoul Felder did not believe Nancy when she told him that

Judge Tyler had lifted all of Andy's lawyer's findings and conclusions verbatim. He asked her to send over both documents. She did. Felder was astonished. In his twenty-five years as a divorce lawyer, he said, he had never seen anything like it.

Felder agreed to waive his usual $50,000 retainer and, instead of charging $450 an hour, accepted a promissory note to be paid at the conclusion of the appeal. Determined to fight for what she believed was rightfully hers, Nancy turned once again to the court's appellate division for justice. She had let Andy make a fool of her during his two-year affair with Bess; she was not going to let him make a fool of her now. "I could have put up with it," she said. "I didn't have to make waves. But that isn't my style."

28
The Fifth Amendment

Bundled up against the cold in a full-length mink coat, Bess strode across the wooden platform in front of City Hall to the center of the stage bedecked in red, white, and blue. It was a few minutes before noon on January 1, 1986, a bright, sunny day, and as the unofficial first lady of New York Bess was presiding over the inaugural ceremonies for Mayor Koch.

Her arrival at the podium quieted the crowd. Almost three thousand people had packed City Hall Plaza in the thirty-nine-degree weather to witness the swearing in. Bess made a few welcoming remarks and spoke with confidence about the future, declaring, "These next four years will be even better years for our city, and for ourselves."

Then, as the band struck up "New York, New York," she introduced the mayor, "our CEO," and Koch bounded down the steps of City Hall, smiling broadly. He was jubilant about beginning his third term, having captured an extraordinary 78 percent of the vote in November.

Koch had come a long way since those days in 1977 when Bess held his hand at campaign rallies. He was now a national celebrity, a best-selling author, even the subject of an off-Broadway play. During his eight years as mayor he had won the respect of most of the city's movers and shakers for improving New York's self-image, lowering the crime rate, and making such tough decisions as cutting services and raising taxes to put the city back on its feet after its prolonged fiscal crisis.

Bess stood only inches away from her old friend as he put his hand on a 160-year-old Bible and recited the solemn oath of office. It was the second time in twelve hours that she had witnessed this scene. The night before, she and Andy had been among the thirty or so guests invited to attend the mayor's private swearing-in ceremony at midnight at a friend's Upper East Side town house.

For the public ceremony at City Hall Plaza, Andy sat in one of the folding chairs arranged in neat rows in front of the Federal-style building that housed the Koch administration. Also in the audience was the U.S. attorney for the southern district of New York, Rudolph

226

Giuliani, an aggressive and ambitious prosecutor who had become known as a latter-day Elliot Ness for having brought indictments against the leaders of New York's most notorious organized crime families and the head of the Sicilian Mafia.

As Giuliani listened to the mayor's inaugural address that day, his eyes roamed across the stage and focused on two of the guests who sat on the dais in seats reserved for the city's most powerful politicians—Queens borough president Donald Manes and Bronx Democratic leader Stanley Friedman.

Giuliani recently had received reports from the FBI office in Chicago about an undercover operation probing payoffs to officials of that city from collection agencies seeking contracts to collect overdue parking ticket fines. The Chicago investigation had turned up information that collection agency owners and public officials were engaged in a similar scheme in New York.

From his folding chair, Giuliani remembered, he wondered "whether it was all true or not," as the FBI reports from Chicago and his own preliminary inquiry suggested, that Friedman and Manes were among the politicians shaking down collection agencies in New York.

Giuliani once said he felt that with the exception of murder, selling away a public office was the worst possible crime. In the three years since he had arrived in New York from the U.S. Justice Department in Washington, Giuliani had developed a reputation for having an unyielding view of what was right and what was wrong.

An only child of Italian working-class parents—his father, whom he idolized, ran a tavern—Giuliani grew up in Brooklyn and Long Island. A devout Catholic, he had considered becoming a priest until he decided at twenty that he did not want to take the vow of celibacy. Instead his vocation would become the law.

The first member of his family to attend college, Giuliani went on to graduate from New York University Law School. He clerked for two years for a federal judge in Manhattan and then joined the U.S. attorney's office in Manhattan in 1975, where he rose to head the anticorruption unit. Giuliani's courtroom reputation for relentless and effective prosecution was sealed after former Brooklyn congressman Bert Podell folded under two days of Giuliani's fierce cross-examination and suddenly pleaded guilty on the stand to the corruption charges he had denied.

In 1975 former federal judge Harold R. Tyler, Jr., a prominent New York attorney, invited Giuliani to go with him to the U.S. Department of Justice in Washington. Tyler had just been appointed deputy attorney general by President Gerald Ford, and he needed an assistant. Giuliani, a lifelong Democrat who had worked on Robert Kennedy's senatorial campaign and had voted for George McGovern in 1972, changed his registration to the Republican party and joined the Ford administration.

He remained in Washington for two years and then followed Tyler back to New York to join Tyler's law firm as a partner. But despite the big salary of private practice, he found the work unsatisfying and returned to government in 1981, soon after Ronald Reagan was elected president. He took the number three job in the Department of Justice under U.S. attorney general William French Smith. Two years later he opted to return to New York to become U.S. attorney for the southern district of New York, a post widely regarded as the best local prosecutor's job in the country.

Back in his hometown, Giuliani announced that his top priorities would be narcotics, organized and white-collar crime, and public corruption. By January of 1986, having already indicted many of the leaders of the city's powerful organized crime families, Giuliani was turning his attention to public corruption.

At first Giuliani believed there was little high-level corruption in the Koch administration, especially when compared to other big cities around the country. But the reports from the FBI's Chicago office implicated some New York politicians as well and caused him to reconsider his views. He began to mobilize his office's considerable investigative powers to focus on some of the city's top elected and political figures.

In his inaugural address Koch spoke that day of "public service as the noblest of professions if it is done honestly and well" and praised his guests on the dais for performing "superbly as public servants."

Though Giuliani had grown suspicious of some of Koch's friends and political allies seated with him on the dais that day, he had no idea that the Chicago probe would soon spawn at least a dozen investigations in New York. Those probes would dramatically change the power structure of the city, fundamentally alter the way city government did business, and provoke an intense debate over ethics in government and the definition of right and wrong.

Eight days after the mayor's inauguration, in the early morning hours of Friday, January 10, a bizarre incident involving Donald Manes provided the first hint of scandal to come.

At 1:50 A.M. two city police officers pulled over Manes's city-owned, 1984 Ford LTD after noticing the vehicle weaving erratically on the Grand Central Parkway in Queens. They found Manes, speaking incoherently and near death, with a two-inch-long Y-shaped wound on his left wrist and a two-inch cut on the inside of his left ankle, near the top of his shoe. He had lost nearly one-third of his blood. A bloody kitchen knife with a stainless-steel four-inch blade was found on the floor in the front of the car.

Concerned that Manes might bleed to death while waiting for an ambulance, the police officers covered him with a blanket, put him into their patrol car, and rushed him to nearby Booth Memorial Medical Center. Slipping in and out of consciousness, Manes muttered something about being "cut" near Queens Borough Hall, which was a few miles away.

At the hospital, as surgeons worked until dawn to repair his wounds, Manes's family, closest friends, and aides arrived. Mayor Koch got there at around 3:15 A.M. after a close aide, Victor Botnik, who screened emergency calls for the mayor, awoke him with the news.

By 4:00 A.M. reporters from the daily newspapers and television stations had gathered outside the emergency room. Sometime around dawn Andy Capasso slipped into the hospital by a back entrance to try to see his old friend. Stanley Friedman arrived there, too.

The mysterious slashing of the powerful borough president dominated news coverage the following day. According to Manes, two men hiding in the backseat of his car had kidnapped him and slashed him. However, some reporters and police investigators suspected a suicide attempt, noting that a Y-shaped wound was more likely to be self-inflicted than the result of an attack. But no one could explain why Donald Manes, who had just won another term as Queens borough president and who talked about running for mayor in 1989, would attempt to take his own life.

Finally, on January 21, after the New York Police Department's chief of detectives announced that his investigators did not believe the kidnapping story, Manes read a five-paragraph statement from his hospital bed admitting that he had tried to take his own life. "There were no assailants, and no one but me is to blame," he said.

He refused to explain why he had been driving around or why he had attempted to kill himself. But two days later, on January 23, newspaper columnist Jimmy Breslin provided the explanation in a story that began on the front page of the *New York Daily News* under the headline "Manes Accused of Extortion":

> Michael Dowd, a Queens Blvd. attorney, last night told the United States attorney's office in Manhattan that Donald Manes, the Queens Borough President, extorted money from him for a period of 18 months. . . .
>
> This revelation causes the city's Parking Violations Bureau scandal to detonate. . . .
>
> It now appears that New York, under Mayor Koch, has the largest political scandal since Jimmy Walker was on the nightclub floor and his people were out stealing even the street lights. . . .

Breslin's column and subsequent reporting, for which he was later awarded the Pulitzer Prize, stunned many of the city's elected officials, including the mayor, who had trusted Manes as an able and honest politician.

The Manes revelations set off a media firestorm, creating new skepticism among law enforcement officials and the press about the way business was being done in New York. Within days Koch appointed a special commission to investigate any allegations of corruption in city government. And over the next few months law enforcement agencies throughout the city opened probes into allegations of corruption in the awarding of cable television franchises and city towing contracts, the operation of the Taxi and Limousine Commission, and the granting of a no-bid contract to a private developer to build a public parking garage in Queens.

The downfall of Manes, widely considered the city's second most powerful politician after Koch, also changed the way many of the city's newspaper and television reporters covered City Hall. Editors assigned additional reporters to probe city government contracts and possible conflicts of interest between elected officials and contractors. Public corruption became the ongoing story on television and in the city's newspapers.

With the cooperation of Dowd and others involved in the extortion scheme at the city's Parking Violations Bureau, Giuliani's investigation was also turning up information implicating Stanley Friedman, the popular Bronx County Democratic leader, who was also a close friend of Andy Capasso's.

Manes, meanwhile, was plunging deeper and deeper into depression. Under the care of a psychiatrist and taking antidepressant medication, Manes spent his days at his Jamaica Estates homes dressed in only a bathrobe. He saw only a few close friends during the weeks following his suicide attempt. Among those permitted to visit with him was Andy.

By the middle of March Manes was so despondent that he began to talk about suicide. His family tried unsuccessfully to persuade him to enter a psychiatric hospital for treatment. On March 13, in the kitchen of his home, Manes stabbed himself in the chest with a carving knife. He died minutes later on his kitchen floor.

Some members of the Koch administration had expected Manes's shocking death to bring an end to the Parking Violations Bureau probe, but Giuliani told reporters at the time that "nothing from this tragic incident creates an impediment to our investigation." The scandal had taken on a life of its own and had extended beyond Manes.

Since Breslin's January 23 column many of the city's reporters had been asking questions about the relationships between politicians and city contracts that had rarely been posed before. They scanned campaign contribution lists, looking for the names of city contractors who had donated heavily.

After two months the pressure on the press and other prosecutors to uncover wrongdoing was still intense. Now five prosecutors, four commissions, and several city and state agencies were all probing allegations of corruption that ranged from contracts for hospital supplies to ferry permits. So many investigations were undertaken by so many different law enforcement agencies that *New York Newsday* frequently ran a chart for readers called the "city scandal rap sheet."

It was only a matter of time before Giuliani's prosecutors would begin taking a closer look at Friedman's and Manes's other friends who held city contracts. By March they were looking at Andy Capasso, who had received $125 million in city contracts since 1981.

After reading about the federal investigation of Donald Manes and Stanley Friedman in the newspapers that spring, divorce lawyer Herman Tarnow called a friend in the U.S. attorney's office and suggested that he consider taking a close look at sewer contractor Andy Capasso and how he had won his lucrative city contracts.

Tarnow had known Assistant U.S. Attorney David Lawrence, a tall, slim, bearded former lawyer, since they had worked out together at a gym two years earlier. Tarnow thought that Lawrence might be interested in what he had learned while representing Andy's ex-wife, Nancy, during her bitter divorce: that Andy was a close friend of both Manes and Friedman and was also romantically involved with the mayor's longtime friend Bess Myerson.

Tarnow also told Lawrence about tape recordings that Nancy Capasso had made of telephone conversations with her estranged husband during their futile divorce negotiations in 1984 and 1985. In the telephone conversations, Tarnow told Lawrence, Andy expressed concern about having committed a crime and going to jail for it.

Lawrence was intrigued by Tarnow's call, and he decided to subpoena the entire sealed *Capasso* v. *Capasso* divorce record, which contained detailed financial records about Andy's company, Nanco, as well as hundreds of pages of depositions documenting the destruction of the marriage.

After reading the record, Lawrence met with Giuliani and suggested they probe Andy's city contracts to see what role, if any, his relationship with Bess, Stanley Friedman, and Donald Manes might have played in the $125 million in city contracts awarded to Nanco since 1981. Lawrence was also interested in trying to find out why Capasso had donated huge amounts of money to political campaigns, including tens of thousands of dollars to city comptroller Harrison J. Goldin, whose office was responsible for settling city claims against contractors.

Giuliani was interested in more than Andy's connections to powerful politicians. At the time, Giuliani was also prosecuting leaders of the city's organized crime families, and he wanted to know more about

Andy's relationships with crime syndicate figures. Andy's name had come up in a conversation among reputed mobsters on a secret tape recording made by the FBI in 1984 at the Palma Boy Social Club in East Harlem.

According to federal authorities, the reputed mobsters were discussing handing out projects in the concrete and construction industries. On the tape Louis DiNapoli, a reputed Genovese family member, can be heard telling Anthony ("Fat Tony") Salerno, the head of the Genovese family, about a talk he had had with Gambino captain Robert ("D.B.") DiBernardo.

"See, he talks smooth," DiNapoli said, describing Andy. "I don't know how to talk smooth. . . . He says that he was going to give us that job anyway. Who the fuck is Andy Capasso? Who the fuck is he to give you a job? I was shocked. D.B. told me that Andy Capasso told him, 'You know, even though they told me to give you the job on this . . . I was gonna give it to you anyway.' He wants to make himself the hero." DiNapoli laughed.

"Yeah, but Andy's looking to build a fucking cement plant," Salerno replied.

Giuliani also knew that Matthew ("Matty the Horse") Ianniello, a reputed captain in the Genovese family, was Andy's friend and former next-door neighbor. So he gave Lawrence the go-ahead to look into Andy's contracts with the city and his relationships with politicians and reputed mobsters.

Tony Lombardi, a former federal agent who had recently joined the U.S. attorney's office as an investigator, was assigned to the case. He had been gathering information about Andy on his own in his previous job as chief investigator for Mayor Koch's short-lived mayoral commission created that January to look into allegations of corruption. The commission had been disbanded because so many different law enforcement agencies were working in the same areas.

One of the first things Lawrence did was gather copies of all of Andy's city contracts with the city's Department of Environmental Protection. He discovered then that Kevin Ford, a lawyer with the city's Department of Investigation, had already been looking at Andy's contracts for several months. Ford was brought over to the U.S. attorney's office and made a special assistant U.S. attorney so that he and Lawrence could work together on the case.

In the middle of March Lawrence sent a subpoena to Nancy Capasso asking her to come to the U.S. attorney's office to talk with him.

Andy heard about her subpoena and offered to provide her with an attorney. But she did not trust her ex-husband and politely refused. She went alone and answered Lawrence's questions. She did not, however, volunteer to turn over the tape recordings or the photocopies of the canceled checks for the phony insurance claims that she had discovered during the divorce case. She suspected that Andy would be in deep trouble if anyone heard his comments on the tape or looked at the canceled checks. As she had told Andy, she had no interest in seeing the father of two of her children go to jail.

On March 31, however, Lawrence did not give her any choice. He sent Nancy another subpoena, this time requiring that she turn over to him the tapes, along with any and all documents, canceled checks, computer disks, electronic wire transfers, invoices, contracts, and financial records pertaining to Andy and his business.

Since she had not even used the tape recordings against Andy at her own divorce trial, she said she complied reluctantly with the subpoena.

After listening to the tapes and examining the photocopies of the canceled checks, Lawrence, Ford, and Lombardi believed that at the very least they could put together a strong case of federal income tax evasion against Andy.

In April Lawrence sent out more subpoenas, to present and former employees at Nanco who he thought might know something about Andy's bookkeeping practices.

Andy retained lawyers for everyone—from officers to clerical and support staff—who had been approached by law enforcement officials. Virtually all who were subpoenaed before the grand jury invoked the Fifth Amendment, refusing to testify even after being told they were not targets of the investigation.

One former employee, an accountant who had quit his job at Nanco after discovering what he believed were questionable bookkeeping methods, declined Andy's offer of a lawyer and retained his own. The day after he was interviewed by government investigators he got what appeared to be a warning to keep his mouth shut.

At 1:30 A.M. he was sitting alone in the living room of his modest red brick home in Queens, having fallen asleep in front of the television set, when he was suddenly awakened by a popping noise. Someone had fired two gunshots into his living room. The .22-caliber bullets pierced the picture window in his living room, traveled only a few feet above his head, and lodged in a wall that separated the living room from the bedroom where his infant daughter lay sleeping.

At dawn that morning police also found a dead bird, with a piece of cloth shoved in its mouth, lying on the front walk. "Now tell me this is not an organized crime case," Tony Lombardi said to Lawrence at the time.

Lombardi had seen a dead bird used as a "message" before in cases that he had investigated for the President's Commission on Organized Crime. But Andy's lawyer, Jay Goldberg, complained that the government's effort to link his client to the dead bird was a "low blow."

The accountant nevertheless agreed to testify before the grand jury about what he had found in the books. So did another former Nanco employee, who feared so much for her life that she moved out of state after testifying.

Her testimony before the grand jury was particularly damaging to Andy. She described in detail how Andy would direct her to pick out of a Coles directory names of people who lived near his sewer construction projects and then make out phony insurance and damage claims for them. She said she was then instructed to endorse the checks for the phony liability claims to generate cash for Andy. "I could not go over fifteen hundred dollars per claim; no more than ten thousand dollars a day," she said.

By the end of April Lawrence was exploring whether or not Andy's relationships with Bess, Stanley Friedman, Donald Manes, and Herb Rickman had affected the awarding of city contracts.

At the end of April Bess called Rickman and told him that she understood Giuliani's office was investigating them to see whether they had used their influence with anyone over at the city's Department of Environmental Protection to help Andy win his city contracts. Rickman was terrified. With dozens of top-level city administrators having been forced to resign since January amid allegations of corruption, he was concerned that he too might be swept up in the scandal. He was prepared to tell all he knew to any federal investigator who asked.

At 4:30 P.M. on Thursday, May 1, Rickman got a phone call from Lawrence asking him if he would mind answering a few questions. Eager to persuade investigators that he had not been involved in any wrongdoing, he volunteered to answer any question that night.

The U.S. attorney's office, tucked behind the federal courthouse on St. Andrew's Plaza, was only two blocks from City Hall. Rickman arrived about an hour after talking with Lawrence, and from the moment he sat down he spewed forth all sorts of information about his frequent visits during the summer of 1983 and early 1984 to Andy's homes in Westhampton Beach and Palm Beach and his trips to the Hamptons with Bess on a seaplane at Andy's expense. He said that Andy had never asked him to influence anyone at City Hall. In fact, he told them that Andy had once said to him jokingly: "I wouldn't ask you for a favor because you don't have any fucking influence anyway."

Rickman also told them he had stopped visiting Andy in Westhampton Beach in the spring of 1984 and had also urged the mayor not to attend a Fourth of July party at Andy's home that year. He said he became concerned about being seen with Andy after reading in the *New York Times* that two of the minority-owned subcontractors Andy had hired to qualify for federally funded contracts were under investigation for allegedly serving as fronts for companies owned by white males.

"From that point on, I no longer took up invitations for further visits," he said.

Before leaving the U.S. attorney's office that night, Rickman decided to tell all he knew about the hiring of Sukhreet Gabel as well. He remembered how Bess had tried to attach his name to the hiring of Sukhreet three years earlier, and if that ever became an issue again, he wanted prosecutors to know that he had had nothing to do with the matter. His comments about Sukhreet Gabel interested Lawrence, who had not yet focused on that aspect of the investigation.

On the same day that Rickman volunteered to go to the U.S. attorney's office for questioning, Barbara Ross and Marilyn Thompson of the *New York Daily News* were finishing up a story to run in the next day's newspaper, quoting sources that said Giuliani was probing Andy's contracts and his relationships with Rickman and Bess.

WNBC-TV's Gabe Pressman, the best-known television reporter in New York, was also working on the story. At eleven o'clock that night he reported on the air that Giuliani had subpoenaed court papers linking Bess and Rickman to Andy Capasso, whom Pressman described as a "Long Island construction man who won a multimillion-dollar city contract to repair a sewage treatment plant."

At the mayor's City Hall press conference the next morning, reporters from the city's other television stations and newspapers crowded into the Blue Room to record the mayor's reaction to the latest news—that the woman who had helped make him mayor in 1977 was now being swept up into the scandal as well.

Disgusted that the press and the prosecutors appeared to be trying to drag Bess into the corruption scandal because of her personal relationship with a city contractor when her city agency had nothing to do with sewers, Koch launched into a diatribe, saying the allegations smacked of "McCarthyism."

Reached for comment at the Department of Cultural Affairs that afternoon, Bess told reporters that the allegations were "absurd." "There is no foundation for it. There's no reason for the story."

But the story would not die.

That Monday, May 5, Mayor Koch was attending a luncheon at *New York Newsday*'s editorial offices in midtown Manhattan to discuss his new $21.5 billion city budget when he got a message from an assistant press secretary that a *New York Daily News* reporter was looking for a comment about another story about Bess. This time the story was going to focus on Bess's hiring of Sukhreet Gabel in 1983 while Sukhreet's mother, Judge Gabel, was ruling on Andy Capasso's temporary alimony payments.

Koch immediately called Bess at her office at the Department of Cultural Affairs and asked, "What the hell is going on?"

Bess replied, according to Koch, that she had already told him about the matter. "I sent you a memo, and you sent me a letter."

Koch had forgotten all about the single-spaced three-page memo that Bess had sent him on October 19, 1983, following the gossip item in the *New York Post* that had raised similar questions about the circumstances surrounding Sukhreet Gabel's hiring. When he returned to City Hall that afternoon, he pulled Bess's memo from the file and ordered that it be given to the *Daily News* reporter, Marcia Kramer, who was working on the story. Koch still did not know that Bess had lied to him in the memo. "I believed it to be true at the time," he said later.

Kramer, a tenacious reporter who had been named the newspaper's City Hall bureau chief that January, had been working on the Sukhreet Gabel angle of the Bess story for weeks. She had assembled all of the court records from the divorce case and had finally persuaded Nancy Capasso to talk with her on a not-for-attribution basis. Inexperienced in dealing with the press, Nancy had been reluctant at first. Finally Kramer's persistence paid off. By the middle of April Nancy had agreed to meet with her and to give her a copy of the letter she had written to Judge Gabel in 1984, asking the judge to remove herself from the case.

With the letter and Bess's October 19 memo from the mayor, Kramer was now almost ready to write a story raising ethical questions about Bess's hiring of Sukhreet Gabel. Bess refused an interview, so Kramer had only one person left to talk to, Judge Gabel. She walked across the street that afternoon and headed three blocks north to the judge's chambers in the state supreme court building. In a brief interview Judge Gabel claimed that she did not remember anything about the Capasso case. "The chances are dollars to donuts that the decision was drafted by a law assistant," Judge Gabel said.

The story, headlined "Bess' Role: All in the Family, Myerson Hired Daughter of Judge Who Cut Beau's Alimony," appeared in the *Daily News* the next day and made public for the first time that just weeks after Sukhreet got the job Judge Gabel had cut Capasso's combined alimony and child support payments from $1,850 to $680 a month. Kramer quoted legal experts who said the canons of judicial ethics generally prohibit judges from participating in cases where "personal or familial interests" are involved.

Within days after the *Daily News* story appeared Judge Gabel, who was seventy-four years old, suffered what she later described as a "mild stroke." She was hospitalized for eight days.

Although the *New York Post* had first reported Sukhreet Gabel's hiring three years before, on October 18, 1983, it was not until Kramer laid out the facts about the slashing of the alimony payments within two weeks of Sukhreet's becoming Bess's special assistant that the story caught the attention of judicial watchdogs. In the anticorruption climate that prevailed that spring, Kramer's story prompted the state Commission on Judicial Conduct to conduct an investigation of Gabel's rulings in the divorce case—three years after they had been made.

Meanwhile, over at the U.S. attorney's office, Lawrence, Lombardi, and Ford were still working to put together a federal tax evasion case against Andy and determine if he had any connections with organized crime. They had not yet turned up any evidence that Bess had used her influence to help him win his city contracts, but they were continuing to look.

On May 20 Lawrence sent a subpoena to the Department of Cultural Affairs requesting copies of Bess's professional daily diaries and telephone logs dating back to 1983. The subpoena arrived in the office of Gwen Hatcher, the agency's inspector general, who was responsible for conducting criminal investigations within the agency. She brought the subpoena upstairs to show Bess so that Bess could help her put the material together.

When Bess heard about the subpoena, Hatcher later recalled, she erupted into a fit of rage, calling Giuliani's federal grand jury investigation a "witch hunt" and promising that he would find "nothing."

Bess said she could not produce all of the documents requested by the subpoena because she had not kept her diaries from 1983 and 1984. She said that she had "lost" her diary from 1986. She did, however, tell Hatcher about a black loose-leaf binder containing copies of her schedule for the past several years.

The next day, Hatcher said, as she was trying to gather the telephone logs and other documents, to comply with the federal subpoena, Bess burst into her office and started screaming that she did not want her working on this matter anymore because she was "tying up" the department. "I don't give a fuck about any of this shit," Hatcher recalled Bess shouted at her that morning. "I'm still the commissioner here, and I don't care what [Department of Investigation commissioner Kenneth] Conboy or Giuliani have to say; I don't want the staff working on this."

Hatcher was astonished. She said Bess then demanded the return of her black loose-leaf binder containing her schedules. Hatcher had to explain to Bess that the binder had been subpoenaed and that she could not remove it from the office. Bess stalked out of the room.

She returned, though, about ten minutes later to apologize for her outburst and to request that Hatcher make copies of the pages in the loose-leaf book. "I'm sorry, but all of this is happening because his wife, who was offered ten million dollars, only got two million dollars in the court," Hatcher recalled Bess told her at the time.

Marcia Kramer had been trying for weeks to get Nancy's former divorce lawyer, Herman Tarnow, to play for her the potentially damaging tapes that Nancy had made during her divorce negotiations with Andy. Tarnow finally agreed, and on Sunday, June 15, Kramer published a story in the *Daily News* headlined "Bess' Guy Begs, Jury Hears Tapes of Contractor Capasso Pleading with Ex-Wife Not to Spill the Beans." The story contained direct quotes from the tape recordings in which Andy begged Nancy not to run "to authorities and put me in jail for four hundred or five hundred years." Kramer revealed for the first time in the press that the tapes, along with copies of bogus insurance and damage claims, were in the hands of federal prosecutors. After reading the *New York Daily News* that Sunday, Andy and Bess probably learned for the first time that Giuliani knew about the tapes. It was now possible that the investigators had enough evidence to put Andy in jail.

At about 9:00 P.M. the next day Bess called Sukhreet Gabel at home and invited herself over to Sukhreet's apartment. Bess must have thought that Sukhreet was a loose cannon and could cause her a lot of trouble. Who could say what Sukhreet might tell federal investigators about the circumstances surrounding her hiring and how that information might be construed during what Bess believed was a "witch hunt"?

Sukhreet was surprised to hear Bess's voice on the phone that night. It had been a long time since they had last seen each other. In the two years since Sukhreet had left her unsuccessful city jobs, she had experienced much pain. But the deep depression that had followed her firing in August 1984 and her British boyfriend's rejection of her had finally lifted, and she was able to maintain a good mood with the help of lithium and other antidepressant drugs. She had not been able to find a steady job, however—in part, she thought, because she was unable to explain to a prospective employer why she had failed at the two city agencies. Sukhreet blamed Bess for this blotch on her résumé because she suspected that Bess had set her up to fail at the Department of Cultural Affairs and had had something to do with her forced resignation from the Commission on Human Rights. She believed that Bess had used her to try to influence her mother, who was then making decisions in Andy's divorce.

At first Sukhreet didn't know Bess was calling out of concern about the federal investigation and the state Commission on Judicial Conduct probe. No reporters or federal investigators had yet contacted Sukhreet, and she had not seen any of the articles in the *New York Daily News*. She knew there was some sort of investigation, but she had been led to believe by her mother that it was no big deal.

On the telephone that night, she recalled, Bess told her she had "wonderful news" and that she would like to come over right away and "talk about it."

About an hour later Bess arrived in the lobby of Sukhreet's modest apartment building on East 69th Street wearing a gray running suit, dark glasses, and white Reebok sneakers. Her hair was hidden under a scarf that she had wrapped around her head. No one would have recognized her that night as Bess Myerson, former Miss America.

Sukhreet said Bess called upstairs on the intercom and asked if anyone else was with her in the apartment. When Sukhreet told her she had a friend staying with her, Bess said that she did not want to come upstairs and insisted that Sukhreet meet her in the lobby.

"And so, I come down," recalled Sukhreet, "and she looks at me and says that I need a sweater . . . in her typical Mother Bess way. Always, you see two sides of her behavior with me. It has two faces: incredible cruelty and sort of babushka motherliness.

"I said, 'Bess, c'mon.' I thought I'd be out for five minutes. But she insisted that I go up and get a sweater, so I trot upstairs dutifully, feeling childish and foolish, to get the sweater, and I put my little sweater on, and down I come."

It was a few minutes past ten o'clock before they stepped out on East 69th Street into the cool summer night. Sukhreet said that Bess opened the conversation by asking her to tell her "exactly" what she had told her mother's lawyer. "I didn't know why she was so worried," Sukhreet said. "I was confused about the whole thing."

As they walked around the Upper East Side, circling a five-block area around Sukhreet's apartment, Sukhreet said Bess told her the investigation was "very serious" and Sukhreet could "make a lot of trouble for everybody." She also said that Bess told her to "keep my big mouth shut."

As Sukhreet recalled, Bess told her, "You've got a terribly big mouth, and I've got to know exactly how you came to be working for me so that we can coordinate our stories."

"Then she told me this cock-and-bull story about Herb Rickman sending her my résumé, and I said, 'No, Bess, that isn't how it happened.'"

Bess then became angry with her, Sukhreet said, and told her, "You could be dangerous. Don't you know what you're doing? . . . Before you talk to your lawyer I would like you to tell me exactly what you're going to say. We should keep in touch at all times. . . . Call me at the Department of Cultural Affairs and tell them that it's Ms. Grant calling. When Barra calls, she always says, 'This is Barra calling.' Use Ms. Grant, and I'm going to know who it is."

It was almost 11:30 P.M. before Bess said good night and they walked home their separate ways. The next morning Sukhreet called her mother's lawyer, Phil Schaeffer, and told him about Bess's visit the night before. Schaeffer suggested she sit down and write out everything she remembered about the conversation and then send a copy to his office. Sukhreet agreed. She said she never called Bess or consulted with her about her testimony or her discussions with her mother's lawyer after that night.

That summer, as Giuliani's office concentrated on building a federal tax evasion case against Andy, the state Commission on Judicial Conduct started interviewing witnesses for its investigation of Judge Gabel. Bess was not among the witnesses asked to testify.

Confident that she would be found not guilty of any wrongdoing, Judge Gabel agreed to testify before the commission in her own defense. After more than forty years of public service, she did not want to leave the bench in disgrace. In her testimony Judge Gabel admitted to having talked frequently with Bess about Sukhreet during the summer of 1983, but she denied ever having asked Bess to give Sukhreet a job. When asked to describe her telephone conversations with Bess, Judge Gabel replied: "It's very hard to. I was very eager for Sukhreet to find this kind of interesting work, and I wanted her to be in public life and I was certainly being nice to Bess, not to be nice to her. But I would have been nice to her anyway."

She said the reason for lowering Nancy Capasso's alimony payments was simple: she was impressed by Andy's lawyers' argument that Nancy had her own substantial income as a real estate broker.

In July Sukhreet testified at the state Commission on Judicial Conduct, but she was not very forthcoming. She admitted later, in federal court, that she had ducked some of the commission lawyer's questions and tried to respond to most of them with a simple yes or no. She was trying, she said, to protect her mother from having to resign from the bench in shame.

All during her divorce proceedings, Nancy Capasso had felt as if she had the "power of an ant" while opposing her politically connected husband in court. Now, with both a federal grand jury and the state Commission on Judicial Conduct trying to determine whether Bess had improperly influenced Judge Gabel while the judge was ruling on Nancy's divorce, she felt vindicated. The system was finally working.

Nancy's new attorney, Myrna Felder, was confident, too, that Nancy would win an appeal of Judge Tyler's December 18, 1985, divorce ruling, which had been so favorable to Andy.

On October 2, 1986, Felder called Nancy with the news that she had won a major victory. A Manhattan appeals court had tossed out the $2 million divorce settlement, voting five to zero that Judge Tyler had divided the assets and marital property improperly between Andy and Nancy. The appeals court ruled that Nancy should get more.

In its decision the court wrote, "We also find an error of law in the trial court's wholesale, verbatim adoption of the husband's requests for findings. At least insofar as they bear on property distribution, these proposals were unacceptable and should have been rejected across the board."

The appeals court directed Judge Tyler to reconsider his decision and come up with a bigger financial award for Nancy. But on February 23 Judge Tyler rebuffed the appeals court and, using the same reasoning he had used in his initial decision, stood by his first ruling. Only this time he explained in detail in his decision why he chose not to grant Nancy any part of Andy's business. "This court finds and determines that defendant's [Nancy's] activities during the marriage were limited, and her contributions as a spouse, parent, and homemaker did not contribute to the career advancement of plaintiff [Andy] or his business," Tyler wrote. "The appreciated value of the plaintiff's separate property is not the result of any direct contributions made by defendant, and indirect contributions of defendant as a spouse, wage earner, parent, homemaker are not considered."

By the end of 1986 Giuliani's federal grand jury was about ready to bring an indictment against Andy for federal tax evasion. During a nine-month investigation David Lawrence reviewed hundreds of documents and talked to more than fifty people. While he did not turn up any evidence that Andy had bribed politicians or city officials to win his city contracts, he did discover that Andy had evaded $774,000 in corporate and personal income taxes.

Working with investigator Tony Lombardi and city investigating attorney Kevin Ford, Lawrence talked to dozens of people whose names had appeared on canceled checks for bogus liability claims against Nanco. None of the people interviewed had ever made a claim against Nanco or had even heard of the company before. Still others could not be interviewed because they were deceased—and had been dead when the checks were made out to them. The checks had generated an estimated $358,323 in nontaxable cash for Andy, according to the government's estimate.

In another tax fraud scheme Andy had charged more than $1.3 million in renovations to his Park Avenue and Fifth Avenue apartments to Nanco as business expenses, which he concealed through a series of false bookkeeping entries as expenses incurred by the company in the course of performing city contracts.

An audit of Nanco's books revealed that another $500,000 had been diverted somehow from his company, but Lawrence and the investigators could not determine where the money had gone. They suspected that Bess, who kept at least thirty separate brokerage accounts, may have been hiding the money there. Since 1980, her net worth had quadrupled from $4 million to $16 million, primarily from investments in real estate partnerships and stocks. A former Nanco chauffeur had told investigators that Bess had given him large amounts of cash in white envelopes to deliver to her stockbroker.

In the middle of December Lawrence called Bess's attorney, Fred Hafetz, and told him that Bess was about to be subpoenaed before the federal grand jury. In addition to questions about her personal finances, Lawrence warned, he intended to ask Bess questions about two other ongoing investigations: the circumstances surrounding the hiring of Sukhreet Gabel and whether she had used any influence to help Andy win city contracts. Lawrence also told Hafetz that Bess was considered a target of the investigation.

After angrily telling the prosecutor that he would advise Bess against testifying before the federal grand jury, Hafetz tried to persuade Lawrence not to force her to appear. Although Lawrence was insistent that she show up, he agreed not to serve the subpoena at the Department of Cultural Affairs, to help protect her privacy and maintain the secrecy that surrounds grand jury proceedings.

On Monday, December 15, a red satin ribbon tied into a huge bow was draped across the front of Carnegie Hall. After a seven-month renovation, the ninety-five-year-old grande dame of West 57th Street was opening its doors for a gala concert and celebration. Among the guests invited to the most important social event of the season were Brooke Astor, Oscar de la Renta, Lally Weymouth, Lee Radziwill, Armand Hammer, Mary and Laurance S. Rockefeller, Nancy Kissinger, Maureen Reagan, Patti Hearst Shaw, Frank and Barbara Sinatra, Gregory Peck, Beverly Sills, and William S. Paley.

Bess, the city's commissioner of cultural affairs, appeared at the reopening wearing a gold embroidered Trigere gown. She looked fabulous at Mayor Koch's side as she talked about the city's role in helping to finance the $50 million face-lift. "This is the best: restoration at its best, New York City at its best, music at its best," she told the audience.

As the flashes illuminated her smile, Bess revealed no trace of the tremendous pressure she must have felt knowing that within a few days she had to appear before a federal grand jury.

Minutes later the concert opened with "The Star-Spangled Banner" played by the New York Philharmonic under Zubin Mehta. Onstage, leading the audience in song, were sopranos Leontyne Price and Roberta Peters, baritone Sherrill Milnes, mezzo-soprano Betty Allen, and Mayor Koch and Bess Myerson.

It was one of her last public appearances.

Bess had decided not to tell Koch that she intended to take the Fifth

Amendment rather than testify before a federal grand jury. She later said she had believed the grand jury process was secret and that no one would know. She didn't want to tell the mayor about her predicament because he would have wanted her to testify and cooperate with the federal prosecutors.

The following Monday, December 22, Hafetz accompanied Bess to the fifth floor of the U.S. District Courthouse at Foley Square. Since no one but the prosecuting attorney and the grand jurors was allowed inside the grand jury room, Hafetz waited in the hallway.

Entering the grand jury room that day, Bess looked nervous. Tiny beads of sweat formed on her forehead as she took a seat at the end of a long oak table facing David Lawrence. Grand jury rooms are not like standard courtrooms. There was no judge at the proceedings. It was just Bess, David Lawrence, and the members of the grand jury, about twenty-five people who sat in a box looking down at the witness and the prosecutor at a long table.

Following her attorney's advice not to answer any questions, Bess gave her name, then invoked the Fifth Amendment protection against self-incrimination in response to every question.

While Bess had exercised her constitutional rights that afternoon, she had also violated a promise that Mayor Koch had made to the public only six months before. Koch had vowed that all of his commissioners and staff members would cooperate fully with the numerous corruption investigations. Anyone who did not cooperate, he had said, would be fired.

29
"The Bess Mess"

M ayor Koch was on his way home to Gracie Mansion on Friday,
January 9, 1987, when the call about Mike Taibbi's bombshell report on the six o'clock news came in over the car
phone. Taibbi, an enterprising reporter then working for WNBC-TV,
had found out that Bess had taken the Fifth Amendment three weeks
earlier while testifying before a federal grand jury investigating municipal corruption.

Koch was stunned by the news. Bess had never mentioned to him
anything about testifying before a grand jury.

After the mayor reached Gracie Mansion, Bess called to apologize for
not having informed him of her refusal to testify. "She said her lawyer
didn't think it necessary to tell me because he didn't think anything
further would result from her appearance there," Koch said later. He
then asked her to meet with his first deputy mayor and top legal adviser
on Monday morning "to explain what happened here."

The disclosure of Bess's decision to take the Fifth Amendment rocked
City Hall and once again made corruption in city government a front-
page story. Reporters who for months had ignored Marcia Kramer's
stories about Bess in the *New York Daily News* were now asking her for
copies. Everyone wondered what Bess had to hide.

Whatever anger Koch felt about Bess's decision, he gave her the
benefit of the doubt, telling reporters that he had a "great deal of
confidence and respect for her and for her integrity." At the same time,
he acknowledged to Joyce Purnick, then City Hall bureau chief of the
New York Times, that "a negative inference has to be drawn when the
Fifth Amendment is used. There is no question an explanation is
required here."

On Monday Bess and her lawyer, Fred Hafetz, met for more than two
hours with the mayor's top advisers, Corporation Counsel Frederick
A. O. Schwarz and First Deputy Mayor Stanley Brezenoff. Afterward,
Schwarz told reporters: "I didn't hear the state of mind of a duplicitous
person. I heard the state of mind of someone who was a little confused

about the situation she was in, concerned about the situation she was in, because it was unfamiliar, and who followed the advice of her lawyer."

Even so, Bess's refusal to testify presented Koch with a personal and political dilemma. How could he fire Bess, the woman who had helped make him mayor, a close friend of more than twenty years, and a top official in his administration? On the other hand, he knew those personal considerations could not color his responsibilities as mayor.

To figure out his next step Koch met with his top two legal advisers following their meeting with Bess to discuss his options. They advised him that he could not fire Bess for exercising her constitutional rights and recommended instead that Koch appoint someone to conduct a formal inquiry to determine whether Bess had abused her public office. They suggested that the inquiry focus on whether Bess had used her influence to help Andy obtain city contracts and whether she had sought to win a favorable divorce ruling for Andy by giving Sukhreet a job. Since the city's commissioner for investigations, Ken Conboy, was already cooperating with the federal probe, they suggested that Koch appoint someone from outside city government to undertake the inquiry.

Koch turned to former federal judge Harold R. Tyler, Jr., a sixty-four-year-old partner in the firm of Patterson, Belknap, Webb, and Tyler who in the past had been called on by city officials to investigate other politically sensitive allegations and who by happenstance was Giuliani's mentor. "He was kind enough on a pro-bono basis to undertake the investigation," Koch said later. "I said to him, 'While you have to look at these questions, it's unlimited. You just make a full investigation and report to me. Whatever your investigation discloses, that's going to be something I am going to accept as factual. That's it, for me.'"

Koch ordered Bess to take a ninety-day leave of absence without pay pending the outcome of Tyler's inquiry. Bess objected to taking the leave without pay, but Koch promised her she would be reimbursed for the time when she returned to work.

On Tuesday, January 13, just four days after Taibbi's broadcast report, Koch announced at a crowded City Hall press conference that Bess would step down as cultural affairs commissioner while Tyler determined whether or not she had done anything wrong.

In a statement released through her lawyer Bess vowed to return to her post in city government. She was defiant, declaring flatly: "I will return as commissioner. . . . I want to make clear: I have done nothing wrong. I state unequivocally that I never in any way helped Mr. Capasso to get any city contract. . . . I agree with the appropriateness of this procedure and expect to testify at this inquiry."

She acknowledged having hired Sukhreet—which she had earlier blamed on one of her employees—but she insisted she had done so because she had believed Sukhreet was "extremely qualified." Bess went on to insist that the hiring was "in no way done to influence in any way the decisions of Justice Gabel." She concluded her statement by saying, "I plan no further comment to the media until I return to my position as commissioner."

The following day Giuliani announced a nine-count federal indictment against Andy, accusing him of having evaded $744,000 in corporate and personal income taxes through his phony liability scheme and of having billed $1.3 million to his company for renovations at his luxurious Fifth Avenue apartment.

Andy's attorney, Jay Goldberg, called the indictment the "last gasp" by federal prosecutors and told reporters, "We view the present indictment, unpleasant as it is and incorrect as we will show it to be, as a vindication of any notion that Mr. Capasso made improper payments to public officials or secured his contracts through any but lawful means."

But Giuliani warned that the federal grand jury had just completed "one aspect" of a "continuing and active" investigation.

In a move that took federal prosecutors by surprise, Andy pleaded guilty to all nine counts in the federal indictment at his arraignment on January 22. Some of the regular court reporters speculated that he had made his decision after learning that his case would be handled by U.S. district judge Charles Stewart, who had a reputation for leniency. But Andy told friends that he wanted to spare his family and friends, particularly Bess, the agony of a long public trial.

The night before Andy's court appearance, Bess called one of her assistant commissioners, Richard Bruno, at home. She respected his abilities as a writer and thought that the prepared statement Andy intended to read to the press following his guilty plea needed to be revised.

Bruno was at home with his sleeping infant daughter when Bess called, so he asked if she could bring the statement over to his apartment, which was only a few blocks away. About fifteen minutes later she arrived at his apartment with Andy and showed him the statement.

After reading it, Bruno went into the bedroom, where he worked on an alternative draft on his computer for about a half hour. Bess seemed to like the revision, and as they got up to leave, Andy pulled out his wallet. Bruno stopped him. "Please don't," he said.

As they were leaving, Bess turned to Bruno and promised him the favor would be returned. "When Mr. Capasso is released, he will probably be needing public relations assistance, and you should keep that in mind," Bruno recalled she said.

But Andy had already left a $100 bill on a table in the apartment.

Because of all of the publicity surrounding her decision to take the Fifth Amendment, Bess did not accompany Andy to his arraignment the next day. After entering his guilty plea, he stood alone on the courthouse steps and read his prepared statement facing the television cameras. "I categorically deny that any improper influence, bribery or bid-rigging was involved in my obtaining contracts with New York City and New York state," he said. "Any claim that Bess Myerson exerted influence with the city or state . . . in my behalf is totally false. . . . I am ready to face whatever punishment the court decides is appropriate. I am also ready to face any continuing investigation secure in the knowledge that my guilty plea today encompasses the totality of my misconduct."

Later that day his attorney, Jay Goldberg, happened to be in the U.S. attorney's office when he ran into Howard Wilson, the chief of the criminal division. According to Goldberg, Wilson said he would like to talk with him about getting Andy's cooperation with the federal investigation into city corruption. Cooperation with the U.S. attorney's office could mean the prosecutors might not ask for a long prison term at Andy's sentencing hearing on March 30.

Goldberg asked Wilson what information he thought Andy could provide.

"He said to me, and this is a quote because I will never forget it," Goldberg later recalled, " 'You know that Andy plays tennis with Stanley Friedman regularly and that he is a very close friend and he also played tennis regularly with Donald Manes. You know what kind of people they are. He must have information about public corruption.' "

Goldberg said that he was astonished that anyone would think Andy might have information on Manes and Friedman "because he is a tennis mate of these people." Goldberg said he asked Andy whether he had any information that could help the government in its investigation, and Andy replied that he didn't have any information at all.

But according to prosecutor David Lawrence, Goldberg told him that Andy would not cooperate with the federal government because Andy did not want to be a "rat" and "it would take more than a tax case to make him talk."

In the two-and-a-half months before Andy's sentencing hearing on March 30, Bess and Andy gathered glowing letters from friends and family on his behalf to submit to Judge Stewart in the hope that these testimonials would convince the judge to spare him from going to prison.

There were letters from longtime family friends, high school buddies, directors of the charities Andy had contributed to over the years, and prominent members of the community. Samuel Peabody, who was president of the cooperative at 990 Fifth Avenue when Andy and Nancy first moved in, wrote a letter asking Judge Stewart to "show leniency." Andy's stepson also wrote a letter praising Andy for being a good stepfather.

Bess sought help from a few of her old friends, including former state supreme court judge Jerome Becker, who wrote that "whatever mistakes Andy made as a citizen cannot diminish in my own mind, the fact that he is a self-made businessman whose professional achievements are marked with excellence. . . ."

Another letter came from Bess's longtime friend and psychiatrist, Dr. Ted Rubin, who had gotten to know Andy well over the past few years. In his letter, Dr. Rubin wrote:

> . . . I have never witnessed so much growth by an incredibly curious human mind in so short a time. The Andy Capasso of old and of confused values is surely the man who is responsible for current difficulties. The Andy of today has become a self-contemplative, ever-changing, growing man, much too wise to ever be the victim of pride or greed again. . . .

All of the letters were attached to a memorandum written by Andy's lawyer and submitted to the judge. Goldberg asked the judge to sentence his client to community service instead of prison so Andy could offer his construction expertise in repairing plumbing systems in shelters for the homeless. "Surely, Mr. Capasso's substantial efforts to alleviate the problems of the homeless would far outweigh any benefit that society would derive from his incarceration," Goldberg argued in his memo.

But Giuliani's presentencing memo to the judge offered a sharp contrast to Goldberg's. The prosecutor portrayed Andy as a greedy and corrupt man who had "achieved every social and economic advantage and used and abused those advantages for criminal ends." In asking for a long prison term Giuliani pointed in his memorandum to an excerpt from the 1984 taped conversation of mob members in which Andy's name came up. He harshly criticized Andy for not assisting the federal government in its ongoing corruption investigations:

> Specifically, he repeatedly refused to discuss his documented and longstanding relationships with various city officials and political leaders who have been at the epicenter of the city's corruption scandal (e.g., former Queens Borough President Donald Manes, former Bronx County Democratic Chairman Stanley Friedman and . . . Myerson) as well as convicted and reputed organized crime leaders (e.g., Matthew "Matty the Horse" Ianniello).

At 9:40 A.M. on March 30 Goldberg and Lawrence presented their arguments in person before U.S. district judge Charles Stewart in the federal courthouse in lower Manhattan.

As Andy sat at the defense table, Goldberg complained that the federal prosecutors were trying to prejudice the judge against his client by saying that Andy had declined to cooperate with investigators. "Your honor, he had no information, because, you see, Mr. Capasso's work was awarded long before . . . Stanley Friedman emerged as a power, before Donald Manes emerged as a powerhouse. His work is awarded on the basis of a sealed low bid. No one, neither Mr. Manes, Mr. Friedman, or Miss Myerson, whose name has been mentioned prominently in the press, could help him one bit, could intercede for him in any way, for him to get a public contract."

Lawrence, representing the U.S. attorney's office, disputed Goldberg's assertions and asked for a "substantial term of incarceration and substantial fines. . . ."

The judge then turned to Andy and asked whether he had anything to say.

"Well, I have never had any information, your honor, which is alluded to in the report about any other public corruption or any other criminal activities," Andy replied.

"All right," Stewart said. "Is there anything else in there that you have any problems with?"

"No, sir," Andy replied.

"Anything you would like to say to me before I impose sentence?"

"Yes," Andy said. "I feel I committed a serious crime and I apologize for it and I am ready to face the consequences."

Stewart sentenced him to four years in jail and imposed $500,000 in fines. "I was amazed that someone with your intelligence, your abilities, and your resources, financial resources, found it necessary to engage in such deliberate, ongoing, long-term fraud," he said.

Andy lowered his head. Goldberg said later it was one of the longest jail sentences for tax evasion that he could remember. He was eventually able to persuade the judge to reduce the sentence to three years. That morning, stunned by the lengthy term, he asked the judge to give Andy a few months to get his business and other matters in order before beginning his prison term. The judge ordered Andy to report to prison in June.

"I'm like a leashed tiger," Bess told her friend, *New York Post* columnist Cindy Adams, in an exclusive interview only hours after she began her ninety-day leave of absence on January 14, the day Andy was indicted. "I am not down. I am not sad nor depressed. When I'm under pressure, I become energized."

While some of Bess's friends had urged her to resign instead of subjecting herself to a specially commissioned mayoral investigation, Bess refused to walk away. She fully expected to return to her job as cultural affairs commissioner at the end of ninety days and was already planning the celebration. She told Cindy Adams that upon her return she intended to hang a banner saying "Bess Is Back and Koch Has Got Her."

She also lashed out publicly against Nancy for the first time, telling Adams, "Mrs. Capasso felt the way to bring her husband down was to bring me down. She didn't want him. She wanted what he has. I appreciate him for what he is—for his vibrancy and sense of humor.

"This is a woman seeking vindictive triumph," Bess continued. "Andy had said that she and her attorney threatened to go to the authorities and they did. And in all these years, I have never once spoken out to defend myself. But I am angry. Angry that for three and a half years, I've had to endure a repetition of the same lies."

In the weeks after taking her leave, Bess became increasingly obsessed with what she believed were Nancy Capasso's efforts to ruin her. She found it impossible to keep her vow not to talk to the press. One of her first calls was to Mike Taibbi at WNBC-TV, on February 3. "There's no validity to any of the charges," she began. "Look, I took the Fifth because I sat with four lawyers, including a criminal lawyer, and that's what they told me to do. And it's the grand jury, they said . . . nobody's gonna know, because you can't talk about it. So I didn't. I held up my end of the bargain, but the prosecutors didn't. . . .

"I mean, really. Do you think, really, I'd make any calls to anyone so Andy could get a contract? Christ, I'm not fucking stupid. And I have too much respect for the man I helped get into office. . . .

"About Horty Gabel's daughter? Look, she went to Oxford, speaks seven languages. It's not like she wasn't qualified for the job. . . .

"I know Andy. I know the kind of man he is. And even though she claims I stole him from her and her five babies, let's face it, the babies are twenty-seven and twenty-eight now. . . . Then she went crying to Giuliani, and she was going to destroy Andy. You know . . . a sixty-two-year-old lady isn't gonna take a forty-year-old man away from his wife, unless that wife had created such a stormy marriage that he was gonna be vulnerable. . . .

"I was talking to the *Times* the other day when [public relations director] Robert Sklar called me. She [Bess's secretary] said 'Page Six' [*New York Post*] was on the line. They got a tip I was dying of cancer. Christ, I *had* cancer. Back in 1974. I beat the shit out of it, just like I'll beat the shit out of this stuff. . . . You know what the Italians say? Andy uses the expression 'I swear on my daughter's eyes.' Well, I swear on my daughter's eyes all this stuff is bullshit. . . .

"Again, I thought this was a country where you weren't guilty just because you took the Fifth. I can fight the big lie. . . . I fought it before for Ed, when they were all saying he was a homosexual. . . .

"I'm coming back after ninety days. I have no doubt at all, even though I know Giuliani isn't through with me. It's not like me to quit: after all, the mayor's gonna have a lot of trouble the next election. . . . I may wanna help him."

Bess also made several calls to Marcia Kramer of the *New York Daily News.* One night, after Bess called the reporter at home and talked for more than an hour about "the big story" she had to tell without ever telling her what it was, Kramer became convinced that Bess was out of control.

At about the same time, writer Patricia Morrisroe was working on a story about Bess for *New York* magazine. At first Bess was reluctant to speak with her, telling Morrisroe that "there is no story here. There is no premise. Mr. Capasso never paid any of my living expenses. No man has ever paid my expenses. I'm sure everybody you've spoken to has said a lot of negative things. They're eyeing my job. They're jealous. So what have they said about me?"

"They've said you were very complex," Morrisroe replied.

"Well, that's nice. I hope when you get to be my age they'll say the same thing about you. There's nothing worse than being simple."

Morrisroe said that Bess called her back a few days later around nine o'clock in the morning and launched into what Morrisroe described as a "monologue" about jealousy and how Nancy Capasso had attacked her because of her celebrity and her name. Eight hours later, Bess was still on the phone.

"The reason this is happening is that I'm a woman. I'm a Miss America. . . . I'm queen of the Jews," she told Morrisroe. "There's a great deal of jealousy because most women haven't achieved what I have and because they don't have more men in their lives. . . ."

"Is it possible to continue this in person?" Morrisroe asked. It was 5:15 P.M.

"No," Bess replied. "My lawyer told me I'm not supposed to talk to the press."

On Monday, March 23, Morrisroe's story about Bess and her troubles appeared as *New York* magazine's cover story, with the headline "Bess and the Mess: Myerson's Slide into Scandal." By describing her eight-hour phone conversation with Bess and quoting her extensively, Morrisroe drew a devastating and unsympathetic portrait of her. With Bess pronouncing to Morrisroe that she was the "perfect route to the downfall of this administration," City Hall insiders thought it would be impossible for Bess to return to the Koch administration gracefully, regardless of the outcome of former federal judge Harold R. Tyler, Jr.'s, investigation.

At the beginning of Tyler's inquiry Bess had agreed to answer questions and explain the circumstances surrounding her decision to take the Fifth Amendment. But on the advice of her lawyer she changed her mind when she learned that she would not be granted immunity. Any information she provided to Tyler, she was informed, could be used against her in court, and with Giuliani's office continuing its grand jury investigation of her and Andy, Bess could not take that risk.

Tyler and the three young attorneys from his law firm who were working with him on the investigation had the full cooperation of the city's Department of Investigation, which was working closely with Giuliani. During the three-month probe they examined hundreds of records from the Department of Cultural Affairs, including letters and memos, staff meeting minutes, and personnel records. They scanned Bess's telephone logs and her schedules for 1985 and 1986, looking for messages and notes that might indicate possible conflicts of interest. They scrutinized the *Capasso* v. *Capasso* divorce papers, listened to the tape-recorded conversations between Andy and Nancy, and read the dozens of letters Judge Gabel had written to her friends on behalf of Sukhreet.

In all they interviewed thirty-five witnesses, including sixteen present and former employees at the Department of Cultural Affairs. Among the others interviewed were Herbert Rickman, former chauffeurs for Andy, and even his former live-in servants in Westhampton Beach. Of all the witnesses, though, Tyler and his investigators became most interested in the testimony, that late February, of Judge Hortense Gabel, her husband, Milton, and their only child, Sukhreet.

Unable to find any evidence that Bess had abused her position as a city commissioner to help Andy win sealed-bid city contracts, they ended up focusing on the circumstances surrounding the hiring of Sukhreet while her mother was ruling on Andy's divorce case.

In her previous testimony before the state Commission on Judicial Conduct and the federal grand jury, Sukhreet insists, she had been careful to protect her mother. An examination of her testimony before the judicial commission does show she responded "I do not recollect" to many of the questions posed to her at the time. And, she said, when she was unsure of how to respond, she would turn to her lawyer, Philip Schaeffer, a longtime friend of her mother's, for guidance. "I was a very good Girl Scout," she said later. "Defending my mother and Bess was second nature."

But during an interview with Tyler and his lawyers at their law offices at Rockefeller Center, Sukhreet decided to break her silence.

One of the lawyers showed her a copy of the October 19, 1983, letter that Bess had written to Mayor Koch after the *New York Post* gossip item about her hiring and then asked whether she had ever seen the letter before. "Something snapped," she said later. "I said, 'Yes, I have seen that letter. It is a pack of lies. There is not one true statement in that letter.' Then I pointed out exactly what the falsehoods were.

"I just had enough lying. I just had enough of protecting people. What the hell have they ever done for me? Had they protected me? No. They had made a monkey of me."

During the three years since she had left city government Sukhreet had pent up anger at her mother and Bess for making her life "a living hell on earth." She blamed them for her deep depression, which, in her words, had turned her into a "zombie," and for her inability to find a full-time job. In her mind it was the fault of her mother and Bess that she now had to depend on her parents for financial support. She had virtually given up her job search, although her father frequently called to inquire about her prospects for employment and to offer ideas. Her mornings were spent reading and studying. To get herself out of her apartment in the afternoons she roamed around the city playing a strange, private game—spending an imaginary $1 million window-shopping. Sometimes her game would take her to a quarry in Queens, where they had the finest marble, or a small fish store in Brooklyn, where she pretended to buy fresh Norwegian salmon. When short on time, she went directly to Tiffany. In just a few minutes she could drop $1 million, not a "penny more or a penny less."

Although her deep depression had lifted after she underwent outpatient shock treatments and started taking antidepressants, she could not help still feeling resentful of her mother and of Bess, whom she blamed for wrenching those years out of her life.

As Sukhreet saw it, if it had not been for those two powerful women "using her" in 1983 to achieve their own separate goals, she would not have to explain to potential employers why she had been pressured to resign from the city's Commission on Human Rights after a few weeks and why she had lasted only nine months at the city's Department of Cultural Affairs.

Could she tell prospective employers what she really thought were the reasons behind her failure? That Bess had originally hired her as a special assistant but, after the press found out that her mother was ruling on Bess's boyfriend's divorce case, Bess had shunned her and made her life miserable?

While Bess had made her tenure at the Department of Cultural Affairs difficult, Sukhreet did not want to take responsibility for her poor job performance. It was as if she needed someone else to blame for all of her unhappiness and failures. And now, sitting in front of her at a table in one of the city's most prestigious law firms were a former federal judge and three attorneys willing to listen to her story of how she believed she had been wronged. "I was absolutely delirious that the truth was coming out," she said later.

In contrast to how they accepted Sukhreet's story, Tyler and his investigators found Judge Gabel's statement that she had known nothing of the relationship between Andy and Bess while deciding on his alimony payments to be "evasive and unconvincing."

Even before Tyler handed over his report to Koch at Gracie Mansion on Wednesday, April 8, there seemed to be too much adverse publicity for Bess to return as an effective commissioner in the Koch administration. The seventy-four-page litany made it impossible. The report portrayed Bess as a scheming, manipulative woman who had abused her city office to help lower her boyfriend's alimony payments by taking advantage of a distraught elderly mother worried about her troubled only child. Tyler had concluded that Bess had been guilty of "serious misconduct" and the mayor should ask her to resign.

In the report Tyler found that "Ms. Myerson's employment of Sukhreet Gabel was intended to, and did, improperly influence Justice Gabel in the conduct of the divorce proceedings. Indeed, even the facts we found just beneath the surface of the allegations quickly began to change our perceptions of the events that occurred in the summer of 1983. Although Sukhreet Gabel was well-educated, we learned she also had a long history of emotional disturbances and had, in her father's words, 'limited talents.' " The report further said that Bess "immersed herself in the Gabel household" and "developed an intense, almost surrogate mother relationship with Sukhreet. . . .

"As a result of these attentions, Ms. Gabel's emotional health blossomed. Her mother said Ms. Gabel had 'a crush' on Ms. Myerson and that she could see a change in her outlook. At the same time, we conclude, Justice Gabel showed in tangible fashion what Ms. Myerson's attentions could achieve. On July 5, 1983, in response to an ex parte motion from Mr. Capasso, she cut his weekly maintenance and support payments in half. . . ."

The summary continued with additional details of the Capasso divorce, of Sukhreet's experience at the Department of Cultural Affairs, and of Bess's having told Sukhreet to keep her "big mouth shut."

The report noted, too, that while its most "significant findings are that Ms. Myerson misused her city office to give employment to Sukhreet Gabel for the purpose of influencing her mother . . . we also find other less serious, improper behavior by Ms. Myerson."

The report harshly criticized Bess for having used city employees for personal errands, for once having directed one of her drivers to falsify travel records when she had him drive her out to Westhampton Beach, for having asked an assistant commissioner to lie on her behalf to cover up Sukhreet's hiring, and for having received "substantial gifts from Mr. Capasso of jewelry, and perhaps furs and the use of credit cards, a Mercedes, and a limousine, none of which had been disclosed to the city in violation of city law."

Tyler noted, however, another conclusion: "No witness had provided us with substantial evidence to support any allegation of misconduct by Ms. Myerson in connection with awarding of contracts to Mr. Capasso."

After reading the report, Koch agreed that Bess should resign. The mayor decided that if she refused to resign he would have to fire her. Peter Zimroth, the mayor's new corporation counsel, conveyed the mayor's thoughts to Bess's lawyer, Fred Hafetz, early that Wednesday evening. Haftez told him the mayor would receive a call from Bess in an hour or two.

At 9:15 P.M. Bess telephoned Koch at Gracie Mansion to offer her resignation. Koch said she also offered an apology for causing him embarrassment: "Her last comment was 'I hope that this won't stop us from having an occasional cup of coffee.'"

Early the next morning, before anyone had arrived in the City Hall offices, Bess walked into the building with her letter of resignation and left it with the police detectives at the front desk.

Typed on personal stationery, the letter read:

Dear Ed:

I will always be proud to have worked with you through the years and for the opportunities that I have had to serve the people of New York City, first, for four years as commissioner of consumer affairs, and then, for nearly that long, as your cultural affairs commissioner.

However, I regret that current circumstances are such that I can no longer be sufficiently effective to warrant my continued service in your administration.

I am therefore resigning my position effective immediately.

I wish you and your administration success in serving the needs of New Yorkers, a cause to which I have dedicated my public life.

Most sincerely,
Bess Myerson

During her three-year tenure as cultural affairs commissioner Bess had proved to be an effective advocate for the arts during budget negotiations with city officials, seeing that the agency's budget doubled from $60 million to $123.5 million, which allowed her to dramatically increase financial support to many of the city's major cultural institutions as well as the more than four hundred smaller cultural programs that the agency supports. At the same time, however, some senior-level managers thought she was a poor administrator.

"I don't think that she knew why she was there," said one senior-level administrator who worked for Bess. "I don't think she had any goals. For a while she tried to approach it like consumer affairs—see who's cheating, see if anybody is spending money on things where they shouldn't be—and then she came to realize that it was an inappropriate role for a cultural affairs commissioner. She was supposed to balance the city's interest against the interest of the arts. I don't think that she realized that. There was just no leadership."

Another important role of the city's cultural czar is to bring visibility to the arts, and many people in the arts faulted Bess for not being as visible as they would have liked her to be.

She also had a reputation for sometimes being embarrassingly unprepared for meeting on important issues affecting the cultural community. "She wasn't professional," complained the director of an arts group. "She showed up for one meeting with me in her curlers."

Staff members at the cultural affairs agency said that Bess frequently arrived at the office in a sweatsuit. She used to plug in her electric rollers in the men's room and change into dresses and suits that she kept in her closet, usually before noon.

With her staff Bess displayed both extremes of her personality. "She could be very tough," recalled a former senior-level administrator. "She was famous for her voice; that voice made people quiver. She was often really ugly to people, but often she was very nice to people. She showed a real motherly quality to everyone, not just Sukhreet."

Koch accepted Bess's resignation. In a letter he dictated that morning he praised her work at the agency and assured her that "our personal friendship will continue undiminished."

At a strained and crowded City Hall news conference a few hours later, Koch appeared unusually subdued as he read from a prepared statement and responded to reporters' questions with terse and abrupt answers. Following Tyler's advice, the mayor did not release the seventy-four-page report to the public that day; instead he provided reporters with only a five-sentence summary of Tyler's conclusions. Tyler had asked the mayor not to make the report public because it might jeopardize the continuing investigation of the U.S. attorney, Rudolph Giuliani, his longtime friend. Noting that bullets had been fired into the home of a former Nanco employee during Andy's investigation, Tyler also requested that Koch keep the report secret so that "witnesses could be protected."

"Judge Tyler's findings are distressing, to say the least," the mayor read from his statement that morning. "Bess Myerson and I have been close friends for more than twenty years. I owe her much as a friend and as the commissioner of cultural affairs, in which capacity she has made significant contributions to the life of this city. While I will not comment on the particular issues or allegations discussed in Judge Tyler's report, I know that professionally and personally this has been a very difficult time for Bess Myerson.

"But Bess Myerson fully recognizes my responsibilities as mayor of the city of New York and recognizes that our friendship can never stand in the way of carrying out those responsibilities. Acceptance of her resignation is personally painful, but as mayor I know it is the only appropriate thing to do."

The pained expression on Koch's face throughout the press conference and his solemn demeanor at the podium suggested that Bess's resignation was for him perhaps the most difficult and embarrassing resignation since the city's corruption scandal first broke out in January 1986 with Donald Manes's attempted suicide.

Although she had not been an "insider" for more than ten years, since his 1977 campaign and the early days of his first term, Bess's departure from Koch's administration was perceived to be extremely damaging to him politically. In the public's mind she had been the unofficial first lady of New York.

Bess turned on her answering machine that day and refused to take calls. Her lawyer, Hafetz, released a statement on her behalf that said: "Although, in retrospect and with hindsight, Ms. Myerson believes it was a mistake of judgement [sic] to have hired Judge Gabel's daughter, Ms. Myerson did not intend to, and indeed did not, commit any wrongful acts. Ms. Myerson is further confident that the grand jury will conclude that there was no wrongdoing on her part."

Hafetz was shocked by the Tyler report. "It was a very unfair document," he said later. "It presented a very one-sided picture. All of what was in there was possibly subject to impeachment or contradiction. Yet it conveyed the impression that it was gospel. Additionally, wherever there was an inference that could be drawn for or against Bess, they drew it against Bess."

The day the report was released, *New York Post* reporter Charles Lachman interviewed Judge Gabel, who insisted it was an "absolute fact" that she had never called Bess on behalf of her daughter. "I can understand how people would think, 'Oh, she was doing it to take care of her kid,'" Judge Gabel told the *Post*. "It's not true. I never recommended her to Bess. I never did. My conscience is as clear as can be. As much as I love my daughter, I have never done anything that my conscience has bothered me with. . . ."

Another reporter called Nancy Capasso that afternoon to ask if she had any comment on Bess's resignation. "Oh, that's too bad," she said, her voice dripping with sarcasm.

After completing the report, Tyler sent it over to Giuliani to assist his grand jury investigation, which had abandoned its probe of Bess influencing city contracts to focus instead on whether Bess had bribed Judge Gabel by giving Sukhreet a job. Since bribery allegations involving state judges were normally handled by the state, some people were surprised that the report had not gone first to Manhattan district attorney Robert Morgenthau. He said he received it from Tyler ten days after it had been sent to Giuliani. "I did not see a case based on the report," Morgenthau said later. He called Giuliani's office and said they should, however, let him know if they were not going to pursue it. "Don't worry about it," Morgenthau said he was told. "We're doing it."

Giuliani's office proceeded with its investigation, interviewing many of the same people as Tyler had, including the former and present employees at the Department of Cultural Affairs, Andy's former live-in servants and drivers, and aides who worked with Judge Gabel. Since the probe seemed to be focused primarily on Bess, Nancy was now less reluctant to cooperate with investigators. She helped the government locate one of her husband's former drivers, and she invited one of Giuliani's investigators to meet Shirley Harrod, her husband's former maid, at her apartment. Nancy had met Harrod through a mutual friend after Harrod had been fired by Andy.

Meanwhile, reporters from six news organizations attempted to persuade the city and the courts to make the Tyler report public under the state's freedom of information act. On May 18, however, their request was denied. Manhattan supreme court justice Bruce Wright agreed the report should be kept secret. He said the report contained "shocking" statements of wrongdoing and noted that there was a "genuine possibility" of criminal prosecution. Despite Wright's ruling, the Tyler report was not to remain secret for very long.

Not long after asking Bess for her resignation, Koch invited her to Gracie Mansion for Passover. Koch later said publicly that he had extended the invitation because he worried that Bess would be so despondent over her fall from grace that she might harm herself. When word of Koch's invitation to Bess appeared in the newspapers, a federal official who had read the secret, politically damaging report believed the mayor intended to "whitewash the whole thing." A few days later writer Jack Newfield, then working for the *Village Voice*, received a copy of the report in the mail.

On Wednesday, June 10, the headline "How Bess Bought Justice" ran on the front page of the *Village Voice*. Inside, Newfield and Wayne Barrett published excerpts from the secret seventy-four-page document. For the first time details about Sukhreet's city job and the reduction of Nancy Capasso's alimony were made public.

The publication of the Tyler report, proclaiming there was "a secret understanding" between Bess and Judge Gabel, set off another frenzy of media coverage. By noon three television news camera crews were at the *Village Voice* to interview Newfield and Barrett. On the front page of the *New York Post* the next day the headline read "Bess Mess Rocks City Hall." Koch was once again under siege. The reporters in City Hall's Room 9 pressed him to make the Tyler report public, and after Giuliani said he no longer had any objection to making it public, Koch finally released it that night.

With the report's details now in full public view, Koch was not as reticent as he had been in the past about his old friend Bess. "I'm aghast at what she did. It's deplorable," Koch said a day after the *Voice* article appeared. "It has to be perceived, though, in the context of a person who I have known, who is without question suffering and has been disgraced.

"Am I going to reject her phone calls? The answer is no.

"Do I have any current plans on having dinner with her? The answer is also no."

"The Bess Mess" dominated the front pages and television news for days. Developer Donald Trump even injected himself into the controversy, calling on Governor Mario Cuomo to launch a special investigation. The pressure for the state court system to take some action against Judge Gabel was intense, and finally Judge Gabel reluctantly decided to retire from the bench. Reporters sought interviews with Sukhreet, who was only too happy to oblige.

Editorial writers were also quick to call for further action.

The *New York Daily News* expressed righteous indignation on its editorial page: "At long last, the Bess Myerson rock has been kicked over, and what's crawling out is sickening: arrogance, abuse of power, payroll manipulation, case-fixing, coverup. Small wonder so many people fought so widely to keep Judge Harold Tyler's report secret."

On Friday, June 12, the *New York Times* ran a strong editorial titled "Ms. Myerson, the Judge, and the Mayor," calling for "more public answers and appropriate prosecution."

"Two public offices were grossly abused when Bess Myerson, then New York City's Cultural Affairs Commissioner, hired the daughter of the judge presiding over the divorce of Carl Capasso, the Commissioner's companion. This transaction demands more public answers and appropriate prosecution. . . .

"Ms. Myerson has resigned, but her conduct as detailed by Mr. Tyler warrants further action. . . ."

In this climate the U.S. attorney's office worked at a furious pace to prepare federal indictments against Bess, Judge Gabel, and Andy.

As the scandal continued to swirl around her, Bess took refuge at Andy's three-acre estate in Westhampton Beach. She drove out there alone on Thursday, the day after the *Village Voice* broke the story, spending most of her time in a second-floor bedroom overlooking Quantuck Bay. "Bess is locked in her room and not even seeing friends," a servant told a *New York Post* reporter. "That poor lady is going through so much, she doesn't want to talk to anybody."

She emerged briefly that afternoon to visit with her daughter, Barra Grant, and her four-year-old granddaughter, who was always able to put a smile on her face. She ignored the large group of photographers and reporters who were camped out at the end of the driveway chronicling her every move.

Before the public release of the Tyler report on June 10, Bess had appeared to be handling her resignation quite well, considering the circumstances. She was keeping busy, working on a book with writer Susan Dworkin about her year as Miss America, and spending as much time as possible with Andy, who was about to enter jail. She said at the time that it would be difficult watching Andy go to jail, but that she would manage. "It has to be done. I will take it in stride."

She also talked about moving forward in her life. "I feel a vibrancy and excitement about life," she said. "It is a good time. It doesn't mean that it is all happy days. It means contentment, peace, and work, and relationships. Sometimes life is problematic and sometimes it is sad. It is all of these things. And one learns to take things in their stride, to move forward. I have had great joy in friends. I have had a lot of time for friends that I didn't have before. And I have had a wonderful time with this book. It is something getting to know myself again."

The renewed interest in her following the *Village Voice*'s article, however, seemed to set her back, close friends said.

That Friday night, June 12, 1987, Andy arrived at his oceanfront estate. It was the last weekend they would have together. On Monday he was scheduled to report to the federal prison camp at Allenwood, in the rolling hills of northcentral Pennsylvania, to begin serving his four-year prison term.

They spent Saturday sitting around his pool with his two children and her granddaughter. According to the reporters who watched them, Bess and Andy appeared to be relaxed as she soaked up the sun and he occasionally went into the water for a swim.

To avoid the photographers Bess left the house in her blue Mercedes early Sunday morning. Andy and his two children emerged from the house at about 11:00 A.M. and packed their belongings into his late-model Lincoln Town Car. Trailed by a caravan of reporters and photographers, he then drove about a mile over to Nancy's luxury condominium complex to drop off the children. He fought back tears as he stood in the parking lot for a last few moments with his children, lovingly smoothing their hair and pulling them near. He watched them enter the lobby of the complex and then drove back home.

On his way back to his Park Avenue apartment in Manhattan early that afternoon, reporters continued to trail him. He tried desperately to lose them, at one point zooming to ninety miles per hour on the Long Island Expressway. At his Manhattan apartment he accepted a pizza delivery at about 5:00 P.M. and later emerged from his apartment toting suitcases and refusing to say where he was going.

That night he was spotted in J. G. Melon's, a neighborhood bistro at

74th Street and Third Avenue, having dinner with two young, pretty blond women, one of whom he had met through Bess at her group therapy sessions. Bess was nowhere to be seen.

The next morning, on Monday, June 15, Andy, wearing khaki slacks and a light blue shirt, left for the federal prison camp at Allenwood in his Lincoln Town Car with his nephew, Michael Capasso. They then drove another fifteen miles to the dormitory-style prison on 420 acres, regarded as a "country club" by some because of its tennis court, two boccie ball courts, a law library, and an indoor gym. There are no bars on the windows. That day Andy moved into a small, linoleum-tiled cubicle equipped with a desk, a closet, and a bed. Once a millionaire contractor, he now would spend eight hours a day on custodial duty earning $.30 to $1.11 an hour.

Prison regulations allowed Andy eight visitors, eight times a month. To arrange for a visit Andy had to put the visitor's name on a list. Bess was not the only woman Andy invited to visit him.

Two weeks later, on July 2, Nancy Capasso got the news she had been waiting for. The state appeals court had reversed the decision of state supreme court justice Andrew Tyler and awarded her a $6.4 million divorce settlement.

In its unanimous decision the Appellate Division voted five to zero to award Nancy three times the $2.2 million she had been awarded at the end of 1985. In a harsh rebuke to Judge Tyler the court found that he had failed to compensate Nancy for contributions she had made to her husband's career and failed to assess properly the total value of the marital property, which they placed at $15 million.

As part of the settlement Nancy was to be awarded the $1.9 million estate in Westhampton Beach and $1.3 million from her husband's company. The court ordered that the $6 million Fifth Avenue apartment be sold by June 30, 1988, and that Nancy get half of the proceeds.

She also got the $200,000 waterfront condominium, $228,552 in furniture and household items from their Fifth Avenue apartment, and her jewelry, worth an estimated $144,650.

Andy got to keep his $400,000 Palm Beach condo and collect half of the proceeds from the Fifth Avenue apartment.

Nancy was ecstatic about her award, and when told that the settlement included Andy's three-acre Westhampton Beach estate she declared, "Oooh . . . that's where Bess the Beauty Queen is ensconced. I wonder how soon I can go in and get her out. This could be fun. I'll ask her for the key."

That July 4th weekend in Westhampton Beach, Nancy was pictured in the newspapers, sipping champagne, celebrating her victory. "I hope that I can start putting the pieces of my life back together," she said.

She talked, too, with Marcia Kramer about her fantasy of going over to the waterfront estate and kicking Bess out. "I know she's there. But I don't know what the law allows. . . . She's got what's coming to her. Bess is a very manipulative woman. I feel she was punished for what she did."

Then, referring to Betty Bienen, a forty-two-year-old former model who was the ex-wife of a handbag manufacturer and had been identified in the *New York Post* as the other woman Andy had invited to visit him at Allenwood, Nancy said: "Just the fact that there is another woman is almost enough."

Sukhreet Gabel had not seen a copy of the Tyler report until she read the excerpts in the *Village Voice*, so she was furious when she read that her father had described her to Tyler as having a history of emotional disturbances and being of "limited talents." She was also indignant that her mother's attorney, Philip Schaeffer, had seemingly portrayed her to reporters and to prosecutors as being troubled, thereby suggesting that her testimony was unreliable. She felt he was trying to make a fool out of her to undermine her credibility so that he could protect her mother.

Out of anger Sukhreet called Assistant U.S. Attorney David Lawrence on June 15, five days after the Tyler report became public, and asked him whether she might come down and meet with him. She had previously testified before the grand jury in March and then again in May. "I felt that there were certain things that had not come up in the grand jury sessions, and there were certain details that I had subsequently remembered that I thought might be useful in getting to the truth of this matter," she said later. Lawrence invited her to meet with him that night.

Sukhreet arrived downtown at around 5:00 P.M. to meet with Lawrence, Lombardi, and Ford as well as other members of the U.S. attorney's staff. On the telephone Lawrence had told her she was free to bring an attorney to the meeting, but Sukhreet said she wanted to come alone. She told them about her concerns that her mother's lawyer was trying to hurt her credibility. To Lawrence and other members of the U.S. attorney's staff, that sounded like a possible violation of federal law, maybe even obstruction of justice.

The next day two FBI agents, along with Lawrence, Ford, and Lombardi, went to Sukhreet's apartment with her consent to install a device on her telephone to record conversations. The intention was that she get Schaeffer on the telephone so they could eavesdrop on the conversation and determine whether there was anything to Sukhreet's allegations.

At 8:10 P.M., while the FBI agents and assistant U.S. attorneys stood in her living room and watched, Sukhreet dialed Schaeffer's office at White and Case, a Manhattan law firm, but he had already gone for the day. She next tried to call him at home, but there was no answer. Then she called her mother to see if Schaeffer was there. Earlier in the day Schaeffer had held a press conference to announce that Judge Gabel would step down from the bench temporarily due to health problems. He told reporters that the judge was suffering from syncope, a sudden fall of blood pressure that can cause fainting or loss of memory, and was unable to fulfill her judicial duties.

When Judge Gabel answered, the tape-recording device continued to run, which Sukhreet did not bother to tell her mother. Judge Gabel told her she thought Schaeffer was out of town. Disappointed, Sukhreet tried to elicit information from her mother about how she had come to know Schaeffer in the first place. She ended the conversation by telling her mother to have Schaeffer give her a call if she heard from him.

Instead of removing the tape-recording device from Sukhreet's telephone that night, the federal officials decided to leave it on in case Schaeffer returned her call. Tony Lombardi showed her how to use the toggle switch to shut the device off so she would not tape anyone inadvertently. Leaving the tape-recording device with Sukhreet turned out to be what everyone involved in the case later acknowledged was possibly the biggest mistake of the investigation.

Sukhreet apparently did not learn how to operate the toggle switch properly. Over the next few days she taped virtually all of her telephone conversations, including a call to her parents on a Saturday night. Her parents did not say anything incriminating on the tapes, so when the tapes became public, the defense lawyers pointed to them as evidence that the government had tried to turn a child against her parents.

According to transcripts of the telephone conversations, Sukhreet asked her father and mother for a "family conference" so that she could learn what was going on: "I think we should try, the three of us, to cooperate, try to reconstruct the events. And then to figure out what the hell is going on today in terms of Myerson's strategy and a lot of other things. Because obviously we are her enemies at this time and she is a very rich, very manipulative lady."

Her mother tried to change the subject, but Sukhreet kept bringing the conversation back to her request for the "family conference."

Finally, in what sounds like an effort to placate her, Judge Gabel agreed, telling Sukhreet, "We've got something to talk about."

"Of course we do," Sukhreet said.

"You know I think you are wonderful," her mother said.

"What do you mean?" asked Sukhreet.

"You're a wonderful woman. I think you've done a lot of good."

"Well, Mother, I tell you the truth—listen, I have been grievously wronged through no fault of my own, and that makes me ever so much more determined to get to the bottom of this and to redeem myself, as it were, and I think there are an awful lot of people out there who for one reason or another do not want to see that happen, and I want to get to the bottom of it."

"Okay, honey, we'll try," Judge Gabel said.

"And figure out why, and I need your help."

"I'm at your service, but I gotta hang up," the judge said.

At their family conference Sukhreet didn't learn anything new. Yet she continued to try to elicit from her parents information that she could provide to her new friends in the U.S. attorney's office, whom she fondly referred to as "the boys."

Sukhreet enjoyed the attention she got from the prosecutors and the press, who called her constantly for interviews. The federal investigation of Bess and her mother was almost like having a full-time job.

Most importantly, Sukhreet believed the federal investigation would finally vindicate her by showing she had been a victim, "a pawn in the chess game," wronged by Bess Myerson and her mother, rendering her unemployable.

During the first week of August, without the knowledge of the federal prosecutors, Sukhreet helped her mother clean out her closet. When she came across boxes and boxes full of her mother's files, she asked, "Can't we get rid of some of this clutter?"

According to Sukhreet, her mother replied, "Dear, I'd be so delighted if you'd help me. That's wonderful of you."

Sukhreet spent hours going through the files and found a number of documents that she thought might be of some relevance to the case. They were mostly letters that her mother had written on Sukhreet's behalf in 1982 and 1983. Sukhreet stuffed the material into four shopping bags and, without her mother's knowledge or consent, took the documents to the U.S. attorney's office. After Lawrence said that he admonished Sukhreet for bringing him the documents, Sukhreet said her mother had given her permission to remove the papers. Instead of examining all of the papers, Lawrence told her he would inspect only those documents that Sukhreet wished to show them. He reminded her that she was under no obligation to produce any records at all.

Nevertheless, the image of a daughter testifying against her mother and taking documents out of her mother's closet and delivering them to the U.S. attorney's office to be used against her in a federal investigation troubled some members of that office.

Although a former assistant U.S. attorney said he argued against bringing an indictment against Judge Gabel, Giuliani said no one approached him with strong objections to the case.

To Giuliani it was about judicial corruption and an abuse of power, and it involved the one member of the Koch administration who mattered most of all to Mayor Koch.

At eleven o'clock on the morning of Wednesday, October 7, almost fifty reporters, photographers, and camera crews crowded into the lobby of the U.S. attorney's office in lower Manhattan. Rudolph Giuliani had called a press conference to announce an indictment, and everyone in the room expected the subject to be Bess. For days rumors had been circulating around the courthouse and City Hall that his grand jury investigation was coming to a close.

"Is everybody set?" Giuliani asked, looking up at the crews pointing eight television cameras at his podium. Then he began his prepared speech: "Former New York City Department of Cultural Affairs Commissioner Bess Myerson was charged today with conspiracy, mail fraud, and the use of interstate facilities to further the crime of bribery. . . ."

The same charges were brought against Andy Capasso and Judge Gabel. An additional charge, obstruction of justice, was filed against Bess for having gone to Sukhreet's apartment that June night in 1986 and having tried to avert justice.

The six-count indictment contained many of the same findings outlined in the Tyler report. There did not appear to be much evidence other than what the government alleged were "secret meetings" between Bess and Judge Gabel, which began soon after the judge began ruling on preliminary motions in the Capasso divorce case in 1983. The indictment also charged that to conceal her efforts to influence Judge Gabel Bess sometimes used "fictitious names" when leaving messages at the judge's chambers. It further charged that Bess had deceived the mayor by lying to him in an October 18, 1983, memo about the circumstances surrounding Sukhreet Gabel's hiring.

"Why this was not the subject of a judicial misconduct proceeding in 1983 and why was the judge found qualified for reappointment is a question the state authorities have to answer," Giuliani said at the press conference, flanked on one side by the city's Department of Investigation commissioner Ken Conboy and on the other by Assistant U.S. Attorney David Lawrence. "If things were working correctly, they should have led to a vigorous investigation of the conduct of the judge," Giuliani said. "At a minimum that should have happened."

Bess remained secluded in her Upper East Side apartment that day. Once again it was her attorney, Fred Hafetz, who released a statement, saying that she "unequivocally asserts her innocence of all of the charges that have been filed against her."

"After many months of rumors that have circulated in the media of an investigation of her, at long last she welcomes the opportunity to confront these charges in the courtroom," Hafetz said. "She is confident that she will be vindicated of all charges at trial."

A few blocks away in the midtown Manhattan offices of the prestigious law firm Shea & Gould, Judge Gabel, wearing a patch over her right eye to protect the eye after a recent bout with glaucoma, used a magnifying glass to read a nine-sentence statement denying any wrong-doing. She spoke slowly, with little emotion, as she sat next to her husband in the law offices of her attorney, Michael Feldberg.

Asked if she was upset, she replied that she was not. "I am totally convinced of the propriety and innocence of my actions," she said.

Sukhreet was not with her mother that afternoon. She was holding court with the television cameras and reporters in her apartment. "The feeling is absolutely glorious that the truth is finally getting out," she said. "This is no longer a deep dark secret that I am going to live with the rest of my life."

She admitted feeling low about the trouble she had caused for her mother. "It is a lousy way for my mother to finish up a forty-six-year career for something that she had no idea was wrong. It was her best way of helping someone who was dear to her. I feel so awfully sorry for her.

"She expected to resign in glory. She expected all the judges would kiss her and hug her when she left. Instead, most of her friends are not calling. The saddest irony is that my mother brought this whole thing down through her own neurotic needs. . . . I blamed only myself until now. It really destroyed me. It all had to do with politics. It had nothing to do with me."

The newspapers had a field day with the indictment that had spun right out of the gossip columns. All of the tabloids devoted their front pages to the story. The *New York Post*'s front page said, "Indicted! Bess Pays the Price of Love . . . and Nancy Capasso has the last laugh."

Following the indictment, Bess once again found photographers staked out outside her Upper East Side apartment and camped at the end of the driveway in Westhampton Beach. She was spending weekends at the three-acre waterfront estate until Nancy got the go-ahead from the courts to take possession of it.

Bess managed to elude the press until the morning of October 12, when a *New York Post* photographer, sitting in his car at the edge of the driveway of Andy's estate, spotted her coming out of the house.

Dressed in a sweatsuit, without any makeup, she looked drawn and haggard as she loaded boxes and household items into a Lincoln Town Car. After noticing the photographer, she went into the house and later emerged in a fresh set of clothes with her hair tied up in a ponytail. When she drove out of the driveway that afternoon, she attempted to avoid being photographed by draping white towels over the side windows.

The next day Bess appeared in her sweatsuit on the front page of the *New York Post*, holding a pair of andirons.

When Nancy picked up the paper, she was "absolutely furious." She told the press that the andirons belonged to her, and she wondered aloud what else Bess might have taken from the house she had been awarded by the courts. "If she's taking little things like that now, I can only imagine what else she's taken," Nancy said at the time. "It's outrageous for her to get away with that. I want to know what else of mine she has taken."

The andirons were the least of Bess's problems that week. On Thursday, October 15, she was to appear with Andy and Judge Gabel for their arraignment on the charges in federal court. Andy had been transferred that week from the federal prison in Pennsylvania to the Metropolitan Correctional Center in Manhattan for the proceeding. She visited him only once, the day before their joint court appearance. They sat together for about thirty minutes in the crowded visiting room.

The next morning, she made her first public appearance since she had resigned in disgrace. She held her head high, like a queen, as she walked up the courthouse steps into the packed courtroom.

The arraignment lasted only a few minutes. All three defendants, Bess, Judge Gabel, and Andy, pleaded not guilty. Bess and Judge Gabel were released on bail. Andy returned to Allenwood. It would be another year before they would appear in court together again.

30
"Oh, No, Bess!"

I t seemed unbelievable to Bess that she had been indicted on federal criminal charges and now had to face trial. "It's as though it started as a little snowball someplace on the mountain and it just gained speed and it gained dimension and it gained weight and it became distorted and destructive," she told CBS correspondent Steve Kroft. "And I feel as though I was standing there and this thing hit me, and it's been a difficult time to keep picking myself up."

In the months since she had resigned from her city job and Andy had gone to jail, the stress she was under had affected all aspects of her life. She lost her appetite and dropped almost fifteen pounds. She started smoking heavily. At night she would lie awake for hours, sometimes not falling asleep until dawn. Most days, she wouldn't get out of bed until eleven o'clock or noon, according to close friends. For the first time in her life she had no place to go.

Not having a job seemed to bother Bess most of all, according to some of her close friends. She had worked hard all of her life, and in the past, whenever she went through a difficult period, she had immersed herself in work. She missed heading for an office so badly that one afternoon she called a friend who ran a small business in midtown Manhattan and offered to come down and organize her files.

Fortunately Bess had one project to keep her busy that fall. For almost two years she had been working with writer Susan Dworkin on a book about the year she had spent as the country's first Jewish Miss America and the difficulties she had faced during her reign. Part cultural history, part biography, *Miss America, 1945: Bess Myerson's Own Story*, was due out in the bookstores November 9, only a few weeks after Bess's indictment.

Despite all of the adverse publicity about Bess at that time, Esther Margolis, the president and founder of Newmarket Press, was determined to go ahead and publish the book on schedule. And even though Bess was under indictment, she remained committed to the project and ready to face the media ordeal of a book publicity tour. She was careful not to speak with reporters about her present troubles, however. She would speak only about her past. Recalling her 1945 triumph, she said later, made it possible to deal with her present troubles.

"I couldn't be happier about the juxtaposition of the book," she said at the time. "It was a wonderful part of my life, so in a way it takes me away from the present. . . . When I became Miss America, I was everybody's daughter. Then, in later years, I became everybody's sister. And then suddenly I found myself making speeches to women's groups, and they were all younger than my daughter. I became everybody's mother. . . . What is curious, no matter what I spoke about, when they came to questions, I could speak about equal wages [for women], I could speak about legislation on the [Capitol] Hill. I could speak as a consumer advocate. I could speak about consumer complaints and industrial mishaps and so on, and when I opened the hall for questions, the first one was always 'Why did you go to Atlantic City, and tell us about that year?' And this was men, women, children, older people. It was just something that was attached to me. Whatever space I occupied, that was on my right or on my left."

Her Miss America title gave her strength in other ways, too, that fall of 1987. One afternoon, she recounted, a woman approached her on the street and said, "Excuse me. Are you Bess Myerson?"

"Yes," she replied.

"I have to tell you something," the woman said.

"She was little more than waist high," Bess remembered. "I am looking down at her, and she was looking up at me, and she said, 'In 1945, I was in a DP [displaced persons] camp. My father had been killed by the Nazis. My mother had to bury him, and children in the family had been killed. I somehow was rescued out of that moment, and my mother survived. And then of course, we went to a DP camp, and one day in September in 1945 there was a paper that was distributed, and it said that a Jewish girl had become Miss America.'

"She said, 'I will tell you that my days were dark and continually dark. It was the only light day of my memory . . . and I had to tell you that.' "

Then the woman reached up to touch Bess's face, pulling her head down so that she could kiss her. "And she said, 'You don't know what it is to come full circle and to finally meet you. I have been nourished and fed by that all my life.' "

A few weeks after the indictment, on November 6, 1987, Nancy Capasso drove out to Long Island to inspect the Westhampton Beach estate for the first time since the court had awarded it to her as part of her new $6.4 million divorce settlement. The court had said that she could not take possession of the house until she had moved out of the Fifth Avenue cooperative. It had taken her almost four months to find another apartment on the Upper East Side.

Since the andirons episode, Nancy wanted to see in what condition

Bess had left the house, which she had continued to use after Andy went to jail. According to a court order, Andy was enjoined from "interfering with, damaging, defacing or removing" any of the items in the house that had been acquired during the marriage and before the divorce proceedings began. The house was supposed to have been left fully furnished for her, but neighbors had already warned her that she might not find it that way. A moving truck had been in the driveway a few weeks before.

When she walked into the house that afternoon, however, she was unprepared for the sight that greeted her. The house had been virtually stripped of all of its furniture and appliances. Gone were four television sets, the VCR, a $10,000 Oriental rug, an antique clock, expensive lamps, and thousands of dollars' worth of sofas, chairs, tables, and paintings.

In the living room, where once had sat two $5,000 couches, two chairs, a coffee table, and an antique side table, she found only a wicker settee. Also missing from the living room were a $7,500 collection of hand-carved wooden decoys, two paintings, an antique barometer, and the andirons.

Upon checking the kitchen, Nancy found more items were missing. Gone were the kitchen chairs, along with all of the dishes, silverware, and glassware that she contends she bought for more than $2,000 at Henri Bendel. A cappuccino maker and a set of Farberware pots and pans that Nancy expected to find were also nowhere to be found.

Upstairs she noticed that a number of valuable items had been taken from the five bedrooms, including an antique doll's cradle that had belonged to her eldest daughter, a Stieff animal collection, all of the antique quilts that she had bought at Sotheby's, and an armoire, a couch, a barrel chair, and two night tables. In the attic she had expected to find the eighteen place settings of Rosenthal china that her mother had bought for one of her daughters, but that was gone, too. Instead all she found was a Saks shopping bag filled with the electronic bugging equipment that Andy must have used during their divorce to record their telephone conversations.

Nancy called her lawyer, Myrna Felder, to ask what she should do. The first thing, Myrna advised, was to photograph each room so they could present the photographs as evidence in court that Andy had violated the court's order.

Within three months, in February 1988, Nancy's attorneys, Myrna and her husband, Raoul Felder, were able to schedule a court hearing to determine whether Bess, acting at Andy's behest, had violated the court's order prohibiting the removal of any items from the house that had been there during the time that Andy and Nancy had been married.

The Felders hired a private detective to find Bess and serve her with a subpoena requiring her to appear in court and answer their questions under oath about the disappearance of the furnishings and other items.

The private detective was Bo Dietl, a highly decorated former New York City police detective who had recently traded in his gold shield to start his own private investigation firm. Dietl assigned four investigators to track down Bess after discovering that she was not staying at her two-bedroom apartment in the East Seventies off Fifth Avenue. They found that she apparently had taken up residence in Andy's huge duplex apartment on Park Avenue.

At six o'clock on Monday, February 22, Dietl left his office in Queens and drove into Manhattan so that he could deliver the court summons to Bess. To make sure that Bess was home, he called Andy's apartment from his car phone, hanging up as soon as he recognized Bess's distinctive voice. "I couldn't let on to her that I was coming," he said later.

When he pulled up outside the Park Avenue apartment, he made his way past the doorman, went upstairs to the apartment, and banged on the apartment door. There was no answer. The law required him to hand her the summons in person. Finally he left, returned downstairs to his Cadillac, got on his car phone, and dialed her telephone number again.

At the same time, he noticed that a black limousine was waiting outside the building, and he suspected it was waiting for Bess to take her to a restaurant or the theater.

"Miss Myerson," he said. "My name is Detective Dietl. I would like to give you your court summons. If need be, I will follow you to dinner, and I will serve you in front of two hundred people. I think it would be a little embarrassing to serve you in public. Please accept it as the gracious lady that you are."

Bess paused for a moment, he said, and then invited him upstairs.

She opened the apartment door just a crack and took the summons. "She gave me a very nice smile," Dietl said.

The summons demanded that she appear in court two days later at 9:30 A.M. on Wednesday, February 24, 1988. Even so Bess had no intention of going to court to answer Nancy's charges.

On that morning Nancy Capasso put on a chic black wool dress and rode downtown to the courthouse with her lawyers in their Silver Cloud Rolls-Royce. Known as the Duke and Duchess of the matrimonial bar, Raoul and Myrna Felder were the flashiest divorce lawyers in town and the most potent team in court. Outside the courthouse were more than two dozen reporters and photographers, plus camera crews, waiting to chronicle the first face-to-face encounter between Nancy and Bess in more than five years.

Nancy let her lawyers do the talking. She was careful not to show her desire for revenge in front of the television cameras. "I have no comment," she told reporters politely as she walked alongside her lawyers into the courthouse. She was clearly enjoying all the havoc she was causing for Bess, though. Smiling widely, she whispered to Myrna, "I don't believe this. This is too much."

When the hearing began that morning at ten o'clock, there was no sign of Bess. Her lawyer, Fred Hafetz, and Andy's divorce lawyer, Samuel Fredman, were trying to quash the subpoena, arguing that Bess's appearance in a Capasso divorce matter might compromise her upcoming criminal trial. Manhattan supreme court justice Walter Schackman, who was assigned to rule on the remaining motions and issues in the *Capasso* v. *Capasso* divorce case, still insisted that Bess respond to the summons, like anyone else, and show up for the hearing. He asked her lawyers to have her in his courtroom by noon.

Out of concern that a face-to-face meeting with Nancy in open court might turn his courtroom into a media circus and cause Bess more adverse publicity, thereby making it even more difficult to pick a non-biased jury for her criminal trial, the judge agreed, however, to hold the hearing in the privacy of his robing room.

While everyone waited for Bess to arrive, Schackman heard testimony from other witnesses whom Felder had called in his effort to prove that Bess had taken items out of the house. One of the witnesses was Tony Jerome, the photographer from the *New York Post* who had captured Bess on film carrying the andirons from the house and into the car. When Felder held up the photograph and asked Jerome if he could identify it, Nancy burst into laughter.

At 12:25 P.M. Bess finally arrived for the proceedings. Accompanied by one of her lawyers, Jeremy Gutman, she managed to avoid the press by slipping into the courthouse through a back door and climbing two flights up a back stairwell leading directly to the judge's robing room.

"The queen has arrived," quipped Raoul Felder.

Moments later the judge walked into the robing room and greeted Bess. He was followed by the lawyers, three pool reporters, and Nancy, who did not take her eyes off the woman she believed had stolen her husband and ruined her life.

Bess took a seat next to the judge, who sat at the foot of the long, battered wooden table. Nancy sat between her lawyers at the opposite end of the table. She stared coldly at Bess, who averted her gaze by twisting around in her chair to face the judge.

Nancy couldn't help feeling somewhat gleeful at Bess's appearance that afternoon. She looked pale and drawn, in a black sweater and skirt. Her shoulder-length hair was pulled back severely from her face by a tortoiseshell hairband. So this was the beauty queen who had become involved with her husband? "I looked at her and thought, this is where it all started," Nancy said later. "What a mess."

Sucking hard on a lozenge, Bess appeared subdued, almost stoic, as she was sworn in and gave her name and address to the court stenographer. She fingered a piece of yellow paper in her hands.

"You were subpoenaed to be here, weren't you?" demanded Felder.

She looked at him quizzically, and then Gutman reminded the court of Bess's upcoming criminal case. "I have advised her to assert the Fifth Amendment," he said. "It is her fundamental, constitutional right to do so."

"What questions do you want to ask?" the judge inquired of Felder.

"What happened to the missing stuff?" Felder shouted. "Who took what where? It seems hard to see how that would affect her criminal case. The Fifth Amendment should be a shield, but it is not a sword."

Turning to Bess, the judge said: "Miss Myerson, is it my understanding that you intend to invoke the Fifth Amendment privilege on any questions asked by Mr. Felder today?"

"I do," Bess replied in a low, firm voice.

"I don't see the necessity of asking all the questions," Schackman concluded.

Felder objected angrily, saying that he wanted to ask Bess about "the looting" of the house. "You can't just wave it like a flag!" he argued, referring to the Fifth Amendment.

Andy's lawyer, Sam Fredman, interjected a contention that Bess's decision to take the Fifth was not an indication of guilt or innocence. "There hasn't been a shred of proof to show that there has been any looting of the house," he said, his voice rising.

Bess nodded in agreement. Nancy continued to stare at her, but Bess never once caught her eye.

Felder repeated his request to be able to ask Bess specific questions. "I want to ask her about the stuff itself," Felder insisted. "Did she take the stuff? What did she do with it?"

But Judge Schackman cut him off. "Miss Myerson has, from her own lips, stated to the court that she intends to invoke the Fifth Amendment. I see no point in going any further."

He told Bess that she could go.

"Thank you," she said to the judge, shaking his hand. Then, without ever looking at Nancy, she headed toward the door and disappeared down the back stairs, out of the courthouse, past a crowd of television reporters, and into a waiting cab.

"This was a case of what the French would call noblesse oblige," Felder complained to reporters after leaving the judge's robing room and returning to the courtroom. "The queen kept us waiting for two-and-a-half hours, and then she took the Fifth Amendment to every question I asked."

Schackman resumed the hearing with Nancy on the witness stand.

She testified for almost three hours about all of the furniture and items that had vanished. She estimated the value of the missing belongings at $65,000.

Several weeks later, "in view of the total lack of defense," Schackman ruled that Andy had, in fact, violated the court order and wrongfully had Bess remove items from the house: "The photographs of Ms. Myerson removing andirons from the premises . . . [are] certainly strong evidence that there was a removal process in effect." Schackman said he could not "conceive" of Bess removing the items without Andy's permission.

Marcia Kramer, the *New York Daily News* City Hall bureau chief, had heard from one of her sources that the FBI had conducted an international background check on Bess, which had turned up records indicating that she had been arrested for shoplifting in London in 1969. After dozens of phone calls to Scotland Yard, she confirmed the arrest and published the story on Sunday May 8, 1988.

Bess had ignored her arrest at the London boutique until after she had been indicted on the federal bribery charges. She must have worried that her London arrest would show up on FBI records when she was fingerprinted and photographed following her arraignment. A few weeks later she quietly pleaded guilty to the charge and paid London authorities a $100 fine.

After the *Daily News* published details about Bess's arrest, many people who knew her found it difficult to believe. Then two weeks after Kramer's story ran, Bess was arrested for shoplifting again.

The arrest was made in South Williamsport, Pennsylvania, just eight miles north of the federal prison camp at Allenwood, where she had gone to visit Andy. He had been in prison for almost a year, and Bess had tried to visit him at least once a month. They could spend hours together at a table in the prison's huge visiting room. On warm days they could move out to the adjacent patio and sit at a picnic table under a white umbrella, looking out at the surrounding five hundred acres of rolling hills.

On Thursday morning, May 26, 1988, she made the four-and-a-half-hour drive from New York City to northcentral Pennsylvania in Andy's gray 1987 Lincoln. Instead of returning to New York that night, she checked into the ten-unit Northwood Motel, across the road from the prison, which cost $23 a night. She planned to visit Andy again the following morning and then drive back along Interstate 80 to New York.

To pass the time between visiting hours, Bess usually drove into nearby South Williamsport, up U.S. 15, to do some shopping. A favorite store was Hill's discount department store, which is similar to K mart. She had visited Hill's eight or nine times during the past year.

At about eleven o'clock on Friday, May 27, Bess parked the Lincoln in Hill's parking lot and walked into the store carrying a Hill's shopping bag that contained a wall clock she had purchased the night before.

Once inside, she took a shopping cart and put her brown leather purse into the cart's seat. She stuffed the shopping bag behind it and then pushed the cart over to the jewelry counter. She picked out a pair of bright red earrings shaped like seashells, and as she tried them on in front of a small mirror she caught the attention of Nancy Hill, the store's security manager, who first became suspicious of Bess when she saw Bess walk into the store carrying the shopping bag. Hill, who is not related to the store owner, decided to watch her every move.

A few minutes later she watched Bess take five pairs of the earrings, ranging in price from $1.97 to $8, and carefully put them on top of the Hill's bag. Bess next moved over to the cosmetics aisle, only a few feet away, and picked up two bottles of red nail polish, three bottles of clear nail polish, and Sally Hansen's "No Chip Acrylic Top Coat." She put them in her purse.

Bess then pushed the cart to the back of the store toward the shoe department. She chose a pair of white woven leather sandals, and put them on top of the Hill's bag, next to the earrings, and then hurried over to the hardware department. Apparently thinking that no one could see her, she put the sandals and earrings into the Hill's shopping bag.

All she needed now were batteries for the wall clock she had bought the night before. She walked over to a display of Duracell batteries and took the clock out of the bag. She opened the box that the clock was packaged in and shoved a package of size AA batteries inside.

Finished with her shopping, she pushed the cart over to the house-wares department, lifted her handbag and her Hill's shopping bag from the cart's seat, and headed for the front of the store, past the cash registers, and out the door.

Nancy Hill was right behind her. She caught up with her in the parking lot.

"Excuse me, ma'am," she said. "I'm with Hill's security, and you have items in your purse and your bag that you didn't pay for."

"I'm going to my car to lock it," Bess told her.

Hill noticed that she didn't have the car keys in her hand.

Bess identified herself, but Bess's celebrity didn't seem to register at all with Hill, who had no idea that the sixty-three-year-old woman wearing white Calvin Klein jeans, a white blouse, and a plastic hairband was the famous former Miss America who was now under federal indictment for bribing a judge.

She asked Bess to turn over the shoes, the earrings, the nail polish, and the batteries. Bess reached into the shopping bag and pulled out the white sandals. "I then asked her for the rest of the items, and she kind of stuttered and gave me the nail polish," Hill said later. "Then I said, 'Please come back in the store with me where we can talk in private.'"

Bess followed Hill to a conference room at the back of the store, and Hill read Bess her Miranda rights. She also asked Bess to turn over the pierced earrings and batteries that were in the bag. Bess insisted that she had purchased the earrings and the batteries the previous day; however, she was able to produce a sales slip for only the clock.

"My daughter will never forgive me. I don't know why I did this," Hill recalled Bess said as she paced back and forth in the room. "What's the matter with me? I should kill myself. Please pray for me. Can't I please just pay for the stuff?"

The stolen goods totaled $44.07. Bess had $160 in cash in her pocket.

Hill declined to drop the charges. Police chief William Smith was already on his way over to the store to make the arrest.

"You don't understand. I'm already in so much trouble, and I have to go to federal court," Bess pleaded. "I don't understand why I did it. I'm sick about it. . . ."

"Hold me, I need to touch someone," Bess said, turning to another employee, Linda Wolfe, who followed them into the conference room to assist Hill. Bess pulled out a photograph of her daughter and her granddaughter.

"She said her daughter would not forgive her and she would be ruined for life," Wolfe recalled. "She also repeated several times that she did not know why she did what she did."

While Hill and Wolfe waited for Chief Smith to arrive to arrest Bess, Hill offered Bess a glass of water. "Please pray for me," Bess beseeched her again.

"I kept telling her not to think about killing herself and that I would pray for her," Hill said later.

When Chief Smith arrived, he issued Bess a citation and told her that she would have to be arraigned on the charges in front of a local district judge because she was from out of state. She followed him outside to his patrol car, and they drove over to Borough Hall, where she was finger-printed and photographed. She begged both Smith and Nancy Hill not to tell the press about the incident.

But the word of her arrest had already reached the city room of the local *Williamsport Sun-Gazette*. When Bess arrived at her arraignment at about one o'clock that afternoon, a reporter, Rick Walker, was standing outside.

She brushed past him, refusing to answer any of his questions, and went upstairs to the tiny courtroom on the second floor of a building next to a submarine sandwich shop. Walker followed her and stood in the back of the courtroom. As soon as the proceedings began, she asked District Justice John McDermott to remove the reporter. McDermott declined her request, saying that he would not bar anyone from a public proceeding.

"So be it," she said, throwing up her hands.

McDermott, who didn't recognize the famous former Miss America standing in front of him at first, set bail at $150 after Bess told him that she had never been arrested for shoplifting in Pennsylvania before. She counted out $150 to him in small bills and told him she did not intend to return to fight the charges and would plead guilty "under protest."

Visibly upset, she walked out of the building with Chief Smith. He took her back to her car, which was parked five miles away in the Hill's store parking lot.

Within an hour the story had spread around the country over the Associated Press wires. Newspaper and television reporters from New York descended on South Williamsport. Bess's arrest made the network news that night. *Life* magazine sent a reporter to buy the same nail polish, earrings, batteries, and sandals that she had attempted to steal so that it could photograph them for a story about shoplifting the magazine was planning for the August issue.

The *New York Post*'s front-page headline the next day read "Oh, No, Bess!"

Bess went into seclusion. Her lawyer, Fred Hafetz, issued a statement saying that Bess, distracted by her pending trial, had mistakenly walked out of the store with the merchandise so that she could lock her car.

Some of Bess's friends, though, dismissed the distraction theory. They believed that Bess wanted to get caught. "It was a cry for help," insisted one woman who has known Bess for more than ten years.

Although Bess was worth at least $16 million that spring of 1988, another friend speculated that Bess had never been able to overcome growing up in the Bronx during the Depression and simply stole the items because she did not like to spend money. "Even though she's rich, she still feels poor," the friend said. "She is incredibly cheap."

But most psychologists and psychiatrists maintain that shoplifters like Bess, who walked into Hill's discount store with $160 in cash and could easily have paid for the items, commit their crimes because they feel "emotionally deprived." In a twisted way they feel that shoplifting is a reward.

Others say that shoplifting reflects the attitude "If you don't give it to me, I'll take it." The stolen item represents what the shoplifter really wants: love, affection, or sex.

Still others say that shoplifting is a sport for those who believe they are above the law.

Fred Hafetz did not want Bess returning to South Williamsport to face trial on the shoplifting charges that summer of 1988 when her federal trial on the bribery charges was to open in September. He appealed to the top county judge there to postpone Bess's shoplifting trial until after her federal trial, but the judge refused.

Bess never returned to South Williamsport for a hearing. On July 16 she pleaded guilty through the mail. Judge McDermott fined her $100 and ordered her to pay $48.50 in court costs.

Within days after Bess's shoplifting arrest in South Williamsport, federal investigators started checking with security directors at New York department stores to see if they had picked Bess up for shoplifting in the past. It was part of an effort to gather as much information as possible against her. A federal grand jury was also continuing to hear testimony about her multimillion-dollar financial dealings. If any of Andy's money from his tax evasion scheme could be traced to Bess, that might be the basis for a federal tax evasion case against her. Bess had come to believe it was all an attempt to pressure her to plead guilty to the bribery charges so that Giuliani's office would not have to bring its weak bribery case to trial.

The prosecutors did not have a strong case against Bess, Andy, or Judge Gabel. To prove there was a conspiracy they would have to show that there was an actual agreement among the defendants. And they did not have a single piece of direct evidence that they could point to as proof that any agreement existed whereby Judge Gabel would lower Andy's alimony payments in exchange for Bess's giving Sukhreet a job. They did not have it in writing, they did not have it on a tape recording, and they did not have an eyewitness who could remember any one of the defendants acknowledging that a conspiracy existed. They did not have what lawyers call "the smoking gun."

Instead what they intended to present to the jury was what they believed to be a strong circumstantial case. By introducing scores of documents and calling more than a dozen witnesses to the stand, they hoped to weave together enough testimony and details to create a scenario suggesting that what had happened during Andy's 1983 divorce proceedings was a federal crime.

From the very beginning of the case the prosecution had been plagued by problems.

Within days after Bess's arraignment on October 15, 1987, Rudolph Giuliani had attempted to persuade the federal judge assigned to the case, U.S. district judge Kevin Thomas Duffy, to remove himself. Giuliani contended that Judge Duffy and his wife were friends of Judge Gabel's. He also charged that Judge Duffy's wife had been appointed as a judge in the state's family court with the help of attorney Milton Gould, whose law firm was representing Judge Gabel.

Duffy adamantly denied Giuliani's charges and refused to remove himself from the case. He was convinced that Giuliani wanted him out of the case because of his "long-established and oft-stated belief that cases should be tried in the courtroom and not in the newspapers." But after Giuliani submitted a formal motion on December 31 requesting that Duffy step down, Duffy decided to give up the case. He could no longer be impartial in the face of the prosecutor's allegations. "I resent the unsupported assertions of the United States attorney and his tactics in attempting to disqualify me," said Duffy. "They apparently arise from a belief that my understanding of the law and the proper conduct of an attorney for the government would hamper the way he wants to prosecute this case. I doubt that I can any longer maintain that impartiality and the appearance of impartiality which are necessary to the proper administration of justice."

In January 1989 another federal court judge, U.S. district judge Constance Baker Motley, was assigned, but she removed herself from the case because she had known Judge Gabel and Bess for years. The wheel was spun again, and U.S. district judge John Keenan's name came up.

As it turned out, Keenan also knew almost all of the parties involved in the case. Before becoming a federal judge, he had worked in the Koch administration as the mayor's criminal justice coordinator. He was still with the Koch administration in 1983 when Bess joined the administration as commissioner of cultural affairs and when the alleged conspiracy occurred.

Even after her mother had been indicted, Sukhreet Gabel continued to cooperate with the federal government. Just five days after she accompanied her parents to the federal courthouse for her mother's October 15, 1987, arraignment, she made copies of her father's financial and tax records and handed them over to the prosecutors. She also gave them her mother's Rolodex, hoping they would find names and telephone numbers that might be useful to their case.

By the time of the indictment Sukhreet had completely convinced herself that she was on a quest for the truth. "I am so concerned with getting to the bottom of this," she said at the time. "If it results in my mother going to jail, so be it. This is as much my trial as it is my mother's."

She ignored the advice of close friends, including her roommate, Ken Chase, who counseled her to stop cooperating with the prosecutors and not to testify voluntarily against her mother. Sukhreet and Ken had met one afternoon in late 1983 at a coffee shop near the Metropolitan Museum of Art. They became such good friends that he eventually moved in with her. Sukhreet appreciated his companionship and his contribution to the rent. Over the years he had come to know Sukhreet's parents well. "Parental loyalty should come before the truth," Chase had told her, but Sukhreet disagreed. "This may very well release me of my guilty finding at the kangaroo court several years ago," she explained matter-of-factly, referring to her firing at the Commission on Human Rights.

Her regular visits to the U.S. attorney's office also gave her feelings of self-importance. She recalls telling one of the federal prosecutors that she thought her case showed "an incredible pattern of corruption" and the prosecutor agreeing that she was "absolutely right." She often insisted that the prosecutors and investigators involved in the case see her whenever she wanted to see them. At one point during the investigation, when they had not called her for several weeks and had declined to meet with her at her request, she became so angry that she threatened "to blow their entire case."

The case became her entire life. She agreed to meet with her mother's lawyers as well. She thought it would help support her contention that she was not motivated by revenge. She told them virtually anything they wanted to know that would help them prepare a defense for her mother.

Her mother's chief lawyer, Michael Feldberg, remained convinced that Sukhreet was acting out of revenge, however. A thirty-seven-year-old, Harvard-educated former assistant U.S. attorney, Feldberg was a partner at Shea & Gould. He intended to present Sukhreet to the jury as an unhappy, troubled young woman whose testimony against her mother was motivated by deep resentment over her unhappy childhood and her mother's success. He intended to point out that she not only taped her mother's telephone conversations gleefully but also took documents from her parents' apartment and carried them in shopping bags to the prosecutor's office. He tried unsuccessfully to block the prosecutors from using the documents that Sukhreet had taken from her mother's apartment, charging in a motion that she "conducted this illegal search and seizure as a government agent."

Sukhreet met with Feldberg and his associate, Steve Gersten, on several occasions, each time giving them more ammunition that they would later use to destroy her credibility as a witness at trial.

During extensive interviews with Feldberg, Sukhreet described a lonely and painful childhood in which she was "cruelly misunderstood by two parents who had different skills and talents and didn't care about me." She told him that she felt unloved and that her parents had no interest in her at all. "No one ever paid attention to me," she said. "No one ever believed me."

As a child, she said she believed that her father was disappointed in her because she was not a natural athlete, as he was. She remembered struggling so hard one day to learn how to jump rope that she broke her foot. She claimed that her parents did not believe at first that she had injured herself and it took her hours to convince them to take her to a hospital.

She openly acknowledged that she did not like her mother very much. "She is excruciatingly lazy," she told her mother's lawyer. "I don't find her a pleasant human being."

She said that her mother was always pushing her to succeed and giving her "insincere compliments." Instead of being grateful that her mother tried to help her find a job, she said that she felt humiliated, degraded, and insulted.

She then told Feldberg of one incident from her childhood in which she had experienced hallucinations that Feldberg declined to bring up at trial. When she was sixteen or seventeen years old, she recalled, as she was sitting in the bathtub she saw a figure in a long, black robe with a white powdered face, stabbing her repeatedly with a dagger. She was so paralyzed by fear that she remained in the bathtub for forty-five minutes.

She told Feldberg that the figure in her hallucination had been her mother.

By late June of 1988 the U.S. attorney's office must have begun to worry about the inherent problem of having a daughter testify against her mother. The office had also heard from Sukhreet and others that Judge Gabel had not been in the best of health in recent months. One friend of Judge Gabel's had told the office that the judge had experienced fainting spells. The U.S. attorney's office expressed concern to U.S. district judge John Keenan about whether Judge Gabel was capable of assisting with her own defense. But her attorney, Michael Feldberg, assured the court that she was competent to stand trial and "wanted very much to fight the charges."

On September 23, the day that jury selection was completed in the case, the prosecution raised the issue again. In a six-page letter to Keenan, the prosecutors, requesting a private hearing, wrote that "if it were determined that the physical or mental conditions were degenerative in nature or not likely to improve, the government would agree to dismiss its case against Judge Gabel in the interest of justice."

At the hearing in Keenan's chambers on Friday, September 30, just four days before testimony in the trial was to begin, Assistant U.S. Attorney David Lawrence asked Keenan to sever Judge Gabel from the case or to grant them an adjournment. "The government is prepared to dismiss the case against Judge Gabel in the interest of justice based upon her medical condition," Lawrence said at the hearing.

For the charges to be dismissed, however, Keenan would have to conclude that Judge Gabel was mentally incompetent to stand trial. The law mandated that he would then have to commit Judge Gabel for hospitalization. For the prosecution, it was the only way to get Judge Gabel out of the courtroom without dismissing the charges against her and still save face.

Feldberg vigorously opposed the application. "These are very serious charges that have been lodged against an extraordinarily distinguished citizen of our community," he argued. "She wants to fight them. If the government has an application to dismiss the charges, that's fine; they can do it for any reason they want. But to put her in the position where she loses the opportunity to fight them and gets put into some kind of suspense for some indeterminate period of time is grossly unfair to her. It is unconscionable of the government to ask it. She deserves an opportunity to fight these horrible charges and prove that there is no proof to support them. . . . We're either going to have a trial or we're not. We either want a dismissal or we want to have a chance to fight the charges."

Keenan decided to look at the law more closely before making up his mind. He asked that both sides return to his chambers on Monday—the day before testimony was to begin—for another hearing. "I seriously urge the government to reconsider the application for a severance and to amend it to be an application to dismiss in the interest of justice."

David Lawrence, Kevin Ford, and Stuart Abrams, another assistant U.S. attorney who had recently joined the government's team, met with Rudolph Giuliani that afternoon and talked over what they should do. They decided that the government could not dismiss the charges against Judge Gabel without a reason. What would the public think? For almost a year the elderly judge had had a federal indictment hanging over her head.

Instead they decided once again to argue before Keenan that the charges should be dismissed against Judge Gabel based on her "neurological condition, and possibly also her physical condition." They also intended to ask Keenan to consider removing Gabel from the case until further neurologic tests could be done.

At 3:15 P.M. on Monday, October 3, Keenan agreed to hear the government on this issue once again in a private meeting in his chambers. Feldberg was there, along with Judge Gabel and her husband. Keenan also called Bess and Andy's lawyer into the hearing.

Opposing the government's motion for further tests, Feldberg argued that Judge Gabel did not want a dismissal of the charges based on a finding that she was mentally incompetent. Then he told Keenan that Judge Gabel was eager to respond to the question of undergoing further examination.

"If it's an examination for neurological condition, I have no objection to that," Judge Gabel said. "But if it's an examination to ascertain whether I am mentally competent to stand trial, I would take grave exception to this. I believe that my judgment, my ability to understand the issues, my experience as a criminal judge . . ."

"Did you serve in criminal court?" asked Keenan.

"Yes, I served in criminal for a number of years. I believe I can do all that, and I have no objection to that. But I do object strenuously to the imputation which will come all over the city and the country that I am mentally incompetent to stand trial. I see no reason for it. I see the statement that I am making today, this very moment, as a statement of evidence that I can handle it."

Keenan agreed. "I find that she is competent to stand trial mentally," he concluded. "The trial is starting tomorrow at 9:30 in the morning."

31
The Trial

At ten minutes past eight on Tuesday, October 4, 1988, the opening day of her trial, Bess emerged alone from the Lexington Avenue subway and bounded up the long granite staircase of the Federal Courthouse in lower Manhattan. Arriving more than an hour before the trial was to begin, Bess was hoping to slip into the courthouse before the press arrived. But she was too late. A huge gathering of photographers, reporters, and television camera crews was already waiting for her on the steps.

"There she is!" shouted a photographer. As the crowd stampeded toward her, waving notebooks and microphones, Bess quickened her pace, walking briskly in her low-heeled patent leather shoes as the crowd surrounded her on the courthouse portico, among the massive Corinthian columns rising four stories high. Bess kept walking straight ahead, ignoring their requests for interviews, slipping inside the white marble lobby through the revolving front entrance door.

Now that her day in court had finally arrived, more than two years after the federal investigation had begun, Bess summoned up all of her strength to project an image of dignity. In an interview with her friend, *New York Post* columnist Cindy Adams, that was published that morning, Bess said she saw the trial as one more tribulation of a hard life.

"Life is very painful," she told Adams. "I had a bad first marriage, but from it came a daughter. I had a bad second marriage, but from it came a second career. I have lived with cancer. I must live even with the foolish parts of me. So now what I have to do is get through this with dignity. That means grace under pressure. Whatever the end may be, so may it be."

Bess had taken the subway to the courthouse in Foley Square on the advice of her lawyer. Fred Hafetz thought that the image of Bessie from the Bronx, the straphanger, would serve their case better than that of Bess, the powerful and wealthy woman stepping out of a chauffeur-driven limousine.

Bess no longer trusted chauffeurs, anyway. "They turn around and talk to the press even if you tell them not to," she complained to *New York Post* reporter Ann Bollinger that afternoon. "And even if you say nothing, they turn around and say you did.

"Nancy was big on chauffeurs," she added, unable to hide her contempt for Andy's ex-wife. Bess told friends that she blamed Nancy for all of her present troubles. She contended that Nancy went to the federal authorities after she did not get what she wanted from Andy during their divorce.

Bess took the elevator to the courthouse's fifth-floor cafeteria, where she bought a large cup of black coffee. She remained there for almost an hour, avoiding Courtroom 318, two floors below, until five minutes before the proceedings were scheduled to begin at 9:30.

She appeared perfectly composed as she entered the courtroom. Two weeks earlier she had arrived for the first day of jury selection pale, trembling, and hiding behind dark glasses. This time she strode into the imposing courtroom with its twenty-two-foot-high ceiling and gray marbled walls as if she were walking into a reception as the guest of honor.

It was one of the largest courtrooms in the thirty-one-story classical-style courthouse. Keenan would have preferred to have held the trial in his own, smaller courtroom on the fourth floor but agreed to move to larger quarters to accommodate the more than fifty reporters covering the case.

The first two rows of the press section were filled with sketch artists, who used binoculars to study Bess close up even though she was seated only a few yards away. Behind them were five rows packed with newspaper, television, and radio reporters from all over the country.

Bess was dressed in a black-and-white striped suit and red silk blouse. At Andy's suggestion she had cut her shoulder-length hair, and curled it into a fluffy bouffant style. Andy thought the curls made her look less severe.

At the defense table Andy was smiling and talking with his lawyer, Jay Goldberg, and Bess's attorney, Fred Hafetz. Dressed in a well-cut navy blue suit and starched white shirt, Andy looked haggard, with deep circles under his large brown eyes. Prison guards had roused him at 4:30 that morning from his jail cell at the Metropolitan Correctional Center on Park Row, next door to the courthouse. Andy was staying there, far from the more comfortable surroundings of the federal prison camp at Allenwood, Pennsylvania, for the duration of the trial. In what would become a daily routine, Andy had already spent several hours in a crowded holding cell in the bowels of the courthouse, waiting to be taken to trial. Some days, so many prisoners would be crowded into the holding pen, waiting for their court appearances, that Andy would have to stand for hours. The stench of urine in the cell was overpowering.

Walking to the well of the court, Bess smiled at Andy and then turned
to the other end of the long defense table to greet Judge Gabel and her
eighty-one-year-old husband. A quiet, soft-spoken man with blue eyes
and thick gray hair combed straight back, Milton Gabel accompanied
his wife to the trial every day, sitting directly behind her and attending
to her needs—from fetching her a snack from the cafeteria to putting
drops in her eyes.

The Gabels had also taken the subway downtown to the courthouse
that morning. Sukhreet had seen them off after going to their apartment
around 7:30 to help her mother put on her makeup and choose a blue
print dress. Sukhreet was furious that she had been barred from attending the proceedings because of her status as a witness. She had hoped at
least to hear the prosecutors and defense attorneys make their opening
statements. "I've spent two years working on this case," she complained
angrily to Marcia Kramer of the *New York Daily News*. "I probably
know more about it than anyone involved. Is this justice?"

Bess chatted briefly with the Gabels and then returned to Andy's side.
They had about fifteen minutes to visit quietly with each other over
coffee before Keenan entered the courtroom and took his place behind
the bench. A short man with a reddish complexion, thinning white hair,
and silver-rimmed glasses, Keenan looked like an Irish priest in his
black robes and stiff white collar. A few minutes later the twelve jurors
and their six alternates filed into the room. Bess watched them as they
took their seats in three rows of green leather swivel chairs arranged on
a platform adjacent to the witness stand.

Choosing a jury for most trials takes about a day. But in this highly
publicized case the judge took nearly two weeks to interview 150
prospective jurors so that he could eliminate those from the jury pool
whose prejudices or biases might prevent them from reaching a verdict
based strictly on the evidence.

Each prospective juror was required to answer a thirty-four-page
questionnaire prepared jointly by the defense attorneys and prosecutors.
The questionnaire was intended to probe their backgrounds, moral
attitudes, and knowledge of the case. Would they be biased against a
man accused of beating his wife or a woman who had had a relationship
with a married man? Did they believe that most public officials tended
to be corrupt? Those who answered yes to those questions and others
designed to ferret out any biases or prejudices were excused immediately. One potential juror lost the chance to sit on the jury after
writing that he had read about Bess's shoplifting "escapade" in Pennsylvania and believed as a result that "her behavior is inherently criminal."

The prosecutors were looking for older, conservative, middle-class
jurors with families. Such jurors, particularly married women, they

believed, would be deeply offended by high-ranking public officials' abusing their power and by a married man who had left his wife for another woman.

The defense team felt it needed an entirely different jury to win its case. The defense wanted well-educated, sophisticated people, who were capable of putting aside whatever personal feelings they might have about the case to return a verdict based strictly on the evidence and the law.

Throughout the interview process both sides could submit questions to the judge to ask prospective jurors. The defense lawyers relied heavily on Jay Goldberg's wife, Rema, for advice. An attractive, intelligent woman, she used her training in psychology and her experience as a career counselor to assess those jurors, who, she hoped, would conclude from the evidence that the government did not have much of a case.

After the judge pared down the original pool of 150 prospective jurors to fifty, the defense and prosecution lawyers chose twelve men and women and six alternates to hear the case.

The defense team counted itself lucky to have what it considered to be a well-educated jury hearing the case. There were six men and six women—a nurse, two engineers, a computer operator, a computer technician, two medical office workers, an administrative assistant in a bank, an artist, an unemployed actor, a nursing home administrator, and a retired postal worker. Rema Goldberg's top choice had been juror number nine. She was Linda Berardi, a pretty, petite, twenty-nine-year-old administrator at a state mental health facility in Westchester County who was also studying for a master's degree in psychology.

She struck Rema Goldberg as smart and tough. She was also single, an important factor, Rema thought, considering that the backdrop of the case was a bitter divorce. The Goldbergs also liked the idea that she lived upstairs from her elderly Italian grandparents, who had worked in the construction business, which they hoped might make her sympathetic toward Andy. "Smile at Linda," Rema would quietly coax Andy as they sat together at the end of the defense table. He would look over at the jury box, where Berardi sat in the middle of the second row, and smile and nod to her now and then. Andy called it "jury patrol."

Turning to the jurors after court was called to order, Judge Keenan reminded them about the seriousness of their job and gave them a few rules to follow: They were not to talk with anyone about the case or share their opinions about the case with one another until the very end. Although the jurors were not sequestered, the judge warned them against reading newspaper articles or watching television reports about the trial. "You have the Mets' play-off game tonight," Keenan said good-naturedly. "You've got the presidential election. Hopefully, you will be able to talk about the Mets in the World Series."

Keenan also explained to the jurors what they could expect in the coming weeks. First they would hear both sides lay out the broad outlines of their case in opening statements. Next the prosecution would present its case by calling witnesses. Those witnesses could be subjected to cross-examination by the defense. Then the defense would have an opportunity to relate its version of the events. Finally, before the jurors began their deliberations, the prosecution and the defense lawyers once again would speak directly to them in closing arguments.

Before turning over the stage to the lawyers, there was one last thought that Keenan wanted the jurors to bear in mind: "The government has the burden of proving each defendant guilty beyond a reasonable doubt."

Lawrence looked a little nervous as he rose from the prosecution's table and walked over to the podium set up in front of the jury box. He opened up a black binder and began reading in a soft voice that belied the dramatic language of his statement.

"This is a case about money and greed and the abuse of power. It is about the use of secrets, deceptions, and lies to keep the truth from the public. It is about local people who decided to use their wealth, their power, their positions of privilege to violate the public trust in exchange for personal gain and profit. This is a case about whether such privileged people are above the law."

From her seat at the defense table Bess stared intently at Lawrence with lips pursed and chin held high, her hands folded in her lap. Her posture was so rigid and her bearing so implacable that she looked as if she wasn't breathing. The only visible sign of tension was in her jaw, which she continuously opened and closed.

From the beginning Lawrence warned the jurors about what would turn out to be the single biggest hitch in the case: no direct evidence. "There will be no one or two witnesses who will be able to tell you the entire story," he said, nor "one or two documents that can reveal everything to you."

He also tried to prepare the jurors for the most distasteful aspect of the government's case, Sukhreet's impending testimony against her own mother. "The government, if it had a choice, would prefer never to call a daughter of a defendant or any child of a defendant. This is not a pleasant situation or something that anyone likes, but Sukhreet Gabel will not be taking the stand simply because she is Judge Gabel's daughter. The evidence will show that she is taking the stand because she is a witness in the case. She was part and parcel of the defendant's scheme."

Lawrence talked for more than two hours. It was ten minutes past noon when he completed his opening statement, too early to break for lunch. Since Bess, Andy, and Judge Gabel were each represented by a lawyer, there were three more opening statements for the jury to hear. The defense attorneys had decided among themselves that Jay Goldberg would go next.

He jumped up and in a booming voice told the jurors "why this unjustified prosecution was brought." Andy leaned back in his chair with a broad smile on his face and watched his attorney, looking as if he were in a nightclub waiting for the entertainment to begin.

Goldberg delivered. Pacing back and forth in front of the jury, he sought to make the jurors so angry at the government for bringing the case that they would disregard all the evidence and return what he called "a repulsion verdict." To accomplish this, he later explained, he needed to create "repulsion characters."

Using one of the oldest tricks in a defense attorney's bag, Goldberg intended to put Nancy Capasso "on trial" in the hope that it would make Andy more sympathetic and enable Goldberg to cast the trial as an extension of the Capassos' bitter divorce instead of as "a federal case."

"There was no fury as intense and mean-spirited as that of Nancy Capasso; no rage as venomous as that of Nancy Capasso once her love for Andy Capasso turned to hate and once her friendship for Bess Myerson turned to hate," he said. "When the case is concluded, and you have heard the evidence, and the judge's instruction, you will conclude that it is Bess Myerson and Andy Capasso who are the victims, and not, as the indictment wrongly charges, Nancy Capasso. . . .

"I pledge to you that you will not see one single, solitary believable witness, not one piece of documentary proof to support the claim that in the divorce case Andy Capasso resorted to any improper means, let alone sought to bribe one of New York's most respected, one of New York's most admired and revered justices of the supreme court, Hortense Gabel."

Goldberg took the jury through the entire divorce case, arguing that Judge Gabel had cut Nancy's alimony payments to shift "the money away from the greedy wife for the benefit of the children."

Knowing that he was not going to win much support from the jury if he kept them much past one o'clock without lunch, he concluded by telling the jury that it would be their "solemn duty, because you will have no choice—it will be your responsibility to return a verdict of not guilty. Thank you."

For the hour-and-a-half lunch break, Andy was led away to a jail cell behind the courtroom. Bess joined *Post* columnist Cindy Adams and *Post* reporter Ann Bollinger for a tuna sandwich on whole wheat in the courthouse cafeteria.

She had taken only a few bites from her sandwich when a woman approached her to wish her well. Bess chatted briefly about Hunter College with the woman, who said she was a fellow alumna.

After the woman left, Bess turned to Adams and Bollinger and sighed. "You can't just tell people to go away," she said.

When she finished her lunch, she lit a Marlboro cigarette and returned to the courtroom with a large cup of black coffee for Andy. They chatted quietly at the defense table until the judge returned and called the jury back in.

Next to present his opening statement was Bess's attorney, Fred Hafetz. He stood in front of the jury box, his hands folded in front of him, and began delivering the statement that he had virtually memorized the week before.

Hafetz spent the first half of his opening statement making a plausible case for Sukhreet's hiring. He outlined her lengthy academic credentials and her fluency in languages. But he also pointed out that Bess was unaware at the time she hired her that Sukhreet had recently been a patient at a psychiatric hospital.

He said that Bess realized that she had erred in giving Sukhreet a job when the *New York Post* ran a gossip item on October 18, 1983, but Hafetz asserted, "There is a world of difference between making an error of judgment and committing a crime. And what Bess Myerson did was to make an error of judgment, she realized, in hiring the daughter; but errors of judgment, thank God for all of us, for we have all made errors of judgment, are not criminal offenses. They are not acts committed with specific intent to commit unlawful criminal acts. They are what they are, errors of judgment."

Hafetz then conceded that following the *Post* gossip item Bess wrote a "misleading letter" to Mayor Koch as " a kind of damage control" in an effort to avoid a potentially embarrassing political problem she feared the *Post* story would trigger.

Bess sat at the edge of her seat, her head tilted slightly toward Hafetz, so that the hearing aid she wore would pick up every word. But when he came to explain why Bess had disguised her identity by leaving messages with false names for Judge Gabel at the judge's court chambers, Bess lowered her head in apparent embarrassment.

Describing Bess as a "complex person," Hafetz dismissed that damaging evidence against his client as "oddities of behavior in her, as indeed there may well be in all of us. But oddity of behavior or occasional unusual behavior does not a crime make."

Michael Feldberg rose to deliver the last opening statement that afternoon. In a voice filled with emotion he spent more than an hour describing Judge Gabel's achievements during her forty years of public service. He called her "a model of integrity and decency" and asserted that the charges against her were unfounded and based on "conjecture and speculation."

Feldberg questioned why Judge Gabel had met with Bess in restaurants, in public view, if she had been engaged in a "secret conspiracy." And he argued that if jurors looked closely at this "so-called horrible decision, this so-called product of the bribe, this tremendous reduction was really not a reduction at all. It was a rearrangement, it was appropriate, and it was justified by the facts."

As he neared the end of his statement, Feldberg walked behind Judge Gabel's chair and lowered his voice for dramatic effect. "We are in the presence of greatness in this room in the person of Hortense Gabel," he said, looking down at the judge. "Hortense Gabel is of a time when honor was everything, when people in public life put their good names ahead of personal gain and would never dream of compromising themselves. . . . You hold in your hands the light of Hortense Gabel's freedom."

It was after five o'clock when Feldberg ended his statement and the first day of the trial came to a close. Bess looked exhausted. She had been fidgeting in her chair for the last twenty minutes of Feldberg's statement and glancing at the jury box as if to study the faces of the twelve men and women who would decide her fate.

The next day, the testimony would begin.

When Bess arrived the following morning, she seemed more relaxed. Inside the courtroom she stopped and chatted with reporters, complimenting WNYW-TV's reporter Barbara Laskin on her on-camera appearance. Bess complained that the lighting was too harsh when the cameras televised her daily entrances and exits on the courthouse steps. "Maybe I should have gotten a face-lift like Nancy Capasso did in 1985," she said.

After that comment was reported in the newspapers the next day, Bess became more cautious in talking to the reporters who were covering her trial.

The first major government witness was Howard Leventhal, Judge Gabel's former top aide. A pale man in his early forties with short-cropped red hair and thick glasses, Leventhal had worked as a civil servant in the back rooms of the state supreme court for more than ten years.

He seemed to enjoy his role as a witness, frequently offering the lawyers—and occasionally the judge—his interpretation of legal points. Observers could not help concluding that testifying at one of the most dramatic and highly publicized cases of the year seemed to be the most exciting thing that had ever happened to him.

He looked directly at Judge Gabel when he was asked to identify his old boss in court. She rose from her chair, half stooped, peering at him through her thick glasses. A clear plastic cup holding two roses and a spray of baby's breath, a gift from her daughter, was on the table in front of her. Goldberg had seated the elderly judge in the direct line of vision of those on the witness stand so that when Sukhreet was called to testify she would face her mother and her father, who sat in a chair behind his wife.

Under questioning by prosecutor Stuart Abrams, Leventhal portrayed Judge Gabel as a veteran of city politics rather than one of the great judicial minds in the city's history. Abrams had Leventhal describe how Judge Gabel had handled the Capasso case differently from the other divorce cases during her two years as the court's presiding matrimonial judge. Of the thirty-seven hundred divorce motions that passed through her chambers, Leventhal testified, he could "count on one hand" the number Judge Gabel had handled herself.

Recounting the history of the rulings in the Capasso divorce case, Leventhal told the jury that the first alimony decision Judge Gabel had signed in June of 1983 granted Nancy $1,500 a week in alimony payments. By September, he said, the judge had reduced those payments by two-thirds, to $500 a week.

When Abrams asked Leventhal if he had agreed with Judge Gabel's decision to lower the payments, he replied, "No."

Since the government had no tape recordings of secret phone conversations or witnesses who could testify that they had overheard Bess and Judge Gabel striking a deal, Abrams attempted to suggest that the quid pro quo might have occurred during telephone conversations between Bess and the judge that summer. He had Leventhal tell the jurors about Bess leaving the phony names.

Leventhal then told the jury about the repercussions that had ensued after he attended a Christmas party that year at the office of Nancy Capasso's divorce lawyers, Raoul and Myrna Felder. While there, he saw one of Andy's divorce lawyers. About a week later, he testified, Judge Gabel called him into her chambers and said apologetically, "Bess heard that you were at Felder's party, and she was livid. So let's not go to any more parties at his place."

On Leventhal's cross-examination Judge Gabel's attorney, Michael Feldberg, set out to show that the judge's handling of the Capasso case had not been out of the ordinary and that the reduction in Nancy's alimony had been justified.

Feldberg got Leventhal to agree that it was "not unusual" for him and the judge to disagree about an award, that it had been "proper" for Judge Gabel to give Andy Capasso a rehearing, and that there had been "nothing unusual" about the judge's changing her first decision.

Jay Goldberg then took his turn. Goldberg had no intention of putting his client on the witness stand or calling character witnesses on Andy's behalf. Doing so would have enabled the prosecutors to question them about what they knew of Andy's tax evasion conviction and whether they had heard stories of his associating with reputed mobsters. To solve that problem Goldberg made Howard Leventhal into a surrogate character witness for Andy. He asked Leventhal to read from the three-inch-thick pile of Capasso divorce papers and affidavits that described Andy as a wonderful father and provider for his family.

From one affidavit written by Nancy's attorneys to show that she should receive substantial alimony payments, Leventhal read how Andy was so generous to his own two children and the three children from her previous marriage that they had lived in "a state of royalty."

"He fed, clothed, housed, educated, and loved those children in every way a father could do, and then some," Leventhal read, quoting Nancy from the affidavit.

Then Goldberg asked Leventhal to turn to the page in the affidavit in which Nancy described her life on Fifth Avenue in her $6 million apartment—a life of unlimited charge accounts, chauffeured limousines, eight telephones, and nine fur coats.

"Did she sound, as you read this, to be impoverished?" Goldberg asked incredulously, throwing his arms out pointedly.

"No, sir," Leventhal said.

"By the way," Goldberg went on, "did you ever make a statement that you believed that Nancy Capasso, from the papers that you read, was more interested in getting a Mercedes for herself than support for the children?"

"Yes, sir," Leventhal answered.

With Leventhal finished on the witness stand, the time had arrived for the prosecution to call on its star witness—a tag that seemed particularly appropriate for Sukhreet Gabel. In the weeks preceding the trial Sukhreet had readily consented to numerous newspaper, television, and radio interviews to address good-naturedly the question of how she could turn on her mother and testify against her in court. A few days before she was to appear on the stand she had flown out to San Francisco to appear on a talk show called "People Are Talking." Sukhreet's quirky charm, engaging personality, willingness to testify against her mother, and volubility with the press had made her the talk of New York.

As she explained shortly before the trial, "My role is neither to prosecute nor to defend. As a witness, my job is to tell the truth, the whole truth, and nothing but the truth." Still, many wondered about her motive and her insatiable appetite for publicity.

For the prosecution Sukhreet was a high-risk witness. Lawrence worried that jurors would be repulsed by the image of Sukhreet secretly taping her telephone conversations with her mother and surreptitiously turning over her mother's papers to the prosecutors.

The prosecutors also worried about whether she would be able to stand up against the furious assault they expected from the lawyers for the defense, some of the best money could buy. The defense had already interviewed the chatty Sukhreet extensively and had reviewed thousands of pages of grand jury testimony and statements to prosecutors to prepare for their attack.

But David Lawrence was hoping that Sukhreet would cut both ways with the jury. Lawrence thought that the jury would see that Sukhreet's eccentric personality had made it difficult for her to find a job and therefore would conclude that there had been no reason for Bess to hire Sukhreet except as part of a secret bargain to fix Andy's divorce. The prosecutors were willing to allow Sukhreet to destroy herself on the stand.

Sukhreet, furthermore, was the only person who could provide evidence that Bess had sought to obstruct justice by visiting her at her apartment in June 1986 and warning her to keep her "big mouth shut." The prosecution intended to argue that, by doing so, Bess had attempted to obstruct a federal grand jury investigation. The basis for the charge rested solely on Sukhreet's testimony.

Sukhreet was led into the courtroom by Tony Lombardi, one of the federal investigators and her favorite among "the boys." She smiled sweetly at her mother as she stepped up to the witness stand. Her mother, leaning forward with her arms resting on the defense table, smiled back. Publicly and privately supportive of her daughter, the inscrutable Judge Gabel had kept the two red roses her daughter had given her a few days ago in a plastic cup on the defense table. The roses had already begun to droop when Sukhreet took the stand.

With her flawless complexion and her brown eyes tinted green by contact lenses, Sukhreet looked much younger than her thirty-nine years. She was calm and composed and was dressed as if she were on a job interview, in a conservative gray wool striped dress that hung neatly over her ample figure. She reluctantly had abided by the prosecutor's request that she not come to court with her "animals"—the brightly colored dresses and blouses emblazoned with huge silk-screened prints of zebras, lions, and bears that she tended to favor.

The only thing odd about her appearance was the bright red wig that she was wearing parted in the middle and hanging neatly to her shoulders. Reporters chalked up the wig to Sukhreet's penchant for flamboyance. But no one, including her parents and the prosecutors, knew that she had recently lost clumps of her short blond hair due to chemotherapy. Four months before the trial, Sukhreet had undergone chemotherapy and surgery after her doctor discovered a lump in her breast.

Unaware of this fact, the defense lawyers would taunt Sukhreet unmercifully on cross-examination for using her parents' money to undergo what they had read in the newspapers to be liposuction surgery to remove fat cells from her upper body so that she could improve her appearance for the trial. Each time they asked her about the liposuction, she refused to tell them about the cancer. She felt that her mother was under enough stress and didn't want to add her health problems to the judge's worries.

Lawrence began by questioning Sukhreet about her job history and academic credentials. Sitting with her hands folded neatly in front of her on the witness stand's gunmetal-gray table, Sukhreet recited her long academic career in a perfectly modulated voice, nodding and smiling for the jurors. She reveled unabashedly in being the center of attention. "It was like dancing with Fred Astaire," she would tell WABC-TV's Doug Johnson after that first day on the witness stand.

At one point Judge Gabel turned to Feldberg and complained that she couldn't hear what her daughter was saying. He rose from his chair and asked, "Could you ask if Ms. Gabel could possibly speak into the microphone a bit so Justice Gabel can hear her testimony?"

"Mother? Is that better?" Sukhreet asked as she adjusted the microphone.

Her mother nodded and smiled.

A couple of jurors exchanged glances and appeared to be uneasy about the drama that was about to unfold before them. One veteran court marshal whispered to a reporter, "I've never seen blood testify against blood."

Lawrence seemed to sense the reaction as well and moved quickly to the most unpleasant aspects of her testimony. He asked Sukhreet to explain the secret tape recordings, the shopping bags full of documents, and her decision to cooperate with the government and testify against her mother. By having Sukhreet explain that she saw herself as only "a witness" who cooperated with her mother's and Bess's lawyers, as well as the prosecution, he was hoping to soften the impact of the defense team's attempts to paint Sukhreet as a troubled woman full of hate and revenge.

Lawrence next asked Sukhreet to tell the jurors about her futile fifteen-month job search after returning home from the University of Chicago in 1982. Sukhreet dutifully explained how her mother had devoted herself to helping her find a job. Then she described how she had met Bess at her parents' apartment. Over the next day of testimony Sukhreet related how Bess had "swooped down" on her that summer by inviting her to dinner, to the movies, and finally, that August, to Andy's estate in Westhampton Beach.

Offering a colorful, humorous, and detailed account of Bess's courting of her that summer, Sukhreet even mentioned the time that Bess

showed her a drawer full of Nancy's bikinis. The courtroom's spectators' section and jury box erupted into laughter. Judge Keenan, however, was not amused. A look of disgust crossed his face. "Let's get away
from the bikinis," he said sternly. "I don't think there's anything
amusing about it."

Up to this point Bess had been listening impassively. Now she was
visibly annoyed and, leaning forward in her chair with her jaw tightened, she glared at Sukhreet while clasping and unclasping her hands.

Bess continued to stare at Sukhreet as the star witness described the
rest of her Westhampton Beach weekend. As she was about to testify
that she also learned that weekend from Andy's maid, Shirley Harrod,
that her mother was presiding over Andy's divorce, Bess's attorney
jumped up to object. Fred Hafetz argued that the federal rules of
evidence do not permit a witness to testify about a conversation with
someone who is not a defendant in the case.

Since the judge needed to determine whether Sukhreet's conversation
with the maid and her subsequent conversations with her parents were
admissible, he asked that she recount them away from the jury.

With the jury out of the courtroom, Sukhreet turned to the judge and
told him that she had called her parents upon learning from the maid
that her mother was involved in Andy's divorce. She said her father
answered the phone and told her to "keep her nose out of it" and "keep
looking for a job."

When Lawrence asked her if she had discussed the matter with her
mother around the same time, Sukhreet paused. Shortly before the trial
had begun, she had told prosecutors that she had recently remembered
talking about the case with her mother. On the witness stand she
frowned and seemed to turn the question over in her mind, appearing
not to want to answer. In numerous interviews with reporters and
investigators in the past, she had mentioned only a conversation with her
father, never with her mother. Were she to testify that she had told her
mother in August that Bess and Andy were romantically involved, she
would directly contradict her mother, who had contended that she
didn't know about Bess and Andy until after she had lowered Andy's
alimony payments on September 14, 1983. It was a turning point for
Sukhreet, who had long maintained that she wasn't testifying against
her mother.

Now, on the witness stand, she was suggesting that she had discussed
the divorce case with her mother before that date. "I just don't remember the words she used," Sukhreet testified. "She said it really
wasn't very important and that it wasn't worth worrying about, just to
ignore it, to forget it."

The next day Judge Keenan ruled in favor of the prosecution and
agreed to allow Sukhreet's testimony about her phone conversation with

her father. She related the conversation in a dramatic tone of voice and almost exactly as she had the day before.

But when she got to the conversation with her mother, her recollection was different from what she had related the previous day. While she still contradicted her mother's contention that the conversation never took place, it was as if, overnight, she had decided that she could go only so far in placing her mother at the center of the conspiracy. "What I remember is a very vague response on my mother's part, which I think involved a shrug of the shoulders," Sukhreet said as she imitated her mother by elaborately raising both hands in a gesture that seemed to say "Who knows?" Then she said quietly, "She had a very sad expression on her face."

On her third day on the stand Lawrence had just one final story for Sukhreet to tell the jury, and it was this testimony that many expected to be the most damaging to Bess. It was Sukhreet's story about Bess's having called her at home after the federal investigation had begun and suggesting that they go for a walk around the block. During that walk, Sukhreet contended, Bess tried to persuade her not to talk with the authorities about the circumstances of her hiring at the Department of Cultural Affairs.

As Sukhreet began testifying about that night, Bess sat at the defense table with her chin held high, looking haughty and disbelieving. A slight smile played around her lips, as if to say to the jury, "Isn't this ridiculous?"

"We've got to get our stories straight," Sukhreet quoted Bess to the jury. "The trouble with you is that you remember too much. You have got to learn to forget more. I have forgotten more than you have ever, ever known."

To reinforce the public's perception of her as a witness in the case, and not exclusively a tool of the prosecution, Sukhreet had agreed to extensive interviews with her mother's and Bess's attorneys during the summer before the trial.

After two days of Hafetz's aggressive and brutal questioning about her background and her knowledge of the case, she had jokingly told government lawyers that she was going to get a T-shirt that read "I Survived Fred Hafetz."

But they had told her that might be premature. They knew that it was difficult for any witness to survive Hafetz in a courtroom. If Sukhreet thought he was tough on her in his office, they warned, she could expect him to be merciless during his cross-examination. They were right.

Outside the courtroom Hafetz is a charming man who speaks with pride about the accomplishments of his four teenage boys. But once he steps into the well of the court, he becomes a fierce advocate.

It was Monday morning, October 17, when he stood up to take his first shot at Sukhreet. She had just finished giving her most damning testimony about Bess.

Of the three defense attorneys, Hafetz had the hardest job. His task was to present Sukhreet as a perfectly suitable—even extraordinary—job candidate for Bess to have hired in 1983. Having established that, Hafetz intended to do his savage best to damage her credibility in the eyes of the jury.

To emphasize to the jurors that Bess might have been fooled by Sukhreet's qualifications, Hafetz asked Sukhreet to recite her academic record for the jury again. She seemed to be delighted to talk about her graduate work one more time and to read from the glowing letters of recommendation from her professors at the University of Chicago and New York University.

Then Hafetz suddenly switched the direction of his questions and went in for the kill, hammering away at Sukhreet so relentlessly that he reminded one reporter of a "terrier gnawing at a bone."

"Am I correct that you received fifteen electroshock treatments to your head at some time after you left DCA?" he began.

"I'm not certain of the number," Sukhreet said without flinching, "but you are certainly in the ballpark there. That is correct."

"And this was over how long a period of time?"

"I believe it was over a period of a month," she replied.

"I see," he nodded, walking toward her. "When you say electroshock treatments, those are electric or electro-current shock treatments to your brain, are they not?"

"That is correct," she said cautiously.

"Is that what we are talking about?"

"Yes." Her voice faltered. A look of fear crossed her face.

"Now, with regard to the electroshock treatment, am I correct, Ms. Gabel, that you have previously testified that the effect of those electroshock treatments on your mind was to make your memory selective, rather like a Swiss cheese with holes in it? Did you make that statement?"

"Yes, I did."

Sukhreet slumped down in her seat, her credibility collapsing in the face of Hafetz's surprise attack. Becoming increasingly rattled by his assault, she was unable to remember names, dates, places, or events from 1983. She told Hafetz that the shock treatments were in 1986, about the same time she had had the walk around the block with Bess Myerson, when in fact they had begun the year before. "I get all confused when it comes to those years," she said. "I have been known to mess up years. More rapidly than seasons generally."

As he continued to shout questions at her in his loud, insistent voice, Sukhreet fell apart.

At the defense table Bess sat on the edge of her seat, opening and closing her mouth. A slight smile crossed Andy's lips. Judge Gabel looked distressed, as if she would jump up at any moment and try to restrain Hafetz from shouting at her daughter.

"In an interview with the *New York Post* yesterday," Hafetz continued, "did you refer to the prosecutors as 'the boys'? Yes or no, Ms. Gabel?"

"I don't remember."

"You don't remember yesterday?"

Sukhreet screwed up her face like an angry little girl. "I don't remember yesterday."

Hafetz paused for a beat. He smiled cruelly and then asked sarcastically, "Do you know what day of the week you took the stand last week, Ms. Gabel? Do you recall that?"

"No, I don't remember."

"I see," he said, raising his eyebrows. "Did you take the stand last week?"

"Yes," Sukhreet said disgustedly.

"No Swiss cheese on that, right?" Hafetz shot back.

Hafetz did not let up, continuing his assault hour after hour through Monday afternoon and the following day. Although he was attacking her relentlessly, the prosecutors did not make frequent objections. It was as if they had decided to let Sukhreet hang out to dry.

Despite his brutal, but brilliant, cross-examination, Hafetz was unable to get Sukhreet to back down from her story. He was, however, successful in systematically challenging her credibility and creating the impression that Sukhreet had trouble remembering things. He suggested it was possible that she even made up events. Quoting grand jury testimony she had given sometime in 1987, Hafetz read to the jury, "I'm getting confused between knowing something and thinking something must have been. . . ."

Then he read aloud from statements that she had given to David Lawrence during the investigation. After telling him an anecdote about life at Andy Capasso's home in Westhampton Beach, she had said, "Oh, dear, am I making this up?"

By the end of the second day of cross-examination Sukhreet had begun to recover. Instead of giving Hafetz a blank look or a silly answer, she began engaging him in a philosophical debate about the meaning of truth. It became a battle of wits.

When, at one point, he asked her if she was committing perjury, she turned to Keenan and said, "I would request a copy of *Black's Law Dictionary*."

Then, after Hafetz sarcastically asked her if "a thunderbolt struck you and gave you that memory recollection," she shot back, "No, I haven't been in the rain lately."

Several times she gave a persuasive explanation for why she had testified differently about the same event. "The more time that you spend thinking about a particular event," she said, "searching your memory, trying to remember what happened, being asked the same question not once but twice and three and four times, the more you find that you do recollect."

But then she would quickly stumble again.

"Both times you were under oath," Hafetz yelled at her, "both times you swore that you were telling the truth, and both times you gave two different answers, am I right?

"You are absolutely correct, Mr. Hafetz," she said with a sigh, a sarcastic tone creeping into her weary voice.

"And, Ms. Gabel," he said, his voice rising, "do we have any guarantee that if you come back next month we are not going to hear yet a third inconsistent story from you?"

"It is conceivable," she said.

Before walking away from Sukhreet, Hafetz had just one more item on his list: he needed to challenge her testimony against Bess on the obstruction of justice charge.

Following the walk around the block in June 1986, Sukhreet had written a memorandum to her lawyer detailing what Bess had told her that night. Hafetz got Sukhreet to admit that there were at least ten statements that she had attributed to Bess in her testimony that were not contained in the memo to her lawyer, including some of the more damning statements, such as "You can make a lot of trouble," "We've got to get our stories straight," and "You've got to keep your mouth shut."

Then he took his line of questioning a bit further. He had found a gold nugget in the thousands of pages of Sukhreet's prior testimony and depositions that the government, under the federal rules of evidence, had to turn over to him and the other defense attorneys.

"Ms. Gabel, am I correct that in an interview of you several months ago by representatives of the defense you stated that your understanding was there was no intent by Ms. Myerson during the course of her discussion with you on that evening to subvert governmental process? Did you make that statement?"

"Yes, I did," she said, her hands folded on the table in front of her.

"Am I correct that you have previously testified that Ms. Myerson during the course of this walk did not ask you to change your memory?"

"That's true," Sukhreet said.

Michael Feldberg took an entirely different approach to challenge Sukhreet. He didn't raise his voice. He was gentle, yet he too was merciless, and he too walked a delicate line. He had to destroy her credibility as a witness while being careful at the same time not to attack too hard, for fear that Judge Gabel would rise out of her chair to defend her daughter.

Feldberg began by asking Sukhreet to describe her mother's reaction when the judge learned that her only child was cooperating with federal investigators pursuing a criminal case against her.

"Isn't it a fact, Ms. Gabel, that with respect to your conduct in this case your mother has consistently said three words to you?" he asked softly.

"Yes," she replied, smiling.

"And would you tell the jury, please, what those three words are?"

Turning to the jury, Sukhreet enunciated each word: "Tell the truth."

"And your mother has said that to you knowing that you have been cooperating with the folks who are prosecuting this criminal case, isn't that correct?"

"Absolutely," she said firmly with a smile, adding later, "My mother's position has never wavered."

With that out of the way, Feldberg used Sukhreet as a character witness for her mother, asking her to tell the jury about her mother's record as a fighter for civil rights and fair housing. More than once he had her acknowledge that she had told a reporter that her mother "absolutely could not be bought."

Feldberg also tried to suggest that her mother had known Bess Myerson well for twenty to twenty-five years and led Sukhreet to tell the jury that Judge Gabel had once told her she thought "Ms. Myerson was a delightful cuckoo."

At the defense table Bess looked unamused, sitting straight up in her chair, sucking her cheeks in. A few feet away, Judge Gabel stared straight ahead.

Then Feldberg slowly began to set the stage for a devastating cross-examination designed to show that Sukhreet chose to cooperate with the government because she felt she had been insulted publicly by her parents.

"Ms. Gabel, you have had difficulties in your life, have you not?"

"Yes, I have," Sukhreet said in a tentative voice.

"Unlike your mother, who is married now for forty-four years, your marriage did not turn out successfully, correct?"

"That's correct."

"Unlike your mother, who completed law school and went on to a career in public service and as a judge, you did not complete your Ph.D. at the University of Chicago, did you?"

"That's correct."

"To date?"

"That's correct."

"And you have not enjoyed professional success yet, is that correct?" Feldberg lowered his voice with each question.

"That's correct."

"You have not enjoyed the kind of public esteem that your mother has enjoyed, correct?"

"That's correct."

"You have told the prosecutors and other people that you feel that you have had little luck in your life, correct?"

"I am not certain about that. I am not a great believer in luck."

"That life has been unfortunate in many respects?"

"In some respects," she replied, frowning. "I don't know that I have said many."

"You have suffered from illness?"

"Yes."

"You suffer from severe unipolar depression?"

"That is the illness that I suffer from, yes."

"You have told the prosecutors that, correct?"

"Yes, I have."

"You haven't hid that from anyone, have you?"

"No."

"You have told the court, you have told the jury, you told the defense lawyers, and you told the prosecutors, is that correct?"

"That's correct."

"You have been very open about the illness with which you suffer, correct?"

"I have always tried to be."

"You underwent electroshock treatment for that illness in an attempt to combat it."

"Yes, I did."

"And you take medication on a daily basis to try to combat the effects of that illness, correct?"

"Yes."

"You sometimes feel that your parents were less than understanding about you, don't you?" Feldberg asked, walking over to Hortense Gabel and putting both hands on the back of her chair.

"Yes," Sukhreet replied matter-of-factly. "I think that's a good characterization."

Feldberg put his hands behind his back and slowly walked toward her.

"And there came a time on June 10, 1987, when a report was released to the public in which your parents were quoted as saying something about you that upset you. Isn't that correct?" he queried as he approached the witness.

"That is correct," Sukhreet answered, an edge to her voice.

"Isn't it a fact, Ms. Gabel," he said, his voice suddenly rising as he sought to suggest that Sukhreet's testimony was motivated by revenge, "that within five days of that, you called up the prosecutors and essentially volunteered to become a member of the prosecution team in this case?"

"I am not certain of the dates, but I think in terms of the timing you are correct."

Feldberg next tried to show that Sukhreet was also motivated by a need for the attention she had received from the prosecution. "They paid attention to you, didn't they?"

"Yes, they did," she admitted.

"At the time you did this, Ms. Gabel, you knew that your mother was under criminal investigation, didn't you?" His voice grew louder.

"Yes, I did."

The jurors were riveted by Feldberg's gentle questioning. Bess leaned forward, straining to listen to every syllable. Judge Gabel sat impassively, staring straight ahead. Dr. Gabel sat directly behind her, his head bowed.

Then Feldberg had Sukhreet recall that the "very next day" the prosecutors and two FBI agents came to her apartment to install a tape-recording device on her telephone to record a conversation with her lawyer, Philip Schaeffer. Although she had not intended to secretly tape-record her mother that night, Feldberg wanted to leave jurors with the impression that she had been manipulated by prosecutors into bringing her mother down.

Feldberg ran no risk in playing the tape, which had been turned over to him during the discovery phase of trial preparation. Judge Gabel had said nothing incriminating during the brief conversation.

A hush fell over the courtroom as Feldberg pushed the cassette into a tape machine hooked up to the courtroom's sound system and distributed copies of transcripts to jurors. Sukhreet lowered her head as she heard her voice asking her mother if she knew where she might be able to find Schaeffer. Her mother listened without any expression.

Feldberg had accomplished what he had hoped. A look of disgust crossed the faces of several jurors as they listened to the recording and read along on their copies of the transcripts.

"Did you say to anybody on the prosecution team, 'Is it really okay for me to tape-record a conversation with my mother for you under these circumstances?'"

"No, I did not ask them."

"Did any member of the prosecution team say to you, 'Wait a minute. We can't do this'?"

"No," Sukhreet answered, glaring at him.

"Did anybody say that in America things like this aren't done?" he yelled.

"No."

"Did it occur to you on the evening of June 16, 1987, that in America things like this are not done?"

"No."

Then he started in on the attack that everyone had been waiting for, trying to compare her actions to those of children who informed on their parents in Nazi Germany.

Lawrence stood up and finally objected to the question, but he was overruled.

Feldberg asked the question again. "You have heard of places where prosecutors have used children to inform on their parents, haven't you?"

"I don't want to comment on the specifics of that," Sukhreet replied.

The defense lawyers debated whether to have Goldberg attack Sukhreet, too. Hafetz didn't think it was necessary, believing that her credibility had been destroyed and that any more hammering at her might be overkill and would evoke sympathy from the jury. But Goldberg wanted to take his shot. "Sukhreet and I were like a perfect combination," he later said with a smile.

It was Thursday, October 27, Sukhreet's eighth day on the witness stand. By now even those in the spectator section who had first taken pity on her felt uneasy in her presence. She seemed to be relishing the attention too much, and the scene played out each morning in the courtroom, when she would greet her parents with an affectionate hug and a kiss and then step up to the witness stand to testify against them, was too bizarre.

For days now she had been joining her parents for lunch in the cafeteria but would leave them whenever reporters asked her to join them on the courthouse steps for a "stand-up" interview for that evening's television news. She seemed thrilled at her newfound celebrity. Every night she happily answered dozens of phone calls at her home from people commenting about her testimony, and even though one caller suggested that she buy "life insurance," she had no intention of changing her published number.

Goldberg set the tone for his cross-examination right away.

"You have in the course of the proceedings given your mother roses?" he said, pacing around the room.

"Yes, I have."

"You have. And at times you have blown her a kiss, isn't that so?"

"I have waved at her."

"You waved at her, and one time you asked her if she could hear as you pulled the microphone to you?"

"Yes."

"But those acts don't reflect your true feelings toward your mother, do they?"

"I believe that they do."

"Did you tell the prosecutors prior to June 17, 1987, that you harbored deep resentment toward your mother?"

"Yes, I probably have," Sukhreet said calmly.

"You have. Now you have said you had a love-hate relationship with Bess Myerson. By May of 1987, you told that to these learned gentlemen, right?"

Goldberg walked behind the prosecutor's table.

"And did there come a time when you prepared for the prosecutors a self-diagnosis of what you are suffering from mentally?"

"Yes, that is correct."

Then Goldberg began to read from a statement that she had written for the prosecutors describing her depression and her mistreatment as a child.

"Did you ever inform the government that your mother had viewed you as mad—M-A-D?"

"Yes."

"And I take it the word *mad* didn't mean angry, did it?"

"Meaning mad crazy," she quickly said.

"Crazy!" Goldberg threw his arms in the air. "And that didn't please you that your mother had viewed you that way, did it?"

"It didn't please me," Sukhreet said curtly. She was glaring at Goldberg as he continued to question her.

"Your father, on the other hand, felt that you were lazy, isn't that so?"

"That is correct." She smiled.

Now the jurors appeared to be riveted by Goldberg's questioning. Their eyes followed him as he approached Sukhreet on the witness stand, where he had noticed her arm was resting on a book, a copy of the *Diagnostic and Statistical Manual of the American Psychiatric Association* that she had brought along with her to court after noticing that Goldberg had a copy of his own on the defense table.

"You want to be prepared?" he asked sarcastically.

"That is correct," she replied, beaming.

"Okay. By the way, are you familiar with a term, as you looked through the book, called *narcissism*?"

"Yes, I am."

"A narcissist is someone, as far as you understand, who had grandiose ideas, grandiose visions of oneself, isn't that correct?"

Lawrence stood up and objected to the question, but once again he was overruled.

"My answer is that's my lay understanding of the term," Sukhreet replied, narrowing her eyes.

Then Goldberg set the dramatic scene of Sukhreet coming to her mother's arraignment on October 15, 1987.

"It was you, the loving daughter, who escorted her up the stairs, is that right?" he asked softly.

"That is correct."

"I see. You held her arm? . . . As you walked up the steps for her public humiliation. . . . You sat right over there, do you remember that day? Because as a matter of fact you want to see not only your mother undergo humiliation but Bess Myerson, isn't that a fair statement?"

"No, I would not say that," Sukhreet snapped.

"You would not say that?" Goldberg asked incredulously.

"No," Sukhreet replied.

"Madam, your presence at the arraignment of . . . Justice Hortense Gabel and Bess Myerson was something that gave you pleasure because it brought them down, as far as you could glean, to your level, isn't that a fair statement?"

"No."

"It was a culmination, was it not, of a long-standing, deep-seated hatred of both your mother and your father, isn't that so?"

"No."

Goldberg was pacing furiously around the room, throwing his arms up in the air, yelling at Sukhreet. "And there came a point in time when you even considered the possibility of a book, isn't that so?"

"I have considered it."

"Have you thought of a title such as 'Daughter Dearest'?"

"No, not that particular title," she said. "Thank you, Mr. Goldberg, for your suggestion."

Then he took the shot he had been saving for last.

"You live, do you not, on the support that your mother and father give you, isn't that so?"

"Yes, I do. Yes, it is."

Goldberg had Sukhreet tell the jury that she was receiving $1,775 a month from her parents for living expenses and that, in April of 1988, she was threatened with eviction because she had not paid $6,981 in rent.

"You took the money, and you used it for some other purpose, isn't that so?" he yelled. "Yes or no! You didn't pay the rent, did you? . . ."

Sukhreet was furious. Judge Gabel looked as if she were finally going to physically restrain Goldberg.

"Because you used that money to buy yourself a wardrobe, isn't that so?"

"No, that's not correct."

"You used that money to do some cosmetic surgery, some liposuction, right?"

"That's incorrect," she said, pushing her hair behind her ear.

"But you did have liposuction, correct?"

"That's incorrect."

Then Sukhreet told him she had spent the money on something else to help battle her depression. "I bought drugs," Sukhreet said. Her voice was low and angry. A hush fell over the courtroom.

Suddenly another voice called out from across the courtroom. It was Judge Gabel, trying to make sure that no one misunderstood.

"Medical drugs," she piped up softly.

32
The Verdict

On the day that Sukhreet Gabel finally left the witness stand Bess was completely relaxed for the first time since the trial had begun. Her attorney had told her that Sukhreet's performance had been so disastrous for the prosecution that he no longer thought it would be necessary to put her on the stand to defend herself. Bess was ready and willing to testify, but Hafetz's reassurances were a big relief. Now it looked as if it was at least possible that she might be vindicated with an acquittal.

That Friday afternoon, October 28, after everyone else had departed for the weekend, Bess sat on a hard oak bench outside the courtroom with a reporter and a friend who had stopped by the trial to lend support. She was feeling so upbeat that she speculated about what she would tell the waiting throng of reporters and television cameramen on the courthouse steps on the day that she was found innocent.

"Do you know what I think I might do?" she said with a sly smile. "I'm going to walk out the door and keep on walking. I'm not going to say anything for the cameras. Fuck 'em. I don't need the press. I don't need to say anything at all."

Bess was going home that night to Andy's Park Avenue apartment to spend "three long hours" soaking in the tub. She talked to her daughter, Barra, in California, on the telephone most evenings. Barra had not come east for her mother's trial because she was working on the television show "Dirty Dancing," which she was helping to write and produce. Bess did not seem to mind that her daughter's work had kept her from being with her.

On most nights Bess made sure she was home and off the phone by ten o'clock. That was when Andy called from prison. She told friends that she had to see the movie *Madame Sousatzka* three times during the trial because she had to keep leaving the Baronet movie theater on Third Avenue to get home in time for his call. Andy, she said, didn't like it when he got the answering machine.

From their demeanor in the courtroom, it was difficult to discern the nature of Bess and Andy's relationship that fall. They exchanged glances and whispers and wrote each other notes during the testimony. She brought him the latest photographs of her daughter and granddaughter. During the court's fifteen-minute recesses she would step outside into the corridor, smoke a Marlboro, and then hurry back to the defense table to be with him. Andy would often put his hand on her back, and she would slip an arm around him, but they did not look like lovers. They looked instead as if they were supporting each other, almost like business partners caught in a terrible mess.

Bess rarely left the courthouse to join her attorneys for lunch in a restaurant. She had arranged for the cafeteria manager to fix her a salad, which she usually carried back with her to the courtroom to eat with Andy. She would often bring him big pastrami sandwiches from the Carnegie Deli for lunch and a snack of M&Ms so he wouldn't have to eat the prison food. Bess occasionally wrapped up Andy's prison sandwiches and took them home for herself so the food wouldn't "go to waste."

Even some of their closest friends were unable to figure out what was going on between Andy and Bess during the trial. At times there seemed to be tremendous tension between them. Before he had gone to prison, Andy had been seen around town with several women much younger than Bess, although he was no longer receiving visits from the former model, Betty Bienen. Sitting next to his lawyer's wife, Rema Goldberg, at the defense table, Andy would occasionally nudge her and ask her if she knew of any women he could meet. He once told a friend that he might be interested in having a few flings when he got out of jail and wondered whether it could be arranged for Bess to be sentenced to prison. "Can't she get a year and a day?" he asked jokingly.

Bess, herself, didn't seem to know what to make of their relationship. "We are very supportive of each other," she told a reporter. "I'm not sure that is love. I'm not sure what it is."

Despite the enormous setback for the prosecution caused by Sukhreet's disastrous appearance on the witness stand, David Lawrence was hopeful that his next witness would corroborate most of her testimony and thus buttress her tale. By the time the jurors began deliberations, Lawrence was hoping, the image of Sukhreet cheerfully testifying against her mother would have dulled in their minds.

But Sukhreet, to the exasperation of prosecutors and the delight of some members of the defense team, was determined to extend her "fifteen minutes" of fame. On Tuesday, November 1, the first day of testimony after she left the stand, Sukhreet showed up in court as a spectator, outfitted in a canary-yellow dress and matching velvet slippers. Not content to be in the background, Sukhreet took a seat in the front row of the spectators' section.

With her testimony over, she was now able to sit in on the rest of the trial, a situation that put Lawrence and the other prosecutors in a bind. They feared that if they asked the court to remove her, she might retaliate against them in some way. But it turned out that they wouldn't have to worry about it. Bess did not want to spend the rest of the trial trying to avoid Sukhreet in the ladies' room and the cafeteria, so her attorney, Fred Hafetz, asked Keenan to exclude Sukhreet from the courtroom. Hafetz told the judge that Sukhreet was "really a diversion from the trial."

Keenan called Sukhreet up to his bench that morning and asked her to leave. She walked out quietly, trailed by about twenty reporters. Outside the courtroom she held an impromptu news conference in the hallway, angrily telling reporters that she wanted to attend the rest of the trial because she "didn't believe in hit-and-run justice." She also wanted to be there, she said, to give her mother "moral and physical support."

With Sukhreet out of the courtroom the prosecution turned toward rebuilding its case. The next witness called to testify was every wealthy person's worst nightmare: the maid under oath.

A spirited woman with curly white hair, a long narrow face, and a lantern jaw, Shirley Harrod, along with her husband, Ray, had worked as a live-in servant for Andy at his Westhampton Beach estate during the summer of 1983. Her husband was fired after only five months because of an argument he got into with Bess's son-in-law. Shirley Harrod was fired seven months later, she said, for "disobeying" Andy by leaving the house to take her son to visit a friend.

Bess and Andy were visibly annoyed that the woman who had made their bed, cleaned their bathrooms, and cooked their meals was now in court to testify against them.

Before Harrod took the stand, Jay Goldberg asked during a conference with the judge for assurance that Harrod's testimony would be limited in scope. He didn't want her mentioning that Donald Manes and Stanley Friedman had been guests at the Westhampton Beach house. The government agreed. Goldberg also received assurances that Harrod would not tell the jury about the time Andy Capasso took an attractive young real estate broker into his bedroom.

There were a couple of important points that the prosecution needed Harrod to make for the jury.

First, under the questioning of prosecutor Stuart Abrams, Harrod corroborated Sukhreet's testimony that she had first discovered from Harrod that her mother was presiding over the Capasso divorce case.

Then Abrams moved on to the main reason the government had put Shirley Harrod on the witness stand—to set the scene of the beginning of the alleged conspiracy. He had her tell the jury in her nasal voice and thick cockney accent about the day in June or July when Andy and Bess were sitting around the dining room table, looking at the divorce papers. "Mr. Capasso threw the papers on the table," she testified, "and said, 'Isn't there something you can do about this?' "

The prosecution wished that Harrod had stayed in the dining room to hear what Bess Myerson said in reply.

Jay Goldberg took the first real crack at Harrod by returning to his theme of Nancy Capasso as the "villainess." From the investigative reports that the prosecution was required to hand over to him on each witness he had discovered that Nancy Capasso had called federal investigators to introduce them to Harrod in her home.

Goldberg tried to throw Harrod off balance by shouting a series of quick questions and suggesting that she was testifying only because she and her husband had been fired by Andy Capasso and that she was doing Nancy Capasso's bidding.

Harrod remained unruffled. She leaned into the microphone with a bemused expression on her face, laughing as he tried to rile her, talking back to him in her distinctive voice, ending a phrase with a high screech as if to say, "Of course not!" Even when he called her a "domestic," drawing out the syllables with just the right amount of condescension in his voice, she refused to rise to the bait. When he kept repeating the fact that she had been "fired," she cut him off and said, "You like that word, don't you?"

She had almost everyone in the courtroom laughing with her. Bess, however, was not laughing. Goldberg finally asked Harrod to stop smiling when she answered his questions. But it seemed to have little effect, because everyone was having so much fun watching her best him.

Fred Hafetz's manner with Harrod was much more effective. His grating voice and serious tone quickly wiped the smile off her face and stopped the laughter in the courtroom. Repeatedly calling her "ma'am," he wanted the jurors to believe that Shirley Harrod was a woman they could not trust. He needed to cast doubt on the damaging testimony she had given about watching Andy throw down the divorce papers at the dining room table and ask Bess for help. Hafetz didn't stop hammering Harrod with questions until he got the answer that he wanted. Finally she gave it to him.

"And how far away were you from Mr. Capasso at that time, approximately?"

"Six feet maybe."

"But you could see the papers he held up, is that right?"

"Yes."

"And what papers did you see, ma'am?"

"They were the divorce papers."

"They were the divorce papers," he repeated, mimicking her. He slowly walked over to the defense table and began to shuffle papers. "Mrs. Harrod," he said, holding up what had been marked 3524 B, "were these the papers that you saw?"

"Similar to that, yes," she nodded.

"I see. And what are these papers, ma'am? Are these divorce papers?"

"I don't know," she said matter-of-factly. "You are not close enough to see."

"And I'm standing approximately six feet from you, ma'am," he announced triumphantly.

"I didn't have to see them to know what they were," she snapped.

Hafetz's hard face softened into a smile. The damage had been done.

Herb Rickman was trembling when he walked into the courtroom. Small beads of sweat formed on his forehead. He was nervous, so nervous that he had brought close to a dozen friends with him to sit in the front row of the spectators' section for support.

For more than two years now, since federal investigators first questioned him about this case, Rickman, a special assistant to Mayor Koch, had been working at City Hall under a cloud, knowing that Bess was intending to use him as a fall guy at her trial.

From the beginning Bess had insisted that Rickman had played a role in the hiring of Sukhreet. When a *New York Post* reporter called her in October 1983 to ask how Sukhreet came to be hired as her special assistant, Bess had replied that Herb Rickman had "sent" her over.

Then, after the Tyler report became public in June 1987, one of Bess's closest friends, Allen Funt's ex-wife, Marilyn Funt, told reporters that Rickman was denying his role in hiring Sukhreet because he was frightened that he might lose his big job at City Hall.

Funt also said at the time that after Rickman found out about the federal investigation he left a message in Yiddish on Bess's answering machine, telling her to meet him right away at a nearby coffee shop. The accusations against Rickman became newspaper stories. "Bess Blames City Hall," read one newspaper's front-page headline, which was accompanied by a large photograph of Rickman, sitting at his City Hall desk, located just a few yards from Mayor Koch's office. Reporters wanted to know what he knew, when he knew it, and, most importantly, when he told Mayor Koch what he knew about Sukhreet's hiring.

Rickman had also complained publicly that he would get anonymous late-night phone calls warning him to keep his mouth shut.

Rickman, who had convinced the federal prosecutors and investigators in the case that he was telling the truth, had over the past two years
developed his own theory of why Bess and Andy had entertained him so
lavishly that summer of 1983 out in Westhampton Beach. They both
knew that he had been close friends with Judge Gabel for years. Rickman believed that perhaps Andy and Bess's invitations to him were all
part of a plan to set him up, to make it look as if he was the one who had
suggested that Bess hire Sukhreet.

On the witness stand Rickman stared straight ahead, away from Bess,
who was sitting on the opposite side of the room at the defense table,
glaring at him. For the first time since the beginning of the trial, Andy
looked truly enraged. Here was a man whom he had generously entertained at his home, a man he had considered a close friend, now
betraying him.

Focusing his gaze on the prosecutor, Stuart Abrams, Rickman began
in a shaky but resonant voice by telling the jury that he was special
assistant to the mayor of the city of New York. His voice grew steadier as
he testified about first meeting Andy Capasso when they were both
visiting Bess Myerson at Lenox Hill Hospital after she had suffered a
stroke. Of the years of his friendship with Bess, he said, "I held her in
great affection."

Hoping to elicit testimony that might establish a motive for Andy to
want to fix the divorce, Abrams asked Rickman about Andy's divorce.
Rickman described Andy as a "bitter man" who complained that "he
was being taken for every penny" by his wife. "Throughout 1983 there
was a lot of upset over the ongoing proceedings," Rickman recalled,
"and invariably it would produce friction, unhappiness. It was not a
particularly good time for Mr. Capasso. He was not feeling well. He
was showing great strain, and obviously that strain affected Ms. Myerson as well."

Then he told the jury that he knew Judge Gabel because they were
both involved in "liberal Democratic circles." He said that for years they
used to get together for lunch every six or eight weeks. In 1983, he said,
the judge frequently talked about Sukhreet's job search. He said that he
met Sukhreet one afternoon for lunch and suggested that she find a job
in the Office of Economic Development, but it never came to pass.

Then Rickman dropped a bombshell. Stuart Abrams asked him about
the reception for Bess Myerson at Gracie Mansion on May 25, 1983, to
celebrate her new appointment as cultural affairs commissioner. He
recounted for the jury that he had seen Judge Gabel sitting down at the
reception and that he had walked over to her to say hello.

"She asked me, 'Is what's-his-name here?'. . . I knew she meant Bess's
friend, and I said, 'You mean Andy Capasso?' and she said yes."

There was suddenly a motion from one end of the defense table to the other as the defendants conferred with their attorneys. Rickman's account surprised Judge Gabel's attorney, Michael Feldberg. It directly contradicted Judge Gabel's long-standing position that she did not know until five months later that Bess was romantically involved with Andy and that that was why she had made no move to disqualify herself from the Capasso divorce case before reducing the alimony.

Then Rickman told the jury that, around Labor Day of 1983, Bess Myerson told him she had hired Sukhreet Gabel.

"What, if anything, did you say to Ms. Myerson at that point?" Abrams asked.

"That's a mistake!" Rickman replied. A day or two later, Rickman said, he talked to Bess again on the telephone: "I asked Ms. Myerson why she had hired Sukhreet Gabel. She replied it was a merit appointment, Sukhreet was found ably qualified at every level of the agency, that she had been interviewed by a number of people. It was a low-level position. She said it was cleared at City Hall. And I also believe she said that the major decisions in the case were already over."

On September 23, 1983, he said he had lunch with Horty Gabel at Hunan Garden. "When I got there, I said, 'Horty, we don't talk about law, I haven't practiced law, we don't talk about cases, but I have some concerns about Sukhreet's ability to survive at the Department of Cultural Affairs. I am concerned on a parallel track about the possible appearance of it. Are you concerned, Horty?'"

"What, if anything, did Judge Gabel say at that point?" Abrams asked.

"Judge Gabel got rather irate with me," Rickman said. "She told me immediately that it had been a merit appointment and for all intents and purposes told me it was none of my concern."

Judge Gabel later said that she had become angry not because Rickman had suggested an appearance of impropriety but because she thought Rickman was suggesting that her daughter was incapable of handling the job.

As Rickman had anticipated, Bess's lawyer, Fred Hafetz, came at him hard. But Rickman counterattacked. He shouted back at Hafetz and pointed at Bess in front of the jury, calling her "*that woman*" over and over again, yelling "No, no, no," and repeatedly telling the jury that Bess had been a lousy administrator whose poor management skills had left the city's cultural affairs agency in chaos.

"Mr. Rickman, isn't it a fact that you have lied in your testimony that you had a conversation with Bess Myerson in the early part of September 1983 regarding the employment of Sukhreet Gabel as you testified about yesterday?"

"Mr. Hafetz, that is a disgusting lie on your part," Rickman said snidely, leaning into the microphone. "It demeans you in every way, shape, or form. You have no right to insinuate that. That conversation took place. You ought to be ashamed, Mr. Hafetz."

Hafetz was undeterred. "Mr. Rickman," he began, his voice surly again, "isn't it a fact, sir, that the reason you have invented this story is because of the fact, sir, that during the summer of 1983 you not only knew that Bess Myerson was considering hiring Sukhreet Gabel, but indeed, you had suggested that she hire Judge Gabel's daughter? Am I right, sir?"

"No," Rickman yelled, his voice booming across the room.

"Mr. Rickman, isn't it a fact that after the October 18, 1983, *Post* article came out, you knew you were in an embarrassing situation, because the mayor of the city of New York knew that you had a close relationship with Bess Myerson and you were concerned that someone might say you had a role in the hiring of the daughter? Am I right, sir?"

"Absolutely wrong," Rickman said disgustedly. "Absolutely wrong again, Mr. Hafetz."

"And in fact, Mr. Rickman, isn't it a fact that you decided after the embarrassing events became—the public embarrassment of October 18, 1983, you, Herb Rickman, decided to invent a story to place yourself as far away from the knowledge of the hiring of Sukhreet Gabel as you possibly could, even if it meant lying against your dear friends Bess Myerson and Judge Gabel? Isn't that correct, sir?"

At the defense table Bess nodded her head at Hafetz's question and then turned to Rickman to listen to his response.

"Mr. Hafetz," Rickman shouted back, his face distorted with rage, "not only is there not a scintilla of truth in anything you have said, but you have just done everything to damage twenty-two years of noble public service. And I hope you earn your thirty pieces of silver for that."

Bess shook her head. Herb Rickman was giving Sukhreet Gabel heavy competition for putting on the best show in town.

Hafetz pressed him, too, on a question that every reporter in New York had been asking Mayor Koch and Rickman since the Tyler report first described in detail the circumstances surrounding Sukhreet's hiring in 1983: what did the mayor know and when did he know it? Did Rickman tell the mayor, four years before Sukhreet's hiring exploded into a full-blown scandal, that Bess had been courting the daughter of a judge ruling on Andy's divorce and had given her a city job?

"Yes or no?" Hafetz demanded.

"I went to the mayor of the city of New York—"

Hafetz interrupted him. "Yes or no, Mr. Rickman?" he insisted.

Finally Judge Keenan leaned across the bench toward Rickman to give it a try. "Did you tell Mayor Koch, 'I said to Bess Myerson that I am concerned about this, and she said to me 'I cleared it [at City Hall]'?"

"No, I did not," Rickman replied. He explained that after the *New York Post* article suggested that he had played a role in the hiring of Sukhreet he had approached Koch and told him that he hadn't had anything to do with Sukhreet's getting the job. "When I walked in and the mayor saw my rage, the mayor said, 'Stop. We received a letter or a letter is on its way [from Bess]. Be calm. She's reassured us about the hiring, and she says the hiring is okay.'

"That was it as far as I was concerned," Rickman stated.

Leaning back in her chair, Bess folded her arms across her chest and fixed her gaze on her once-close friend. She looked at Rickman as if she had the power to turn him to stone.

And that's how it went for hours, Fred Hafetz hammering away at Herb Rickman. During a brief recess Bess, enraged at Rickman's testimony, furious that he had repeatedly referred to her in his testimony as "*that woman*," walked up to a reporter, lit a Marlboro, and spewed forth. "We were like brother and sister," she said rapidly, her face hard with anger. "I never had a brother. He never had a sister. Do you know what he used to call me in Yiddish? Little sister! Do you think that he would speak to a man like that if I were a man?"

Then, suddenly realizing she was talking to a reporter, she abruptly walked away.

After the recess Hafetz resumed his attack by trying to get Rickman to say that Koch had committed perjury.

"Mr. Rickman," he began, "the reason that you are fighting on the dates and acknowledging your role in the hiring of Ms. Gabel is because you, sir, as a high-level Koch administration person, would have to acknowledge that he committed perjury and you would be out on your derriere, isn't that right, sir?"

"That's a lie," Rickman yelled. Hafetz tried to ask his next question, but Rickman continued to yell back at him. Finally Judge Keenan intervened.

"Now wait," Keenan lectured Rickman. "You answered the question quite vehemently. You made your point. Next question."

"Your honor, if I may—" Rickman said, turning to face the judge.

"No, next question. Just stop."

"I am being badgered here over and over," he complained. His voice suddenly took on a whining tone.

"No," Keenan insisted. "I said stop it. Don't be a baby. Stop it."

But the two men didn't stop, and finally Keenan sent the jury out of the room and delivered a lecture to the witness and the lawyer.

Jay Goldberg joined in. "Judge," he said, "this witness makes personal comments with respects to Mr. Hafetz's state of mind which I find to be supremely improper—"

Keenan just stared at him. "Did you ever hear of a two-edged sword?"
"Yes."
"Might cut both ways. The jury may think he is protesting too much. The jury may think he is too defensive."

Michael Feldberg began his cross-examination of Rickman by getting him to confirm that he thought Horty Gabel was a "heroine" and that she had "incredible integrity" and that he had testified during the investigation that "in no way do I believe the judge would ever have allowed, you know, the daughter, the daughter's hiring or employment in government to have in any way influenced her decision making."
Then Feldberg moved to the most important point he sought to make: that Rickman had spoken to law enforcement officials on eighteen occasions but had never before recalled the conversation he claimed he had had with Judge Gabel on May 25, 1983, at Gracie Mansion.
"That's correct," Rickman said quietly.

The next witness was Walter Canter, a tall, thin, soft-spoken man in his sixties who had worked for Bess Myerson from 1968 to 1983, writing speeches and magazine articles for her and helping her to produce consumer reports while she worked as a reporter for WCBS-TV.
When she was named cultural affairs commissioner in April 1983, she brought him into the department. A former assistant cultural affairs commissioner recalled, "She sat us all down and said, 'I want to tell you about Walter. He's very important to me. I worked with him for twenty years. I want you all to try your best and be nice to Walter. I care a lot about Walter.'"
Then, just a few months later, the assistant commissioner got a call from Bess, asking him to fire Canter for her. "I don't think that's fair," he told her at the time. "I didn't bring him in."
Bess asked him if she could fire him by sending him a letter. "Well, legally, yes," he told her. "But I don't think it's very nice."
But that's exactly what Bess did in October 1983. She wrote a letter to Canter dismissing him.
What the prosecutor, Stuart Abrams, wanted to suggest to the jurors was that Bess had forced out her loyal old friend to make room for the judge's daughter.
Then, at the end of the direct testimony, Abrams surprised the defense lawyers by asking Canter, "After leaving the Department of Cultural Affairs, did you have any further dealings with Bess Myerson after that time?"
"No," Canter replied, "except for a telephone call which I received about two or three weeks ago."

"Could you please describe for the jury what was said during the course of that telephone call?"

Jay Goldberg jumped to his feet. "Judge, could we have a side bar on this?"

Keenan told the jurors they could take their morning break. The government and defense lawyers approached the bench and talked in whispers so that reporters or spectators could not hear them.

Abrams was telling the judge that if Canter were allowed to answer the question he would say that Bess called him to ask him to talk about hostility against her within the Department of Cultural Affairs. This would help her lawyer describe future witnesses from the cultural affairs agency called to testify against her as disgruntled. "At the end of the conversation," Abrams said in a low voice to the judge, "she said to him that she was thinking of starting a foundation and that he would be a good person to head the foundation."

Keenan asked if Abrams intended to draw the inference that Bess was "trying to buy him off by offering him something at a foundation."

"I think that is a fair inference," Abrams said, adding that Canter "did not take it particularly seriously."

Keenan refused to allow Canter to testify about the telephone call, ruling that the testimony would be ambiguous and unfair to the other defendants.

The defense attorneys were pleased with the judge's ruling and expected to hear nothing more about it. But late that afternoon Paul Moses, who covered the courts for *New York Newsday*, picked up a copy of the court transcript of that day's proceeding to check it against his notes and to read what the lawyers had discussed in whispers at the side bar conference about Bess's phone call to Canter.

The next morning the front page of *New York Newsday* carried a large color photograph of Bess and a bold headline: "Myerson Prosecutor: Bess Tried to Buy Off Witness."

When Hafetz lost his temper over the headline in the courtroom, Judge Keenan reminded him that he had told the jurors not to read the newspapers. They wouldn't know anything about it.

It was two days before Thanksgiving when Mayor Edward I. Koch finally took the witness stand. His only appearance as a witness in a criminal case was billed on all the local radio and television shows that morning with the one-line lead "Mayor Koch testifies today in first corruption trial."

The press section was packed with City Hall reporters, out-of-town correspondents, and virtually every newspaper columnist in town. Members of the public, who had been attending the highly publicized murder trial of Joel Steinberg, accused of killing his six-year-old adopted daughter, left the Manhattan Criminal Court building and crowded into the spectator's section of Bess's trial in federal court. In the front row were Mayor Koch's three lawyers, his press secretary, George Arzt, and his closest adviser and friend, Dan Wolf.

Ever since Mayor Koch had first learned from the television news in January 1987 that Bess was caught up in a federal investigation and had taken the Fifth Amendment, his advisers had worried that this case would be the final blow to his administration. For all of the city officials who resigned or went to jail in the wake of the city's municipal corruption scandals, none of them were as closely tied to him in the eyes of the public as Bess Myerson, the woman who had held his hand at rallies during his first mayoral campaign. His political future was at stake. There were rumors that Giuliani was considering running for mayor.

Over the past two years Koch's advisers had been carefully trying to get out the message that this was a case of a troubled woman who happened to be a city commissioner and not another example of city corruption. By now, two months into the highly publicized trial, it seemed as if the public had begun to see it as just that.

Koch had two concerns as he took the witness stand. He did not want to come across as a man out to betray an old friend, and he did not want to testify to anything that he had not said before.

When he stepped up to the witness stand at 10:35 A.M., Koch was not his normal ebullient, irrepressible self. Subdued and appearing uneasy, Koch sat slumped in his chair, staring straight ahead and avoiding eye contact with Bess.

From her seat at the defense table Bess looked perfectly composed. She put on her glasses to look at him across the room as she waited for Lawrence to begin asking questions of her old friend. She watched him steadily until Lawrence asked Koch to identify her. He looked over to Bess for the first time. She lowered her eyes. Fred Hafetz jumped up during that awkward moment, telling the court, "We will acknowledge the identity."

Then Lawrence got to why he wanted Mayor Koch in the courtroom: to dramatize to the jury that Bess had lied to him in October 1983, following the publication of the *New York Post* article about Sukhreet's hiring. He was hoping Koch's testimony would leave the jury with the impression that Bess was conscious of her own guilt.

Koch, responding dutifully to Lawrence's questions, told the jury that the first time he heard about Sukhreet's hiring was when he returned from a trip to Puerto Rico and saw a copy of the *New York Post*, accompanied by a letter from Bess about the article. Then he explained that he had "no other information" about Sukhreet's hiring other than what was contained in the article and the letter. But the federal rules of evidence prevented Lawrence from further dramatizing the matter by asking Koch how he felt four years later when he learned that the letter had been a lie and that he had been betrayed.

One of Koch's lawyers, Henry White, had slipped into the back of the courtroom one afternoon while Herb Rickman was on the stand under cross-examination. White reported back to City Hall that the best tack for the mayor to take while under Hafetz's tough cross-examination was to answer the questions quietly, with a simple yes or no.

Following that advice, Koch was a dutiful, docile witness on cross-examination. He did not volunteer anything. He sat there, blowing air in and out of his cheeks, remaining completely under control.

Hafetz had him tell the jury that a commissioner did not have to conduct an "exhaustive search" to fill the job and had "absolute discretion" in hiring someone for a job under $20,000 a year. But the most important task for Hafetz that afternoon was to get the mayor to cast doubt on Herb Rickman's testimony that he had walked into Koch's office to talk to him about the *New York Post* article shortly after it appeared.

The government lawyers knew it was coming.

"I have no recollection of that incident," Koch said calmly. Then he added, "It could have occurred, but I have no recollection of it."

On redirect examination David Lawrence tried to get Koch to remember the conversation with Rickman, reminding him of a City Hall press conference the mayor gave right after the Tyler report was released. What the mayor said that day could be interpreted to mean that he had, in fact, discussed the *New York Post* article and Bess with Rickman back in 1983.

But Koch could not be budged, not to save Herb Rickman, not to save the government, not to save the government's case. He was not going to testify to something under oath in court that he had not told the government in a sworn deposition in September of 1987.

David Lawrence handed a transcript of the press conference to the mayor. "Does that refresh your recollection?" he asked.

"Of what?"

"As to when was the first time that you had a conversation with Mr. Rickman concerning the hiring of Sukhreet Gabel."

"It doesn't add to my recollection over and above what I have testified to this morning."

Over the next couple of weeks the prosecution wrapped up its case by calling a series of witnesses, including city officials, to testify that Bess had not followed city hiring regulations to put Sukhreet on the payroll; former employees at the Department of Cultural Affairs to testify about Bess's decision to hire Sukhreet; former employees of Andy's to testify about his anger and obsession over his divorce; and close to a dozen witnesses who could corroborate parts of Sukhreet's story.

Among those corroboration witnesses was a doorman from Sukhreet's apartment building who recalled the night in June 1986 when Bess appeared in the lobby, wearing a jogging suit, to meet Sukhreet for a walk around the block. The government arranged for Sukhreet's old boyfriend, Tony Babinec, to fly in from Chicago to tell the jury that Bess had picked up the $66 tab for Sukhreet's birthday celebration with her parents. And then, after Jay Goldberg had suggested in court that $66 was not enough for food and liquor for five people, the government called the woman who ran the Chinese restaurant. It was a low point in the prosecution's case. As the woman testified through a Chinese interpreter about the 1983 prices of fried rice and spareribs, a few jurors giggled. One shook his head in disgust and turned his chair away from the witness, as if to say, "C'mon, give us some real evidence."

To establish the "affair of the pocketbook" motive, the government called a Mercedes-Benz salesman who testified that Bess had picked up a 380 SL roadster with a hefty $41,000 price tag. The government also called Andy's loyal secretary to show that he had paid the bill on the Diners Club card used by Bess Myerson at the Chinese restaurant for Sukhreet's birthday celebration.

Some of the most embarrassing testimony in those final weeks came from Bess's former secretary and her former city driver.

An elderly woman with snow-white hair and short tight curls, Barbara Kennedy told the jury about the day in May or June of 1983 when she placed a call to Judge Gabel on behalf of Bess and left the message that Bess Myerson had called. "Ms. Myerson was very upset with me at the fact that I had left her name, and she said I was in the future to leave my name when I made calls and Judge Gabel was not available at the moment."

"Would you describe Ms. Myerson's tone of voice when she told you this?" asked David Lawrence, hoping that Bess's use of aliases would demonstrate "consciousness of guilt."

"She was very—she was angry with me and upset, and she spoke rather sharply to me."

Bess looked down, as if embarrassed, and started scribbling on a yellow legal pad.

Another embarrassing moment came when her former driver, Nelson Pagan, told the jury about the time that Bess put a new card addressed to Judge Gabel on a bouquet of flowers that she had received and then sent them to Judge Gabel's home.

It may have been these embarrassing moments that motivated Bess to insist that her close friends and family not join her in the courtroom. On the day that Pagan testified, an old friend from Los Angeles, Roz

Wyman, was sitting in the spectators' section. Wyman, a Democratic power broker who had served on the Los Angeles City Council and had known Bess for years, was in New York for only a couple of days and wanted to lend Bess support. But Bess seemed uncomfortable in her presence. During a recess, she walked up to her friend and began explaining that she never would have given away flowers sent to her. "No one would have any reason to send me flowers in October, anyway," Bess insisted.

When the proceedings resumed, Bess struck a pose at the defense table, looking incredulous at the testimony of her former driver.

A big, handsome man in his late twenties with black hair and a thick neck, Pagan was not allowed to testify about everything that Bess had said to him in the car. Keenan decided to strike from the record Pagan's testimony that, following the publication of the *New York Post* story, he overheard Bess mumbling in the car, "I should have never hired her. I should have listened to him." Pagan assumed she was referring to Herb Rickman. The prosecution, desperately trying to find some direct evidence, argued to keep Pagan's testimony in the record because it supported Rickman's story that he had advised Bess against placing Sukhreet on the city payroll. But Keenan refused and acceded to a defense request to strike his testimony, noting that Bess could have been referring to anyone, even "President Reagan."

Under the questioning of prosecutor Stuart Abrams, Pagan told the jurors next that he had twice driven Bess and Judge Gabel to dinner. The government did not have any evidence at all that Bess and the judge struck a deal at these dinners, but the prosecutors were hoping that the jury would believe a conspiratorial conversation might have taken place.

Then Pagan told the jurors a story that went right to the heart of the prosecution's case: Bess's obsession with Nancy Capasso. One afternoon during the summer of 1984, he recalled, he was driving Bess somewhere near Fifth Avenue when she told him to stop the car. Then she pointed out Nancy Capasso walking along the sidewalk.

"Did she say anything about Mrs. Capasso at that time?" Abrams asked.

". . . She was talking about the case as to how vicious this woman was and how she wants to destroy Andy."

"Did she say anything about Mr. Capasso's property or wealth at that time?"

"Well, she was just stating, you know, she [Nancy] wanted everything he had and she was trying to destroy him."

"Did Ms. Myerson make any comment about her feelings about the divorce case?"

"Yes," Pagan said. "She said that she is very evil, and she wouldn't get a penny from her, you know, meaning him, over her dead body."

Bess smiled broadly and turned her head to face Andy. They broke into laughter.

There was one final witness the defense was waiting for the govern-ment to call. His name was Tony Bailey, and he had worked as a driver for Andy and Nancy for a couple of years before Andy fired him in late 1983, while in the middle of his divorce. Andy accused Bailey of giving information to Nancy to use against him in his divorce case. After he was fired, Bailey found out that Bess had arranged to have his telephone changed to an unlisted number so that Nancy would have trouble locating him.

Andy and Nancy shared Bailey until Andy became so involved with Bess that he had to hire another driver to take care of Nancy. Bailey did not approve of Andy's affair with Bess. Bailey was fond of Nancy, who had been kind to him. Bailey later said he found Bess to be cold, haughty, and imperious.

Andy instructed him to drive Bess wherever she wanted to go. He remembered frequently picking Bess up at her apartment and driving her over to the West Side to WCBS-TV, where she was working as a television reporter at the time. He took her shopping on Madison Avenue and drove her to Rhode Island, Connecticut, and southern New Jersey to deliver speeches. He also delivered to her apartment divorce papers for Bess to read.

The government would have liked Bailey to tell the jury about deliver-ing the divorce papers because it would have helped support their obsession theory. And the government would also have liked Bailey to testify about a few other things that he had overheard Andy and Bess discuss in the car. Bailey had the strongest evidence of all against Andy and Bess.

According to Bailey, Andy once said, "I can buy any judge." Bailey also supposedly heard Bess say, "I can do anything I want with respect to this litigation."

Considering that the government needed every piece of evidence it could get, it seemed strange at first to many reporters covering the trial that the prosecution did not intend to call Bailey at all.

But David Lawrence did not want to take the chance of putting Bailey on the stand. He worried that the defense lawyers were laying a trap for him.

For one thing, Jay Goldberg was prepared to use a transcript of a telephone conversation between Bailey and Nancy just before her 1985 divorce trial. On the tape Nancy and Bailey are gleefully talking about how Andy would have a "heart attack" when he saw Bailey at the divorce trial prepared to testify against him.

But what convinced Lawrence and the other prosecutors and investi-

gators involved in the case not to take a chance with Bailey on the stand
was not so much his connection with Nancy Capasso. They learned that
Bailey had an attorney at the time. The attorney was a former partner of
Jay Goldberg's, and Andy Capasso was paying the bill.

The day after the prosecution rested its case, the defense began. It
lasted a total of one hour and forty-five minutes. Fred Hafetz brought
one witness, Mayor Koch's former counsel, Pat Mulhearn, to the witness stand to tell the jury that Rickman never told him about his
discussions with Bess Myerson in 1983. Then, to disprove the government's theory that money was a motive in the case, Hafetz read into the
record a list of Bess's assets, totaling millions of dollars. He did not call
any character witnesses because he did not want to run the risk of the
prosecutors asking them if they had heard about Bess's shoplifting.

Jay Goldberg called no witnesses. He introduced a couple of documents, including a long computer printout that showed that Andy
Capasso had paid his divorce lawyers $480,600 to represent him in the
divorce case. He thought it would show that, if the divorce case was
fixed, he could have "gotten a firm out of the yellow pages."

Michael Feldberg brought a series of character witnesses to testify
about Judge Gabel's reputation for honesty and integrity. Former mayor
Robert Wagner took the stand, followed by former U.S. housing and
urban development secretary Robert Weaver, former city council president Paul O'Dwyer, and Robert Caro, the author of the Robert Moses
biography *The Power Broker: Robert Moses and the Fall of New York*.

Caro was the most eloquent witness, telling the jurors how Judge
Gabel had a reputation "for honesty, for courage, and for having been
unusually concerned for thirty years about the plight of poor people in
the city of New York." He said that Hortense Gabel had been the only
one "who would listen to the poor" when Robert Moses's slum clear-
ance project was forcing tens of thousands of poor people out of their
homes. "Hortense Gabel was the only official in the city government
who was interested in what happened to them," he said.

Now that both sides had finished presenting their cases, no one
mattered to Bess Myerson but the twelve strangers sitting in the jury
box. The words of encouragement from friends and others who showed
up in the courtroom to lend their support were no longer relevant. One
afternoon a former Miss America contestant, Miss Detroit of 1957,
who described herself as the "other Jewish beauty queen," sat in the
back of the courtroom. She was too shy to introduce herself to Bess, but
she walked up to one reporter to tell her, "I think it's a terrible injustice,
a terrible injustice."

When court recessed for the day, the reporter ran into Bess Myerson as she was heading down a stairwell. "Miss Detroit of 1957 was here today," she told Bess. "I told her to introduce herself to you, but she didn't want to. She said she thought this was a terrible injustice."

Bess Myerson stopped for a second and glared at the reporter as if to say that she was tired of hearing words of encouragement. Then she lit a cigarette, opened the door to the stairwell, and on her way out said, "She's not the jury."

It was Tuesday, December 13, less than a dozen shopping days before Christmas. The holiday season had once again turned Manhattan into a glittering, magical place. Twinkling lights hung across Fifth Avenue. The Salvation Army volunteers, dressed as Santa Claus, rang bells at street corners for donations. Choirs gathered in building lobbies. It was a time of goodwill and peace toward men—the perfect season, the defense lawyers said half-jokingly, for a criminal case to go to the jury.

Inside the courtroom that morning, where closing arguments were to begin, however, there was no sign of the holiday season. The room was darkened by a gray sky that hinted at snow. After eleven weeks of testimony almost everyone involved in the case seemed tired and eager for the trial to come to an end.

Stuart Abrams stood up to deliver the closing argument for the government. A shy, polite, scholarly lawyer, he had an earnest, boyish manner that seemed to command the attention of the jurors as he sought to summarize the government's complex, circumstantial case following testimony from thirty-four prosecution witnesses. His straightforward style was a sharp contrast to the ridiculing theatrics of the defense team.

His voice was tinged with anger and indignation as he addressed the jury, punctuating his points by striking his fist in the air while pacing back and forth along the length of the jury box. It was as if he was trying to instill in the jurors his own sense of personal outrage over the "overwhelming evidence" demonstrating that Bess had abused her public office and manipulated the emotionally fragile daughter of Judge Gabel out of "greed and vengeance."

To underscore the weight of the evidence against the defendants Abrams used the words "no doubt" seventeen times during the four-and-a-half hours he addressed the jury as he recounted the critical facts of the government's case.

"There is no doubt that in 1983, when the divorce case came before Hortense Gabel, all of a sudden Bess Myerson swoops in . . . and . . . scoops up Sukhreet Gabel. In fact there is no doubt that the same day Sukhreet Gabel got her job with the Department of Cultural Affairs, Justice Gabel . . . told her law clerk she had granted Mr. Capasso's motion" to reduce his alimony.

"We are here to decide whether or not city jobs get used to pay bribes or whether they get assigned fairly," Abrams said in a stern voice.

He took the jury through the entire case, pointing frequently to a five-foot-high chart set up on an easel that listed the events as they had unfolded in 1983. With the date of each event—from the beginning of the divorce action to Sukhreet's hiring—clearly marked and the names of the three defendants highlighted in different colors, it was easy for the jury to see how Bess, Andy, and Judge Gabel had interacted that year. Abrams was hoping that the chart would diagram for the jury how a conspiracy to commit bribery, and not mere coincidences, had brought the defendants together that year.

As Abrams meticulously laid out the government's case, Bess sat stone-faced at the defense table, alternately watching Abrams and then the jurors, who were listening intently to the prosecutor. This would be the first and only time they would hear the government tie together all of its circumstantial evidence into a compelling argument that Bess had bribed Judge Gabel by hiring Sukhreet in return for the judge's lowering Andy's alimony payments.

Abrams's closing was so powerfully persuasive and charged by his own indignation at the crimes he alleged that one of the jurors later said she was moved to tears. Another juror, who was leaning toward acquittal, said nonetheless that he thought for sure that Abrams's summation would compel the other jurors to vote to convict.

After Abrams finished, the defense team looked visibly worried for the first time since Sukhreet had left the stand. "That was a ten, a ten," Jay Goldberg told reporters somberly in the courthouse corridor after court was adjourned for the day. Andy's lawyer was scheduled to appear next in front of the jury to deliver his summation.

The next morning, in a closing argument filled with ridicule, sarcasm, and one-liners that kept everyone in the courtroom laughing uproariously, Goldberg worked the room like a borscht-belt comedian.

Comparing the government's witnesses to bad vaudeville acts, Goldberg said the prosecution's case reminded him of "The Gong Show." "The jurors should have a button on their chairs to sound the gong on witnesses," he said to laughter from the jurors and the spectators.

He said that the government case was like a television soap opera. "Never have so many days, so much time, energy and taxpayers' money . . . been spent on such trivial pursuits. . . .

"How important was it that you learn Bess Myerson didn't want people to know she was sleeping with Andy Capasso?" he asked the jury.

"Was it important for you to know that Bess Myerson tried on Nancy Capasso's bathing suits or that Bess Myerson threw out Nancy Capasso's potted plants?"

He blasted the prosecutors for manipulating Sukhreet, this "sick and disturbed woman," and for giving her "a forum for the unfair destruction of her parents.

"They take this disturbed girl in 1986, a girl who has a self-professed love-hate relationship with her parents and with Bess Myerson. . . . A girl who has no friends. . . . They take this woman . . . and they put her up to taping her own parents. . . .

"There has got to be a level of decency beneath which even an advocate will not sink in a quest to make a case. . . . The prosecutors, in their quest to make a case, struck blows so low that their knuckles scraped the pavement."

Returning to his tactic of blaming Nancy, he asked the jurors not to mistake Andy's ex-wife for "some virginal victim."

"Pity poor Nancy," he said, his voice dripping with sarcasm. "She couldn't make ends meet with a piddling $2 million a year."

Then, in his very best Brooklyn accent, Goldberg delivered his best line of the day. "Where I grew up in Brooklyn, we have an expression," he said, pausing for dramatic effect. "Don't make a federal case out of it."

The courtroom erupted in laughter. Smiling broadly, Linda Berardi, the juror Goldberg and his wife were most hopeful would vote to acquit, nodded her head in agreement.

Late that afternoon Michael Feldberg changed the tone in the courtroom with his quiet, serious manner. "Is there any direct proof of a secret agreement?" he asked the jurors. "Is there any witness who came before you and said, 'I saw it, I heard it, I smelled it, I tasted it'? The answer to that is no."

Then, continuing his summation the following morning, he tried to evoke sympathy for his client. He walked behind the judge's chair and, resting his hands on her shoulder, looked up at the jurors and said, "Don't convict this good woman, ladies and gentlemen. If you do, God forbid . . . in the end you will say, 'Oh my God, what have I done?'"

Fred Hafetz had worried throughout the trial that the jurors wouldn't like Bess. The government had presented a succession of Bess's former employees as witnesses, and they had described her as a demanding, imperious, and inconsiderate boss. Having concluded as a result of that testimony that he wouldn't win any sympathy for Bess, Hafetz drafted a closing argument intended to tear apart the government's case fact by fact and cast doubt on virtually every bit of circumstantial evidence against Bess.

"If Bess Myerson were going to use Sukhreet Gabel as the instrument for a bribery conspiracy," he asked, "why do it in such a public, identifiable way? . . . Why make her special assistant? Why let her have cards printed up to be given out to the world as 'special assistant to the commissioner'?"

Then, addressing what he feared would be the most damaging evidence against Bess—her use of aliases when she left messages for Judge Gabel—Hafetz once again referred to Bess's "strange behavior. It is eccentric behavior. But criminal cases are not made of eccentric or strange behavior."

Bess leaned back in her chair and laughed aloud at this. But as Hafetz brought his summation to a close, she looked somber when he reminded jurors of the importance of their decision to Bess's life.

"At this point in Bess Myerson's life the most important thing—the most important event—from the time of her birth until now will be the decision that you will make in this case."

Throughout the trial Judge Keenan did nothing to camouflage his opinion about the government's case. It was apparent to everyone in the courtroom—the defendants, the spectators, the press, even members of the jury—that he thought little of the government's case and the way the prosecutors were handling it. He repeatedly told the prosecutors that he did not want his courtroom turned into "a daytime soap opera," and he frequently snapped his criticisms of them in front of the jury.

While his rulings had been straight down the middle, favoring neither prosecution nor defense, his expressive face had revealed whenever he was annoyed, amused, or disgusted. More than once he had rolled his eyes upward and swiveled his chair to face the courtroom's paneled wall when a prosecution witness was testifying.

Before the case went to the jurors on Monday, December 19, Keenan instructed the jurors on the laws of conspiracy, bribery, mail fraud, and obstruction of justice—the legal framework from which they were to find Bess, Andy, and Judge Gabel guilty or innocent.

In what Jay Goldberg would later say was the defense team's luckiest break in the case, Keenan also defined circumstantial evidence for the jurors in a way that may have suggested that such evidence carried less weight than it normally carries in federal court.

Then the defense got what it considered a second break in the case when Keenan broke with tradition that morning and chose the foreman of the jury. He picked juror number nine, Linda Berardi, to lead the deliberations. In federal court cases in Manhattan judges usually select juror number one as the jury foreman. In this case, however, that juror, a Cuban exile, did not speak English well. But Keenan's selection of Linda Berardi as jury foreman surprised both sides, because both the prosecutors and the defense lawyers had concluded from watching Berardi's reaction to the testimony that she had little use for the government's case.

Judge Keenan did not explain his choice, but Berardi later told Jeannie Kasindorf of *New York* magazine her theory about her selection. "I think the judge chose me because he saw I was pro-defense," she said. "I think he tended to favor the defense and he saw there was no case and that was part of the reason he chose me. There were moments between myself and the judge during the trial when I felt him glancing at me. I felt at certain moments that he knew what I was thinking."

There was another person in the courtroom whom she felt in sync with at certain moments and who laughed when she laughed. That was Andy Capasso. "There's something warm about him," Berardi told Kasindorf. "He's got a nice sense of humor. . . . He seemed to have the same family values I have."

As the jurors filed out of the courtroom that morning to begin discussing the case among themselves for the first time in weeks, Jay Goldberg was smiling. Whenever he worried about a conviction during the ensuing four days of jury deliberation, Goldberg would repeat what he had come to call his mantra: "Linda will never say Andy is guilty. Linda will never say Andy is guilty. Linda will never say Andy is guilty."

Returning to the jury room following Keenan's instructions, the jurors revealed to each other for the first time what they thought of the case. Their initial poll made it clear that a consensus would not be reached easily. Five jurors thought Judge Gabel was not guilty, three said she was guilty, and four were uncertain. In Andy's case, four jurors favored acquittal, three thought he was guilty, and five were uncertain. And three jurors believed Bess should be found innocent, three thought she was guilty, and six were unsure.

Although Berardi felt strongly that the government had not proved its case against the defendants, she signaled in the poll that she was undecided. As jury foreman she believed that it was important in the beginning of the deliberations to be the "gatekeeper" and the "facilitator."

After reading the indictment for the first time, the jurors began discussing the government's central charge against the defendants, conspiracy to commit bribery, and the battle lines were drawn: Nelson Marty, a forty-four-year-old electrical engineer, and Lucy Gray, a sixty-three-year-old computer operator, argued for conviction. Daniel Handley, a quiet and aloof forty-one-year-old unemployed actor who had spent the past few months reading a book in the corner of the jury room during breaks, surprised his fellow jurors with his forceful, emphatic arguments for acquittal.

Handley later said that Sukhreet's testimony against her mother had deeply disturbed him and as a result he had discounted much of what she had said. He also said the soap opera aspects of the case had turned him off: "I guess you could take Joan Collins's character on 'Dynasty' and make her into Bess, and people have very strong feelings on those types, but that's nothing you can judge a crime on. . . . The more they just painted an ugly personality picture, the more I just started pulling back; they were pushing that idea too hard."

Joining Handley in his argument for acquittal were Zenaida Alvarez, a fifty-seven-year-old administrative assistant in a bank, and Gerald Purcell, a sixty-four-year-old retired postal worker who thought that the key prosecution witnesses—Sukhreet, Herb Rickman, and Shirley Harrod—were all lying.

Unable to reach a consensus that afternoon, the jury, now sequestered, boarded a bus that took them to a midtown Manhattan hotel for the night. They returned to the courthouse at nine o'clock the following morning and resumed deliberations. With the jurors still unable to reach a decision on the conspiracy charge, Berardi, as the foreman, suggested they consider the obstruction of justice charge that had been filed only against Bess. The charge stemmed from Sukhreet's testimony that Bess had told her to keep her mouth shut about her hiring after the federal investigation had begun, during a late-night walk around the block in June of 1986. Since the charge was based virtually entirely on Sukhreet's testimony, most of the jurors dismissed it outright with little discussion.

Before returning to the conspiracy charge, Berardi decided it was time to make her opinions known. "I had explored some of the evidence, and I felt comfortable saying not guilty," she later said. Handley was pleased to have her as an ally.

She requested that the judge provide her with a flip chart and felt-tip pens so that she could illustrate her arguments for an acquittal. She diagrammed three columns—labeled "innocent," "reasonable doubt," and "guilty."

"Almost none of us feel complete innocence—most of us are here in the middle," she remembered telling the jurors at the time as she pointed to the chart. "We feel they are guilty of some things. We feel they are not guilty of other things, but we still have to come in with a not guilty verdict, because we're not beyond a reasonable doubt."

While the chart convinced some jurors to switch their votes from undecided to not guilty, others switched their votes back and forth between guilty and not guilty. Several jurors brought up the possibility that Judge Gabel was the mastermind of the conspiracy, and juror Sheila Adler remembered that one juror suggested that Gabel was "pushing all of the buttons." By late Tuesday night, the second day of deliberations, three jurors who had been undecided on the conspiracy charge had moved their votes into the not guilty column. Berardi was pleased that she was making some progress.

By the following day, several jurors concluded there were possibly reasons for Judge Gabel to have lowered Andy's alimony payments other than getting her daughter a job. They also concluded that Bess might have hired Sukhreet based on her résumé. With many of the jurors now conceding these points, the element of reasonable doubt about a conspiracy had been introduced into the deliberations, and the defendants could be convicted only if the jury was convinced of their guilt beyond a reasonable doubt.

Handley even sought to explain away what some jurors considered suspicious behavior by Bess, such as wearing sunglasses the night she walked around the block with Sukhreet. Celebrities, he said, wear sunglasses at night because they don't want to be recognized. They use aliases when they make telephone calls, he added, because they want to protect their privacy.

And Bess's misleading letter to Mayor Koch about Sukhreet Gabel's hiring, Handley and Berardi argued, was simply a matter of political expediency. "She did not out-and-out lie really terribly; she was just apologizing publicly for an error in judgment," Berardi recalled telling her fellow jurors. "I would send a letter, too. I would do something to bandage it."

By Wednesday night, the end of the third day of deliberations, most of the jurors favored acquittal. Only two jurors were inclined to vote to convict—Nelson Marty, the electrical engineer, and Lucy Gray, the computer operator.

By lunchtime of the following day, Thursday, December 22, all but Lucy Gray were prepared to vote for acquittal on all charges. Berardi had persuaded Nelson Marty to vote for an acquittal that morning after asserting that it was not his fault that the government had not provided him with enough quality evidence to find them guilty.

Berardi, however, had no luck in convincing Gray. "Tell the judge it's a hung jury, Linda," Gray told her.

"Are you kidding?" Berardi replied. "I am not going to embarrass myself by going out there and telling the judge that on such a high-publicity case."

The tension in the jury room was palpable. Jurors began shouting at each other. Berardi demanded that Gray explain why she believed they should be found guilty. "This is all wrong," Berardi told her angrily, reminding her that the defendants were entitled to a presumption of innocence. "You should be standing up and trying to prove guilt to me."

But Gray would not budge from her position that afternoon, nor would she explain her vote. "They're guilty. They're guilty," is all she would say.

On that Thursday afternoon, the fourth day of jury deliberations, the hot and stuffy courtroom was packed with reporters and spectators milling around, waiting for a verdict. No one had any idea what was going on in the jury room, but everyone agreed that lengthy deliberations were not a good sign for the defense.

With each passing hour Bess grew more worried about her fate. She spent most of the time seated at the defense table with Andy and his sixteen-year-old son, who had spent each day of the deliberations with his father in the courtroom. Occasionally Bess would wander into the press section or the corridor to chat with reporters. To one reporter she compared herself to the central character in the movie *A Cry in the Dark*, about an Australian woman, portrayed by Meryl Streep, who was wrongfully accused of murdering her child.

A few of her friends came down to the courthouse during deliberations to offer her encouragement and support. Dr. Ted Rubin and his wife, Ellie, were there, along with Esther Margolis, who had published the story of Bess's Miss America triumph, and Bess's longtime friend Sandy Stern, who had won a Bess Myerson look-alike contest sponsored by *New York* magazine.

Noticeably absent was Bess's daughter, Barra, who remained in California working on her television show. Bess said she understood why her daughter couldn't be there, and in any event, Bess had her six-year-old granddaughter, Samantha, staying with her that week. When she returned home from the courthouse each night, Bess said, her granddaughter's presence helped take her mind off the deliberations.

The Gabels sat at the other end of the defense table during jury deliberations. Judge Gabel and her husband would occasionally doze off for a half hour or so. Dr. Gabel was deeply distressed that it was taking the jurors so long to return with a verdict. "I thought that after they heard what Mayor Wagner and the other people said they would return quickly with a not guilty verdict," said a despairing Dr. Gabel.

Judge Gabel was also worried that the deliberations were dragging on. Perhaps that is why she decided to call Sukhreet at four o'clock that morning to ask her to join her at the courthouse that day.

For days Jay Goldberg had been trying to convince the Gabels' lawyer, Michael Feldberg, to get Sukhreet to return to the courtroom and sit in the spectators' section. Goldberg was hoping that the jurors would spot her if they returned to the courtroom for further instructions from the judge or to listen to the court reporter read back parts of the testimony. He was hoping that seeing her in the courtroom would remind the jurors of how repulsive it was for a daughter to testify against her mother.

"You tell me whether any old-time trial lawyer wouldn't do this," Goldberg later said with a sly smile. "I said to Michael Feldberg, 'Ask Milton Gould [the senior partner at his law firm] if any war-horse wouldn't see this as the greatest fucking move.' I wanted her in the first row during the judge's charge."

Worried about Bess's reaction to Sukhreet's presence, Hafetz was adamantly against Sukhreet's returning to the courtroom. Feldberg wasn't too excited about the prospect, either. There wasn't much they could do about it, though, when the judge called her daughter before dawn that Thursday morning to ask her to join her in the courtroom at ten.

At fifteen minutes past ten that Thursday morning, Sukhreet, dressed in a gold brocade suit, walked into the courtroom. Goldberg was delighted. With a big smile on his face, he stood up and said, "Oh, Sukhreet is here. Have her sit in the front."

David Lawrence and Tony Lombardi were furious. Since Sukhreet had stepped down from the stand, she had been appearing on radio and television talk shows, including the nationally broadcast "Larry King Live." On the very day that Stuart Abrams was delivering his closing argument, Sukhreet was on the television show "People Are Talking," undergoing a complete cosmetic and fashion makeover. And while testimony was still being given by government witnesses, Sukhreet made her singing debut at the El Morocco nightclub in a zebra-striped dress, belting out the song "Let the Punishment Fit the Crime."

"We expected some mugging for the camera," Lawrence said later. "Did we think she would go to the El Morocco? No, we didn't think she would do that."

When reporters surrounded Sukhreet that morning to ask why she had decided to return, she told them she had been invited. "I learned I was welcome," she said with a broad smile. "I'm glad to be here. I didn't want to show up where I wasn't welcome. I'm on coffee duty. I'm going to get coffee for Mummy."

Bess was not happy about Sukhreet's presence. Walking over to the other end of the defense table, she said to Judge Gabel, loudly enough for reporters to hear, "I don't want to talk to Sukhreet, so don't bring her over. I love you, dear, but I don't want to talk to her." The judge nodded her head in understanding.

When the jurors filed back into the courtroom that morning to ask the judge about a legal point, Sukhreet sat at the very back of the press section, out of the jury's sight. But the second time the jury returned to listen to the court reporter read back testimony, Sukhreet was seated at the front of the spectators' section, in full view of the jury.

Sheila Adler was the first juror to spot her. She turned and whispered to the juror next to her that Sukhreet was sitting in the courtroom. As the word spread to the other jurors, several of them covered their mouths to hide their laughter. Taking care to make sure the entire jury spotted her, Jay Goldberg rose from his seat and elaborately looked over at her. Andy was laughing so hard at Goldberg that he bit the back of his hand to stop.

Goldberg was on the mark with his old trial-lawyer trick. Sukhreet's presence in the courtroom was a powerful weapon for his cause. Other jurors later said that Lucy Gray was shaken when she saw Sukhreet. She told them back in the jury room that seeing Sukhreet reminded her of how much she didn't like her and how much of the government's case depended on her testimony.

Gray's position was beginning to waver, but she was not yet convinced that an acquittal was proper.

Berardi tried a new approach to win Gray over. She called for an unofficial tally of how many of her colleagues thought the defendants were guilty but that the government had failed to prove the case against them. Nine of the jurors, including Berardi, raised their hands. "I think most of us felt there might have been a conspiracy there," said Sheila Adler. "We all felt that something happened. But in no way did the prosecution prove it."

Berardi had hoped that this poll would illustrate to Gray that it was possible to find Bess and the others not guilty even if there was doubt about their innocence. Gray was still unmoved. She said that there might have to be a hung jury.

Determined to return a verdict, Berardi suggested they request the judge to repeat his instructions on the issue of the presumption of innocence.

At about 7:25 P.M. the jurors filed back into the courtroom to listen to Keenan define presumption of innocence for them once again. As he explained that the burden of proof rested with the government, beyond a reasonable doubt, Berardi nodded her head in approval. The judge had just validated the argument she had been making to Gray in the jury room.

As the jurors slowly filed back into the jury room, Lucy Gray pulled Linda Berardi aside. Raising her arm slightly, Gray looked at Berardi and said softly, "Linda, I'm ready to vote now." Berardi smiled, and as soon as everyone had returned to the jury room she called for another vote. A look of surprise crossed many of the jurors' faces. After Gray raised her hand with them, voting not guilty on all counts, the jurors let out a cheer.

"There's a verdict."

A hush fell over the courtroom as everyone hurried to take a seat. Bess's best friend, Sandy Stern, began to sob uncontrollably. Andy, who had sat through the whole trial with his lawyer carefully placed between him and Bess, took a seat next to her for the first time. Then Bess took her place in her chair, sitting, as she had sat every day of the trial, with her back straight and her chin held high, her arms folded in her lap. She looked more composed than her noticeably nervous friends.

Judge Gabel looked frightened as her attorney escorted her toward her seat at the defense table, with her husband behind her. Sukhreet took a seat in the back of the press section.

It was 8:02 P.M. by the courtroom clock when the judge and the jury returned and took their seats. The judge's clerk stood up at her desk in front of the defendants and asked Linda Berardi to rise. Then the clerk began going down the list of the sixteen counts in the case, asking Berardi the verdict on each count. Each time Berardi's crisp, clear voice rang loudly through the courtroom as she replied, "Not guilty."

When Berardi recited "not guilty" for the thirteenth of the sixteen counts, Bess reached up and took off her oversized glasses and wiped a tear from one eye. She turned to Andy and touched his arm, then turned back to listen. The last count was the obstruction of justice charge that had been lodged only against her. Berardi considered pausing long enough to make Bess sweat. ("I wanted Bess to squirm for the last one," she said later.)

Finally Berardi said "not guilty" one last time, and for the first time in the nearly four months of the court proceedings Bess abandoned her proud posture. She lay down her head, stretched her arms out on the defense table before her, and began to cry.

Andy pulled her next to him and kissed her on the cheek. Then she hugged her attorney and got out of her chair and walked over to the other end of the defense table to the Gabels. She embraced Dr. Gabel and put her hand on Judge Gabel's shoulder.

Returning to her seat, Bess started sobbing. Andy wrapped his arms around her and put her head on his shoulder. He whispered something in her ear and rubbed her back. She quickly became composed again while the judge thanked the jurors and they filed out of the room.

Bess's friends crowded into the well of the court to embrace her. Andy hugged his son and then lit a cigarette, his hand shaking. When asked how he felt, he replied with a big smile, "Outstanding."

Sukhreet made her way through the crowd, pushing her way gently, hesitantly toward her mother and father in the front of the courtroom. Her mother grabbed her arm as soon as she spotted her and smiled. "She told the truth all the way," Judge Gabel said. "I'm proud that she stood by me the whole way." When reporters asked what she thought of the verdict, Sukhreet replied with a tight smile, "Justice has been done."

Bess kissed Andy one last time and tenderly touched his arm before the court marshals led him away to his holding cell for his return to prison. Surrounded by friends, Bess turned and headed for the ladies' room to put on lipstick and smooth her hair before facing the huge crowd of television cameras and photographers waiting for her on the courthouse steps.

"Do you have any comment, Bess?" one of the dozen or so reporters asked, following her into the corridor.

"No," she said, still smiling, as if she were floating on air.

When she emerged from the ladies' room, she was wearing a colorful silk scarf tied around her neck. She was now ready for the cameras. Still smiling, she stepped into the crowded elevator and rode down to the lobby with her friends and attorneys.

Sukhreet was a few feet ahead of them, walking behind her parents, who were surrounded by reporters and friends. "C'mon, Sukhreet," her father said, turning to her.

"I don't go where I am not wanted," she snapped. She felt shunned as her parents' friends surrounded Judge Gabel to wish her congratulations. Then she walked over to a bench in the courthouse's lobby, sat down, and opened a book. Her parents continued on to the courthouse portico.

The Gabels were the first to step outside the revolving door and into the throng of reporters and camera crews waiting on the courthouse steps.

Bess paused for a moment before following them out the door.

"Wait," she told her friend, Sandy Stern. "How does my scarf look?"

"Just fine," Stern said. "Just fine."

"Okay," she said. "Let's go."

Bess pushed open the doors and stood on the top of the courthouse steps, the same steps that she had first walked up more than a year ago on that October day to answer the criminal charges at her arraignment.

"Bess!" "Bess!" "How does it feel?"

She waded through the crowd, still smiling, a frozen smile, until she reached a bank of microphones set up at the bottom of the stairs. Speaking in a firm and deliberate voice and beaming happily before the cameras, she said, "I'm grateful for the American judicial system, and I thank the jury for exonerating me." Having made her statement, she stepped away from the microphones and moved slowly, as if in a daze, through the crowd of reporters and spectators toward a waiting cab. The reporters continued to shout questions at her.

"Were you always hopeful it would happen, Miss Myerson?"

"Did the delay have you somewhat worried there?"

"Bess, did you have some rough moments during the week?"

"Turn around, Bess."

"Any message for Ed Koch? Should this prosecution have been brought?"

"What about the allegations of the job to Sukhreet, the coincidences of the phone calls, the cuts in Capasso's alimony?"

"It's over," Bess replied, a frown crossing her face. "It's over."

Then a photographer shouted for her to give the crowd a victory sign.

Turning her head to face the cameras, she flashed her dazzling smile once again and held up her fingers in a V before climbing into her cab and speeding away.

Afterword

Rudolph Giuliani was about to walk out of his office to buy a Christmas present for his wife when he got the call about the verdict. The acquittal of all three defendants ranked as one of the biggest—if not *the* biggest—embarrassments of his otherwise impressive tenure as U.S. attorney. The case, two years in the works, had collapsed under its star prosecution witness, whose testimony in court and antics outside the courtroom had made her a citywide joke. It was not the outcome Giuliani had hoped for as he considered entering the 1989 mayoral race.

An hour after Bess walked down the courthouse steps, a calm and composed Giuliani met with reporters in his office and explained that he had "never argued with a jury's verdict and I will not do so here. The jury concluded there was insufficient evidence." But he stood by his decision to bring the case into court: "This case was a case that should have been brought to a jury. Obviously we are disappointed with the result. . . . I made the decision to go forward because of the corruption that was involved here. It was serious."

Without a doubt Giuliani's aggressive prosecution of corrupt city officials and Wall Street executives had helped change the moral climate of New York dramatically. When the circumstances of Sukhreet Gabel's hiring were first revealed on the *New York Post*'s gossip page in 1983, no one in journalism or law enforcement bothered to follow it up. It was not until 1986, after Giuliani had begun to delve into charges of municipal corruption, that the old *Post* story finally attracted the attention of investigators and led to the federal charges against Bess.

However, while the allegations were serious—a high-ranking member of the Koch administration bribing a state judge to fix a case—Giuliani's decision to prosecute Bess raises questions about his political ambition and also underscores his critics' most frequent complaint: that he brought high-profile cases to draw attention to himself and his office.

The Tyler report, prepared at the request of Mayor Koch, convicted Bess in the court of public opinion. But the standard of proof is much higher in a court of law. And this is where prosecutorial discretion became important.

Considering all of the law enforcement problems in New York, it seems now, in hindsight, a waste of limited resources to prosecute a public official and an elderly judge who had already stepped down from their public offices in disgrace. And looking at the case now, the problems of prosecuting Bess seem formidable and should have been apparent to a prosecutor of Giuliani's skill and experience.

Giuliani and his team of prosecutors should have anticipated how disturbing it would be for a jury to watch a daughter testify against her elderly and nearly blind mother; to hear testimony that she taped her mother's telephone conversation; to listen to her as she recounted carting shopping bags filled with her mother's private papers to federal investigators. They should not have used a woman with a long history of depression to testify against her mother.

On Tuesday, January 11, two weeks after the verdict, Giuliani, then forty-four years old, announced his resignation as U.S. attorney of the Southern District. Three months later he formally announced that he would seek the Republican nomination for mayor of New York and run on an anticorruption platform. Although he easily won the Republican nomination, he was unable to make the transition from effective federal prosecutor to successful mayoral candidate in the general election. He lost to Democrat David Dinkins, who became the city's first black mayor, ending Koch's twelve-year reign over New York.

Sukhreet Gabel had mixed feelings about the verdict. While she insists that she did not want to see her mother convicted, she says that she would have liked to see Bess found guilty. She still blames Bess for the unhappiness and the difficulties she faced finding a job after she left the Department of Cultural Affairs and the city's Commission on Human Rights in 1983. She had hoped that the trial testimony would show that it wasn't her fault that she had lost both of her city jobs.

The days after the verdict were filled with more media appearances for Sukhreet. She showed up on news programs and interview shows all over town, including another appearance on "People Are Talking." The Gabels declined to appear as guests but could be seen by viewers in the audience, applauding and smiling as Sukhreet defended her decision to testify against her mother. It was a sad, pathetic sight. They had gone to the television studio to show support for Sukhreet, but they might have helped her more if they had stayed at home and insisted that she do the same.

Sukhreet's behavior was not unexpected because by the midpoint of the trial she had already become a sideshow act. While her mother was sitting in court, Sukhreet was making the rounds of the city's television and radio stations, candidly answering questions about her chronic depression and electroshock therapy. She believed her appearances would show the public that she was a "real person" and allow them to judge whether she was, in her own words, "crazy" or sane. She ignored advice from friends who told her that she was being made a fool of. She didn't seem to care. She was basking in the attention. After seven years of looking for a job, she had a full-fledged career in her newfound celebrity.

In the months following the trial she posed topless with a snake draped around her shoulders for a gay lifestyle magazine. She worked on an album that included one song titled "Who Am I to Judge?" and accepted singing engagements at downtown Manhattan nightclubs and Greenwich Village bars, hiring Tiny Tim's agent to represent her. Then there was her line of greeting cards, called "Sukhreet's Sassy Tips," featuring her in an assortment of odd or revealing costumes. One card shows her in a broad-brimmed hat and a matronly dress with one hand raised and one hand on a Bible. A blindfolded and bare-chested young man in a white toga stands in the background holding the scale of justice. "Witnesses claim you're such an ol' prude," the front of the card says. Inside the message continues: "You can't even get off on a well-hung jury! Happy Birthday."

In the end Sukhreet may have found what she was looking for when she first made Bess Myerson's acquaintance in the summer of 1983: a little attention and a career.

As for her relationship with her mother, Sukhreet claims that the ordeal of the trial actually brought them closer together and that they are the best of friends. For Mother's Day the judge was in the audience at a Greenwich Village cabaret where Sukhreet was singing. For her mother she sang "Let the Punishment Fit the Crime." Sukhreet is hoping her celebrity will help her get more singing engagements and possibly launch her on the lecture circuit.

Nancy Capasso was packing for a Caribbean vacation when she got word of the verdict. Even though she had been preparing herself for an acquittal in the wake of Sukhreet's testimony, she was disappointed, as she explained that night on the telephone, "that Bess did not get it." For the sake of her children Nancy had hoped that Andy would be acquitted. But Bess was a different matter entirely. Nancy blamed Bess for tearing her family apart and uprooting her from her palatial Fifth Avenue co-op to a $5,000-a-month rental on Third Avenue on the Upper East Side.

Nancy was hoping that by the time she returned from her vacation the press and the public would have forgotten about the case and she could get on with her life. The wounds the divorce and the ensuing public drama had inflicted on Nancy's family would take time to heal. The case had taken a heavy toll on Nancy's five children. Just a few days before the case went to the jury, one of her three children from her previous marriage, twenty-six-year-old Steven, living in California, publicly condemned Nancy, saying that her greed and selfishness, not Bess, had been responsible for the breakup of her marriage to Andy.

The bitter denunciation, printed on Friday, December 16, in the *New York Post* under the byline of Bess's friend, columnist Cindy Adams, divided Nancy's family even more. The following Monday Nancy's other two children from her previous marriage told the *Post* that they had severed their relationship with their brother. "I am truly ashamed, but not totally surprised, that my brother said what he did," Nancy's eldest daughter, Helené, said. "My brother has always been driven by greed, and maybe he believes that the best way to guarantee his financial future is to sing Andy's praises and put down our mother."

With the federal case lost in an acquittal Nancy dropped a multimillion-dollar civil racketeering case that she had brought against Andy, Bess, Hortense Gabel, and the city of New York, charging them with defrauding her by scheming to lower her alimony payments. She was continuing, however, to battle insurance companies in court over her divorce settlement.

Even though an appeals court had awarded Nancy $6.4 million, she learned months later that Andy had arranged their affairs so that she would not be able to collect a penny of it. Almost all of their money was tied up in three Long Island properties and in the couple's luxurious Fifth Avenue apartment. Before going off to federal prison in June of 1987, Andy had arranged to turn over the properties to his creditors—mostly insurance companies that held the bonds for his major sewer construction projects. As a result his creditors would get the proceeds from the sale of those properties—including the Fifth Avenue apartment, on the market at the time for $7.5 million. Since Nancy had signed her name as a co-guarantor for the sewer projects before her marital problems began, the insurance companies contended that she too was liable for paying the bonds.

After fighting Andy in divorce court, she now finds herself fighting insurance companies. Her alimony ended when her divorce became final in 1985, and she is now making ends meet as a $100,000-a-year realtor in Manhattan. At the end of 1989 the case was still unresolved and wending its way through the courts. It is entirely possible that she could end up without a dime from Andy.

On the day after the verdict Judge Gabel received a steady stream of well-wishers at her East Side apartment. She also met with a few reporters to discuss the case. At the end of their interview as they were about to leave, one of them asked the judge whether she thought that Bess had been trying to influence her decisions in the Capasso divorce case, as the prosecution had alleged.

"It's possible," the judge conceded in a startling response. Her two-word acknowledgment appeared to undermine the defense's contention that Sukhreet's hiring and the lowering of Andy's alimony payments were unrelated because she was unaware that Bess and Andy were lovers at the time.

Had Judge Gabel known of that relationship, she should have removed herself from the Capasso case immediately. New York's judicial canon of ethics expressly forbids judges from mixing their personal business with their official duties.

From the testimony presented during the trial it is difficult to believe that Judge Gabel didn't know Bess and Andy were lovers and that Bess's sudden interest in Sukhreet Gabel had nothing to do with the fact that Judge Gabel was presiding over Andy's divorce. Both Bess and the judge were veteran city political figures who had been practicing the you-scratch-my-back-and-I'll-scratch-your-back school of politics for decades. In that school of politics words are not always necessary to strike a deal.

In the months after the trial Judge Gabel thought about looking for another job, possibly as a mediator. Instead she chose retirement.

After climbing into a taxi outside the courthouse, Bess headed uptown to the Upper East Side to celebrate her acquittal at the home of her good friend, Sandy Stern. In the company of a few close friends she toasted her victory with a shot of vodka.

The following day she talked with Andy over the telephone. She would visit him at the federal detention center in lower Manhattan several times over the next two weeks before he returned to Allenwood. He had six months to go before completing his sentence for income tax evasion and returning to New York to rebuild his sewer business, which he had left in the hands of a trusted nephew.

Bess continued to live at Andy's huge Park Avenue duplex apartment until just a few weeks before his release from prison on June 26, 1989, when she returned alone to her smaller, two-bedroom apartment off Fifth Avenue. Andy wanted time and space to start his life over again. No one, including Bess, seemed to know what would become of their relationship now that he was finally free. They were seen early in the summer in the Hamptons. By August, however, the gossip columns were reporting that Andy and Bess were apart. Although he was no longer seeing the former model who had visited him in jail, he was spotted with a woman the *New York Daily News* described as "a younger

version of Bess." Then, by the end of the summer, Bess and Andy were
together again.

In looking back over the events in her life, Bess once wondered aloud
whether her troubles were a confirmation of the old Jewish superstition
her mother had warned her about as a child—that the "evil eye" jinxes
anyone too rich, too beautiful, and too successful. It was an easy way of
absolving herself of responsibility for her downfall.

Sukhreet's hiring arose out of the corrupting influences of power.
Politics is a business of trading favors, and in the New York of the
1980s the lines of ethics and legality were blurred both in city government and on Wall Street. In that milieu Bess's hiring of Sukhreet was
business as usual.

Bess was also beset by weaknesses and character flaws that caused her
problems throughout her life, and those flaws may help to explain her
rise and fall. She had a tremendous need to control people and situa-
tions. She remained anxious about money even after she had become a
millionaire many times over. And her years as a powerful figure in
government and politics made her an imperious and demanding taskmaster who expected to get what she wanted.

It was almost as if the fierce ambition that had propelled her to fame
and fortune was also responsible for her troubles. In the later years of
her life she became obsessive about getting what she wanted—whether it
was the man who rejected her for a younger woman, control over her
boyfriend's divorce case, or $44 worth of merchandise from a discount
store in Pennsylvania.

At the same time, her shoplifting and her other erratic behavior
suggest that Bess may have been crying out for help. She had never
seemed able to overcome the feelings of inadequacy that stemmed from
her complicated relationship with her mother. Her shoplifting could be
seen as an attempt to sabotage her own success to prove that her mother
was right and that she did not deserve the admiration and accolades that
she had received for so long.

Although Bess was acquitted of all charges, her ordeal forever tar-
nished the image of the beautiful and accomplished woman that she had
polished for so long. The reign of Queen Bess had come to an end. But
when I spoke with Bess in the months following the trial, she seemed
almost relieved that she no longer had to project the image of the
perfect woman that came with her crowning as Miss America in 1945.
Forty years is a long time to have to maintain the larger-than-life public
persona called Bess Myerson.

After almost two years in seclusion, however, she has returned to the
social circuit, appearing once again on Andy's arm in the fall of 1989 at

charity balls and at parties at the Rainbow Room and Tavern on the Green. On Saturday, October 7, Bess and Andy made a public appearance and posed for photographers at a dinner sponsored by the Columbus Society at the Waldorf-Astoria Hotel. At the same dinner was Rudolph Giuliani, but he was seated across the crowded room and did not run into Bess or Andy that night.

At last, Bess no longer seems to hear her mother, Bella, demand that she continue to achieve. "Everybody asks me, 'So, what are you doing now?'" she told *New York Post* columnist Cindy Adams. "Why must I be doing something? All my life I've been doing something. All my life I've been doing. For now, I'm being—being quiet, being grateful. Finally, finally, it's time for me. Not the public Bess Myerson, the private me."

Notes

These chapter notes do not include all of the names of the more than two hundred people interviewed for this book or all of the documents and published sources consulted. They are intended to provide readers with an overview of the author's sources of information.

Chapter 1: A Fall from Grace

Most of the material in this chapter comes from my own reporting and observations that day. I covered Bess Myerson's arraignment on October 15, 1987, as a reporter for *New York Newsday*, and I later interviewed her for the newspaper. Several of the details included in this chapter were provided by my colleagues who were also there: Paul Moses, Anthony DeStefano, Christopher Hatch, Marcia Kramer, Gail Collins, Jack Newfield, Gabe Pressman, and Doug Johnson. In addition, I drew from an unpublished interview that Bess Myerson gave in 1987 to another journalist who requested anonymity.

Page 1. **She was shocked:** Bess Myerson, interview with author, October 15, 1987.
Page 2. **In her prayers she asked her mother and father:** Bess Myerson, interview with author, October 15, 1987.
Page 3. **she thought it would be best to go to the courthouse without Helen:** Bess Myerson, interview with author, October 15, 1987.
Page 4. **She thought Sukhreet looked like a clown:** Bess Myerson, unpublished interview with confidential source, 1987.

Chapter 2: A Shtetl in the Bronx

Much of the history and details about life in the 1920s and 1930s at the Sholem Aleichem Cooperative Houses and Bess's early life comes from more than two dozen interviews with Bess's childhood friends, former neighbors, Bronx historians, and relatives of the Myersons who grew up at the Sholem Aleichem Cooperative Houses. Bess Myerson also talked about her childhood, her family, and growing up in the Bronx during an interview with the author on October 15, 1987. The author also examined state and federal census records, plans for the apartment complex on file at the New York City Department of Buildings, and files in the archives of YIVO Institute for Jewish Research and in New York City's Municipal Archives. In addition, the author consulted numerous clippings from the *Bronx Home News*, *Jewish Daily Forward*, *New York Post*, *New York Daily News*, *New York Herald Tribune*, and *Boston Globe*. The author also obtained material from several books, including Susan Dworkin, *Miss America, 1945: Bess Myerson's Own Story* (New York: Newmarket Press, 1987); Bronx Museum of the Arts, *Building a Borough: Architecture and Planning in the Bronx, 1890-1940* (New York: Bronx Museum of the Arts, 1986); Hutchins

Hapgood, *The Spirit of the Ghetto: Studies of the Jewish Quarter of New York* (New York: Schocken Books, 1966); and Irving Howe, *World of Our Fathers* (New York: Simon and Schuster, 1976).

Page 7. **"See that? . . ."**: Marian Christy, "The Myerson Mood," *Boston Globe*, October 28, 1987.

Page 7. **"I think I spent a lot of time trying to get my mother's approval."**: "The Myerson Mood."

Page 7. **she stopped by a Bronx hospital**: Bess Myerson, interview with author, fall 1988.

Page 8. **Bella Podelaky Myerson arrived in New York:** Description of Bella Myerson comes from Susan Dworkin, *Miss America, 1945: Bess Myerson's Own Story* (New York: Newmarket Press, 1987), 26.

Page 8. **December 19, 1922**: Date, cause of death, and burial come from Joseph Myerson's death certificate: New York City Municipal Archives.

Page 8. **Family friends remember that the death of Bella's little boy transformed her**: Description of Bella Myerson's depression after Joseph's death comes from *Miss America, 1945: Bess Myerson's Own Story*, 25-27.

Page 8. **her mother would tie a red ribbon in her hair**: Bebe and Sidney Barkan (cousins who were close to Bella Myerson), interview with author, 1988.

Page 9. **Louis Myerson was eighteen when he arrived in New York:** *Miss America, 1945: Bess Myerson's Own Story*, 10.

Page 9. **When soldiers descended on the shtetl:** *Miss America, 1945: Bess Myerson's Own Story*, 12-13.

Page 9. **"No Catholics, Jews, or dogs"**: Bronx Museum of the Arts, *Building a Borough: Architecture and Planning in the Bronx, 1890-1940* (New York: Bronx Museum of the Arts, 1986), 60.

Page 10. **Bella decided soon after moving in**: Bess Myerson, unpublished interview with confidential source, 1987. A similar anecdote is described in *Miss America, 1945: Bess Myerson's Own Story*, 11.

Page 10. **Worried that Helen's asthma might be exacerbated**: *Miss America, 1945: Bess Myerson's Own Story*, 11.

Page 10. **Louis and Bella gave up their five rooms for three**: Bess Myerson, interview with author, October 15, 1987. A similar anecdote appears in *Miss America, 1945: Bess Myerson's Own Story*, 11.

Page 10. **Bella and Louis were among the original 135 members**: Sholem Aleichem Cooperative Houses file, Archives, YIVO Institute for Jewish Research.

Page 10. **Peretz Kaminsky**: Interview with author, 1987.

Page 10. **Ruth Singer**: Interview with author, 1987.

Page 10. **The complex had been designed with artists' studios**: Sholem Aleichem Cooperative Houses file, Archives, YIVO Institute for Jewish Research.

Page 11. **Judy and Sam Sanderoff**: Interview with author, 1988.

Page 11. **her father stayed above the political divisions**: *Miss America, 1945: Bess Myerson's Own Story*, 18.

Page 11. **She recalls marching with her father**: *Miss America, 1945: Bess Myerson's Own Story*, 18.

Page 11. **"You had a very safe and secure feeling here. . . . "**: Bess Myerson, unpublished interview with confidential source, 1987.

Page 11. **ruled her home with an iron hand and barked out commands**: Quotes and description of Bella Myerson are drawn from Bess Myerson, interview with author, October 15, 1987; unpublished interview with confidential source, 1987; and Bess Myerson, "My Mother, My Piano and Me," *Redbook*, June 1974.

Page 11. **"I was not allowed to have friends. . . ."**: "The Myerson Mood."

Page 12. **"I realized that people just hugged little girls. . . ."**: Bess Myerson, unpublished interview with confidential source, 1987.

Page 12. **"Hey, Stretch . . ."**: Description of Bess's anxiety about her height comes from "My Mother, My Piano and Me."

Page 12. **She was mortified**: Details about the school play come from Bess Myerson, interview with author, October 15, 1987.

Page 12. **"She taught me discipline. . . ."**: "The Myerson Mood."

Page 12. **an irony to Bella's nagging**: Information on Bella's habits comes from Riva Lieberman, interview with author, 1988, and from *Miss America, 1945: Bess Myerson's Own Story*, 27–32.

Page 12. **"My mother and father lived in conflict. . . ."**: Bess Myerson, unpublished interview with confidential source, 1987.

Page 13. **"His work was so good. . . ."**: Bess Myerson, interview with author, February 1989.

Page 13. **Pearl and Sam Pochoda**: Interview with author, 1988.

Page 13. **the cooperative went bankrupt**: Sholem Aleichem Cooperative Houses file, Archives, YIVO Institute for Jewish Research.

Page 13. **the residents of Sholem Aleichem did not go sheepishly into tenancy**: Details about rent strike come from Sholem Aleichem Cooperative Houses file, Archives, YIVO Institute for Jewish Research, *Building a Borough: Architecture and Planning in the Bronx, 1890–1940*, 76.

Page 14. **"independently poor"**: Bess Myerson, interview with author, October 15, 1987.

Page 14. **"Baby, I would give it to you. . . ."**: Bess Myerson, interview with author, October 15, 1987.

Page 14. **Bella saw music as a way**: Details about the importance she attached to music come from "My Mother, My Piano and Me."

Page 15. **"You don't appreciate it now. . . ."**: Quotes and details on Bella and Bess are drawn from "My Mother, My Piano and Me" and from Bess Myerson, unpublished interview with confidential source, 1987.

Page 15. **"She was like Ingrid Bergman. . . ."**: Bess Myerson, interview with author, October 15, 1987.

Page 15. **Mrs. LaFollette's elegant apartment**: Ruth Singer, interview with author, 1987.

Page 15. **"It's not the altitude, Bess; it's the attitude."**: "My Mother, My Piano and Me."

Page 15. **Her father had declined her pleas**: Bess Myerson, interview with author, October 15, 1987.

Page 15. **"I don't know what you're planning to wear. . . ."**: Bess Myerson, interview with author, October 15, 1987.

Page 15. **Tension hung in the air**: Bess Myerson, interview with author, October 15, 1987.

Page 15. **"Walk fast and don't forget to breathe. . . ."**: "My Mother, My Piano and Me."

Page 16. **dreamed of becoming a concert pianist**: Bess Myerson, interview with author, October 15, 1987.

Page 16. **"My mother wanted for me what she never had. . . ."**: "The Myerson Mood."

Chapter 3: Beauty from the Bronx

Among the people interviewed for this chapter were Murray Panitz, Ruth Singer, Shirley Schwartz, Marjorie Wallis, three other high school classmates, two college classmates, and a former music teacher. Details about Hunter College come from material in the college's archives. Other sources include newspaper clippings and an unpublished interview Bess Myerson granted to another journalist in 1987. Material was also obtained from Susan Dworkin, *Miss America, 1945: Bess Myerson's Own Story* (New York: Newmarket Press, 1987), and Benjamin M. Steigman, *Accent on Talent: New York's High School of Music and Art* (Detroit: Wayne State University Press, 1964).

Page 17. **Fiorello La Guardia**: Details about the school are drawn from Benjamin M. Steigman, *Accent on Talent: New York's High School of Music and Art* (Detroit: Wayne State University Press, 1964), 11–31.

Page 17. **Shirley Schwartz**: Interview with author, 1988.

Page 18. **Ruth Singer**: Interview with author, 1987.

Page 18. "physical appearance had no meaning at all. . . .": Bess Myerson, interview with confidential source, 1987.

Page 18. "I always took the price tag and slashed it. . . .": Bess Myerson, unpublished interview with confidential source, 1987.

Page 19. "My mother sabotaged any attempt I made at dating. . . .": Bess Myerson, unpublished interview with confidential source, 1987.

Page 19. Frenchie: The entire anecdote about Bess returning home and confronting her parents is drawn from Susan Dworkin, *Miss America, 1945: Bess Myerson's Own Story* (New York: Newmarket Press, 1987), 25.

Page 20. "We lived four years without dating.": Bess Myerson, interview with author, October 15, 1987.

Page 20. All of Hunter's seven thousand students: Details about Hunter College during the war come from issues of the student newspaper, yearbooks, and other documents on file at the college's archives.

Page 20. dreamed of becoming a conductor: Bess Myerson, interview with author, October 15, 1987.

Page 20. Hunter's "Personality Girl": *Hunter College Bulletin*, December 19, 1944.

Page 20. Marjorie Wallis: Interview with author, 1987.

Page 21. "You see, I did not live in a family. . . .": Bess Myerson, interview with author, October 15, 1987.

Page 21. John C. Pape: Bess Myerson, interviews with author, October 15, 1987, and February 1989.

Page 21. Sylvia encouraged her to pose for Pape: Bess Myerson, interview with author, October 15, 1987.

Page 21. Sylvia sent a couple of John Pape's photographs: Details about Bess's attempts at starting a modeling career come from *Miss America, 1945: Bess Myerson's Own Story*, 64-68.

Page 22. "I felt that I wanted to be like everybody else. . . .": Bess Myerson, interview with author, October 15, 1987.

Chapter 4: Miss New York City

Among the people interviewed by the author for the chapters on the 1945 Miss America pageant and reign were Virginia Freeland Berry, Mary Corey, Arnold Forster, Candy Jones, Al Marks, Ruth McClandliss, Bess Myerson, Judy Sanderoff, Shirley Schwartz, Mildred Schwartzman, Ruth Singer, Lenora Slaughter, Louise Sugarman, and Marjorie Wallis. Documents, including correspondence about the pageant, were obtained from the archives at the Miss America Pageant's headquarters in Atlantic City, New Jersey. Other sources include articles published in the *Atlantic City Press, Chicago Tribune, Hartford Times, New York Journal American, New York Daily Mirror, New York Post, New York Daily News, Newsday, Philadelphia Bulletin, Philadelphia Daily News, Philadelphia Inquirer, P.M.*, and *World Telegram*. The author also obtained material from Susan Dworkin, *Miss America, 1945: Bess Myerson's Own Story* (New York: Newmarket Press, 1987); Frank Deford, *There She Is: The Life and Times of Miss America* (New York: Viking Press, 1971); Joseph C. Goulden, *Best Years of Our Lives* (New York: Atheneum, 1976); and David S. Wyman, *The Abandonment of the Jews: America and the Holocaust, 1941-1945* (New York: Pantheon Books, 1984). Much of the material in the following chapters comes from an unpublished interview that Bess Myerson granted to a journalist who requested anonymity, 1987.

Page 23. Miss New York City contest: Penny Fox, "Myersons to Do Sister Act at Camp," *Newsday*, January 10, 1961.

Page 23. Louise Sugarman: Interview with author, 1988.

Page 23. she looked confident playing a three-minute arrangement: Susan Dworkin, *Miss America, 1945: Bess Myerson's Own Story* (New York: Newmarket Press, 1987), 69.

Page 24. Lenora Slaughter: All quotes from Slaughter come from an interview with author, 1988.

Page 24. Bess was stunned: Bess Myerson, interview with author, October 15, 1987.

Page 24. "Never forget who you are.": All quotes from Bess Myerson in this chapter come from an interview with author, October 15, 1987.

Chapter 5: Atlantic City, 1945

Page 26. "When I explained that I might also bring back a black baby grand. . . .": Bess Myerson, unpublished interview with confidential source, 1987.

Page 26. she began feeling anxious: The description of Bess's feeling depressed about the upcoming pageant is drawn from Susan Dworkin, *Miss America, 1945: Bess Myerson's Own Story* (New York: Newmarket Press, 1987), 76–77.

Page 26. "I thought I didn't have a good physical appearance. . . .": Marian Christy, "The Myerson Mood," *Boston Globe*, October 28, 1987.

Page 27. Bess still felt blue: *Miss America, 1945: Bess Myerson's Own Story*, 77.

Page 27. "We've never been away from home. . . .": Bess Myerson quoting her sister, Sylvia, in an unpublished interview with confidential source, 1987.

Page 28. "We got there, and here are these lovely girls. . . .": Bess Myerson, interview with CBS correspondent Steve Kroft on CBS-TV's "West 57th Street," broadcast November 1987.

Page 28. It also seemed to Bess that all the other girls were dressed in stylish clothes: Bess Myerson, unpublished interview with confidential source, 1987.

Page 28. "First you have the all-blue outfit. . . .": Bess Myerson, unpublished interview with confidential source, 1987.

Page 28. Virginia Freeland Berry: Interview with author, 1988.

Page 28. Lenora Slaughter: Interview with author, 1988.

Page 30. "filled with a flaming competitive spirit": Robert Williams, "Miss America, 1945," *New York Post*, November 16, 1955.

Page 30. "no matter how insecure I felt. . . .": "The Myerson Mood."

Page 30. Lenora thought it rode too high: Lenora Slaughter, interview with author, 1988.

Page 30. "I looked like a frog. . . .": Bess Myerson, unpublished interview with confidential source, 1987.

Page 30. "She slept in it all night. . . .": Bess Myerson, unpublished interview with confidential source, 1987.

Page 30. Sylvia sewed the straps shut: Details about the bathing suit come from "Miss America, 1945"; Frank Deford, *There She Is: The Life and Times of Miss America* (New York: Viking Press, 1971), 63; and *Miss America, 1945: Bess Myerson's Own Story*, 133–135.

Page 30. "I heard this shriek. . . .": Bess Myerson, unpublished interview with confidential source, 1987.

Page 31. "They're going to take it away from you. . . .": Bess Myerson, interview with author, 1988.

Page 31. Candy Jones: Interview with author, 1988.

Page 32. "there were people there who were not rooting for me. . . .": Bess Myerson, interview with author, October 15, 1987.

Page 32. parents remained at home: *New York Daily Mirror*, September 10, 1945.

Page 32. curtain rose at 8:00 P.M.: Description of the pageant comes from Jack Boucher, "Bess Myerson Is Crowned Nation's Queen of Beauty," *Atlantic City Press*, September 9, 1945, and "Miss New York Wins Nation's Beauty Title," *Philadelphia Inquirer*, September 9, 1945.

Page 32. "She seemed to me to have complete beauty requirements. . . .": *World Telegram*, January 15, 1955.

Chapter 6: Pride and Prejudice

Page 34. Earl Wilson: "It Happened One Night," *New York Post*, September 10, 1945.

Page 35. "Hollywood to them meant bad girls. . . .": Bess Myerson, unpublished interview with confidential source, 1987.

Page 35. "She's pretty and she's a nice girl. . . .": *New York Post*, September 10, 1945.

Page 35. "I wouldn't say she's bad-looking. . . .": *New York Post*, September 10, 1945.

Page 35. Judy Sanderoff: Interview with author, 1988.

Page 35. Mildred Schwartzman: Interview with author, 1987.

Page 36. "When I came back as Miss America. . . .": Bess Myerson, interview with author, October 15, 1987.

Page 36. Ruth Singer: Interview with author, 1987.

Page 36. press conference: *New York Post*, September 11, 1945.

Page 37. "featured acrobatics . . .": Frank Deford, *There She Is: The Life and Times of Miss America* (New York: Viking Press, 1971), 162.

Page 37. "I came out in a high-necked gown. . . .": Robert Williams, "Miss America, 1945," *New York Post*, November 16, 1955.

Page 37. Marjorie Wallis: Interview with author, 1987.

Page 37. Lenora Slaughter: Interview with author, 1988.

Page 37. Virginia Freeland Berry: Interview with author, 1988.

Page 37. "anxious to hear word from you": Postcard, Bess Myerson to Lenora Slaughter, dated October 2, 1945. Miss America archives, Atlantic City, N.J.

Page 38. "we contestants listened to endless tales of sponsors. . . .": *Parade*, February 1, 1977.

Page 38. caught in a messy dispute: Susan Dworkin, *Miss America, 1945: Bess Myerson's Own Story* (New York: Newmarket Press, 1987), 161.

Page 38. Lenora Slaughter: Interview with author, 1988.

Page 39. "I wasn't invited to attend as many events as I should have been.": Carole Agus, "Bess, Wherever She Goes," *New York Newsday*, February 28, 1986.

Page 39. "In some instances I thought they really wanted a blond. . . .": Bess Myerson, interview with author, October 15, 1987.

Page 39. former Miss America Jean Bartel . . . earned a total of $3,000: *There She Is: The Life and Times of Miss America*, 157.

Page 39. Venus Ramey . . . collected $8,500: *There She Is: The Life and Times of Miss America*, 277.

Page 39. "But it's nice to be a Miss America": *There She Is: The Life and Times of Miss America*, 278.

Page 39. "Sometimes they said it subtly. . . .": Bess Myerson, interview with author, October 15, 1987.

Page 40. "It was a lovely place. . . .": Bess Myerson, interview with author, October 15, 1987.

Chapter 7: "You Can't Be Beautiful and Hate"

Page 41. She felt that as a public person . . . she could be a positive influence.: Jack Helsel, "Bess Was Urging Human Rights in '46," *Philadelphia Daily News*, February 2, 1946.

Page 41. "And I realized that this title was mine, forever. . . .": "Bess Was Urging Human Rights in '46."

Page 41. "We can't live through a Holocaust. . . .": Bess Myerson, interview with author, October 15, 1987.

Page 41. Arnold Forster: Interview with author, 1988.

Page 42. "If I'm supposed to be representative of the American girl. . . .": *World Telegram*, March 16, 1946.

Page 42. Bess began her speaking tour in Chicago and Milwaukee: *Chicago Tribune*, February 26, 1946.

Page 42. "I talked to them about tolerance. . . .": *World Telegram*, January 18, 1958.

Page 42. "I said, 'There were girls. . . .' ": Bess Myerson, interview with author, October 15, 1987.

Page 42. The concert opened with *Fantasia on Themes*: "Pop Concert Role for Bess Myerson," *New York Times*, June 1, 1946.

Page 43. "Of course I never would have had the chance to play at Carnegie. . . .": Associated Press, August 13, 1949.

Page 43. "My teacher, Mrs. LaFollette, and my mother were backstage. . . .": Bess Myerson, interview with author, October 15, 1987.

Page 43. "It seems incredible that all the doors won't stay open. . . .": May Okon, "Want Your Daughter to Be Miss America?", *New York Daily News*, November 7, 1954.

Page 43. **Candy Jones**: Interview with author, 1987.

Page 44. **What Bess was really yearning for was a man**: Bess Myerson, interview with author, October 15, 1987, and Robert Williams, "Miss America, 1945," *New York Post*, November 16, 1955.

Chapter 8: A Practical Prince

Among the people interviewed for this chapter were Bebe Barkan, Gilda and Samuel Kramer, Pearl Maged, Bess Myerson, Stephen Posner, Lenora Slaughter, and three close friends of the late Allan Wayne. Other material from this chapter comes from an unpublished interview that Bess Myerson granted in 1987 to a journalist who requested anonymity and articles published in the *New York Daily News, New York Daily Mirror, New York Post*, and *P.M.* In addition, material was drawn from Susan Dworkin, *Miss America, 1945: Bess Myerson's Own Story* (New York: Newmarket Press, 1987).

Page 45. **Lenora Slaughter**: Interview with author, 1988.

Page 46. **knew that evening that she wanted to marry Allan Wayne**: *P.M.*, December 8, 1946.

Page 46. **he didn't seem intimidated**: Susan Dworkin, *Miss America, 1945: Bess Myerson's Own Story* (New York: Newmarket Press, 1987), 212.

Page 46. **The Myersons approved of Allan**: Bebe Barkan, interview with author, 1988.

Page 46. **"No woman left to get her own apartment. . . ."**: Bess Myerson, unpublished interview with confidential source, 1987.

Page 46. **"The best thing that can happen to a beauty contest winner. . . ."**: Associated Press, July 15, 1953.

Page 47. **"We were never taught. . . ."**: Bess Myerson, unpublished interview with confidential source, 1987.

Page 47. **how he had proposed**: *P.M.*, December 8, 1946.

Page 48. **Bebe Barkan**: Interview with author, 1988.

Page 48. **Gilda and Sam Kramer**: Interview with author, 1988.

Page 48. **"She would always leave the living room. . . ."**: Confidential source, interview with author, 1988.

Page 48. **"We used to go up to Dyckman. . . ."**: Confidential source, interview with author, 1988.

Page 49. **"And I thought, that's right. . . ."**: Bess Myerson, unpublished interview with confidential source, 1987.

Chapter 9: The Lady in Mink

Among the people interviewed for this chapter were Walt Framer, Lloyd Gross, Betty Ann Grove, Jeff Hayden, Louise McKinney, and friends and relatives of the late Allan Wayne. The author consulted files at the New York Public Library's Performing Arts Research Center and viewed tapes of old television shows at New York's Museum of Broadcasting. Material for this chapter was also drawn from articles published in *Newsweek, Newsday, New York Daily News, New York Daily Mirror, New York Herald Tribune, Time*, and *Variety.*

Page 50. **"It was a tremendous training ground. . . ."**: *New York Daily News*, August 15, 1959.

Page 51. **"She takes only those jobs she thinks she can do. . . ."**: Associated Press, August 13, 1949.

Page 51. **Walt Framer**: Interview with author, 1988.

Page 52. **Jeff Hayden**: Interview with author, 1988.

Page 52. **Betty Ann Grove**: Interview with author, 1988.

Page 52. **"I've always made it my business. . . ."**: May Okon, "Want Your Daughter to Be Miss America?", *New York Daily News*, November 7, 1954.

Page 53. **"She was making a bigger income. . . ."**: Confidential source, interview with author, 1988.

Page 53. **Stephen Posner**: Interview with author, 1987.

Page 53. **"Allan was crazy about his dad. . . ."**: Confidential source, interview with author, 1988.

Page 54. **Pearl Maged**: Interview with author, 1987.
Page 54. **Allan underwent a radical change**: Susan Dworkin, *Miss America, 1945: Bess Myerson's Own Story* (New York: Newmarket Press, 1987), 214.
Page 54. **Louise McKinney**: Interview with author, 1988.
Page 54. **"I wanted some kind of emotional support. . . ."**: Bess Myerson, unpublished interview with confidential source, 1987.
Page 54. **Betty Ann Grove**: Interview with author, 1988.
Page 54. **Allan beat her savagely**: George Carpozi, Jr., "Custody to Bess Myerson as Mate Yields; Child Hugs Him in Court," *New York Journal American*, September 9, 1956.

Chapter 10: The Custody Battle

The author interviewed Samuel Kramer, Stephen Posner, Anne Rudell, and three close friends of Allan Wayne's, including an ex-girlfriend who requested anonymity. Other material from this chapter comes from articles published in the *New York Daily News*, *New York Daily Mirror*, *New York Herald Tribune*, *New York Journal American*, *New York Post*, and *New York* magazine.

Page 55. **August 26, 1956**: Description of Bess's departure that night comes from interviews with a confidential source and Allan Wayne's court testimony on September 8, 1956, in state supreme court.
Page 56. **Justice Matthew Levy**: *New York Daily News*, September 5, 1956.
Page 57. **"working like a horse. . . ."**: Josephine DiLorenzo and Jack Smee, "Girl, 9, Fails to Pull Bess, Dad Together," *New York Daily News*, September 9, 1956.
Page 57. **Judge Levy**: George Carpozi, Jr., "Custody to Bess Myerson as Mate Yields; Child Hugs Him in Court," *New York Journal American*, September 9, 1956.
Page 57. **Anne Rudell**: Interview with author, 1988.
Page 57. **Sam Kramer**: Interview with author, 1988.
Page 57. **Barra**: Patricia Morrisroe, "Bess and the Mess," *New York*, March 30, 1987.
Page 58. **"He ripped my pajamas off. . . ."**: *New York Daily News*, November 3, 1957.
Page 58. **Richard Rudell**: *New York Daily News*, November 3, 1957.
Page 59. **"If I love her the way I do. . . ."**: *New York Daily News*, November 3, 1957.
Page 59. **"That's his statement. . . ."**: *New York Daily Mirror*, November 4, 1957.
Page 59. **Benjamin Robinson**: *New York Daily News*, November 5, 1957.
Page 59. **Richard Rudell**: *New York Daily News*, November 5, 1957.
Page 59. **"I don't really know when I stopped. . . ."**: *New York Daily Mirror*, November 5, 1957.
Page 59. **"She's still a wonderful girl."**: *New York Daily Mirror*, November 5, 1957.
Page 60. **"I fear that he will attempt to sell. . . ."**: "Bess Says Hubby Plays Big Shot on Her Stock," *New York Daily News*, December 31, 1957.
Page 60. **"It took a long time finishing. . . ."**: Bess Myerson, interview with author, 1989.
Page 60. **"He couldn't take what had happened to him. . . ."**: Confidential source, interview with author, 1988.
Page 60. **"He had too much respect for women. . . ."**: Confidential source, interview with author, 1988.
Page 61. **Just after eleven o'clock**: Details about the circumstances of Allan Wayne's death come from family and friends of Allan Wayne's and the autopsy report, New York City Medical Examiner's Office.
Page 61. **"They felt that Bess had deliberately kept her away. . . ."**: Confidential source, interview with author, 1988.

Chapter 11: "I've Got a Secret"

For this chapter, among the people interviewed were Chester Feldman, Lloyd Gross, and Henry Morgan. The author also consulted files at the New York Public Library's Performing Arts Research Center and viewed tapes at the Museum of Broadcasting. Material for this chapter was also drawn from articles published in the *Philadelphia Inquirer*, *Philadelphia Bulletin*, *New York Daily News*, *New York Herald Tribune*, *New York Times*, and *New York Post*. The author also consulted several books, including Gil

Fates, *What's My Line? TV's Most Famous Panel Show* (New York: Cornerstone Library, 1978).

Page 62. **"An Emma Schultz can go through it. . . .":** Alan Gill, "For Beauty with Brains—Take Bess Myerson, for Example," *Philadelphia Inquirer*, August 26, 1962.
Page 62. **"It's hard to just pick up and go. . . .":** *New York Daily News*, August 18, 1959.
Page 62. **dismissed questions about becoming a serious actress:** *New York Herald Tribune*, April 24, 1959.
Page 63. **Chester Feldman:** Interview with author, 1988.
Page 63. **Henry Morgan:** Interview with author, 1988.
Page 63. **Bess knew she couldn't be the funniest panelist:** Susan Berman, "One Tough Customer," *New York*, November 14, 1977.
Page 64. **"By the end it all boiled down to finding a new dress. . . .":** "For Beauty with Brains—Take Bess Myerson, for Example."
Page 64. **Lloyd Gross:** Interview with author, 1988.
Page 65. **"People in New York might say. . . .":** "One Tough Customer."
Page 65. **she wanted very much to marry again:** Confidential source (close friend of Bess Myerson's), interview with author, 1988.

Chapter 12: A Pygmalion on Sutton Place

Among those interviewed for this chapter were Joseph Baum, Lilly Bruck, Chester Feldman, Al Marks, Henry Morgan, two close friends of Bess Myerson's who requested anonymity, and close friends and associates of Arnold Grant's who requested anonymity. Bess Myerson also spoke briefly to the author about Arnold Grant. In addition, the author consulted court records from Bess Myerson and Arnold Grant's divorce on file in the clerk's office at Surrogate's Court, New York County, in Manhattan. Material was also obtained from published articles in *New York* magazine, *Commentary*, the *New York Post*, *New York Daily News*, *Newsday*, *New York Times*, *Washington Post*, *Washington Star*, *Philadelphia Bulletin*, and the *Philadelphia Inquirer*.

Page 66. **Arnold Grant sat on the dais:** Margaret McManus, "Miss America Crown Wore Well for Bess," *Philadelphia Bulletin*, March 22, 1964.
Page 66. **"only if the lovely mistress of ceremonies will have dinner with me. . . .":** "Miss America Crown Wore Well for Bess."
Page 66. **Lilly Bruck:** Interview with author, 1988.
Page 67. **His client list:** Walter H. Waggoner, "Arnold Grant, Corporate Lawyer in the Film Industry, Dead at 72," *New York Times*, November 18, 1980.
Page 67. **Human Relations Award:** "Award Winner," *New York Post*, November 25, 1964.
Page 67. **"I'm the luckiest man in the world":** Chester Feldman, interview with author, 1988.
Page 68. **Henry Morgan:** Interview with author, 1988.
Page 68. **he became her Pygmalion:** Confidential source, interview with author, 1988.
Page 69. **Queen Bess felt very much like Bessie from the Bronx:** Confidential source, interview with author, 1988.
Page 69. **Arnold would fly into a rage:** Patricia Morrisroe, "Bess and the Mess," *New York*, March 30, 1987.
Page 69. **"He was great fun around the track. . . .":** Jane Perlez, "Bess v. Liz," *New York Daily News*, July 20, 1980.
Page 69. **"our home on Sutton Place began to look like a prison. . . .":** Susan Berman, "Bess Myerson Is One Tough Customer," *New York*, November 14, 1977.
Page 69. **"One night we had some political people over. . . .":** "Bess Myerson Is One Tough Customer."
Page 70. **signed a separation agreement:** Court records, Surrogate's Court, New York County, Manhattan.
Page 70. **Chester Feldman:** Interview with author, 1988.
Page 70. **subject of bitter dispute:** Confidential source, interview with author, 1988.

Page 71. **it was Bess who first broached the subject of marrying again**: Confidential source, interview with author, 1988.

Page 71. **she wanted another child**: Confidential source, interview with author, 1988.

Page 71. **"No way in the world did he want to have more kids."**: Confidential source, interview with author, 1988.

Page 71. **Bess was ecstatic**: Confidential sources, interviews with author, 1988.

Page 71. **He saw a sinister motive**: Confidential sources, interviews with author, 1988.

Page 72. **"Wasn't I good enough?"**: Al Marks, interview with author, 1988.

Page 72. **she found herself slipping again into depression**: Confidential sources, interviews with author, 1988.

Chapter 13: An Urban Folk Hero

Among the people interviewed for this chapter were George Arzt, Joseph Baum, Robert Blum, Lilly Bruck, Sid Davidoff, Rita Delfiner, Owen Fitzgerald, Joseph Fitzpatrick, Betty Furness, Moe Greenspan, former mayor Edward I. Koch, Simon Lazarus, Victor Marrero, Edward O'Neil, Edward Sadowksy, Philip Schrag, Henry Stern, Howard Tisch, and several others who worked with Bess in the Lindsay administration at that time and requested anonymity. In addition, the author reviewed hundreds of pages of reports, speeches, city regulations, and press releases located at the city's Department of Consumer Affairs and the Municipal Reference Library. Material from this chapter also comes from articles published in the *Chicago Tribune*, *New York* magazine, the *New York Post*, *New York Daily News*, *Newsday*, *New York Times*, *Philadelphia Bulletin*, and *Philadelphia Inquirer*. The author also consulted several books, including Philip Schrag, *Counsel for the Deceived* (New York: Pantheon Books, 1972), and Simon Lazarus, *The Genteel Populists* (New York: Holt, Rinehart & Winston, 1974).

Page 73. **she wanted to devote more time to her new marriage**: Betty Furness, interview with author, 1988.

Page 73. **Robert Blum**: Interview with author, 1988.

Page 74. **Lenora Slaughter**: Interview with author, 1988.

Page 74. **"When you were brought up the way. . . ."**: Bess Myerson, unpublished interview with confidential source, 1987.

Page 74. **"I thought it would be a fantastic chance. . . ."**: Susan Berman, "Bess Myerson Is One Tough Customer," *New York*, November 14, 1977.

Page 74. **"simple to identify with people. . . ."**: Lynn Litterine, "Beauty Is Fine, but Achieving Is Her Raison d' Etre," *Philadelphia Inquirer*, November 4, 1978.

Page 75. **Edward Sadowsky**: Interview with author, 1988.

Page 75. **"See, the Miss America title became part of my name. . . ".**: Bess Myerson, unpublished interview with confidential source, 1987.

Page 76. **Simon Lazarus**: Interview with author, 1988.

Page 76. **Sid Davidoff**: Interview with author, 1988.

Page 76. **Victor Marrero**: Interview with author, 1988.

Page 76. **"Come through with what you have promised. . . ."**: Judy Michaelson, "Consumer's Friend at City Hall," *New York Post*, March 15, 1969.

Page 77. **Bess Myerson's acceptance speech**: New York City Department of Consumer Affairs.

Page 77. **"new—and tough—commissioner of consumer affairs"**: Edward O'Neill, "City's Glamour Lady Vows to Fight Gypsters," *New York Daily News*, March 5, 1969.

Page 78. **Better Business Bureau speech**: New York City Department of Consumer Affairs.

Page 78. **Henry J. Stern**: Interviews with author, 1987 and 1988.

Page 79. **"They were mostly young kids. . . ."**: Confidential source, interview with author, 1987.

Page 79. **Moe Greenspan**: Interview with author, 1988.

Page 80. **"she gave the Department of Consumer Affairs a fantastic reputation"**: Confidential source, interview with author, 1988.

Page 80. **Rita Delfiner:** Interview with author, 1988.
Page 80. **Bess's first public hearing:** Owen Fitzgerald, interview with author, 1988, and his description of the event in *New York Daily News*, May 27, 1969.
Page 81. **"Most people believe. . . .":** *New York Times*, May 27, 1969.
Page 81. **Edward I. Koch:** New York City Department of Consumer Affairs.
Page 82. **Joseph Baum:** Interview with author, 1988.
Page 82. **She was so wrapped up:** Confidential source, interview with author, November 1988.
Page 83. **Henry Stern:** Interview with author, 1988.
Page 84. **"She called up Mayor Lindsay. . . .":** Confidential source, interview with author, 1988.
Page 84. **Sid Davidoff:** Interview with author, 1988.
Page 84. **Bess's objections to Barra's decision:** Bess Myerson, interview with author, 1988.

Chapter 14: For Love and Money

Among the people interviewed for this chapter were Joseph Baum, Lilly Bruck, Marcia Kramer (who broke the story in the *New York Daily News* about the London shoplifting arrest), Henry Stern, and two other close friends of Bess's who requested anonymity, along with longtime friends and associates of Arnold Grant's. Law enforcement sources also provided information. Other material in this chapter was obtained from articles in the *New York Post, New York Daily News, Newsday, New York* magazine, and the *New York Times*.

Page 85. **"theft from a shop":** Police report; confidential sources, interviews with author; and Metropolitan Police Department, London, England.
Page 87. **"I have little or no illusions. . . .":** Patricia Morrisroe, "Bess and the Mess," *New York*, March 30, 1987.
Page 87. **"if A [Arnold] would die. . . .":** "Bess and the Mess."
Page 87. **"more like a thing. . . .":** "Bess and the Mess."
Page 87. **"With his ego, it just blew his mind. . . .":** Confidential source, interview with author, 1988.
Page 88. **locked closets:** Joseph Baum, interview with author, 1988.
Page 88. **formal separation:** Alfred Albelli, "Bess, Pal of Homemakers, Sues to Unmake Her Own," *New York Daily News*, July 16, 1970.
Page 89. **letter from Arnold:** Provided to author by confidential source.
Page 89. **new locks were opened:** Joseph Baum, interview with author, 1988.
Page 90. **"He blackmailed her with the diaries. . . .":** Confidential source, interview with author, 1988.
Page 90. **she sought refuge:** Lilly Bruck, interview with author, 1988.
Page 90. **Bess was worth roughly $1 million:** "Bess' Husband Fights Support," *New York Daily News*, February 10, 1971.
Page 90. **Pyrex double boiler:** "Bess and the Mess."
Page 91. **exclusive occupancy:** "Sued by Bess, Grant Files Action of Own," *New York Daily News*, August 25, 1970.
Page 91. **asked for a postponement:** "Won't Cooperate with Wife Bess," *New York Post*, September 9, 1970.
Page 91. **filed a suit for divorce:** "Bess' Husband Asks for Divorce," *New York Daily News*, October 27, 1970.
Page 91. **exclusive occupancy:** "Bess Fights Husband for Support," *New York Daily News*, February 10, 1971.
Page 92. **"To qualify for financial relief. . . .":** "The Grants Granted Nothing in Court Test," *New York Daily News*, February 28, 1971.
Page 92. **"separation, alimony, counsel fees and a property settlement":** "Notes On People," *New York Times*, April 29, 1971.
Page 92. **Alzheimer's disease:** Arnold Grant's death certificate.
Page 92. **"If I had known he was sick. . . .":** "Bess and the Mess."

Chapter 15: "Bess Myerson for Mayor"

Among the people interviewed for this chapter were George Arzt, Joseph Baum, Lilly Bruck, Sid Davidoff, Rita Delfiner, Moe Greenspan, Simon Lazarus, Philip Schrag,

Henry Stern, and Howard Tisch. Others who requested anonymity included two close friends of Bess's, a television producer who worked with Bess, three former high-ranking officials in the Lindsay administration, a former high-ranking official in the Department of Consumer Affairs, two officials in the Koch administration, and a veteran political operative. The author also consulted hundreds of documents and records, including Bess Myerson's speeches, reports, and press releases on file at the New York City Department of Consumer Affairs. Other material in this chapter was obtained from articles in the *Chicago Tribune*, *New York Post*, *Newsday*, *New York Daily News*, *New York* magazine, the *New York Times*, *Washington Star*, and *Life* magazine.

Page 93. **"you may call me Bess Myerson. . . ."**: Peter Coutros, "By Any Name, Bess Means Biz," *New York Daily News*, March 21, 1971.

Page 93. **"I moved from one space to another space. . . ."**: Tom Buckley, "Bess Myerson, the Drive Behind the Koch Drive," *New York Times*, September 16, 1977.

Page 93. **"I've had the Norell dresses. . . ."**: "A Consumer's Best Friend," *Life*, July 16, 1977.

Page 94. **"a horror. . . ."**: Confidential source, interview with author, 1988.

Page 94. **"very condescending with people. . . ."**: Confidential source, interview with author, 1988.

Page 95. **"voluntarily became her slaves"**: Confidential source, interview with author, 1988.

Page 95. **Lilly Bruck**: Interview with author, 1988.

Page 95. **Howard Tisch**: Interview with author, 1988.

Page 95. **"She was a publicity saint. . . ."**: Confidential source, interview with author, 1988.

Page 95. **Sid Davidoff**: Interview with author, 1988.

Page 95. **put the rumors to rest**: May Okon, "A Day in the Life of Bess Myerson," *New York Daily News*, October 15, 1972.

Page 96. **"not in keeping with 'my image'. . . ."**: Confidential source, interview with author, 1988.

Page 96. **"wide-eyed innocence and embarrassment. . . ."**: "A Day in the Life of Bess Myerson."

Page 96. **"I wanted to put my life together. . . ."**: Jane Perlez, "Bess v. Liz," *New York Daily News*, July 20, 1980.

Page 97. **Henry Stern**: Interview with author, 1988.

Page 97. **"overwhelming pressure. . . ."**: Rita Delfiner, *New York Post*, March 9, 1973.

Page 98. **"I'm very moved by this show of confidence. . . ."**: *New York Post*, March 13, 1973.

Page 98. **final press conference**: Owen Fitzgerald, *New York Daily News*, March 31, 1973.

Page 99. **Meade Esposito**: Judith Michaelson, *New York Post*, April 4, 1973.

Page 99. **"it was not easy for a woman to run. . . ."**: Confidential source, interview with author, 1988.

Page 99. **Bess was also dating another man**: Information on the men Bess dated at this time comes from confidential sources, interviews with author, 1988.

Page 100. **"I wanted to work for companies where I could make changes."**: Frances Cerra, "Bess Myerson's Expertise Now Benefiting Business," *New York Times*, June 10, 1977.

Page 101. **"At the moment, I'm not running. . . ."**: Sam Roberts, "Meade: Listen, Bess, You Can Beat Javits," *New York Daily News*, March 28, 1974.

Chapter 16: The Struggle Against Cancer

Among the people interviewed for this chapter were Bella Abzug, Lilly Bruck, David Garth, former mayor Edward I. Koch, Bess Myerson, and other friends and associates of Bess Myerson's who requested anonymity. The author also consulted the *Chicago Sun-Times*, *New York* magazine, the *New York Daily News*, *Newsday*, *New York Post*, *New York Times*, *Philadelphia Inquirer*, and *Washington Star*.

Page 102. **she felt tired and run-down**: Bess Myerson, interview with author, November 1988.

Page 102. **the call from her doctor**: Bess Myerson, interview with author, November 1988.
Page 102. **"I was on my way down in the elevator. . . ."**: Bess Myerson, interview with author, November 1988.
Page 103. **"The big C was much more scary. . . ."**: Patricia Morrisroe, "Bess and the Mess," *New York*, March 30, 1987.
Page 103. **"unlikely that any of the recipients will be more deserving. . . ."**: Carol Kramer, "Bess Myerson Is a 'Woman of the Year,' Too," *Chicago Sun-Times*, April 7, 1974.
Page 104. **"She became hard. . . ."**: Confidential source, interview with author, 1988.
Page 104. **"This was the priority. . . ."**: Bess Myerson, interview with author, 1989.
Page 104. **"I felt that because I was ill I would need to be very independent. . . ."**: Bess Myerson, interview with author, 1989.
Page 104. **Bess stood up and announced**: Bess Myerson, interview with author, 1989.
Page 105. **"There was this really bizarre behavior. . . ."**: Confidential source, interview with author, 1988.
Page 105. **David Garth**: Interview with author, 1988.
Page 106. **"It's an extremely harsh experience for any candidate. . . ."**: Associated Press, September 21, 1977.

Chapter 17: First Lady Bess

Among the people interviewed for this chapter were George Arzt, Bella Abzug, Maurice Carroll, Pam Chanin, Maureen Connelly, David Garth, former mayor Edward I. Koch, John LoCicero, Joyce Purnick, Bernie Rome, and Jerry Skurnik. The author also obtained material from *New York* magazine, the *New York Daily News*, *Newsday*, *New York Post*, *New York Times*, and *Washington Star*.

The author also consulted four books: Jack Newfield and Wayne Barrett, *City for Sale* (New York: Harper & Row, 1988); Arthur Browne, Dan Collins, and Michael Goodwin, *"I, Koch" A Decidedly Unauthorized Biography of the Mayor of New York City, Edward I. Koch* (New York: Dodd, Meade & Company, 1985); and Mayor Edward I. Koch, *Mayor, An Autobiography, Edward I. Koch* (New York: Simon and Schuster, 1984), and *Politics* (New York: Simon and Schuster, 1985).

Page 107. **Mayor Edward I. Koch**: Interview with author, 1988.
Page 107. **David Garth**: Interview with author, 1988.
Page 109. **Bella Abzug**: Interview with author, 1989.
Page 109. **"She was a prima donna. . . ."**: Confidential source, interview with author, 1988.
Page 109. **"She could be a nightmare. . . ."**: Confidential source, interview with author, 1988.
Page 110. **"subliminal message"**: David Garth, interview with author, 1988.
Page 110. **"the most important person of the campaign"**: Joy Cook, "And Then the Cool Koch Relaxed," *New York Post*, September 9, 1977.
Page 111. **Pam Chanin**: Interview with author, 1988.
Page 111. **"But then I figured that if I didn't, it would be cowardly. . . ."**: Gene Spagnoli, "Will Bess Be First Lady Come November?," *New York Daily News*, September 21, 1977.
Page 111. **"My role from the start of the campaign was to help Ed. . . ."**: Associated Press, September 21, 1977.
Page 112. **"I have had such trouble with fat, ugly reporters. . . ."**: Susan Berman, "Bess Myerson Is One Tough Customer," *New York*, November 17, 1977.
Page 112. **"See, That's Bess Myerson. . . ."**: *New York Times*, October 11, 1977.
Page 112. **"I have enormous respect and deep affection for Ed. . . ."**: "Will Bess Be First Lady Come November?"
Page 112. **"It's always a possibility. . . ."**: "Will Bess Be First Lady Come November?"
Page 112. **Bernie Rome**: Interview with author, 1988.

Page 113. **"I didn't hold press conferences denying the substance of that fantasy. . . ."**: Edward I. Koch, interview with author, 1988.

Page 113. **"dispel rumors of any hint of homosexuality"**: Beth Fallon, "Frayed Mayoral Rivals in Cutting TV Debate," *New York Daily News*, October 31, 1977.

Page 113. **"ugly, scurrilous and deliberate attempt"**: Jane Perlez, "Koch: The Media Whispers," *Soho Weekly News*, November 10, 1977.

Page 113. **Joyce Purnick**: Interview with author, 1989.

Page 114. **"I must have my privacy. . . ."**: "Bess Myerson Shuns a N.Y. City Hall Job," United Press International, November 10, 1977.

Page 115. **"Bess is coming back from vacation. . . ."**: Bernie Rome, interview with author, 1988.

Chapter 18: Obsession

The material from this chapter comes primarily from interviews with confidential sources and the woman identified as Charlotte Ames. The pseudonyms Charlotte Ames and J. Gordon Marcus have been used in this chapter to protect their privacy. The author also consulted the *New York Daily News, New York Post, New York Times*, and *New York* magazine.

Page 117. **"I should have married someone like you. . . ."**: Charlotte Ames, interview with author, 1988.

Page 117. **"Here was someone who was Jewish. . . ."**: Confidential source, interview with author, 1988.

Page 117. **Charlotte had no idea there was another woman**: Charlotte Ames, interview with author, 1988.

Page 118. **"a little bit too crazy for him."**: Confidential source, interview with author, 1988.

Page 118. **"He appeared to be really enamored with Bess. . . ."**: Patricia Morrisroe, "Bess and the Mess," *New York*, March 30, 1987.

Page 118. **"If I were twenty years younger, this never would have happened. . . ."**: Confidential source, interview with author, 1988.

Page 118. **"Men go after me, and I choose among them."**: Confidential source, interview with author, 1988.

Page 118. **Bess told him that a chambermaid had let her in.**: Confidential source, interview with author, 1988.

Page 119. **"unidentified woman"**: Charlotte Ames, interview with author, 1988.

Page 119. **Gordon suspected Bess was responsible**: Confidential source, interview with author, 1988.

Page 120. **"I have never confused my personal life. . . ."**: Liz Smith, *New York Daily News*, November 8, 1978.

Page 120. **"We have absolute evidence of adultery. . . ."**: "Bess Myerson Named in Divorce Case," *New York Post*, March 26, 1979.

Page 120. **"My God, of course it's not true. . . ."**: "Bess Myerson Named in Divorce Case."

Page 121. **A woman was on the other end**: Charlotte Ames, interviews with author, 1988 and 1989.

Page 121. **She has since told friends that she went to Miami for cosmetic surgery**: Confidential sources, interviews with author, 1988.

Page 122. **Armed with this information, Gordon confronted Bess**: Charlotte Ames, interviews with author, 1988 and 1989.

Page 122. **"Dear Nothing, . . ."**: Anonymous letter, obtained from confidential source.

Chapter 19: "Too Tall, Too Beautiful, Too Rich"

Among the people interviewed for this chapter were Maurice Carroll, Pam Chanin, Maureen Connelly, Linda Davidoff, Dick Eaton, David Garth, former mayor Edward I. Koch, Ken Lerer, and Joyce Purnick. Other people interviewed for this chapter include three people who worked closely with Bess on the campaign who requested that their names not be used. Material for this chapter was also drawn from the *New York Times*,

New York Post, New York Daily News, and *New York* magazine. The author also consulted records on file with the Federal Election Commission.

Page 123. **"I don't have anything more to do. . . ."**: Confidential source, interview with author, 1988.

Page 124. **"who's who" of the rich and famous**: Federal Election Commission campaign records.

Page 124. **Gloria Steinem**: "Steinem to Bess: Don't Run," *New York Post,* November 19, 1979.

Page 125. **"I've always been Queen Bess. . . ."**: Andrew Kopkind, "Bess Bets, The Candidate of the 'New Crowd,'" *Village Voice,* December 12, 1979.

Page 125. **Dick Eaton**: Interview with author, 1989.

Page 125. **"emotionally bind"**: Gail Sheehy, "Women and Leadership: Bess Myerson," *New York Times,* December 20, 1979.

Page 125. **"boat people"**: Frank Lynn, "Three Democrats on the Road in Quest for Javits's Seat," *New York Times,* March 14, 1980.

Page 125. **"special magic"**: "Women and Leadership: Bess Myerson."

Page 125. **"I have a history of really impacting. . . ."**: Michael VerMeulen, "They Remember Bess," *New York,* September 1, 1980.

Page 126. **"Bess had no concept of money. . . ."**: Confidential source, interview with author, 1988.

Page 126. **"She thought that the volunteers who came to work at the apartment were helping themselves. . . ."**: Confidential source, interview with author, 1988.

Page 127. **"liberation of the typewriter"**: Confidential sources, interviews with author, 1988.

Page 127. **"She knew the doorman. . . ."**: Confidential source, interview with author, 1988.

Page 127. **"If you want to work on the campaign. . . ."**: Confidential source, interview with author, 1988.

Page 127. **"Her favorite thing to say. . . ."**: Confidential source, interview with author, 1988.

Page 127. **"She showed many sides of her personality. . . ."**: Confidential source, interview with author, 1988.

Page 127. **"She is a very smart, very shrewd person. . . ."**: Confidential source, interview with author, 1988.

Page 128. **"In the campaign she always had to be in control. . . ."**: Confidential source, interview with author, 1988.

Page 128. **"I told her I want to stay out of the Senate race. . . ."**: "Garth Says No to Bess," *New York Post,* April 6, 1979.

Page 128. **"There was no way that Bess was going to beat that. . . ."**: David Garth, interview with author, 1988.

Page 129. **"I'm very proud of her. . . ."**: Maurice Carroll, "Bess Myerson Formally Declares Her Bid to Unseat Senator Javits," *New York Times,* May 8, 1980.

Page 130. **Nancy Capasso**: Interview with author, 1988.

Page 130. **"Andy Capasso was really putting on the moves. . . ."**: Confidential source, interview with author, 1988.

Page 131. **Ken Lerer**: Interview with author, 1988.

Page 131. **Candy Jones**: Interview with author, 1988.

Page 131. **John Lindsay**: Jane Perlez, "Bess Wears Turncoat Well, Lindsay Charges," *New York Daily News,* August 20, 1980.

Page 131. **"I have no question about my loyalty to consumers at all."**: "Bess Wears Turncoat Well, Lindsay Charges."

Page 131. ***New York Daily News* published a poll**: Joan Nassivera, "Bess Is the Primary Favorite with New Yorkers," *New York Daily News,* September 1, 1980.

Page 131. ***New York Times* poll**: Frank Lynn, "Poll Shows Bess Myerson Drawing Varied Support in Race for Senate," *New York Times,* September 2, 1980.

Page 132. **Maureen Connelly**: Interview with author, 1988.

Page 132. **The *Times* polls worried members of Holtzman's staff**: "Miss Holtzman Livens Campaign," *New York Times,* September 3, 1980.

Page 132. **Holtzman launched her harshest attack**: Description of debate comes from interviews with the candidate's campaign aides and from "Miss Holtzman Livens Campaign" and Bella English, "Liz Belts Bess over Job with Israel Boycotter," *New York Daily News*, September 3, 1980.

Page 132. **"against every defense appropriation . . ."**: E. J. Dionne, Jr., "Bess Myerson Steps Up Her Attack on Holtzman Arms Budget Votes," *New York Times*, September 6, 1980.

Page 133. **"If I win, he can sing. . . ."**: Maurice Carroll, interview with author, 1988.

Page 133. **"She was yelling and screaming at everybody. . . ."**: Confidential source, interview with author, 1988.

Page 133. **Marilyn Funt**: Patricia Morrisroe, "Bess and the Mess," *New York*, March 30, 1987.

Page 133. **Pam Chanin**: Interview with author, 1988.

Page 134. **"too tall, too beautiful, too rich"**: *New York Daily News*, March 31, 1981.

Page 134. **"Queen of the Jews"**: "Bess and the Mess."

Page 134. **Ken Lerer**: Interview with author, 1988.

Chapter 20: The Letters

Most of the material for this chapter comes from the woman identified as Charlotte Ames and interviews with other confidential sources. Charlotte Ames and J. Gordon Marcus are pseudonyms used to protect the privacy of these sources.

Other material in this chapter is drawn from articles published in the *New York Times* and *New York Daily News*. The letters mentioned in the text were provided by a confidential source. Bess Myerson declined to discuss the letters, her relationship with the man identified as J. Gordon Marcus, and the police investigation.

Page 135. **Charlotte Ames**: All quotes and description of her feelings and thoughts come from Charlotte Ames, interviews with author, 1988 and 1989.

Page 135. **Gordon had immediately suspected that Bess might be responsible**: Confidential source, interview with author, 1988.

Page 135. **She had been furious with him**: Confidential source, interview with author, 1989.

Page 135. **Gordon was convinced that Bess was responsible for the letters**: Charlotte Ames, interviews with author, 1988 and 1989.

Page 135. **Bess angrily suggested . . . that Charlotte might be writing the letters**: Confidential source, interview with author, 1989.

Page 136. **July 15**: Description of telephone calls with Bess's secretary and Bess comes from Charlotte Ames, interviews with author, 1988 and 1989.

Page 140. **Gordon was spending most of his time with a young woman who worked as a producer**: Confidential source, interview with author, 1989.

Page 141. **Bergdorf Goodman shopping bag**: Details about the incident come from Charlotte Ames, interview with author, 1988, and confidential sources, interviews with author, 1989.

Page 141. **Gordon called Bess**: Confidential source, interview with author, 1989.

Page 142. **November 14**: Confidential source, interview with author, 1989.

Page 142. **O'Meara's report**: Joyce Purnick, "Behavior of Myerson Cited in '80, Police Report Found Obsessive Conduct," *New York Times*, June 20, 1987.

Page 142. **Years later Bess refused to discuss**: Bess Myerson, interviews with author, 1989.

Page 143. **McGuire recalled telling Koch that Bess might be "acting out. . . ."**: "Behavior of Myerson Cited in '80."

Page 143. **Koch acknowledges**: Interview with author, 1988.

Page 143. **"It was a very low time. . . ."**: Bess Myerson, interview with author, February 1989.

Page 143. **"telephone relationship"**: Bess Myerson, interview with author, February 1989.

Page 143. **"When she lost that campaign. . . ."**: Confidential source, interview with author, 1988.

Page 144. **"He is a stand-up guy. . . ."**: Confidential source, interview with author, 1988.

Page 144. **"After the election was over. . . ."**: Patricia Morrisroe, "The Bess Mess," *New York*, March 30, 1987.

Page 144. **"I watched him, and my memory came back. . . ."**: Bess Myerson, interview with author, February 1989.

Page 144. **Andy would tell his wife he had to attend late-night meetings**: Nancy Capasso, interviews with author, 1987 and 1988.

Page 145. **"Sweat came pouring down my face. . . ."**: *New York Daily News*, April 15, 1981.

Page 145. **"She was completely disoriented. . . ."**: Confidential source, interview with author, 1988.

Page 145. **Nancy Capasso**: Interview with author, 1988.

Chapter 21: Andy and Nancy

Among the people interviewed for this chapter were Nancy Capasso, Myrna Felder, Raoul Lionel Felder, Sam Fredman, and Judith Yeager. Many of the details about Andy's early life were drawn from court records, including divorce papers from *Capasso v. Capasso*. The author also consulted records from the New York City Department of Environmental Protection and articles published in *Newsday*, the *New York Times*, *New York Daily News*, *New York Post*, *New York* magazine, and *Vanity Fair*. Except where noted, all of the quotes from Nancy Capasso come from several interviews with the author in 1987 and 1988. Andy Capasso declined to be interviewed for this book.

Page 146. **"I've received a press release. . . ."**: *New York Times*, January 2, 1981.

Page 146. **"She would call him Mr. Capasso. . . ."**: Confidential source, interview with author, 1988.

Page 146. **"sleazy"**: Confidential source, interview with author, 1988.

Page 146. **Carl Andy Capasso was born**: Details about Andy Capasso's early life come from interviews with his ex-wife, Nancy, and from his presentence memorandum, filed March 24, 1987, with the U.S. District Court, Southern District of New York.

Page 147. **Andy still remembers the electric company**: Andy Capasso's presentence memorandum.

Page 147. **Allyn Kandel**: Letter from Allyn Kandel to U.S. district judge Charles B. Stewart, February 5, 1987.

Page 147. **Richard Haas**: Letter from Richard Haas to U.S. district judge Charles B. Stewart, undated.

Page 148. **"There was instant chemistry."**: All quotes and details about Nancy Capasso's background come from Nancy Capasso, interviews with author, 1987 and 1988.

Page 148. **"So when are you going to invite me in for a cup of coffee?"**: Nancy Capasso, interview with author, 1988.

Page 149. **Judith Yeager**: Interview with author, 1989.

Page 149. **"He was madly in love. . . ."**: Judith Yeager, interview with author, 1989.

Page 149. **He claimed the *N* in Nanco stood for Naples**: *Capasso v. Capasso* divorce papers.

Page 151. **former Teamster boss John Cody**: Murray Weiss and Doug Feiden, "Capasso Wheels and Deals," *New York Post*, September 22, 1977.

Page 151. **"There isn't a person who is using cement. . . ."**: Marie Brenner, "Compromising Positions: Bess Myerson and Her World," *Vanity Fair*, December 1988.

Page 152. **"social Sahara."**: "Compromising Positions: Bess Myerson and Her World."

Page 152. **"Things were bad before Bess. . . ."**: Cindy Adams, *New York Post*, December 16, 1988.

Page 153. **"light and space of an Italian piazza"**: *Architectural Digest*, April 1983.

Page 154. **Judith Yeager**: Interview with author, 1988.

Chapter 22: The Other Woman

Among the people interviewed for this chapter were Nancy Capasso, Raoul Lionel Felder, Myrna Felder, Mort Fleischner, Sam Fredman, and Judith Yeager. The author also consulted records from *Capasso* v. *Capasso*. The author also drew material from articles published in *Newsday*, the *New York Daily News*, *New York Post*, *New York Times*, *New York* magazine, and *Vanity Fair*. All of the quotes from Nancy Capasso in this chapter come from several interviews with the author during 1987 and 1988. Andy Capasso declined to be interviewed for this book.

Page 155. **"I had a bad fall...."** "Bess: 'Off my back and feeling great!'", *New York Daily News*, February 4, 1981.

Page 155. **"I think he was in total awe of her...."**: Confidential source, interview with author, 1988.

Page 155. **"You think I don't want to go out...."**: Confidential source, interview with author, 1989.

Page 155. **"table manners"**: Confidential source, interview with author, 1988.

Page 155. **"He seemed like such a nice man...."**: Confidential source, interview with author, 1988.

Page 156. **Judith Yeager**: Interview with author, 1988.

Page 156. **"Bess gave him all of that...."**: All quotes from Nancy Capasso come from interviews with author, 1987 and 1988.

Page 156. **"The best is for Bess...."**: Confidential source, interview with author, 1988.

Page 157. **"took the whole diet out of context...."**: Jane Brody, "Assessing the 'I Love New York Diet,'" *New York Times*, March 10, 1982.

Page 157. **"It was a curiosity...."**: Confidential source, interview with author, 1988.

Page 157. **six-figure contract**: "TV Agent Suing Bess Myerson," *New York*, November 15, 1982.

Page 157. **Mort Fleischner**: Interview with author, 1989.

Page 158. **he saw investment potential**: *Capasso* v. *Capasso* divorce papers.

Page 159. **"just friends"**: Nancy Capasso, interview with author, 1987.

Page 159. **Bess was not thrilled**: Confidential source, interview with author, 1988.

Page 159. **"Be nice to Nancy."**: Patricia Morrisroe, "Bess and the Mess," *New York*, March 30, 1987.

Page 159. **Some of Bess's friends were appalled**: Confidential source, interview with author, 1988.

Page 160. **Tony Bailey**: Confidential source, interview with author, 1988.

Page 160. **"I never knew whether he was going to be there...."**: Confidential source, interview with author, 1988.

Page 162. **she had put cyanide in his food**: *Capasso* v. *Capasso* divorce papers.

Page 162. **"You just worry about making money...."**: *Capasso* v. *Capasso* divorce papers.

Page 162. **Judith Yeager**: Interview with author, 1989.

Page 163. **"Where are you going?..."**: *Capasso* v. *Capasso* divorce papers.

Page 163. **Andy was enraged**: Description of beating comes from Nancy Capasso, Judith Yeager, and court testimony before family court judge Bruce Kaplan.

Page 164. **"seriously depressed..."**: *Capasso* v. *Capasso* divorce papers.

Page 164. **"Mr. Capasso is the sweetest, gentlest of men...."**: "Bess and the Mess."

Page 165. **Judge Bruce Kaplan**: Court transcript, family court hearing, December 28, 1982.

Page 165. **"cruel and inhuman treatment"**: *Capasso* v. *Capasso* divorce papers.

Page 165. **she was thinking about dumping Andy**: Confidential source, interview with author, 1988.

Page 165. **"other woman"**: Confidential source, interview with author, 1988.

Page 165. **"coarse manners"**: Confidential source, interview with author, 1988.

Page 165. **"She was ready to get rid of him...."**: Confidential source, interview with author, 1988.

Page 166. **She decided to stay.**: "Bess and the Mess."

Chapter 23: Cultural Affairs

Among the people interviewed for this chapter were Walter Canter, Nancy Capasso, Raoul Lionel Felder, Sam Fredman, former mayor Edward I. Koch, Nelson Pagan, and Herb Rickman. Much of the information in this chapter is drawn from *Capasso* v. *Capasso* divorce papers and sworn testimony at Bess Myerson's federal trial on conspiracy and bribery charges in U.S. District Court, Manhattan. The author also consulted articles published in the *New York Times*, *Newsday*, *New York Daily News*, *New York Post*, and *New York* magazine.

Page 167. **"superstar status"**: Michael Goodwin, "Bess Myerson Is in Line for Cultural Affairs Post," *New York Times*, February 23, 1983.

Page 167. **he thought that she would make a superb commissioner of cultural affairs**: Mayor Edward I. Koch, interview with author, 1988.

Page 167. **"is as important a commodity as wheat is in Kansas and steel in Pittsburgh"**: Richard Walker, "Do One-Night Stands Lead to Permanent Relationships?", *ARTnews*, Summer 1984.

Page 168. **$5.62 billion**: Amei Wallach, "Arts a $5.6 Billion Bonanza for City," *New York Newsday*, February 16, 1983.

Page 168. **She seemed enthusiastic about her return to government**: Confidential source, interview with author, 1988.

Page 168. **she saw her life coming full circle**: Bess Myerson, unpublished interview with confidential source, 1987.

Page 168. **"It took me five years to get her into government. . . ."**: Quotes from press conference come from press release issued February 23, 1983, by the mayor's office; Bruce Lambert, "Cultural Affairs Post to Myerson," *New York Newsday*, February 24, 1983; and David Dunlap, "Miss Myerson Plans Arts Strategy," *New York Times*, February 24, 1983.

Page 169. **"Between the time I knew of it. . . ."**: Marcia Kramer, "Bess Tied to Hate Mail," *New York Daily News*, June 27, 1987.

Page 169. **He was furious**: Tom Iovino, sworn testimony in *United States of America* v. *Bess Myerson, Carl A. Capasso, Hortense W. Gabel*, December 2, 1988.

Page 169. **"Serious allegations have been made by the defendant. . . ."**: *Capasso* v. *Capasso* divorce papers.

Page 169. **"That's right. I told you I was going to have you thrown out of here."**: *Capasso* v. *Capasso* divorce papers.

Page 170. **"He was angry, and he went into the closets. . . ."**: Nancy Capasso, interview with author, 1988.

Page 170. **"You will get nothing."**: Nancy Capasso, interview with author, 1988.

Page 170. **Tony Bailey**: Confidential source, interview with author, 1988.

Page 170. **"Newly named Cultural Affairs Commissioner Bess Myerson. . . ."**: "Irate Wife Evicts Escort of Bess Myerson," *New York Post*, March 7, 1983.

Page 170. **"It made me more supportive of him. . . ."**: Patricia Morrisroe, "Bess and the Mess," *New York*, March 30, 1987.

Page 171. **Andy had become preoccupied**: Confidential sources, interviews with author, 1987 and 1988.

Page 171. **"The divorce was getting the best of him."**: Confidential source, interview with author, 1987.

Page 171. **"She said Mr. Capasso was going through a very messy divorce. . . ."**: All quotes from Shirley Harrod come from her sworn testimony in *U.S.* v. *Bess Myerson et al.*, November 1, 1988.

Page 172. **"The official version was that their marriage had been troubled long before. . . ."**: Confidential source, interview with author, 1988.

Page 172. **Tony Bailey**: Confidential source, interview with author, 1988.

Page 173. **"He has cut me off. . . ."**: *Capasso* v. *Capasso* divorce papers.

Page 174. **"artificially inflated her expenses . . ."**: *Capasso* v. *Capasso* divorce papers.

Page 174. **Alan Jay Lerner**: *New York Times*, October 26, 1979.

Chapter 24: Mother and Daughter

Among the people interviewed for this chapter were Roma Conable, Judge Hortense W. Gabel, Sukhreet Gabel, and Herbert London. The author also consulted documents contained in former mayor Robert Wagner's papers on file in New York City's Municipal Archives, the Tyler report, and sworn testimony before the state Commission on Judicial Conduct and in the federal trial of *United States of America* v. *Bess Myerson, Carl A. Capasso, and Hortense W. Gabel* in 1988. Other material was drawn from articles published in the *New York Times*, *Newsday*, *New York Post*, and *New York Daily News*.

Page 175. **"lady against the slums"**: Gertrude Samuels, "Lady Against the Slums," *New York Times Magazine*, August 12, 1962.
Page 175. **"Government was always a topic. . . ."**: "Tough Housing Idealist: Hortense Wittstein Gabel," *New York Times*, April 3, 1962.
Page 176. **"a complete case of father identification"**: Bennett Schiff, "Daily Close-up," *New York Post*, August 27, 1959.
Page 176. **"The situation was so bad with men going off to the war. . . ."**: Hortense W. Gabel, interview with author, 1989.
Page 176. **"endorsement"**: Hortense W. Gabel, sworn testimony, Commission on Judicial Conduct, May 26, 1987.
Page 176. **"Since I had a good record. . . ."**: Hortense W. Gabel, interview with author, 1989.
Page 176. **"It was such a breathtaking thing. . . ."**: Robert Caro, *The Power Broker* (New York: Random House, 1975), 962.
Page 177. **"She's proud of me. . . ."**: Bennett Schiff, "City Hall Aide on Slum Rehabilitation," *New York Post*, August 13, 1955.
Page 177. **two hundred city blocks**: "Lady Against the Slums."
Page 178. **April 2, 1962**: Press release announcing appointment from Office of the Mayor, Municipal Archives.
Page 178. **"I don't know why I'm looking forward to this job. . . ."**: Joseph Wershba, "The City's Rent Chief Is No Stranger to Landlords," *New York Post*, April 4, 1962.
Page 178. **"many-sided woman . . ."**: "Tough Housing Idealist: Hortense Wittstein Gabel."
Page 178. **"slumless New York"**: "Lady Against the Slums."
Page 179. **Sukhreet Gabel**: All quotes from Sukhreet Gabel and the description of her childhood come from interviews with author, 1987, 1988, and 1989.
Page 180. **"She was very precocious. . . ."**: Confidential source, interview with author, 1989.
Page 181. **"She was always daydreaming, fooling around. . . ."**: Confidential source, interview with author, 1988.

Chapter 25: Seduction

Among the people interviewed for this chapter were Nancy Capasso, Raoul Lionel Felder, Sam Fredman, Judge Hortense W. Gabel, Sukhreet Gabel, and Herb Rickman. The author also drew on court records, notes, transcripts, and sworn testimony from Bess Myerson's federal trial, the state Commission on Judicial Conduct, the *Capasso* v. *Capasso* divorce case, and the Tyler Commission. Articles published in the *New York Times*, *Newsday*, *New York Post*, *New York Daily News*, and *New York* magazine were also consulted.

Page 186. **May 25, 1983**: Description of gala comes from Judge Gabel and Herb Rickman, interviews with author, 1988, and sworn testimony in the federal trial *United States of America* v. *Bess Myerson, Carl A. Capasso, and Hortense W. Gabel*.
Page 186. **"We were friendly, rather than friends. . . ."**: Hortense Gabel, sworn testimony, Commission on Judicial Conduct, May 26, 1987.
Page 186. **"Is what's-his-name here?"**: Herb Rickman, sworn testimony, *U.S.* v. *Bess Myerson et al.*

Page 187. **Sukhreet Gabel**: All of the quotes and information from Sukhreet Gabel come from numerous interviews with the author, 1987 and 1988, and from her sworn testimony, *U.S.* v. *Bess Myerson et al.*

Page 188. **"Bess told me she liked Sukhreet. . . ."**: Hortense W. Gabel, Commission on Judicial Conduct.

Page 188. **Howard Leventhal**: All of the quotes and information from Howard Leventhal are drawn from his sworn testimony, *U.S.* v. *Bess Myerson et al.*

Page 189. **she was pleased with the judge's decision**: All of the quotes from and information on Nancy Capasso in this chapter come from interviews with author, 1987, 1988, and 1989.

Page 189. **Andy was outraged**: Description of Andy's outrage over having to pay alimony comes from Herb Rickman and Shirley Harrod, sworn testimony, *U.S.* v. *Bess Myerson et al.*

Page 189. **"He was angry as all get-out. . . ."**: Herb Rickman, sworn testimony, *U.S.* v. *Bess Myerson et al.*

Page 189. **"obviously overlooked and or misapprehended material facts"**: *Capasso* v. *Capasso* divorce papers.

Page 190. **"one of the biggest . . ."**: Hortense W. Gabel, sworn testimony, Commission on Judicial Conduct.

Page 190. **Although Judge Gabel was more impressed**: Hortense W. Gabel, sworn testimony, Commission on Judicial Conduct.

Page 191. **Bess later said she found Sukhreet to be charming**: Bess Myerson, interview with author, 1988.

Page 191. **"And Sandy is not impressed by anyone."**: Bess Myerson, interview with author, 1988.

Page 192. **"Sometime in July, if I'm not mistaken. . . ."**: Hortense W. Gabel, sworn testimony, Commission on Judicial Conduct.

Page 192. **They had at least five face-to-face meetings**: Harold R. Tyler, Jr., special counsel, *Report to the Mayor on the Investigation of Bess Myerson, Commissioner of Cultural Affairs*, April 8, 1987.

Page 192. **Bess left messages under assumed names**: Howard Leventhal, Brenda Shrobe, sworn testimony, *U.S.* v. *Bess Myerson et al.*

Page 192. **"I was very eager for Sukhreet to find this kind of interesting work. . . ."**: Hortense W. Gabel, sworn testimony, Commission on Judicial Conduct.

Page 192. **"Mr. Capasso was extremely distressed by the divorce. . . ."**: Patricia Morrisroe, "Bess and the Mess," *New York*, March 30, 1987.

Page 193. **Nancy Capasso**: Interviews with author, 1987 and 1988.

Page 193. **Bess was convinced that Nancy was following them**: "Bess and the Mess."

Page 195. **Shirley Harrod**: Sworn testimony, *U.S.* v. *Bess Myerson et al.*

Page 196. **"legalistic"**: Howard Leventhal, sworn testimony, *U.S.* v. *Bess Myerson et al.*

Page 197. **Brenda Shrobe**: Sworn testimony, *U.S.* v. *Bess Myerson et al.*

Page 197. **Nelson Pagan**: Interview with author and sworn testimony, *U.S.* v. *Bess Myerson et al.*

Chapter 26: "Tough Love"

Most of the material for this chapter was drawn from extensive interviews with Sukhreet Gabel and sworn testimony of former city employees at the federal trial, *United States of America* v. *Bess Myerson, Carl A. Capasso, and Hortense W. Gabel*, 1988. The author also conducted interviews with several sources who requested anonymity. In addition, the author consulted the Tyler report, records from the city's Department of Cultural Affairs, and articles published in the *New York Post, New York Times, New York Daily News*, and *Newsday*.

Page 199. **Bess encountered hostility**: Bess Myerson, interview with author, 1988.

Page 199. **Randall Bourscheidt, was bitterly disappointed**: Confidential source, interview with author, 1988.

Page 199. **"Maybe she sat on the stage and played the piano. . . ."**: Confidential source, interview with author, 1988.

Page 199. **"tough love"**: Deirdre Carmody, "Evaluating Bess Myerson's 4 Years as Cultural Affairs Leader," *New York Times*, February 16, 1987.

Page 199. **"knew all about city employees"**: Confidential source, interview with author, 1988.

Page 199. **she felt that her secretary could take care of whatever**: Richard Bruno, sworn testimony, *United States of America* v. *Bess Myerson, Carl A. Capasso, and Hortense W. Gabel.*

Page 199. **"Nobody had a clue. . . ."**: Confidential source, interview with author, 1988.

Page 200. **Gray was stunned.**: Harold R. Tyler, Jr., special counsel, *Report to the Mayor on the Investigation of Bess Myerson, Commissioner of Cultural Affairs*, April 8, 1987.

Page 200. **"acted as though the commissioner could not do anything. . ."**: Harold R. Tyler, Jr., special counsel, *Report to the Mayor on the Investigation of Bess Myerson, Commissioner of Cultural Affairs.*

Page 200. **Sukhreet Gabel**: All quotes and descriptions of her feelings come from extensive interviews with the author and from her sworn testimony, *U.S.* v. *Bess Myerson et al.*

Page 200. **"it was no coincidence"**: Susan Mulcahy, *My Lips Are Sealed: Confessions of a Gossip Columnist* (New York: Doubleday, 1988), 216.

Page 201. **Richard Bruno**: All quotes and information from him are drawn from his sworn testimony, *U.S.* v. *Bess Myerson et al.*

Page 201. **Bess was furious**: Richard Bruno, sworn testimony, *U.S.* v. *Bess Myerson et al.*

Page 202. **"New York is a big city. . . ."**: Richard Johnson, "Small World: Bess Hires Kin of Divorce Judge," *New York Post*, October 18, 1983.

Page 203. **"I felt, when I saw the clipping. . . ."**: Hortense W. Gabel, sworn testimony, Commission on Judicial Conduct, May 26, 1987.

Page 203. **"Did you people see this story? . . ."**: Howard Leventhal, Brenda Shrobe, sworn testimony, *U.S.* v. *Bess Myerson et al.*

Page 203. **"I think we have been dealt with squarely. . . ."**: Quotes from the proceedings come from court transcripts, *Capasso* v. *Capasso*, October 18, 1983.

Page 203. **Raoul Lionel Felder**: Interviews with author, 1987 and 1988.

Page 203. **Herb Rickman**: All quotes and information are drawn from interviews with author, 1988, and sworn testimony, *U.S.* v. *Bess Myerson et al.*

Page 209. **Marcella Maxwell**: All quotes and information are drawn from sworn testimony, *U.S.* v. *Bess Myerson et al.*

Page 210. **"Sukhreet came in with a lot of very strange notions. . . ."**: Confidential source, interview with author, 1989.

Page 212. **"She was in pretty bad straits when I visited in October. . . ."**: Carole Agus, "The Sukhreet Story," *New York Newsday*, November 2, 1988.

Chapter 27: *Capasso* v. *Capasso*

Most of the material for this chapter was drawn from hundreds of pages of testimony, affidavits, and other court records from the *Capasso* v. *Capasso* divorce trial. The author also consulted transcripts of tape-recorded telephone conversations between Andy and Nancy in 1984 and 1985 and interviewed Nancy Capasso and the lawyers from both sides of the case.

Page 213. **Nancy Capasso**: Interview with author, 1987.

Page 214. **"I have seen absolutely no evidence. . . ."**: Letter, Raoul Lionel Felder to Nancy Capasso, January, 16, 1984.

Page 214. **"realistic and just in terms. . . ."**: *Capasso* v. *Capasso* divorce papers, March 1, 1984.

Page 214. **Andy was reluctant**: Andy Capasso, transcript of telephone conversation with Nancy Capasso, July 1984.

Page 215. **Herman Tarnow**: Transcript of telephone conversations between Andy Capasso and Nancy Capasso, July 1988.

Page 215. **Over the years he had developed a scam that generated $1.5 million**: Indictment, *United States of America* v. *Carl A. Capasso*, January 14, 1987.

Page 216. **Andy became worried**: Andy Capasso, transcript of telephone conversation with Nancy Capasso, July 31, 1984.

Page 216. **"I want to talk to you about an issue. . . ."**: Andy Capasso, transcript of telephone conversation with Nancy Capasso, July 31, 1984.

Page 218. **Tarnow opened the conversation by calling him an "asshole"**: Andy Capasso, transcript of telephone conversation with Nancy Capasso, August 14, 1984.

Page 218. **He despised people who did not treat him with respect**: Andy Capasso, transcript of telephone conversation with Nancy Capasso, August 14, 1984.

Page 220. **"Dear Justice Gabel. . . ."**: Letter, Nancy Capasso to Hortense W. Gabel, December 1984.

Page 220. **Judge Gabel later acknowledged**: Hortense W. Gabel, sworn testimony, Commission on Judicial Conduct, 1986.

Page 221. **Herman Tarnow**: Interview with author 1988.

Page 221. **Patrick Mulhearn**: Interview with author, 1987.

Page 222. **July 8, 1985**: Quotes and testimony come from transcript of *Capasso* v. *Capasso* divorce trial, Manhattan Supreme Court, July 8, 1985, through October 11, 1985.

Page 222. **Andrew R. Tyler**: Jack Newfield and Wayne Barrett, *City for Sale: Ed Koch and the Betrayal of New York* (New York: Harper & Row, 1988), 409–11.

Page 224. **Raoul Lionel Felder**: Interview with author, 1987.

Page 225. **"I could have put up with it. . . ."**: Nancy Capasso, interview with author, 1987.

Chapter 28: The Fifth Amendment

Among the people interviewed for this chapter were Nancy Capasso, Michael Feldberg, Kevin Ford, Sukhreet Gabel, Jay Goldberg, Fred Hafetz, former mayor Edward I. Koch, Marcia Kramer, David Lawrence, Tony Lombardi, Herb Rickman, Barbara Ross, and Marilyn Thompson. The author also examined more than a hundred pages of testimony from a grand jury, the Tyler Commission, and the state Commission on Judicial Conduct. The author also drew from court records and transcripts involving Andy Capasso's indictment and sentencing on federal tax evasion charges. Much of the information about the city's corruption scandal comes from the author's work as a City Hall reporter in 1986 for *New York Newsday*. The author also drew on articles published in *Newsday*, the *New York Times, New York Post*, and *New York Daily News*, where reporters Barbara Ross and Richard Rosen provided a detailed reconstruction of the scandal. The author also consulted Jack Newfield and Wayne Barrett's superb account of the corruption scandal in *City for Sale: Ed Koch and the Betrayal of New York* (New York: Harper & Row, 1988).

Page 226. **January 1, 1986**: Description of mayoral inaugural ceremonies comes from reports published in the *New York Times, New York Daily News*, and *New York Post* on January 2, 1986. Additional details were drawn from the detailed reconstruction of the inauguration and scandal by Barbara Ross and Richard Rosen, "The Fat Boys," *New York Daily News*, December 14, 1986.

Page 226. **Rudolph Giuliani**: Interviews with author, 1988 and 1989.

Page 227. **"whether it was all true or not"**: Rudolph Giuliani, interview with author, 1989.

Page 229. **Andy Capasso slipped into the hospital**: Confidential source, interview with author, 1989.

Page 229. **"Michael Dowd, a Queens Blvd. attorney. . . ."**: Jimmy Breslin, "Manes Accused of Extortion," *New York Daily News*, January 23, 1987.

Page 231. **Herman Tarnow**: Interview with author, 1988.

Page 231. **David Lawrence**: Interview with author, 1989.

Page 231. **Tarnow thought that Lawrence might be interested**: Herman Tarnow, interview with author, 1988.

Page 231. **Giuliani was interested in more**: Rudolph Giuliani, interview with author, 1988.

Page 232. **secret tape recording**: *United States of America* v. *Carl A. Capasso*, U.S. attorney's presentencing report, March 24, 1987.

Page 232. **Tony Lombardi**: Interview with author, 1989.

Page 232. **Kevin Ford**: Interview with author, 1989.

Page 232. **Andy heard about her subpoena**: Confidential source, interview with author, 1989.

Page 233. **Andy retained lawyers**: *U.S.* v. *Carl A. Capasso*, U.S. attorney's presentencing report.

Page 233. **he got what appeared to be a warning**: *U.S.* v. *Carl A. Capasso*, U.S. attorney's presentencing report.

Page 233. **"Now tell me this is not an organized crime case."**: Confidential source, interview with author, 1989.

Page 233. **Jay Goldberg**: Interviews with author, 1988 and 1989.

Page 233. **"low blow"**: *U.S.* v. *Carl A. Capasso*, sentencing hearing, March 30, 1987.

Page 234. **She described in detail how Andy would direct her**: Former Nanco employee, federal grand jury testimony, April 20, 1986.

Page 234. **"I could not go over fifteen hundred dollars. . . ."**: Former Nanco employee, federal grand jury testimony, April 20, 1986.

Page 234. **Bess called Rickman**: Herb Rickman, interview with author, 1988.

Page 234. **Rickman was terrified**: Herb Rickman, interview with author, 1988.

Page 235. **"From that point on, I no longer took up invitations. . . ."**: Herb Rickman, interview with author, 1988.

Page 235. **the mayor's City Hall press conference**: Author attended the press conference as a reporter for *New York Newsday*, May 2, 1986.

Page 235. **"absurd. . ."**: Joanne Wasserman, "Bess Denies Helping Beau Win City Contracts," *New York Post*, May 3, 1986.

Page 235. **Koch immediately called Bess**: Mayor Edward I. Koch, deposition submitted to the federal grand jury, September 23, 1987.

Page 236. **"I believed it to be true at the time"**: Mayor Edward I. Koch, deposition submitted to the federal grand jury.

Page 236. **Marcia Kramer**: Interview with author, 1988.

Page 236. **"The chances are dollars to donuts. . . ."**: Marcia Kramer, "Bess' Role: All in the Family, Myerson Hired Daughter of Judge Who Cut Beau's Alimony," *New York Daily News*, May 7, 1986.

Page 236. **"mild stroke."**: Hortense W. Gabel, sworn testimony, Commission on Judicial Conduct, May 26, 1987.

Page 237. **Gwen Hatcher**: Testimony, *United States of America* v. *Bess Myerson, Carl A. Capasso, and Hortense W. Gabel.*.

Page 237. **"witch hunt"**: Gwen Hatcher, testimony, *U.S.* v. *Bess Myerson et al.*

Page 238. **Bess called Sukhreet**: Sukhreet Gabel, interview with author, 1987.

Page 238. **Sukhreet was surprised**: Sukhreet Gabel, interview with author, 1987.

Page 238. **state Commission on Judicial Conduct**: Witnesses began testifying on July 24, 1986.

Page 240. **Judge Gabel agreed to testify**: Hortense W. Gabel, sworn testimony, Commission on Judicial Conduct, July 24, 1986.

Page 240. **she did not want to leave the bench in disgrace**: Hortense W. Gabel, interview with author, 1989.

Page 240. **"It's very hard to. . . ."**: Hortense W. Gabel, sworn testimony, Commission on Judicial Conduct, May 26, 1987.

Page 240. **Sukhreet testified**: Sukhreet Gabel, sworn testimony, Commission on Judicial Conduct, July 23, 1986.

Page 240. **"power of an ant"**: Nancy Capasso, interview with author, 1987.

Page 240. **Myrna Felder**: Interview with author, 1987.

Page 240. **"We also find an error of law. . . ."**: Appellate Division, *Capasso* v. *Capasso*, October 2, 1986.

Page 241. **Andy had evaded $774,000**: Indictment, *U.S.* v. *Carl A. Capasso*, January 14, 1987.

Page 242. **Fred Hafetz**: Interviews with author, 1988 and 1989.
Page 242. **Bess had decided not to tell Koch**: Cindy Adams, "I'm Like a Leashed Tiger," *New York Post*, January 15, 1987.
Page 243. **Bess looked nervous**: Confidential source, interview with author, 1989.

Chapter 29: "The Bess Mess"

Among the people interviewed for this chapter were George Arzt, Wayne Barrett, Nancy Capasso, Ken Conboy, Michael Feldberg, Myrna Felder, Kevin Ford, former mayor Edward I. Koch, Marcia Kramer, Hortense W. Gabel, Sukhreet Gabel, Rudolph Giuliani, Jay Goldberg, Fred Hafetz, Leland T. Jones, David Lawrence, Tony Lombardi, Patricia Morrisroe, Jack Newfield, Larry Simonberg, and Mike Taibbi. The author also consulted the Tyler report, investigative reports, grand jury testimony, transcripts from the state Commission on Judicial Conduct's investigation, and court records from the federal tax evasion case against Andy Capasso and the federal bribery case against Bess Myerson, Andy Capasso, and Judge Gabel. The author also drew from articles published in the *New York Daily News*, *New York Post*, *New York Times*, and *Village Voice*, as well as articles reported and written by the author in *New York Newsday*.

Page 244. **"She said her lawyer didn't think it necessary. . . ."**: Mayor Edward I. Koch, deposition for federal investigation, September 23, 1987.
Page 244. **A "great deal of confidence and respect"**: Marcia Kramer and Stuart Marques, "'Distressed' Koch Wants Answers, Ed Orders Bess to Talk," *New York Daily News*, January 11, 1987.
Page 244. **"a negative inference. . . ."**: Joyce Purnick, "Myerson, at Grand Jury, Invoked 5th Amendment," *New York Times*, January 11, 1987.
Page 244. **"I didn't hear the state of mind of a duplicitous person. . . ."**: Joyce Purnick, "Myerson Is Stepping Aside as Koch's Culture Chief," *New York Times*, January 14, 1987.
Page 245. **"He was kind enough on a pro-bono basis. . . ."**: Mayor Edward I. Koch, deposition for federal investigation, September 23, 1987.
Page 245. **"I will return as commissioner. . . ."**: Bess Myerson, statement released to press, January 13, 1987.
Page 246. **"We view the present indictment. . . ."**: Marvin Smilon and Marsha Kranes, "Bess' Beau Is Busted," *New York Post*, January 15, 1987.
Page 246. **But Giuliani warned that the federal grand jury**: "Bess' Beau Is Busted."
Page 246. **But Andy told friends**: Confidential source, interview with author, 1988.
Page 246. **Richard Bruno**: Sworn testimony, *United States of America* v. *Bess Myerson, Carl A. Capasso, and Hortense W. Gabel*, November 1988.
Page 247. **"I categorically deny that any improper influence. . . ."**: Andy Capasso, statement released to press, March 30, 1987.
Page 247. **Jay Goldberg**: Interview with author, 1988.
Page 247. **"He said to me, and this is a quote. . . ."**: Jay Goldberg, sentencing hearing, *United States of America* v. *Carl A. Capasso*, March 30, 1987.
Page 247. **David Lawrence**: Interview with author, 1989.
Page 247. **"rat"**: David Lawrence, sentencing hearing, *U.S.* v. *Carl A. Capasso*, March 30, 1987.
Page 247. **Samuel Peabody**: Letter contained in Andy Capasso's presentence memorandum, March 24, 1987.
Page 248. **Andy's stepson**: Letter contained in Andy Capasso's presentence memorandum.
Page 248. **Jerome Becker**: Letter contained in Andy Capasso's presentence memorandum.
Page 248. **Dr. Ted Rubin**: Letter contained in Andy Capasso's presentence memorandum.
Page 248. **The prosecutor portrayed Andy as a greedy and corrupt man**: Andy Capasso's presentence memorandum, March 30, 1987.

Page 249. **"Your honor, he had no information. . . ."**: Jay Goldberg, transcript, sentencing hearing, *U.S. v. Carl A. Capasso*, March 30, 1987.

Page 249. **"Well, I have never had any information. . . ."**: Andy Capasso, transcript, sentencing hearing, *U.S. v. Carl A. Capasso*.

Page 249. **"All right. . . ."**: Judge Stewart, transcript, sentencing hearing, *U.S. v. Carl A. Capasso*.

Page 249. **"I'm like a leashed tiger. . . ."**: Cindy Adams, "I'm like a leashed tiger," *New York Post*, January 15, 1987.

Page 250. **Bess became increasingly obsessed**: Three confidential sources, interview with author, 1988.

Page 250. **Mike Taibbi**: Interview with author, 1989.

Page 251. **Marcia Kramer**: Interview with author, 1987.

Page 251. **Patricia Morrisroe**: Interview with author, 1988.

Page 251. **"there is no story here. . . ."**: Patricia Morrisroe, "Bess and the Mess," *New York*, March 30, 1987.

Page 252. **she changed her mind**: Tyler report, April 8, 1987.

Page 252. **During the three-month probe they examined**: Tyler report.

Page 252. **"I was a very good Girl Scout. . . ."**: Sukhreet Gabel, interview with author, 1987.

Page 254. **"evasive and unconvincing"**: Tyler report.

Page 255. **"I hope that this won't stop us. . . ."**: Mayor Edward I. Koch, deposition for federal investigation, September 23, 1987.

Page 255. **"Dear Ed: I will always be proud. . . ."**: Bess Myerson, letter to Mayor Edward I. Koch, April 9, 1987.

Page 255. **"I don't think that she knew why she was there. . . ."**: Confidential source, interview with author, 1988.

Page 256. **"She wasn't professional. . . ."**: Confidential source, interview with author, 1988.

Page 256. **"She could be very tough. . . ."**: Confidential source, interview with author, 1988.

Page 256. **City Hall news conference**: Author attended news conference, April 9, 1987.

Page 257. **"Although, in retrospect and with hindsight. . . ."**: Bess Myerson, statement released to press, April 9, 1987.

Page 257. **"absolute fact"**: Charles Lachman, "Capasso Judge 'Didn't Know They Were Lovers,' " *New York Post*, April 10, 1987.

Page 257. **Nancy Capasso**: Interview with author, April 9, 1987.

Page 257. **Robert Morgenthau**: Interview with author, 1989.

Page 258. **Jack Newfield**: Interview with author, 1988.

Page 259. **"I'm aghast at what she did. . . ."**: Mayor Edward I. Koch, press conference attended by author, June 12, 1987.

Page 259. *Daily News*:"The Myerson Report: Time to Prosecute," *New York Daily News*, June 11, 1987.

Page 259. *New York Times*: "Ms. Myerson, the Judge, and the Mayor," *New York Times*, June 12, 1987.

Page 259. **"Bess is locked in her room. . . ."**: Ann Bollinger and Jim Nolan, "Farewell, My Lovely," *New York Post*, June 13, 1987.

Page 260. **"It has to be done. . . ."**: Bess Myerson, interview with author, 1987.

Page 260. **Description of weekend at Westhampton**: Details were drawn from articles published in the *New York Post*, *New York Daily News*, and *New York Newsday*.

Page 261. **$6.4 million divorce settlement**: *Capasso* v. *Capasso* divorce records, July 2, 1987.

Page 261. **"Oooh . . . that's where Bess. . . ."**: Marcia Kramer, "Three Sea Belles By Seashore," *New York Daily News*, July 4, 1987.

Page 262. **she was furious**: Sukhreet Gabel, interview with author, 1987.

Page 262. **David Lawrence**: Interview with author, 1989.

Page 263. **transcripts of the telephone conversations**: Evidence, *U.S. v. Bess Myerson et al.*

Page 264. **"Can't we get rid of some of this clutter?"**: Sukhreet Gabel, interview with author, 1987.

Page 264. **October 7, 1987**: Author attended press conference.

Page 265. **"unequivocally asserts. . . ."**: Fred Hafetz, statement released to press, October 7, 1987.

Page 266. **"I am totally convinced of the propriety. . . ."**: Hortense W. Gabel, press conference, October 7, 1987.

Page 267. **"If she's taking little things like that. . . ."**: Marcia Kramer, "Bess Fails to Get Delay," *New York Daily News*, October 4, 1987.

Chapter 30: "Oh, No, Bess!"

Among the people interviewed for this chapter were Nancy Capasso, Michael Feldberg, Myrna Felder, Raoul Lionel Felder, Kevin Ford, Sukhreet Gabel, Rudolph Giuliani, Jay Goldberg, Fred Hafetz, Marcia Kramer, David Lawrence, Tony Lombardi, John McDermott, Paul Moses, Bill Smith, and Rick Walker. The author also consulted court transcripts and records from the federal government's case against Bess and Andy and Nancy Capasso's divorce case. In addition, the author examined police records from Bess's May 27, 1988, arrest on shoplifting charges in South Williamsport, Pennsylvania, and reviewed articles published in *Life* magazine, the *New York Daily News*, *New York Post*, and *New York Newsday*.

Page 268. **"It's as though it started as a little snowball. . . ."**: Bess Myerson to CBS correspondent Steve Kroft, "West 57th Street," broadcast November 1987.

Page 268. **Esther Margolis**: Interview with author, 1987.

Page 269. **"I couldn't be happier about the juxtaposition. . . ."**: Bess Myerson, interview with author, October 15, 1987.

Page 269. **"Excuse me. Are you Bess Myerson?. . ."**: Bess Myerson, interview with author, October 15, 1987.

Page 269. **Nancy Capasso**: Interviews with author, 1987 and 1988.

Page 270. **Myrna Felder**: Interviews with author, 1987 and 1988.

Page 271. **Bo Dietl**: Interview with author, 1988.

Page 271. **the first face-to-face encounter between Nancy and Bess**: Author attended the court proceedings, February 24, 1988.

Page 272. **"The queen has arrived."**: Raoul Lionel Felder, interview with author, February 24, 1988.

Page 274. **Marcia Kramer**: Interview with author, 1988.

Page 274. **Bess was arrested for shoplifting again**: South Williamsport police chief William Smith, district justice John McDermott, and *Williamsport Sun-Gazette* reporter Rick Walker, interviews with author, May 27 and May 28, 1987. The author also reviewed a copy of the police report, which contained transcripts of interviews with the people who were involved in Bess's arrest.

Page 275. **Nancy Hill**: Police investigative report, May 27, 1988.

Page 276. **Linda Wolfe**: Police investigative report.

Page 276. **Rick Walker**: Interview with author, May 27, 1988.

Page 276. **John McDermott**: Interview with author, May 27, 1988.

Page 277. **"It was a cry for help."**: Confidential source, interview with author, June 1988.

Page 277. **"Even though she's rich. . . ."**: Confidential source, interview with author, June 1988.

Page 277. **"If you don't give it to me. . . ."**: *Life*, August 1988.

Page 278. **federal investigators started checking with security directors**: Confidential source, interview with author, February 1989.

Page 278. **Bess had come to believe**: Bess Myerson, interview with author, 1988.

Page 278. **Rudolph Giuliani**: Interview with author and court records from *United States of America* v. *Bess Myerson, Carl A. Capasso, and Hortense W. Gabel.*

Page 278. **Kevin Thomas Duffy**: Court records and transcripts from *U.S.* v. *Bess Myerson et al.*

Page 279. **Sukhreet Gabel**: Interviews with author, 1987–89.

Page 280. **Michael Feldberg**: Interviews with author, 1988–89.

Page 282. **At the hearing in Keenan's chambers**: Court records and transcripts from *U.S.* v. *Bess Myerson et al.*

Page 282. **Monday, October 3**: Court records and transcripts from *U.S.* v. *Bess Myerson et al.*

Chapter 31: The Trial

This and the following chapter are based on the author's observations from attending the trial and interviews with dozens of people on both sides of the case, including Tony Bailey, Walter Canter, Michael Feldberg, Kevin Ford, Hortense W. Gabel, Dr. Milton Gabel, Sukhreet Gabel, Jay Goldberg, Rema Goldberg, Fred Hafetz, former mayor Edward I. Koch, David Lawrence, Tony Lombardi, and Herb Rickman. The author also interviewed the jurors in the case and examined hundreds of pages of court records, grand jury testimony, FBI investigative reports, and other documents that were introduced as evidence.

Page 284. **Bess was hoping to slip into the courthouse**: Bess Myerson, interview with author, 1988.

Page 284. **Bess summoned up all of her strength**: Bess Myerson, interview with author, 1988.

Page 284. **saw the trial as one more tribulation**: Cindy Adams, "Toughening Up for the Test," *New York Post*, October 5, 1989.

Page 284. **Fred Hafetz**: Interviews with author, 1988 and 1989.

Page 284. **Bess no longer trusted chauffeurs**: Ann V. Bollinger, "Easy Rider: Subways Tell No Lies," *New York Post*, October 5, 1988.

Page 286. **Sukhreet Gabel**: Interviews with author, 1988 and 1989.

Page 286. **The prosecutors were looking for older, conservative, middle-class jurors**: David Lawrence, interview with author, 1989.

Page 287. **The defense team felt it needed an entirely different jury**: Jay Goldberg, interview with author, 1988.

Page 287. **Rema Goldberg**: Interviews with author, 1988 and 1989.

Page 287. **Andy called it "jury patrol."**: Confidential source, interview with author, 1989.

Page 290. **"You can't just tell people to go away"**: "Easy Rider: Subways Tell No Lies."

Page 292. **Goldberg had seated the elderly judge**: Jay Goldberg, interview with author, 1988.

Page 293. **"My role is neither to prosecute. . . ."**: Sukhreet Gabel, interview with author, 1988.

Page 295. **"I've never seen blood. . . ."**: Court marshal to author, October 13, 1988.

Page 304. **Jay Goldberg**: Interview with author, 1988.

Chapter 32: The Verdict

Page 308. **Bess was completely relaxed**: Bess Myerson, interview with author, October 28, 1988.

Page 308. **She was feeling so upbeat**: Bess Myerson, interview with author, October 28, 1988.

Page 308. **On most nights Bess made sure**: Bess Myerson, interview with author, October 18, 1988.

Page 309. **"go to waste"**: Confidential source, interview with author, 1988.

Page 309. **"Can't she get a year and a day?"**: Confidential source, interview with author, 1988.

Page 309. **"We are very supportive of each other. . . ."**: Marie Brenner, "Bess Myerson and Her World," *Vanity Fair*, December 1988.

Page 310. **Bess did not want to spend the rest of the trial**: Bess Myerson, interview with author, November 1, 1988.

Page 312. **Marilyn Funt told reporters**: Confidential sources, interviews with author, 1988.

Page 316. **"We were like brother and sister. . . ."**: Bess Myerson, interview with author, November 1988.

Page 317. **former assistant cultural affairs commissioner**: Confidential source, interview with author, 1988.

Page 318. **Paul Moses**: Interview with author, 1988.

Page 322. **"No one would have any reason to send me flowers. . . ."**: Bess Myerson, interview with author, 1988.

Page 323. **Tony Bailey**: Interview with author, 1988.

Page 326. **one of the jurors later said she was moved to tears**: Sheila Adler, interview with author, 1988.

Page 326. **he thought for sure that Abrams's summation would compel the other jurors to vote to convict**: Daniel Handley, interview with author, December 1988.

Page 328. **"I think the judge chose me because he saw I was pro-defense. . . ."**: Jeannie Kasindorf, "How Bess Got Out of the Mess," *New York*, January 16, 1989.

Page 329. **Berardi felt strongly**: Linda Berardi, interview with author, December 1988.

Page 329. **Daniel Handley**: Interview with author, December 1988.

Page 331. **Bess grew more worried**: Bess Myerson, interview with author, December 21, 1988.

Page 332. **Bess said she understood why her daughter couldn't be there**: Bess Myerson, interview with author, December 21, 1988.

Page 332. **"I thought that after they heard what Mayor Wagner. . . ."**: Milton Gabel, interview with author, December 21, 1988.

Page 332. **Judge Gabel was also worried**: Judge Gabel, interview with author, December 21, 1988.

Index